About the A

Dr John Abolarin is a seasoned chartered b... researcher and a Barrister at Law, in Engla... of experience in all four distinctive professional disciplines. ... ... of theoretical knowledge and twenty years of practical industry experience in a commercial bank gave him a bird's eye view of the endemic problems in the banking sector, which he evaluated with a depth of insight.

Among other suggestions, John argued that whilst regulatory reforms are *sine qua non* to safeguarding the economy, maintaining stability in the banking sector begins with empowering banks' internal auditors and compliance officers who should have unfettered access to the bank's Chief Executive Officer when needed. In addition, John argued that headhunting for the right people to manage the affairs of a vast multinational banking corporation and a succession plan are crucial success factors that have the potential to make or break a banking group.

John argues that while capital adequacy and liquidity ratios are essential, maintaining bank stability goes far beyond satisfying those requirements.

For example, the collapse of a 200-year-old investment bank, Barings Capital in 1995 and the narrow escape of Union Bank of Switzerland (UBS) from a major catastrophe in 2011 perfectly illustrates how business operations in a bank could rapidly spiral downward leading to the ruin of a bank if not nipped in the bud quickly enough.

In the case of Barings Capital, unauthorised derivative offshore trading in Singapore by an unsupervised staff led to an accumulated deficit of £208 million over time, but in just two months, it escalated to £830 million. Inevitably, the bank collapsed.

Out of a potential loss of $12 billion, UBS managed to escape with a staggering loss of $2.3 billion. The losses were incurred through unauthorised trading of an unsupervised staff whose web of elaborate concealments remained undetected for three years. Later investigations revealed that he acted alone. No one suspected foul play throughout the three years until the staff owned up to the wrongdoing.

Giving powers to an individual to commit a bank to an exposure of up to $100 million while unsupervised as was the case of the staff involved in the UBS should give real concerns to supervisory institutions and the public.

Suggesting that such failures could happen in the banking sector may sound fictional, but it truly happened.

John's point is that maintaining stability in the banking sector should take a holistic approach. A bank with a strong capital base and adequate liquidity ratios could run aground easily where there is room for what happened in Barings Capital and Union Bank of Switzerland.

Dedication

I dedicate this work to the memory of my late wife, **Funmilayo Adejoke Abolarin**, a companion for thirty years and an adept English literature teacher who gave me insights on writing prose.

John Abolarin

BANKING LAW AND FINANCIAL REGULATIONS

The Imperatives for Managing
Stability in the Banking Sector

LONDON * CAMBRIDGE * NEW YORK * SHARJAH

Copyright © John Abolarin 2025

The right of John Abolarin to be identified as the author of this work has been asserted by the author in accordance with sections 77 and 78 of the Copyright, Designs and Patents Act 1988.

All rights reserved. No part of this publication may be reproduced, stored in a retrieval system, or transmitted in any form or by any means, electronic, mechanical, photocopying, recording, or otherwise, without the prior permission of the publishers.

Any person who commits any unauthorised act in relation to this publication may be liable to criminal prosecution and civil claims for damages.

The story, experiences, and words are the author's alone.

A CIP catalogue record for this title is available from the British Library.

ISBN 9781035854523 (Paperback)
ISBN 9781035854530 (Hardback)
ISBN 9781035854547 (ePub e-book)

www.austinmacauley.com

First Published 2025
Austin Macauley Publishers Ltd®
1 Canada Square
Canary Wharf
London
E14 5AA

Acknowledgements

I want to seize this opportunity to thank Dr Damian Mather, Dr Melanie Latham, Paul Raby (FCIB), and Professor Stephen Whittle of Manchester Metropolitan University. They took time from their hectic schedules to read this material and provided helpful feedback at each milestone, which immeasurably enriched this piece of work.

I also thank Prof Jay Cullen, a Banking Law and Financial Services Regulation Professor at Edge Hill University, Ormskirk, whose attention to detail and critique tremendously contributed to lifting the book to a higher level.

Similarly, I want to thank Mrs Pamela Boffey, a retired mathematics teacher who volunteered to read through the manuscript to see if the content would make sense to lay readers.

I would like to thank the publishers, Austin Macauley Publishers Ltd, London, for their kind and uplifting words following their initial review of the manuscript. Without any hesitation, they agreed to publish the material. Their encouragement and support throughout the production process are well appreciated.

I thank my darling wife, Esther, and our children, Abdul Momen Jameli, Maria, David, Daniel and Joseph. They endured the frustration of seeing a formerly known fun-loving father turning into a recluse 'old man' endlessly locked up in the study. In the process, wasted four consecutive summer holidays for them. Please accept my apologies for this.

Most importantly, I thank God Almighty, the giver of life, knowledge, wisdom and understanding.

I take responsibility for grammatical errors and other mistakes that may still be lurking within the book.

Table of Contents

Chapter 1: A General Overview: The Problem, Context, Content and the Focus of the Book 3

1.1. Introduction: The Problem of Instability in the Banking Sector and the Damaging Socio-economic Consequences Over Time. 3

1.2. The Tension Between the Need to Make More Restraining Laws And Advantages of Granting Discretionary Powers to Responsibly Manage Depositors' Funds 5

1.3. The Aims of the Study 8

1.4. Ring-fencing in Brief 13

1.5. Research Objectives 15

1.6. Research Questions 16

1.7. Research Hypothesis 17

1.8. The Importance of the Banking Sector 17

1.9. Monetised Costs and Benefits of the Ring-fencing Policy 19

1.10. The Context of the Study: The Fallout of the 2007–2009 Global Financial Crisis 24

1.11. The Law: The Provisions of the Financial Services (Banking Reform) Act 2013 28

    1.11.1. Part 1—Banking Reform Act 2013: Ring-fencing 29

    1.11.2. Part 2—Banking Reform Act 2013: Financial Services Compensation Scheme 30

    1.11.3. Part 3—Banking Reform Act 2013: Bail-in Stabilisation Option 30

1.11.4. Part 4—Banking Reform Act 2013: Conduct of Persons working in the Financial Services Sector … 31

1.11.5. Part 5—Banking Reform Act 2013: Regulation of Payments System … 32

1.11.6. Part 6—Banking Reform Act 2013: Special Administration for Operators of Certain Infrastructure Systems … 32

1.11.7. Part 7—Banking Reform Act 2013: Miscellaneous … 33

1.11.8. Part 8—Banking Reform Act 2013: Final Provision … 33

1.11.9. Summary … 33

1.12. The United Kingdom Financial System … 33

1.13. Contribution to Knowledge … 37

1.14. Content and Structure of the Book … 39

Chapter 2: Literature Review: Literature Survey Strategies and Review Questions … **42**

Section A … 42

2.1. Introduction … 42

2.2. The Aims of Literature Review … 42

2.3. The Objectives of the Literature Review … 43

2.4. Literature Sources Consulted and Some of the Subject Leaders … 45

2.5. Approaches to Literature Review … 45

2.6. Steps Taken to Minimise Incidences of Bias and Lack of Academic Rigour … 47

Section B … 48

2.7. Introduction … 48

2.8. Some of the Causes of the Financial Crisis … 49

2.9. Estimate of the Impact of the Global Financial Crisis on the Stock Market Capitalisation in the Banking System … 51

2.10. The Contributions of Collateralised Debt Obligations to the
       Financial Crisis   53

2.11. The Relevance and the Implications of the Causes of the
       Financial Crisis to this Study   56

2.12. Summary of the Causes of the 2007–2009 Global Financial Crisis 57

Section C   58

2.13. Introduction   58

2.14. Sources of Banking Law and Regulations Applicable to
       the Banking Sector   58

2.15. The Principal Laws and Regulations that Governed the Banking
       Sector Before the Global Financial Crisis in 2007–2009   59

2.16. Regulated Areas in the Banking Sector and Applicable Laws and
       Regulatory Framework Before the Global Financial Crisis
       in 2007–2009   60

   2.16.1. Accounting Standards   61

   2.16.2. Basel Accords: Basel Committee on Banking Supervision   63

   2.16.3. Basel I: The Basel Capital Accord   64

   2.16.4. Financial Services Markets Acts 2000   66

   2.16.5. Basel II, 2004: The New Capital Framework   72

   2.16.6. Bank's Capital Adequacy Requirements Considering the
      Global Financial Crisis in 2007–2009   73

   2.16.7. Argument for the Justification of Bank Regulation   77

   2.16.8. Conclusion   79

Section: D   81

2.17. Introduction   81

2.18. The Scope of Banking Supervision Activities   82

2.19. The Nature of Banking Supervision   83

2.20. The Hierarchy of Supervisory Institutions Overseeing
       the Banking   87

2.21. The Treasury	87
2.22. The Ascendance of the Bank of England to the Position of the Banking Sector Supervising Authority and a Review of Previous Remarkable Bank Failures	88
2.23. Banking Supervision Reforms in the 1990s–2000	96
2.24. The Emergence of the Financial Services Authority (the 2000s)	101
2.25. The Financial Services Authority 2001–2009: How Did They Fare?	105
2.26. Why Did the Bank of England and the Financial Services Authority Fail to Meet Expectations in their Roles as Supervisors of the Banking Sector?	107
2.27. Regulatory Changes in the Aftermath of the Global Financial Crisis	113
2.28. The Background to the Ring-fencing Policy	114
2.29. Basel III: Responding to the 2007–2009 Financial Crisis at Supranational Level	115
2.29.1. Conclusions	119
Section: E	121
2.30. Introduction	121
2.31. The Business of Banking	125
2.32. Other Financial Institutions	129
2.33. The Driver of Economic Regulation: Structuralism and Neo-Liberalism Socio-Economic Ideologies	130
2.34. Structuralism	131
2.35. Neo-liberalism	132
2.36. Argument for and against Structuralism (Protectionism) and Neo-liberalism (Deregulation/Free Market Economy)	135
2.37. The Impact of Neo-liberalism on the Banking Sector	143

2.38. Would the Ring-fencing Policy Established in the Banking Reform Act 2013 Prevent future Occurrence of Financial Crises in the Banking Sector?   152

2.39. Summary of Findings and Conclusions   155

Chapter 3: Research Design: Methods and Methodology   158

3.1. Introduction   158

3.2. Research Design   159

    3.2.1. Aims of the Study   159

    3.2.2. Research Objectives   160

3.3. Guiding Research Philosophies   161

3.4. Fig. 4 Research Philosophy in the 'Research Onion Model'.   164

3.5. Philosophical Positions   166

    3.5.1. Positivism/Empiricism   167

    3.5.2. Realism   168

    3.5.3. Interpretivism   169

    3.5.4. Pragmatism   170

3.6. General Features and Debates Around Qualitative and Quantitative Approaches to Doing Research and What that Means to this Study   171

3.7. Methods   173

3.8. The Variety of Data Gathering Options Available to the Researcher   173

    3.8.1. Observation   174

    3.8.2. Interview   174

    3.8.3. Questionnaires   176

    3.8.4. Documents (Secondary Data Sources)   176

3.9. The Documentary Data Sources in the Context of this Study   177

3.10. How the Objectives Stated in Chapter 1 Were Achieved   180

3.11. Profitability Models as Performance Measurement   185

3.12. Analysis, Interpretation and Written Presentation — 187

3.13. Limitations and Justification of the Choice of Method Adopted — 188

3.14. Training, Qualifications and Practical Work Experience of the Researcher in Law, Business Management, Economics, Accountancy and Banking & Finance — 192

3.15. Ethical Consideration — 192

3.16. Conclusion — 192

Chapter 4: Presentation and Analysis of Data Collated from Banks Selected as Case Studies — 194

4.1. Introduction — 194

Section A—The Royal Bank of Scotland Group — 199

4.2. The Background of the Royal Bank of Scotland Group and the Nature of its Business Model Over Time — 199

4.3. Constituents of RSB Group Prior to the Financial Crisis — 201

 4.3.1. Insurance Brand (RBS Insurance) — 201

 4.3.2. Wealth Management/Private Banking — 202

 4.3.3. Banks Within the Group — 202

 4.3.4. Strategic Divisions within the RBS Group — 203

4.4. The Constituents of Table 5 — 206

4.5. Analysis and Interpretation of Extracted Information Collated from the Annual Financial Accounts of the Royal Bank of Scotland in the Light of the Aim and Objectives of the Study — 212

4.6. Conclusions: Final Review on the Performance of RBS in the Light of the Aim of the Study — 219

Section B: Barclays Plc (Group Accounts) — 225

4.7. Barclays Plc: Historical Background, Size and Structure of the Bank — 225

4.8. The Nature of Barclays' Business Model and International Outreach — 226

4.9. The Constituents of Table 6	232
4.10. Analysis and Interpretation of the Extracted Information Collated from the Annual Financial Accounts of Barclays Bank Plc in the light of the Aim and Objectives of the Study	239
4.10.1. Analysis for 2004–2006	240
4.10.2. Analysis for 2007–2009	242
4.10.3. Analysis 2010–2012	246
4.10.4. Analysis for 2013–2018	248
4.11. Contributions to the Operating Income Before Tax by the Investment Banking Division of Barclays Group	252
4.12. Insurance Services Contributions to the Operating Profit Before Tax	255
4.13. Wealth Management's Contributions to the Operating Profit Before Tax	256
4.14. Findings and Conclusions Regarding Barclays Group in the Light of the Aim of the Study	256
Section C: Standard Chartered Bank (Group Accounts)	260
4.15. Introduction	260
4.16. Standard Chartered Bank Plc: Historical Background and Basic Statistics	261
4.17. The Size, Markets and Business Model of Standard Chartered Bank Over Time	262
4.18. Constituents of Table 8	265
4.19. Analysis and Interpretation of the Extracted Information Collated from the Annual Financial Accounts of Standard Chartered Bank Plc in Light of the Aim and Objectives of the Study	273
4.20. Findings and Conclusions Regarding Standard Chartered Bank Group in the Light of the Aim of the Study	279
Section D: HSBC Holdings Plc (Group Accounts)	283

4. 21. HSBC Plc: Historical Background, Size and the Corporate Services Provided by the Bank ... 283

4.22. Constituents of Table 9 ... 289

4.23. Analysis and Interpretation of the Extracted Financial Data Collated from the Annual Accounts of HSBC Group ... 295

    4.23.1. Analysis for 2004–2006 ... 295

    4.23.2. Analysis for 2007–2009 ... 296

    4.23.3. Analysis for 2010–2013 ... 298

    4.23.4. Analysis for 2014–2018 ... 300

4.24. Conclusions ... 301

Chapter 5: Comparative Evaluation of the Performance of the Four Case Studies ... 303

5.1. Introduction ... 303

5.2. Similarities in the Circumstances of the Case Studies: People, Objectives, Structure and Business Models ... 305

5.3. The Differences in the Circumstances of the Four Case Study Banks: RBS, Barclays, SCB and HSBC ... 309

5.4. The Royal Bank of Scotland ... 309

5.5. Barclays Group ... 311

5.6. Standard Chartered Bank ... 312

5.7. HSBC ... 313

5.8. Conclusions ... 315

Chapter 6: Findings and Conclusions ... 317

6.1. Introduction ... 317

6.2. The Varied Long-term Impacts of the GFC on RBS, Barclays, SCB, HSBC and the Undulating Trips of these Case Studies to Recovery from 2004 to 2018 ... 318

6.3. The Desirability of the Ring-fencing Policy as a Suitable Regulatory Measure in Response to the Global Financial Crisis in the UK ... 320

6.4. Suitability or otherwise of the Ring-fencing Policy as a Measure that is Capable of Deterring Financial Crises in the Future   *323*

6.5. The Commonly Accepted Causes of the Global Financial Crisis in 2007–2009   *324*

6.6. Some of the Dire Consequences of the Global Financial Crisis in 2007–2009 to Different Classes of People and Organisations   *325*

6.7. The Gold Rush: Mergers, Acquisition and Leadership Failure in the Banking Sector Before The Global Financial Crisis   *326*

    6.7.1. The Benefits of Mergers and Acquisitions and Potential Harms   *327*

    6.7.2. The Response of the Banking Regulators to M&A and Why.   *328*

    6.7.3. The Impact of Poor Management Decisions, Which Often Led to Incessant Changes in the Leadership of Banks   *332*

    6.7.4. Suggestions About Internal Control Mechanisms   *334*

6.8. Justification of the Hypothesis Proposed at the Beginning of the Study   *336*

6.9. Recommendations on the Way Forward and Further Research   *338*

6.10. Contributions to Knowledge   *340*

Bibliography   **341**

List of Abbreviations

ABN AMRO Algemene Bank Nederland AMRO
ABS Asset-Backed Securities
ATM Automated Teller Machine
AUM Assets Under Management
BCBS Banking Committee on Banking Supervision
BCCI Bank of Credit and Commerce International
BGI Barclays Global Investors
BoE Bank of England
CEO Chief Executive Officer
CET Tier 1 Common Equity Tier 1 Capital
CDO Collateralised Debit Obligation
CLO Collateralised Loan Obligation
CMBS Commercial Mortgage-Backed Securities
CDs Credit Derivatives
CRD Capital Requirements Directive Regulation
DCO Dominion Colonial Overseas
DSO Debit Securitisation Obligations
DPS Dividend Per Share
DCM Dual Control Mechanism
EPS Earnings Per Share
EBRD European Bank for Reconstruction and Development
EU European Union
EURIBOR Euro Interbank Offered Rate
FCA Financial Conduct Authority
FF&P Fleming Family & Partners Ltd
FIS Financial Infrastructure System
FSA Financial Service Authority
FSCS Financial Services Compensation Scheme
FSMA Financial Services and Market Act

GDP Gross Domestic Product
GFC Global Financial Crisis
GSIB Global Systemically Important Banks
HSBC Hongkong Shanghai Banking Corporation
HQLAs High-Quality Liquid Assets
IC Impairment Charges
IMF International Monetary Fund
IRFSs International Reporting Financial Standards
KPI Key Performance Indicator
LIBOR London Inter-Bank Offered Rate
LCR Liquid Coverage Ratio
M & A Merger and Acquisition
OPBT Operating Profit Before Tax
OCT Over-the-Counter Trade
PIDA Public Interest Disclosure Act
PPI Payment Protection Insurance
PRA Prudential Regulation Authority
QC Queen Counsel
RPB Recognised Professional Bodies
ROCE Return on Capital Employed
RBS Royal Bank of Scotland
RMBS Residential Mortgage-Backed Securities
SCB Standard Chartered Bank
SIB Security and Investment Board
SRO Self-Regulatory Organisations
SWOT Strengths, Weaknesses, Opportunities and Threats
TA Total Asset
TIBOR Tokyo Interbank Offered Rate
UBS Union Bank of Switzerland
UDT United Dominion Trust
UK United Kingdom

List of Figures

Figure 1: Gross Domestic Product: Claimed Volume Measures Seasonally Adjusted 1948–2016 — 147

Figure 2: Breakdown of Gross Value Added at Basic Prices by Industry 2015 UK — 149

Figure 3: Compensation of Employees by Industry 2015 — 150

Figure 4: Research Philosophy in the Research Onion Model — 164

Figure 5: RBS Group: The Relationship Between Income and Profit Before Tax 2004–2018 — 207

Figure 6: RBS Group: The Relationship Between Assets, Deposits and Loans 2004–2018 — 208

Figure 7: RBS Group: Trend of Growth/Decline in the Total Assets 2004–2018 — 209

Figure 8: RBS Group: The Percentage of Contribution of Earnings From the Investment Banking to the Profit Before Tax 2004–2013 — 210

Figure 9: RBS Group: Impairment Charges 2004–2018 — 211

Figure 10: RBS Group: Trend of Growth/Decline in the Employees' Profile from 2005–2018 — 212

Figure 11: Barclays Group: The Relationship Between Income and Operating Profit Before Tax from 2004–2018 — 233

Figure 12: Barclays Group: The Relationship Between Assets, Deposits, and Loans from 2004–2018 — 234

Figure 13: Barclays Group: Trend of Growth/Decline in the Total Assets from 2004–2018 — 235

Figure 14: Barclays Group: Trend of Growth/Decline in Impairment
Charges from 2004–2018   236

Figure 15: Barclays Group: The Percentage of Contributions of the
Investment Banking to the Profit Before Tax from 2004–2018
    237

Figure 16: Barclays Group: Trend of Growth/Decline in the
Employees' Profile from 2004–2018   238

Figure 17: Barclays Group: Trend of Growth/Decline in Earnings Per
Share and Dividend Per Share from 2004–2018   239

Figure 18: SCB Group: The Relationship Between Income and
Operating Profit Before Tax 2004–2018 US $ (B)   266

Figure 19: SCB Group: The Relationship Between Assets, Deposits
and Loans 2004–2018 US$ (B)   267

Figure 20: SCB Trend of Growth/Decline in the Total Assets
For 2004–2018 US$ (B)   268

Figure 21: SCB Trend of Growth/Decline in Impairment Charges
2004–2018 US$ (b)   269

Figure 22: SCB Group: The Proportion of Contribution of Investment
Banking Division to the Operating Profit Before
Tax 2004–2018   270

Figure 23: SCB Group: Employee Profile 2005–2018   271

Figure 24: SCB Group: Trend of Growth/Decline in Earnings per
Share and Divided Per Share 2004–2018   272

Figure 25: SCB Group: Trend of Growth/Decline in Income from
Wealth Management 2004–2018 US$ (b)   273

Figure 26: HSBC Group: The Relationship Between Operating
Income and PBT 2004–2018 US$ billion   290

Figure 27: HSBC Group: The Relationship Between Assets, Deposits and
Loans 2004–2018 US$ billion '000   291

Figure 28: HSBC Group: Trend of Growth/Decline in Impairment
Charges 2004–2018 US$ billion   292

Figure 29: HSBC Group: The Proportion of Contributions to PBT from Investment Banking Division, Insurance Business and Private Banking 2004–2018 US$ billion ... 293

Figure 30: HSBC Group: Employee Profile 2004–2018 ... 294

Figure 31: HSBC Group: Investment Banking Contributions to the Profit Before Tax 2004–2018 US$'000 billion ... 295

Figure 32: The Impacts of GCF on the Case Studies and Their Difficult Trips Through 2004–2018 ... 319

List of Tables

Table 1: The Impact of the Credit Crunch on the Stock Market Capitalisation of the Banking System Among Twenty-four foremost Industrialised Countries   52

Table 2: Gross Domestic Product Chained Volume Measures Seasonally Adjusted £ (m) 1948–2016   148

Table 3: The World's Biggest Banks 2018/2019   151

Table 4: Analysis of the Research Onion Model   165

Table 5: Tabulated Data Extracted from the Annual Reports and Consolidated Financial Accounts of the Royal Bank of Scotland Group From 2004–2018 (Financial Year Ending on 31st December Annually)   204

Table 6: Tabulated Data Extracted from the Annual Reports and Consolidated Financial Accounts of the Barclays Group From 2004 to 2018 (Financial Year Ending on 31st December Annually)   231

Table 7: Contributions of the Investment Banking to the Profit Before Tax Relative to Other Divisions: Barclays Group   253

Table 8: Tabulated Data Extracted from the Annual Reports and Consolidated Financial Accounts of the Standard Chartered Group From 2004 to 2018 (Financial Year Ending on 31st December Annually)   264

Table 9: Tabulated Data Extracted from the Annual Reports and Consolidated Financial Accounts of HSBC Group From 2004 to 2018 (Financial Year Ending on 31st December Annually)   288

List of Appendices

Appendix 1: The Royal Bank of Scotland Group: References to Page Numbers on the Annual Reports and the Financial Accounts — 362

Appendix 2: Barclays Group: References to Page Numbers on the Annual Reports and the Financial Accounts from 2004–2018 — 365

Appendix 3: Standard Chartered Bank Group: References to Page Numbers on the Annual Reports and the Financial Accounts from 2004–2018 — 368

Appendix 4: HSBC Group: References to Page Numbers in the Annual Financial Reports 2004–2018 — 371

Appendix 5: Data for Figure 5: The Royal Bank of Scotland Group: The Relationship Between Income and Operating Profit Before Tax 2004–2018 £ (b) — 373

Appendix 6: Data for Figure 6: The Royal Bank of Scotland Group The Relationship Between Assets, Deposits and Loans 2004–2018 £ (b) — 374

Appendix 7: Data for Figure 7: The Royal Bank of Scotland Group Trend of Growth and Decline in the Total Assets 2004–2018 £ (b) — 375

Appendix 8: Data for Figure 8: The Royal Bank of Scotland Group: The Contributions of Earnings from the Investment Banking to the Profit Before Tax 2004–2013 £ (b) — 376

Appendix 9: Data for Fig. 9: The Royal Bank of Scotland Group Impairment Charges 2004–2018 £ (b) — 377

Appendix 10: Data for Figure 10: The Royal Bank of Scotland Group Trend of Growth and the Decline in the Employees' Profile 2005–2018 ... 378

Appendix 11: Data on Fig. 11. Barclays Group: The Relationship Between Income and Operating Profit Before Tax From 2004–2018 £ (b) ... 379

Appendix 12: Data for Fig. 12 Barclays Group: The Relationship Between Assets, Deposits and Loans From 2004–2018 £ (b) ... 380

Appendix 13: Data for Fig. 13–Barclays Group: Trend of Growth/Decline in the Total Assets for 2004–2018 £ (b) ... 381

Appendix 14: Data for Figure 14–Barclays Group: Trend of Growth/Decline in Impairment Charges from 2004–2018 £ (b) ... 382

Appendix 15: Data for Fig. 15–Barclays Group: The Proportion of the Contributions of the Investment Banking to the Operating Profit Before Tax 2004–2018 £ (billion) ... 383

Appendix 16: Data on Fig. 16–Barclays Group: Trend of Growth/Decline in the Employees' Profile 2004–2018 ... 384

Appendix 17: Data on Fig. 17 Barclays Group: Trend of Growth/Decline in Earnings Per Share and Dividend Per Share in Pence 2004–2018 ... 385

Appendix 18: Data for Figure 18 S.C.B. Group: The Relationship Between Income and Operating Profit Before Tax 2004–2018 ... 386

Appendix 19: Data for Figure 19 S.C.B. Group: The Relationship Between Assets, Deposits and Loans 2004–2018 ... 387

Appendix 20: Fig. 20 S.C.B. Group: Trend of Growth/Decline in the Total Assets Employed 2004–2018 US$ (b) ... 388

Appendix 21: Fig 21 S.C.B. Group: Trend in Growth/Decline in Impairment Charges 2004–2018 US$ (b) ... 389

Appendix 22: Fig 22 S.C.B. Group: The Proportion of Contributions of the Investment Division to the OPBT US$ 2004–2018 ... 390

Appendix 23: Fig 23 S.C.B. Group: Employees' Profile — 391

Appendix 24: Fig. 24 S.C.B. Group: Trend of Growth/Decline in Earnings Per Share and Divided Per Share 2004–2018 — 392

Appendix 25: Fig. 25 S.C.B. Group: Trend of Growth/Decline in Income from Wealth Management 2004–2018 US$ (b) — 393

Appendix 26: HSBC Group: The Relationship Between Operating Income and PBT 2004–2018 US$ billion — 394

Appendix 27: HSBC Group: The Relationship Between Assets, Deposits and Loans 2004–2018 US$ billion '000 — 395

Appendix 28: HSBC Group: Trend of Growth/Decline in Impairment Charges 2004–2018 US$ billion — 396

Appendix 29: HSBC Group: Contributions to the PBT by Investment Banking, Insurance Business and Private Banking 2004–2018 US$ billion — 397

Appendix 30: Figure 30, HSBC Group: Employee Profile 2004–2018 — 398

Appendix 31: HSBC Group: Investment Banking Contributions to PBT 2004–2018 — 399

Appendix 32: Fig 32 The Impacts of GFC on the Case Studies and their Difficult Recovery Trips Through 2004–2018 — 400

Preface

Maintaining stability in the banking sector is believed to be critical to promoting everyone's welfare, including those who may not even have a bank account.

With the benefit of hindsight, the book evaluated key historical events that threatened to cause disruptions in the banking industry in the UK from the late 1970s to the 2000s. There are assumptions that learning from history may assist with the avoidance of repeating costly mistakes made in the past.

The analysis began with the impacts on the banking sector, the introduction of the free market economy policy of the 1970s through the troubling financial crisis from 2007 to 2009 and the recovery period between 2017 and 2018.

The book evaluated the evolution of banking theories, neoliberalism, and structuralism and how these philosophies shaped legal responses to stabilise the banking industry in the past forty years.

Applying the case study model, the book evaluated the annual reports and financial accounts of the Royal Bank of Scotland Group, Barclays Group, Standard Chartered Bank Group and HSBC Plc Group for fifteen years, revealing a taste of the sweetness of success when banking operations are going well. It also demonstrated all that could possibly go wrong in a mega bank, the crippling price of failure and the hard road to recovery.

The overarching objective is to present to the new generation of bankers, policymakers, banking sector regulators, supervisors, corporate lawyers, and banking and finance students a digestible overview of what transpired in the banking legal environment in the past forty years. The hope is that these accounts will serve as an essential guide to avoid making the same mistakes in the future.

The Methods and Methodology Chapter would be an indispensable companion for Postgraduate students and other researchers.

John Abolarin, LL B, LL M, M Sc, PhD, FCIB.
Barrister at Law England & Wales.

30th October 2024.

Chapter 1
A General Overview:
The Problem, Context, Content and Focus of the Book

1.1 Introduction: The Problem of Instability in the Banking Sector and the Damaging Socio-economic Consequences Over Time.

The duty to maintain stability in the banking sector is at the heart of the essential functions of banking regulators and supervisors. This book is concerned with managing the endemic instability problem in the banking sector.

The book emphasises the importance of the banking sector as an agent of wealth creation and why the banking industry merits diligent safeguarding in the public's best interest. The question concerns how best to protect the banking sector and, by extension, the public's best interest.

Given some of the failings in the banking sector in the past forty years, such as excessive risk-taking, poor liquidity, and sharp practices in selling controversial products to unsuspecting customers discussed in Chapter 4, some may argue that perhaps the public needs more protection against bankers' excesses.

The banking sector serves as the storehouse for most people where life savings and personal wealth are kept. A general crisis in the financial system can mean hardship, liquidation of businesses, job losses, liquidity crunch and irrecoverable losses for many. Financial crises affect everyone in different ways, including those who do not even have a bank account.

A disruption in the banking sector is comparable to a fire disaster. Few agents can rapidly cause more widespread devastation, grief, and catastrophic financial ruin than a fire outbreak. Sometimes, a fire outbreak may leave little or nothing to salvage after the event. For example, a deliberate act of arsonists may cause a fire disaster. People may also harness the power of fire, turning it into a weapon of warfare to cause incalculable destruction. Likewise, environmental hazards may trigger a fire catastrophe. However, regardless of how caused, the pain of the losses is still the same.

In the same way, a financial crisis in the banking sector may occur due to poor banking practices, lack of suitable internal control mechanisms, inadequate capital and liquidity base, financial mismanagement, recklessness of bank officials, fraud, excessive risk-taking, leadership incompetence and inadequate banking supervision.[1]

Under the Deposit Guarantee Scheme, the Financial Services Compensation Scheme offers protection up to £85 000 for losses relating to funds in personal and business accounts held within a banking group if there is a banking crisis.[2] However, outside of this Deposit Guarantee Scheme, a financial crisis in the banking sector can potentially obliterate personal or family wealth accumulated over the years. Therefore, in the public's interest, it is vital to watch over and safeguard the financial system keenly and by every means possible on an ongoing basis.

For example, catastrophic losses followed the collapse of Johnson Matthey Banks Ltd in 1984.[3] The same thing happened in the aftermath of the Bank of Credit and Commerce International failure in 1991.[4] Worse still, in 1995, the bankruptcy of Barings Capital, an investment bank that had been in business for over two hundred years (1762–1995) before it failed, inspired a general condemnation and public outrage against the banking sector and banking regulators.[5] In addition, the most recent global financial crisis in 2007–2009 is considered the worst of its kind.[6] On each occasion, the failings and

---

[1] Financial Services Authority, 'The Failure of the Royal Bank of Scotland: Financial Services Authority Board Report' (December 2011, pp 314–315)
[2] https://www.prarulebook.co.uk/rulebook/Content/Chapter/213753/14-05-2019
[3] R, Cranston, 'Principles of Banking Law 2nd Ed' (Oxford University Press, 2002, pg. 65)
[4] Bingham, Lord Justice, 'Inquiry into the Supervision of the Bank of Credit and Commerce International' (HMSO, 1992)
[5] E.A J George and A. Hardcastle, "Report of the Board of Banking Supervision Inquiry into the Collapse of Barings" (HMSO, 1995)
[6] C. R Morris, 'The Trillion Dollar Meltdown' (Perseus Books, 2008)

consequences of the economic turmoil in the banking sector left in their trail job losses, bankruptcies, and a hard-hit economy.

It has been well over fifteen years since the world faced a first-of-its-kind global financial crisis in 2007–2009, which rocked the financial systems of some of the most sophisticated world economies to their foundations. As the effects of that financial crisis are dying out, the question is not whether there will be other financial crises in the future. The concern should be when and how soon before another one hits some parts of the world. As we speak (On 11th March 2023), reports are emerging about the collapse of another bank in the USA, Silver Valley Bank. Whilst the re-occurrence of another financial meltdown cannot be ruled out, we can first study the causes of previous financial crises. Understanding the roots of past failures in the financial system can aid in developing plans and informed courses of action to mitigate the effects of future disasters wherever they may rear their ugly heads again.

The book's introductory section sets the scene, stating this work's aims and objectives. It also states the research questions and the rationale for embarking on the study. The section also highlights the broader socio-economic context of the study, defining the area of law visited. Furthermore, it states the importance of the research and the expected contributions to knowledge. Finally, it concludes by tabling the structure of the book.

Although the study is primarily law research, it sits within multiple disciplines. The related subjects include law, socio-economic policy, banking and finance, and business management. Also, it engages critical financial accounting tools required to analyse the annual reports and financial accounts of the banks chosen as case studies for the research.

1.2 The Tension Between the Need to Make More Restraining Laws And Advantages of Granting Discretionary Powers to Responsibly Manage Depositors' Funds

The study raises the point that there is a delicate balance between safeguarding the economy by using legal restraints on banks. At the same time, it emphasises the importance of refraining from stifling creativity in managing banks' funds through over-regulation. Creativity, in this sense, means the discretion and options available to banks' management to resourcefully invest banks' funds at their disposal to increase the wealth of the beneficial owners of banks and, generally, to assist in growing the economy.

One of the challenges that banks' regulators face has to do with contending with the tension between the duty to protect the public against greed and recklessness on the part of the bankers, who may be prone to taking undue risks in managing depositors' funds while at the same time, there is an understanding that the public interests are better served when the financial intermediation capabilities of banks are not unduly fettered by over-regulation.[7, 8]

There is increasing recognition that banks are the engines that drive the economy and the most important source of external funding needed to grow businesses and the economy.[9] Due to the importance of the banking sector to the economy, rightly so, the banking sector is also held to be one of the most regulated institutions in the world.[10] Guiso et al. argued that there is a rational justification for government intervention through regulation when there are incessant bank failures.[11] Persaud and Barth et al. also extensively discussed the justification for government intervention through regulation based on a need for consumers' protection and mitigation against systemic risks.[12, 13]

That said, since the new wave of free-market capitalism promoted by Friedman and which took root in the 1970s, some have argued that banking regulation took on a damaging laissez-faire approach, which may have culminated in the global financial crisis in 2007–2009.[14, 15] Nevertheless, others argued that the free-market economy policy era ushered in unprecedented

---

[7] J. Sinkey, 'Commercial Bank Financial Management 5th Ed' (Prentice-Hall, 1998, P. 13)

[8] D. Hillier, et al., 'Financial Markets and Corporate Strategy, 2nd European Ed' (McGraw-Hill, 2012, P. 4)

[9] F. S. Mishkin, et al., 'The Economics of Money, Banking and Financial Markets', (Pearson Educational, 2013, p. 151)

[10] Ibid (S. Mishkin et al.)

[11] L. Guiso et al., 'The Cost of Banking Regulation', National Bureau of Economic Research Massachusetts Cambridge, Working paper 12501, (2006).

[12] A. Persaud, 'Reinventing Financial Regulation: A Blueprint for Overcoming Systemic Risk' (Apress Publishers, 2015)

[13] J. Barth et al., 'Rethinking Banking Regulation' (University Press, Cambridge, 2006)

[14] M. Friedman, 'Capitalism and Freedom' (University of Chicago Press, 1962)

[15] K. Popper, 'The Open Society and Its Enemies' (Princeton University Press, 1994)

prosperity since the end of World War II.[16] Doubtless, a contributory factor may have been due to the less restrictive regulation at that time. That situation tacitly allowed high leverage (low equity ratio to high debt) in the banking sector and what appeared to be an abundant supply of cheap depositors' funds, which subsidised bank lending operations.[17, 18]

The question then is, when could it be said that a particular piece of regulation has crossed the borderline, transforming from a necessary protective firewall meant to shield and alleviate the costs of taking undue risks into a law that has become an inhibitor of progress? Over-regulation in this context refers to a situation where there are too many laws and regulations, some of which are unnecessary because they do not add justifiable value. Their presence hinders productivity and the facilitation of trade and commerce.

Generally, academics are not always united in their views on the effectiveness and adequacy of the law and regulations in the banking sector. Whilst some concluded that the banking sector was, in fact, already over-regulated, others are of the view that more laws are still needed to stem the recklessness in the banking sector.[19, 20, 21]

Writing in 2013, Baber believed that the regulatory response to the global financial crisis might be inadequate given the contributory economic factors to the global financial crisis in 2007–2009.[22] Admati faulted the range of laws and regulations before the 2007–2009 global financial crisis on the basis that the regulatory architecture then, and with time, attempts to reform it failed to pay

---

[16] Please see page 147, Fig. 1 Gross Domestic Product 1948–2016 and Table 2 on page 148.

[17] R A Admati, 'The Compelling Case for Stronger and More Effective Leverage Regulation in Banking' (2014) Vol. 43 (2) The Journal of Legal Studies.

[18] J. Cullen, 'Executive Compensation in Imperfect Financial Markets' (Edward Elgar, 2014) p. viii

[19] C. Goodhart et al. 'Financial Regulation or Over Regulation' (Institute of Economic Affairs, 1988)

[20] A. Hudson, 'Banking Regulation and Ring-fence' (2013) 107, 1–23 Compliance Officer Bulletin

[21] T. Arthur and P. Booth, 'Does Britain Need a Financial Regulator?' (The Institute of Economic Affairs, 2010)

[22] G. Baber, 'A Critical Examination of the Legislative Response in Banking and Financial Regulation to Issues' (2013) Vol 20 (2), 237–252. Related to Misconduct in the Context of the Crisis of 2007–2009

well-deserved attention to the problematic issue of inadequate equity-cum debt ratio. She opined that this was prevalent within the banking sector.[23] She further contended that dealing with the thorny issue of a high debt/equity ratio is central to maintaining stability in the banking sector and, by extension, the economy.

Nevertheless, others advocated for caution, pointing out that the crisis in 2007–2009 was not a result of failure in the then prevalent regulation alone, but the fault is partly shared by the ineffective supervisory strategies adopted by the regulators who were believed to have often failed to identify difficulties in the financial system ahead of their occurrence or sometimes failed to respond quickly enough when problems were spotted.[24, 25]

1.3 The Aims of the Study

The book briefly reviews a few major UK banks that failed in the past forty years to illustrate and provide lessons for the future. These include Johnson Matthey Bank, Bank of Credit and Commerce International, Baring Capitals, and, most recently, the troubled Royal Bank of Scotland and Barclays Group.

Following the turbulent global financial crisis from 2007–2009 and as the dust settled, the study, with the benefit of hindsight, evaluated the varied long-term impacts of the crisis on the performance of four of the largest UK banks to highlight what went wrong during and after the Global Financial Crisis.

Evaluating the Group financial accounts of the Royal Bank of Scotland Plc, HSBC Plc, Barclays Group, and Standard Chartered Bank Plc from 2004–2018, the outcomes demonstrate what could go wrong in a megabank. It indicates the crippling price of failure, the downward journey of the banks in the period under review and the long, challenging route to recovery.

The study evaluated the ring-fencing policy after the global financial crisis (GFC) of 2007–2009, particularly in the particular circumstances of the UK banks that are considered Global Systemically Important Banks (GSI-Bs).

As mentioned, it has been more than fifteen years since the GFC occurred in 2007–2009 and eleven years after the enactment of the Banking Reform Act 2013. Through evaluation of the financial accounts of the case studies from 2004

---

[23] Op. Cit., A. Admati (n. 17)

[24] A. Arora, 'The Global Financial Crisis: A New Global Regulatory Order?' (2010) 8, 670–699, Journal of Business and Law.

[25] Verrill, L. 'Regulation Hit the Rock?' (2008) 21 (1), 16 Insolvency Intelligence.

to 2018, the study aimed to determine the varied long-term impacts of the GFC on the performance of four of the largest UK banks chosen as case studies. Lest we forget too soon, the study lays out for the future some of the direct consequences and costs of the downward journey of these banks starting from 2004–2018 and the difficult road back to recovery.

The study's stated aims acknowledge that the global financial crisis had some long-term detrimental impacts on the banking sector's financial performance. It also underscores the importance of the long-term effects of the other regulatory responses designed to reduce the consequences and frequency of likely financial crises in the banking sector in the future.

The global financial crisis has often been described as the worst of its kind in modern banking history. In order to forestall a total collapse of some of the UK's banks classified as Global Systemically Important Banks affected by the crisis, the government was constrained to commit bail-out packages which peaked at £1.162 trillion (including pledged cash support of £612.58 billion, but which later reduced to £456.33 billion) as of 31st March 2010.[26] Out of these pledges, the government provided £123.92 billion in loans and shares acquired with cash transferred to the banks that took the government bail-out.[27] Furthermore, the government undertook a contingent liability wherein the government promised to provide cash support of up to £323.40 billion in the likely event that the banks needed additional cash support at a future date.[28]

Thus, the study evaluated the annual financial accounts of some of the largest UK banks and whose collapse could have had the most damaging consequences for the UK economy and the global level. The banks in this category chosen as case studies are RBS, Barclays, Standard Chartered Bank and HSBC Holdings Plc.

In order to appreciate the extent of the knock-on effects of the hard free fall that some of these banks had, the study evaluated fifteen years of their annual financial accounts from 2004–2018. The study highlights the extent of losses incurred by the banks. It also points to the consequences of the inability of some of the banks to pay dividends, which in some cases spanned about ten years. In

---

[26] National Audit Office, 'HM Treasury, the Comptroller and Auditor General's Report on Accounts to the House of Commons (July 2011) NAO Report: The Treasury's 2010-11 Accounts: the financial stability interventions
[27] Ibid.
[28] Ibid.

addition, there were large-scale redundancies in some of the banks. Finally, it points out the negative impacts on the wealth of the equity owners of the banks.

Over the period evaluated, thirteen Key Performance Indicators (KPI) were extracted from the annual financial accounts of the case studies. Among others, these include Operating Profit Before Tax (OPBT), Operating Income, movements in the Total Assets, Earnings Per Share (EPS), Dividend Per Share (DPS), the state of the Liquidity Ratios of the banks, number of employees engaged over time, Annual Impairment Charges, Insurance Income, Earnings from Investment Banking and some other performance indicators discussed in Chapter 4. Some of the Key Performance Indicators chosen are markers of sensitive response to cost, asset accumulation or reduction thereof and factors that had overall effects on the earning capacity of the banks chosen as case studies. Each of the KPIs selected has its own story to tell about the reasons behind the increase or decrease in the profitability of the case studies. This is amply discussed in Chapter 4.

Notably, the study also evaluated legislative measures made at both national and supranational levels in response to the global financial crisis. These were designed to encourage stability in the banking sector through enhanced capital requirements, improvements in the liquidity ratios, enhancement of assets' quality and generally, to reduce the need for future taxpayer-funded bail-outs to the banks.

In the case of the UK, in addition to the need to follow international banking regulations, the ring-fencing policy was also enacted into law, which came into effect on 1st January 2019. The ring-fencing policy is an aspect of the protective measures introduced into the Financial Services (Banking Reform) Act 2013 following the financial crisis of 2007–2009.[29] While the Banking Reform Act was enacted into law on 18th December 2013, preparation for compliance with the policy was ongoing, with mandatory compliance starting on 1st January 2019.

In effect, the affected banks had a six-year moratorium to become ring-fencing policy compliant.

The effect of the legislation is to separate core depositors' accounts from risky investment banking activities in a non-ring-fenced bank into a safe ring-fenced bank. The legislation aimed to prevent banks from using government-

---

[29] The Financial Services (Banking Reform) Act 2013, Part 1 (2), (i) & (ii)

insured core deposits to fund risky investment activities. From the policy's commencement date, core depositors' accounts were removed into a separate ring-fenced bank within the group. The objective is that in the event of any difficulty arising from the non-ring-fenced bank, its adverse effects would not spill over to the separate entity ring-fenced. It is held that this arrangement would make the bail-out of banks by the government less likely and avoid disruptions in the payment system within the economy if difficulties arose in the non-ring-fenced bank.

The legal changes introduced into the banking sector are usually referred to as systemic risks (undiversifiable market risks) common to the participants in the banking sector. Undiversifiable market risks refer to macroeconomic factors that generally affect the profitability of all the market participants. Such factors include changes in interest rates, taxation, legal requirements, inflation, and a natural disaster.[30, 31] These factors are termed 'Undiversifiable risks' because they are unavoidable. Market participants can only respond to mitigate the negative impact of undiversifiable risks. The ring-fencing policy affected the banks in the case studies differently, as explained in Chapters 4 and 5 of this book.

Although the regulatory changes generally affected the banking sector, some banks had more difficulty dealing with the ensuing challenges. Conversely, others thrived in the midst of it because they were more proactive and better equipped to respond to the challenges than others. Examples include HSBC and the Standard Chartered Bank, discussed in Chapters 4 and 5.

Notably, the study helps us appreciate how other broader issues, including the varied circumstances of each bank, such as their different sizes and diverse business strategies, affected them differently. In addition, it also helps us appreciate how their wide-ranging market environments, different leadership approaches and the extent of their respective exposure to American subprime securities affected the banks in different ways.

HSBC Bank Plc, RBS and Barclays were listed as part of the Global Systemically Important Banks[32] by the Financial Stability Board (FSB) in

---

[30] C. Drury, 'Management and Cost Accounting 6th Ed' (Thomson, 2004, p. 563)

[31] G. Arnold, 'Corporate Financial Management, 3rd Ed' (Prentice-Hall, 2005)

[32] C. Hofmann, 'Global Systemically Important Banks (GSIBs): Operating Globally, Regulated Nationally?' (2017) 2, (155-179) Journal of Business Law.

2011.[33] However, eight years later, RBS fell off the list due to the massive reconstruction that had taken place in the bank.[34] The vast sizes of the banks rated Global Systemically Important Banks before and after the crisis led to concerns over the likely damaging consequences to the economy in the event of any of them possibly collapsing. In the period leading to the global financial crisis in 2007–2009, each of these banks had total assets of more than £2 trillion except the Standard Chartered Bank. The large-scale sizes of these banks led to the concern that the collapse of any of them could lead to irreparable damage to the economy and could trigger a crisis at the international level.[35, 36, 37]

This concern was genuine. As much as possible, part of the concerted efforts of the international community to forestall future government bail-outs focused on ensuring that banks are resilient and capable of weathering future financial crises with little or no assistance from the public.[38] As a result, the need to shore up confidence in the banking sector by boosting its soundness, stability, equity capital and liquidity became more imperative.

---

[33] Financial Stability Board, 'Policy Measures: List of Global Systemically Important Banks', (2011)

[34] Financial Stability Board, 'Policy Measures: List of Global Systemically Important Banks', (2019)

[35] Royal Bank of Scotland, 'Annual Report and Financial Account' (2008, p. 175)—Total assets as of 31/12/2008 were £2.4 trillion. This figure has been criticised as over-inflated, as discussed in Chapter 4.

[36] Barclays Plc, 'Annual Report and Financial Accounts' (2008, p. 205)—Total assets as of 31/12/2008 were £2.05 trillion. This was also criticised as over-inflated.

[37] HSBC Holding Plc, Annual Report and Financial Accounts' (2008) p. 1

[38] E. Ligere, 'Legislative Comment, The Future of Banking in the EU' (2014), 29, (5) 308–311, Journal of International Banking Law and Regulation

1.4 Ring-fencing in Brief

The ring-fencing policy relates to the structural separation of core depositors' accounts from non-ring-fenced banks undertaking investment banking activities. The purpose of ring-fencing is to prohibit the use of core depositors' funds in the risky investment banking division of banks considered to be GSIBs. The structural separation will have the effect of protecting core depositors' funds from the impact of the risk of systemic failure on the economy due to losses arising in the investment banking arm of a banking group.[39]

Only banks with a total average of £25 billion in core deposits over three consecutive years are required to be compliant with the ring-fencing policy.[40]

Part of the policy's objectives is to ensure adequate plans for a controlled and orderly winding down of any big bank that may run into difficulties and, as much as possible, to avoid ripple effects on the other banks.[41] This will enable the ring-fenced bank to continue to carry on undisturbed core banking activities in compliance with the ring-fencing policy.[42]

An essential effect of the ring-fencing policy is that, by separating a ring-fenced bank from the investment banking arm of a group, the chances of a disruption in the financial system affecting the retail banking services, especially the payment system, would be largely reduced.[43] The separation between the ring-fenced entity and the non-ring-fenced arm of a group also means the need to use taxpayers' money to fund bail-out is obviated. In addition, the need for the government to pay crystallised contingent liability under the depositors' guarantee scheme would be avoided, assuming there were difficulties in the non-ring-fenced arm of the group only.

---

[39] Op. Cit., Banking Reform Act 2013, (n. 29)

[40] Financial Conduct Authority, 'Ring-fencing: Guidance on the FCA's Approach to the Implementation of Ring-fencing and Ring-fencing Transfer Schemes (2015) Guidance Consultation 15/5

[41] Banking Act 2009, s. 1, ss (2) (3)

[42] FSMA 2000 Part VII Banking Business Transfer Schemes s. 106 B (3)(a)

[43] Banking Reform Act 2013, Article 142 B s. 4 (b) "To protect the continuity of the provision in the UK of Services provided in the course of carrying on the regulated activity of accepting deposit."

Ring-fenced banks are prohibited from dealing as a principal in risky investment banking services except where exempted.[44] The implication is that ring-fenced banks could only act as agents on behalf of non-ring-fenced bodies regarding these aspects of investment banking services. Generally, RFBs are prohibited from dealing in commodities except when trading in commodities is required for their use or consumption.[45] RFBs can securitise their assets and use derivatives for risk management.[46] Ring-fenced banks may carry out corporate banking services, structured finance and traditional core banking activities.[47]

Restrictions are placed on ring-fenced banks to prevent them from providing facilities to financial institutions, branches, and subsidiaries outside the EEA.[48] The rationale for all that restriction is that transactions of this kind would subject RFBs to more difficulties in making claims in the event of a need to wind down a non-ring-fenced entity in a group. That would also be the case when a subsidiary outside the EEA is involved. This would be the likely result, especially if the ring-fenced bank were exposed to such non-ring-fenced arms of a group. Groups with RFBs are allowed to use similar brands if desired. Data sharing within a group with an RFB is also allowed, provided this provision does not lead to an outcome where there is a misleading impression of whether a group member is ring-fenced.[49]

As observed by Goodhart, an equally important implication of the ring-fencing policy is that the non-ring-fenced part of a group will suffer disadvantages relating to more expensive and difficult funding conditions for itself and large customers.[50]

A matter of particular concern is that the UK universal banks may likely face adverse competition because of the inability of the non-ring-fenced arm to have access to cheap depositors' funds, unlike their European counterparts, which are

---

[44] Statutory Instrument 2014/2080 FSMA 2000 (Excluded Activities and Prohibitions) Part II Article 4.

[45] Ibid. Part II Article 5 (2)

[46] Ibid. Part II Article 7 (2) & Article 9

[47] Op. cit. Statutory Instrument 2014/2080 (n. 44)

[48] Op. Cit., Ring-fencing Guidance para. 1.6 (n. 40)

[49] Ibid.

[50] C A. Goodhart, 'The Vickers Report: An Assessment', (2012) Vol. 6 (1), Law and Financial Market Review.

not faced with similar restrictions. The issues raised in this section are elaborated under the literature review in Chapter 2, Section E, paragraph 2.38.

As stated on the preceding page, the notion of ring-fencing retail banks was initiated by the UK government as part of regulatory measures in response to the financial crisis in 2007–2009. It is a crucial component of the UK's regulatory response to the financial crisis in 2007–2009. So far, no other nation is known to be following in the footsteps of the UK in this regard. The research aimed to determine whether there are any potential detriments to UK banks and bank customers arising from the ring-fencing policy. The aim is to evaluate the possible impacts of the ring-fencing policy on the economy post-GFC and whether there are strong enough reasons to call for a policy review on an ongoing basis in the near future. It is hoped that this study will inspire other researchers and bank regulators to take a keen interest in the subject so that performance in the banking sector is kept on the radar in the next decade following the implementation of the policy. This is to determine in the ensuing years whether there are avoidable adverse effects on banks' performance and notable significant disadvantages to banks' customers that have a causal link to the policy on ring-fencing, which should call for regulatory changes.

1.5 Research Objectives

The research objectives concern defining and setting limits on the evidence used in the study.[51] They focus on how the planned processes led to discovering the study's aims. Chapter 3 elaborates on these, including methods and methodology.

Thus, the researcher undertook the following exercise to achieve the study's aims stated earlier.

(i)

    (a) as a background to the study, a review of extant literature was undertaken on the causes of the global financial crisis in 2007–2009,

    (b) a review of the prevailing laws and regulations before 2007–2009 was undertaken to determine whether gaps in the statute and supervisory regimes may have contributed to the global financial crisis.

---

[51] M. Saunders, et al. 'Research Methods for Business Students 5th Ed. (Pearson Education, 2009, p.10).

Also, a review of the newly introduced changes to the laws after the global financial crisis was conducted, evaluating their impacts on the banking sector, (ii) a theoretical critique of the ring-fencing policy was conducted as it applies to the UK banking sector and against the backdrop of the UK's core competencies in providing financial services, a sphere in which the UK has comparative and competitive advantages.

Core competence is a term borrowed from business management which refers to cultivated or learnt specialist's skills, knowledge, expertise, capabilities, and attributes that can become a critical success factor in the administration of an organisation in a rapidly changing business environment, as happened in the aftermath of the global financial crisis.[52]

(iii) An evaluation was conducted of the effectiveness of the ring-fencing policy as a measure that is capable of deterring financial crises in the future.

(iv) The annual financial accounts of RBS, Barclays, SCB, and HSBC Plc between 2004–2018 were evaluated using case studies to determine the impacts of the global financial crisis on the performances of these banks over the period stated and the likely effects of the new regulatory changes. This exercise aids our understanding of some of the direct costs of the downward journey of these banks in the period evaluated and the difficult road back to recovery as a recorded lesson for the future.

1.6 Research Questions

The research questions include: what are the likely benefits of the regulatory changes? Are there any aspects of the regulatory changes that may potentially hurt the banking sector and the economy in ways that were not intended?

There is also the question of whether the ring-fencing route is appropriate in the prevailing circumstances of the UK. Alternatively, perhaps, there are other equally or even more effective ways of safeguarding the economy without unduly stifling creativity in managing the vast resources placed in the hands of the bankers for the benefit of the economy. Nevertheless, it is without a doubt that there is a public interest justification for regulating the banking sector in some ways to protect the economy.

---

[52] L. J Mullins, 'Management and Organisational Behaviour 11th Ed' (Pearson Education, 2016)

Arguably, there are good economic reasons to support competition law, which discourages unhealthy monopoly situations in the banking sector.[53] However, on the other hand, this study raises the question of whether the UK is insidiously reverting to the discredited protectionist ideology of the Bretton Woods era. Or perhaps, could it be the case that the ring-fencing policy will prove to be one of the regulatory models that would ultimately be the panacea to myriad problems that were notable in the banking sector in the years preceding the catastrophe of 2007–2009?

Concern over returning to the protectionism ideology discussed in Chapter 2 is common among bankers. For example, the Chairman of HSBC Group, Mark Tucker, voiced out this fear when in 2017; he said,

"The threat of <u>protectionism</u> and a lack of inclusive growth all have the potential to <u>disrupt economic activities</u>."[54]

1.7 Research Hypothesis

The hypothesis is that "Notwithstanding some benefits that may accrue from the ring-fencing policy, the banking sector and, by extension, the economy in the UK may likely face long-term detriments arising from the implementation of some aspects of the ring-fencing policy."

This researcher contends that the long-term effects of that aspect of the ring-fencing policy need revisiting and objective evaluation.

The research hypotheses and questions were derived from the literature review on the subject area.

1.8 The Importance of the Banking Sector

What is the significance of this study, and why would the outcome of the study matter to anyone?

The study would be a valuable guide to banking and law academics, banking sector regulators, supervisory authorities, government policymakers, lawyers, banking and finance students, and the public.

---

[53] A. Jones and B Suffrin, 'E C Competition Law 3rd Ed' (Oxford University Press, 2008)
[54] HSBC, Annual Report and Financial Accounts, (2017, p. 5)—Mark Tucker was then the incoming Chairman of the bank.

This is because the study underscores the importance of the banking sector to the economy as the facilitator of wealth creation, helping to mobilise funds from individuals, corporate bodies, and the public, lending the funds thus gathered to borrowers to grow their businesses. This emphasises the role of banks in financial intermediation and their pivotal position as the lever that turns the wheel of economic progress. However, this is not the sole purpose of the banking sector.

Banks serve wide-ranging customers, including small savers, salary earners, sophisticated investors, businesses and multinational corporations. In their role, banks generally facilitate payments for transactions on sales of goods and services between people and organisations, thereby dispensing with the need to carry cash about and notwithstanding the different geographical locations of the parties in the transaction.[55] For example, due to the enormous capital outlay required to buy a home, most people would not have been able to afford to buy a home of their own in a lifetime without the assistance of a bank.

Given the critical roles of the banking sector to society, assorted stakeholders mentioned earlier would be interested in knowing that the financial intermediation capacity of the banking sector is not unduly hampered and that the banking sector is generally safe and stable. In addition, this study may potentially help to identify fault lines in the regulatory and supervisory architecture, if any.

There is a recognition that an ailing banking sector could mean loss of jobs across the board within the economy where credit facilities may become scarce, as was the case during the global financial crisis in 2007–2009.[56] It could mean limitations on the availability of mortgage facilities, thus pushing up prices in the housing market. Difficulties in the banking sector could trigger high costs of banking services in terms of bank charges. Disruptions in the banking sector could lead to instability in the economy, as was the case in the ensued violent protests in Greece, Ireland, Portugal, and Spain, for example, when unemployment and liquidity problems threatened people's sense of security in the wake of the 2007–2009 financial crisis.[57] Dislocation in the banking sector

---

[55] A. Salz, and R. Collins, 'An Independent Review of Barclays' Business Practices' (Barclay Plc, 2013)

[56] D. Murphy, 'Unravelling the Credit Crunch' (CRC Press Taylor and Francis Group, 2009, p 28)

[57] ibid

could worsen standards of living. In the worst-case scenario, failure in the banking sector and general economic hardship could ultimately precipitate a change of the government in power if the public believes that the government has become inept at managing the economy. Thus, a collaborative effort is required to ensure that the banking sector in the UK remains healthy and thriving in the best interests of all.

1.9 Monetised Costs and Benefits of the Ring-fencing Policy

There are two sides to the long and hard debates on regulatory changes in the wake of the global financial crisis and afterwards. This was especially concerning the ring-fencing policy on imposed structural reforms in the banking sector. As Goodhart, Haynes, Campbell and Moffatt exemplify, the underlying assumption in the literature is that the ring-fencing policy may be excessively costly to banks and large corporate customers.[58, 59, 60]

The costs mentioned by these authors relate to the one-off establishment costs of the ring-fenced banks. In addition, there are many other running costs, including expenses associated with the additional heightened burden of compliance with supranational laws. Included are regulatory fees, higher costs of compliance with the ring-fencing policy, and costs of legal advice relating to what the regulations might mean and how they would affect the banks. Finally, the banks and their large customers have the challenge of facing hiked operation and transaction costs.

In July 2013, consultations were still ongoing regarding evaluating available options on what to do to resolve the issue of 'too big to fail'. Through the HM Treasury, the UK government released a document on the monetised full economic impact and the cost implications of the adoption of the ring-fencing policy or its forbearance, not adopting the policy.[61] On pages 77 and 78 of the

---

[58] Op. Cit., C. Goodhart, 2012, (n. 50).

[59] A. Campbell and P. Moffatt, 'Bank Insolvency: The Introduction of Ring-fencing in the UK: An Example to be Followed?' (2019) 4, 241–261 Journal of Business Law

[60] A. Haynes 'Banking and Financial Services Regulation' (2016) 37 (9) 265–266, Company Lawyer

[61] HM Treasury, Department for Business Innovation & Skills, 'Banking Reform: Draft Secondary Legislation' (2013)

document, Option 1 relates to refraining from adopting the ring-fencing policy. In this case, there would be no additional direct or indirect cost to the economy, provided there were no financial crises.

Option 2 relates to the implementation of the ring-fencing policy. The estimate of the monetised costs to the main affected groups annually would be:

- The direct private costs to UK banks–about £1.7 billion–£4.4 billion annually
- The indirect costs on the GDP are about £0.4 billion–£1.9 billion annually
- A reduction in tax receipt is about £150 million–£690 million annually
- The assumed benefits of adopting the ring-fencing policy stated in the document are (i) greater financial stability, (ii) a reduction in the likelihood of the government providing bail-out as crises become less frequent and severe, (iii) a reduction in the implicit subsidies to the huge banks, and a reduction in the probability of future crises by 15% which would generate an annual benefit of £7.1 billion.[62]

These were the estimated costs and benefits of the ring-fencing policy computed in July 2013. However, since the implementation of the ring-fencing policy only began in 2019, we do not have complete data to see the actual costs of implementing it.

Campbell and Moffatt's contention is that there has been improvement in prudential regulation since 2009 after the crisis. In addition, ongoing efforts are directed towards recovery and resolution in the banks following the global financial crisis. These steps arguably led to significant improvement in the stability of the banks. Therefore, they cannot justify the enormous cost of ring-fencing under those circumstances.[63]

Hofmann sees it differently because the costs attributable to the adoption of the ring-fencing policy are worth it. The argument is that even though the costs of implementing the ring-fencing policy may be expensive, the price is

---

https://assets.publishing.service.gov.uk/government/uploads/system/uploads/attachment_data/file/223566/PU1488_Banking_reform_consultation_-_online-1.pdf
[62] Ibid.
[63] Op. Cit., Campbell and Moffatt 2019, (n. 59).

worthwhile because it would be far lower than the costs of a rescue package where there is a bail-out situation after a possible financial crisis.[64]

The outcome of research previously conducted by Barth *et al.* suggests that banks tend to be more robust and more stable when they have broad powers to diversify income sources. In addition, they argued that with more extensive resource bases and wider investment outlets, banks could make the most of economies of scale, thereby enjoying a reduction in the cost of capital and ultimately leading to better services to the economy.[65]

The principles stated by Bart *et al.* and Goodhart have practical implications for implementing the ring-fencing policy in the banking sector. For example, following the restructuring of a universal bank, the resource base previously available for lending by the universal bank would be split between the ring-fenced and non-ring-fenced banks within the group. Thus, due to capital adequacy rules and other lending constraints, each unit may be unable to fully meet the multinational customers' financial needs. As such, at extra costs, conglomerate bank customers in dire need of large capital outlay would have the additional burden of searching for multiple sources of finance to meet their financial needs. This is more so that an important part of cheap deposits previously available to a universal bank is now ring-fenced.

Although the ring-fenced part of the group can perform corporate lending, the group will be missing out on the reduction in administration costs afforded by the economies of scale if there were no separation between the ring-fenced and non-ring-fenced parts of the group.[66]

The rationale behind the policy to restructure the banking sector, as stated in the Banking Reform Act 2013, is to mitigate the adverse effects of future financial crises on the economy. This is especially so in light of concerns that some of the financial institutions in the UK, such as the Royal Bank of Scotland, HSBC Plc, and Barclays Bank, have grown too big over the years. As a result, if any of these financial institutions faced a crisis, they would be considered too

---

[64] Op. Cit., C. Hofmann, 2017, (n. 32).
[65] Barth et al, 'Bank Regulation and Supervision: What Works Best?' (2004) Vol 13 (2) 205–248
[66] Op. Cit., C. Goodhart, 2012, (n. 50).

big to fail and too big to rescue without the government's intervention.[67, 68] As well, if any of them were inevitably allowed to collapse, the impact of such liquidation could substantially damage the economy.

Thus, in the likely event of a financial crisis, the government would be forced to provide an expensive bail-out, as happened in the wake of the last global financial crisis. The problem this research is concerned with is examining regulatory responses to the crisis and determining whether some aspects of the ring-fencing policy are indeed in the economy's best interests or that that part of the banking law is a disproportionate response that went far beyond what is necessary to safeguard the economy. This is more so that competitors in Europe of similar sizes are not faced with the restrictions imposed through the ring-fencing policy.

It is argued that the UK occupies a unique position that gives the country an edge and comparative and competitive advantages, which made the UK stand tall above most other nations of comparable status on the world stage.

These comparative and competitive advantages include the strength of the pound sterling and its attractiveness as a store of wealth for foreign investors and international governments willing to keep their nation's reserves in the UK. London is persistently rated as the leader of the world's leading financial capitals.[69] The United Kingdom is famous for its expertise in law, provision of financial services and wealth management facilities. There is a recognition that the UK is a nation with an abundance of astute innovators and entrepreneurial spirit. The English language occupies an important position as a medium of communication worldwide. The UK government wields political clout and soft power influence that cuts across the globe, starting with allied nations such as America to the commonwealth countries covering more than half of the world population. That influence is a product of over 200–300 years of historical alliances.[70]

---

[67] I. Moosa, 'The Myth of too big to fail' (2010) 11 (4), 319–333, Journal of Banking Regulation

[68] R. Nattrass, 'The Too Big to Fail Problem: Fault Lines Open UP' (2010) 6 (353) Journal of International Banking and Financial Law

[69] Z/Yen, 'The Global Financial Centre Index 22' https://www.longfinance.net/media/documents/gfci_22.pdf

[70] P. Mathias, 'The First Industrial Nation: The Economic History of Britain 1700–1914' (Routledge, 2001)

This book argues that not many nations of equal status as the UK combine all these attributes. In the circumstances of the UK, the fruits of these unique attributes are that they naturally attract funds and investors to the UK.

Applying the ring-fencing policy implies that part of the funds thus generated around the globe would be held in the non-ring-fenced body of a group whilst the other part of the funds would fall within the ring-fenced retail bank. As mentioned earlier, splitting up total available funds in this way would vastly curtail the bank's capacity to provide financial assistance to some of the largest multinational corporations and other gigantic institutions.

The argument is that even where ring-fenced retail entities can perform corporate lending within the scope of funds available, there would be limitations on how far they can assist huge conglomerate organisations with equally huge needs for financial assistance. For example, the extent to which ring-fenced banks can lend will, among other factors, be determined by the value of equity capital and liquidity they hold to support their lending as a separate legal entity. Like every other bank, ring-fenced banks must build their equity capital base over time to support their lending capacity.

These limitations could have been reduced if not avoided altogether had it been that only the risky investment arm of a bank was removed instead of the other way round, where core depositors' funds were removed from the mainstream bank.

Suppose only the risky investment elements of a bank's operations are removed, licences could then be given to qualified banks that are interested in incorporating separate companies that could engage in speculative proprietary trading, commodity trading and swap deals should they wish to do so. In effect, the regulators should require banks to take the risky investment elements off the mainstream banks, not the core deposit accounts. That way, core depositors' accounts would be protected in the same way that the ring-fencing policy would assist. The added advantages are that the cheap core deposits would still be available for traditional corporate lending, where huge multinational corporate customers' financial needs could be met. The availability of cheap depositors' funds would also assist in sustaining mortgage accounts with a very low yield to the banks. Also, the UK universal banks would have been able to retain their competitiveness in relationships with the other European counterparts that did not adopt the ring-fencing policy.

This researcher also contends that the financial sector encompasses banking, securities, the stock market, pension funds, insurance, and credit card service providers. These subsectors have a symbiotic relationship, depending on one another. The point is that although ring-fenced banks can provide corporate and retail banking services by separating banks along ring-fenced and non-ring-fenced banks, the ring-fencing policy limits the support from ring-fenced banking to the entire financial system. This is because, to some extent, restrictions are placed on the ring-fenced banks to prevent them from providing facilities to financial institutions, branches, and subsidiaries outside the EEA.[71] That prohibits RFB from supporting NRFB if they run into difficulties.

The argument is that the banking sector needs an effective monitoring and compliance regime in addition to increasing equity capital and liquidity ratio. The absence of an effective monitoring system was one of the primary causes of failure in the banking sector in the past.[72]

Suppose the hypothesis in this study proves to be true. In that case, other researchers may be interested in this study area, using different methods and methodologies to test the same hypothesis. Moreover, the collective efforts of such work may hopefully spearhead a policy change in the near future if it is considered desirable.

1.10 The Context of the Study: The Fallout of the 2007–2009 Global Financial Crisis

The global financial crisis in 2007–2009 was remarkably a monumental catastrophe[73] which, at the time, precipitated a general sense of deep concern and brought home the reality of potential harm that could arise in the economy when there is a failure in the banking sector.

Although the financial crisis happened almost fifteen years ago, issues around the crisis are still gaining currency. For example, attention towards those issues is accentuating given that the deadline for fully implementing the Financial Services (Banking Reform) Act 2013, slated for 1st January 2019, lapsed four years ago. Also, in relation to the existing collaborative efforts of the

---

[71] Op. Cit., Financial Conduct Authority, 2015, (n. 40).
[72] Op cit., L. Verrill. (n. 25)
[73] F.S Mishkin, and S. G Eakins, 'Financial Markets and Institutions 7th Ed' (Pearson, 2012, p. 211)

European Union to reduce the prospect of global financial crises, the impact of the exit of the UK from the European Union is still unfolding. Thus, discussion around stability in the banking sector, as in other sectors, is again heightened.[74]

At the national level, the financial crisis led to various curative and preventative measures, including nationalising banks where appropriate, providing financial rescue packages and increasing deposit guarantee schemes to safeguard depositors' interests.[75] There were also coordinated responses from closely linked economies. Part of the UK government's response to the global financial crisis includes the introduction of the Financial Services (Banking Reform) Act 2013. As stated earlier, its full implementation was on 1st January 2019. The legislation is a comprehensive enhancement of the FSMA Act 2000. The changes introduced are discussed in Chapter 2.

The other side of the coin is the legitimate concern of the government over the huge losses and the resultant expensive bail-out during the financial crisis that may have prompted the government to take whatever step deemed necessary to forestall future crises.

Whilst news about regional banking failure and localised financial crises are not new in themselves,[76] the unique features of the 2007–2009 crisis are that it was global and nearer home, in fact, too close home for comfort. For example, in the UK, Northern Rock was the first casualty in a run-up to the events leading to September 2007, when the Northern Rock finally capitulated. Likewise, Iceland tasted the bitter pill as one of its banks, Glitnir Bank, went into receivership in September 2008.[77] The whirlwind the financial crisis brought across Europe was such that hardly any European State remained completely untouched.

In the past hundred years or so, there have been different waves of financial crises of varying degrees of intensity, such as the 1929 financial crisis in

---

[74] R. Plato-Shimar, 'Principles of Financial Regulation' (2018) 33 (3) 108–110. Journal of International Banking Law and Regulation

[75] Directive 2014/49/EU of the European Parliament and of the Council on Deposit Guarantee Scheme

[76] G R Hubbard, 'Money, the Financial System and the Economy 4th Ed' (Addison Wesley, 2002, p. 364) In the late 1990s, Russian States and Asian countries had serious financial crises, so also, was America in the 1930s.

[77] S. Valdez and P. Molyneux, 'An Introduction to Global Financial Market 8th Ed' (Palgrave 2016, p 289)

America,[78] the debt crisis of the 1980s in Latin American countries, especially Mexico, Brazil, and Argentina, and the financial upheaval of the emerging markets in the 1990s.[79]

However, the immediate past financial crisis in 2007–2009 has been rated as one of a kind regarding global spread, the magnitude of losses incurred by banks, and the unprecedented impact on national economies worldwide. Moreover, the scale of the losses incurred by banks was then measured in trillions of dollars, which gave genuine reasons for deep concern.[80] The fallouts of the crisis at that time included bank failure, job losses, credit crunch, banks' expensive financial bail-out to stabilise the economy, and harsh austerity measures that inspired public outrage. Whilst some financial institutions were rescued at an unprecedented cost, the collapse of others, such as Lehman Brothers and Bear Stearns, became inevitable.[81]

Huge losses were sustained, especially concerning Collateralised Debt Obligations and hedge funds.[82] Following the crisis, the prospect of widespread unemployment as high as it was after World War II[83] triggered violent protests in Greece and France, and it created a state of unrest in Ireland. Icelandic banks shared in the fallouts of the crisis, as mentioned earlier. Royal Bank of Scotland and Lloyd Group found themselves in the eye of the storm, as it were.

While it is one thing to be supportive and commiserate with others in faraway places where they often experience one financial crisis after another, it is a different scenario when the crisis is in one's backyard this time. One of the foremost issues highlighted by the 2007–2009 global financial crisis, which originated in America and mainly affected the leading industrialised nations that taught the world good banking practices, is that no region in the world is immune to financial crises. The crisis also emphasised the reality of a contagion effect and how closely allied economies can be affected by difficulties they had no hand in creating. More than ever appreciated, the crisis brought home what failure in the banking sector could potentially cost the economy.

---

[78] H. Kaufman, 'Financial Crises: Market Impact, Consequences, and Adaptability' (John Wiley & Sons, 1977, p. 153)
[79] J O Joyce, 'The IMF and Global Financial crises' (Cambridge University Press, 2013)
[80] Op. Cit. (C. R Morris, n. 6)
[81] Op. cit., D. Murphy, p 28, (n. 56).
[82] Op. cit., C R Morris, 2008, (n. 6)
[83] J Galbraith, 'The Great Crash 1929' (Penguin Books, 1954)

A natural response to this catalogue of woes is automatically assuming that tighter control and more laws should be the solution.

This research focuses on the changes in the banking regulations and supervisory regimes to determine whether the regulatory responses to the crisis, including the ring-fencing policy introduced into the Financial Services (Banking Reform) Act 2013,[84] in response to the financial crisis in the aftermath of 2007–2009 are in the economy's best interests. In the alternative, whether parts of the legislation went far beyond what is necessary to safeguard the economy in the long run. The concern is whether these laws would promote or hinder trade and commerce.

Given the importance of the Banking sector to the economy and the dire consequences that could ensue in the likely event of a systemic failure in the banking sector, there has always been an intense debate among leading banking law academicians. Also included in the debate are banking practitioners, policymakers, economists, concerned laypeople, and corporate lawyers. The debaters fall into either of two camps. The classical **structuralism** such as Hudson[85] and Brink[86], or **neo-liberalism** theorists, such as Arora,[87] Persaud,[88] Arthur & Booth,[89] Larosiere[90] and Haynes[91], regarding the propriety or otherwise of the government's action in imposing more legislative restraints on the banking sector as it did following the financial crisis in 2007–2009. Part of Chapter 2 will expound on structuralist and Neoliberal socioeconomic theories.

Having had such a severe financial crisis, which some may argue was avoidable, the debate is concerned with what the regulatory response to the disaster should be. More laws? Assuming making more laws is one of the

---

[84] Op. Cit., Financial Services (Banking Reform) Act 2013, (n. 29).

[85] Op. cit., A. Hudson (n. 20).

[86] B. Brink, 'The Tragedy of Liberalism: An Alternative Defence of a Political Tradition' (State University of New York, 2000)

[87] Op. cit., A. Arora (n. 24).

[88] A. Persaud, 'A Critique of Current Proposal to Reform Bank Regulation' (2010) 3 (147) Journal of International Banking and Financial Law.

[89] Op. cit., T. Arthur and P. Booth (n. 21)

[90] J. Larosiere, 'Structural bank Reforms: An Illusion' (2015) Vol 30 (10), 636 Journal of International Banking and Financial Law

[91] A. Haynes, A. 'Banking Reforms Struggles On' (2015) 36, (2) 123 Statute Law Review

available options, the next question would be: what areas in the financial sector have holes that need plugging? Then, what should be the nature of the laws required to safeguard public interests in the circumstances of the causes of the crisis? Finally, how far should these regulations go to safeguard the interests of the public without unduly hurting the economy in the process?

Consequently, safeguarding the economy and giving the banking sector a measured scope of freedom to exercise its expertise and talents in creatively managing the resources at its disposal is likened to a skilful balancing act between proportionate use of the accelerator and brake pedals in a vehicle. Of course, it would be reckless not to have an efficient braking system in a vehicle. However, at the same time, placing a foot on the brake pedal indiscriminately when the car should be moving forward at 70 miles per hour would only guarantee that the vehicle goes nowhere quickly enough.

Assuming the brake is working efficiently, the essence of having a brake in a car is to enable the vehicle to move fast, as the driver is conscious that he can stop the car at will if there is a need to stop or slow down the vehicle. Similarly, assuming regulatory controls are working correctly in the banking sector, there would be less need to unduly hold down the banking sector by more regulations than are necessary.

During and in the immediate aftermath of the 2007–2009 financial crisis, debates focused on what caused it and the appropriate ways to respond. The literature review in Chapter 2 of this book deals extensively with these debates.

1.11 The Law: The Provisions of the Financial Services (Banking Reform) Act 2013

A significant part of this study's subject is the provisions of the Financial Services (Banking Reform) Act 2013. The legislation refers to the Insolvency Act 1986, Building Societies Act 1986, Competition Act 1998, the Banking Act 2009, and significantly enhanced the Financial Services and Markets Acts 2000.

At the onset, it is considered essential to highlight the key provisions of the Financial Services (Banking Reform) Act 2013 in this section of the book since the legislation occupies a place of prime importance in the research.

There is an emphasis on Part 1, which spells out what ring-fencing is about and what the policy attempts to achieve. Also, emphasis is laid on Part 4, which holds senior management staff of banks accountable whose actions, decisions, and failure to act could lead to severe consequences for the banks they manage.

So, in addition to indictable activities in criminal law, Part 4 created offences arising from mismanagement in the banking sector. It specifies stiff penalties for dereliction of duty on the part of the senior managers holding positions of trust in the banks.

The Banking Reform Act is a volume of 204 pages comprising eight parts summarised as follows:

1.11.1 Part 1—Banking Reform Act 2013: Ring-fencing

This section of the Act revisits section 2B of the Financial Services and Market Act 2000, which deals with amendments to the powers and functions of the regulatory institutions Prudential Regulation Authority (PRA). S.1(i) gives the body the mandate to see that the implementation and transition to the ring-fencing regime do not cause disruptions to core banking activities.

This part also deals with modifications of the objectives of PRA, as previously stated in section 11 of FSMA 2000, to reflect the new policy on ring-fencing.

s.4 also amends Part 9A of FSMA 2000, introducing Part 9B. The Banking Reform Act 2013 is cited as s.142A 'Ring-fenced bodies'. Thus, s.4 (i) defines a ring-fenced body as *"a UK institution which carries on one or more core activities to which it has Part A permission."*[92]

Core activities relate to deposit-taking banks and high street banks such as Barclays, RBS, and Lloyd Banks, the kind of services familiar to most people. These are banks that operate demand deposit accounts.

Within the meaning of the Building Societies Act 1986, s.4 (2) excludes Building Societies from the ring-fencing rules.

The section indicates the general purposes of the ring-fencing policy in the following terms:

(a) to secure an appropriate degree of protection for the depositors concerned, or (b) to protect the continuity of the provision in the United Kingdom of services provided in the course of carrying on the regulated activity of accepting deposits.[93]

---

[92] Financial Services (Banking Reform) Act 2013 Part 1, s.4 (1)
[93] Financial Services (Banking Reform) Act 2013 s.4 (1)/ FSMA 2000 s.142B (4) (a & b)

Other important matters under Part 1 relate to administrative issues and compliance.

1.11.2 Part 2—Banking Reform Act 2013: Financial Services Compensation Scheme

This part deals with the administration of the Financial Services Compensation Scheme, where issues about the insolvency of the ring-fenced body arise. These are concerned with categories of preferential debts and eligible deposits for compensation.

1.11.3 Part 3—Banking Reform Act 2013: Bail-in Stabilisation Option

This part relates to the bail-in stabilisation option, which applies to Building Societies. There is no need to emphasise this part as Building Societies are outside the scope of this study since they are excluded from the ring-fencing policy.

However, that part of the Banking Reform Act 2013 is linked with the Banking Act 2009. In recognition of the potentially devastating consequences of the failure of GSI-Bs, the Banking Act 2009 significantly addresses transitional contingent management resolution plans for about-to-fail banks. This is so that the failure of any of such megabanks poses little or no disruption to the financial system. Moreover, losses arising from failed banks are, as much as possible, not borne by the public but by beneficial owners of the banks.[94] Thus, the primary objective of this part of the legislation is to ensure that banks do not fail in a disorderly manner.[95]

The Banking Act 2009, Part 1, provides five special resolution mechanisms to either rescue a bank through restructuring (Bail-out) or to let go of a bank through liquidation (Bail-in option). The resolution tools that are available to the Bank of England Resolution Division are (a) transfer to a private sector

---

[94] Bank of England, 'Executing Bail-in: An Operational Guide from the Bank of England' (2021) Resolution

[95] P. Carabellese and D. Zhang, 'The Legal Nature of the Recovery and Resolution Plans' (2019) 30 (7) 380–398 International Company and Commercial Law Review

purchaser, (b) transfer to a bridge bank, (c) transfer to an asset management vehicle, and (d) bail-in option.[96]

1.11.4 Part 4—Banking Reform Act 2013: Conduct of Persons working in the Financial Services Sector

This part deals with the regulation of senior management employees of banks, the functions of bank employees that require prior approval of regulatory bodies and the vetting of candidates applying for senior managerial posts. It also includes changes in the responsibilities of senior managers, certification of qualified bank management officials, rules of conduct and disciplinary procedures concerning senior managers.

Senior management function relates to regulated activity by an authorised person on matters concerned with (a) functions that require the person performing it to be responsible for managing one or more aspects of the authorised person's affairs, (b) aspects involving risks of severe consequences.[97]

This part of the legislation seeks to hold senior bank managers criminally liable for any dereliction of duty, conduct and decisions that may put the bank at serious risks and losses. The legislation also makes it mandatory that regulatory bodies must be involved in the vetting and appointing of key bank operators. The vetting process imposes a responsibility on the regulatory authority to ensure that a prospective candidate applying for a position of high responsibility in the bank has the prerequisite qualifications and training. Applicants should also possess the appropriate level of competence. In addition, applicants must have the personal character required to hold a responsible post in the bank.[98] Part 4, s.63F requires authorised bodies such as PRA and FCA to give licences/certificates to qualified individuals before such a person can hold a responsible position in the bank.[99]

This is a welcome development as it would enhance the quality of the hiring processes and ensure that only the most qualified candidates are appointed to manage very sensitive management positions in the banking sector.

---

[96] Banking Act 2009, Part I Special Resolution Regime
[97] Financial Services (Banking Reform) Act 2013 Part 4, s.19 (1) (2)
[98] Financial Services (Banking Reform) Act 2013 Part 4, s.21 (2 a-d)
[99] Financial Services (Banking Reform) Act 2013 Part 4, s.63F (3)

Part 4, s.36 provides the basis of an indictment of senior management personnel of banks and the terms of a custodial sentence for offences relating to recklessly putting a bank's assets at risk of crippling losses. The custodial sentence ranges from 6 months to 7 years.[100]

1.11.5 Part 5—Banking Reform Act 2013: Regulation of Payments System

This section deals with the administration of payment systems and regulations. This is a vital part of a bank's smooth running and survival. A payment system is a process that enables the transfer of funds services.[101] In recognition of the importance of the administration of an efficient payment system in the economy, s.39 provides for the appointment of a new 'Payment System Regulator'.[102] S.49 to 53 specify the general duties of the Payment System Regulator. This part of the Banking Reform Act 2013 is an offshoot of the Banking Act 2009, Part 5 s.182 (1), concerning working towards avoidance of disruption to payment services arising from the failure of a bank.[103] The connection with the ring-fencing policy is that the section supports that part of the objectives of the ring-fencing policy, which, as far as possible, aims to minimise incidences of bank failure that could disrupt core banking services.

1.11.6 Part 6—Banking Reform Act 2013: Special Administration for Operators of Certain Infrastructure Systems

This section relates to managing Financial Infrastructure Systems (FIS), which is responsible for the inter-bank payment system. This is an extension of Part 5. These areas are also crucial to the smooth running of the banking system because a failure could disrupt the provision of banking services.

---

[100] Financial Services (Banking Reform) Act 2013 Part 4, s.36 (1) (2) (3) & (4)
[101] Financial Services (Banking Reform) Act 2013 Part 4, s.40
[102] Financial Services (Banking Reform) Act 2013 Part 4, s.39
[103] The Banking Act (2009) Part 5, s.182 (1)

1.11.7 Part 7—Banking Reform Act 2013: Miscellaneous

Part 7 is concerned with defined functions and wide-ranging enhanced powers of the Prudential Regulation Authority (PRA) and the Financial Conduct Authority (FCA) to see to the public's protection and the financial system's smooth running in the UK.

As with other issues, the regulatory authorities, the PRA and the FCA, have a very important role in meeting with bank auditors at least once every year.

This is a unique feature of the Financial Services (Banking Reform) Act 2013. Typically, auditors of companies are only responsible to members of the company they provide auditing services. However, given the importance of the banking sector to the economy, there is an exemption which compels auditors of banks to report matters of concern directly to the bank regulatory authorities. This is also a welcome development for three important reasons: (i) it will ensure transparency and an unfettered flow of information; (ii) it will enable the regulatory authorities to be aware in good time in the event a bank has difficulty and (iii) timely remedial steps could be taken when it becomes known that a particular bank is in difficulty.

1.11.8 Part 8—Banking Reform Act 2013: Final Provision

This section contains Schedules 1–10. It includes interpretations, meanings of keywords used, powers to review, and powers to enact subordinate legislation. Schedule 1 relates specifically to ring-fencing.

1.11.9 Summary

The provisions in Part 4 relating to the vetting of prospective candidates of key managers by regulators and the requirements in Part 7, which impose obligations on auditors of banks to report directly to regulators, are considered innovative and highly welcomed ideas.

Incorporating these ideas into the Banking Reform Act is seen to be some of the lessons learnt from past failures in the banking sector. These aspects of the legislation are discussed further in the literature review Chapter 2.

1.12 The United Kingdom Financial System

As noted in the previous paragraph, **1.9,** which dealt with the substance of the Banking Reform Act 2013, the legislation only covers deposit-taking banks, otherwise referred to as commercial/retail banks. That is only a segment of the financial system. This section deals with how the banking sector, which is the focus of this study, sits within the entire financial services sector. A distinction or classification of the participants in the financial system is essential because each subsector plays a differentiated role.

The United Kingdom is reputed to have a well-developed industrial and commercial economy with a first-class, world-renowned financial system that is the envy of other developed world economies.[104] More than 100 years ago, concerning the Bank of England, Professor Andreades of the University of Athens said,

"... No existing bank can boast a history at the same time so long, so continuous, and so distinguished; nor has any played so large and so worthy a part, not merely in the fortunes of a great nation, but also the general financial activities of the world."[105]

Such glowing tribute coming from a foreigner suggests the extent of the high esteem others have for the UK financial system.

The UK financial system comprises various classes of banks delineated by their functions.[106, 107]

The financial system in the UK comprises the following institutions under the following general headings–Banks and banking institutions: this includes the Bank of England, deposit/clearing banks such as Lloyds Bank, Royal Bank of Scotland, Barclays Bank, Standard Chartered Bank, HSBC Plc (these are the class of banking institutions that this research is concerned with). These banks were traditionally known as Clearing and Deposit-taking Banks.[108] Others under that classification include the Co-operative Bank and Trustee Savings Bank.

---

[104] D. Palfreman and P. Ford, 'Elements of Banking, 2nd Ed' (Pitman Publishing, 1992, p. 43)

[105] Andreades, A. (1909) History of the Bank of England (P. S. King & Sons Publishing, Preface Page)

[106] A. Arora, 'Practical Banking and Building Society Law' (Oxford University Press, 1997)

[107] D. Blake, 'Financial Market Analysis 2nd Ed.' (John Wiley, 2000)

[108] P. E Smart, 'Chorley & Smart Leading Cases in the Law of Banking 5th Ed.' (Sweet & Maxwell, 1983)

These are categorised among banking institutions on the account that they have access to the Clearing House.[109]

Another class is the Discount Market. These specialist banks discount bills of exchange, earning their income from the commission and the differences in the discounted value of the financial instrument they trade in.[110] Usually, they take deposits from the banking sector and lend such money to the government on a short-term basis through gilt-edge securities and local authority bonds. There are also Finance Houses. This class of financial institutions specialise in financing hire-purchase transactions. Also included are Savings Banks, Building Societies, Insurance Companies, Pension Funds, Investment Trust Companies and Unit Trusts, Special Investment Agencies such as Consortium Groups, Finance Corporations for Industry, Industrial and Commercial Corporations, Financial Markets including the stock exchange, Securities Brokers and Dealers, the Gilt-edge Market and Investment Banking.[111, 112, 113] From this long list, readers will note that the financial sector has wide-ranging specialist functions.

In the UK, investment banks used to be called merchant banks, while Americans called them investment banks. However, nowadays, they are mostly referred to as investment banks, even in the UK.

Primarily, investment banks help raise venture capital through consortium lending and lease finance. In addition, they provide advice to companies preparing to enlist on the stock exchange.[114] They typically do not have an extensive network of branches. Usually, they have their offices in London. They only keep accounts for a few high net-worth private and corporate customers. Hence, they are called 'Wholesale Bankers'.[115]

The importance of financial institutions to the economic development of a nation cannot be overemphasised. In the case of commercial banks, this research relates to their role in modern industrialised society, which includes enabling

---

[109] P. Fidler, 'Practice and Law of Banking 11th Ed.' (McDonald & Evans, 1982, p. 2)

[110] J. Revell, 'The British Financial System' (The Macmillan Press, 1973)

[111] Ibid.

[112] A. Saunders and M. Cornett, 'Financial Institution Management: A Risk Management Approach 7th Ed.' (McGraw-Hill, (2011, p. 17)

[113] P. Howells, and K. Bain, 'Financial Markets and Institutions 5th Ed.' (Pearson Education, 2007)

[114] Op. cit., A. Saunders and M. Cornett (n. 112)

[115] Op. cit., P. Fidler, 1982 (n. 109)

customers to deposit their money into current or other interest-bearing deposit accounts. In addition, they lend money to their customers and facilitate payment and collection of cheques on behalf of their customers.[116]

Primarily, this research concerns the regular banks with which most people have bank accounts, through which they receive their pay and make daily transactions. Until the promulgation of the Banking Act 1979, there was no clear definition of what a 'Bank', 'Banking business' and a 'Banker' meant. The Court has, over time, followed the definition suggested by Lord Denning M. R and Diplock L. J in *United Dominions Trust v. Kirkwood*.[117]

This is stated as,

"…accept money on current accounts, payable by cheques drawn upon such account on demand and collect cheques for customers… "[118]

So, essentially, the court intended that these characteristics should distinguish a 'Bank' and a 'Banking Business'—acceptance of deposits withdrawable on demand with cheques. The decision of the Court of Appeal, in that case, was that, though the definition was not applicable in the circumstances of United Dominions Trust (UDT), it was nevertheless a bank carrying out banking business because the organisation had a reputation among other banks that they were operating as a bank.

Specifically, Part 4A FSMA 2000 makes it a prerequisite to obtaining a prior authorisation licence before an incorporated body can carry out the business of banking in the UK.

In the context of this research, the case studies are clearly recognised as banks carrying out banking business with their Headquarters in the UK.

Before the 1980s, the financial activities of the differentiated financial institutions mentioned earlier had highly specialised functions. However, as noted by Howells and Keith, this banking model was at odds with other European countries, such as Germany and France, favouring a universal banking

---

[116] E. Ellinger, et al., 'Ellinger's Modern Banking Law 5th Ed' (Oxford University Press, 2011, p. 213)
[117] United Dominion Trust v. Kirkwood [1966] 1 Q.B. 431
[118] Ibid (United Dominion Trust)

model.[119,120,121] Part of the disadvantages to the UK banks before the 1980s was that they were competing against international financial institutions with very mobile capital and less restrictive laws in their home country.[122] This was part of the environment that led to the growth of conglomerate financial institutions in the UK in the 1980s after the restrictions were removed.

The implication was that the line of demarcation between the institutions became blurred as their services merged under the umbrella of their respective parents' institutions.[123] Thus, from the 1980s, the merging of these various financial institutions led to grotesquely big banks. Today, those banks are referred to as "Too big to fail and too big to rescue." Moreover, a failure among these large banks led to debates on dealing with problems associated with a crisis in huge banks.[124]

Regulatory authorities introduced various regulatory changes in response to the global financial crisis in 2007–2009, which threatened the international banking system. The benefits and limitations of these regulatory changes, including the ring-fencing policy, are discussed in Chapter 2 of this book.

Thus, one of the identified weaknesses of the ring-fencing policy is that once the ring-fenced part of a bank structurally separates from its universal banking roots, the non-ring-fenced arm cannot have the full benefits of the cheap sources of finance held within the ring-fenced bank. Notably, there is a cooperative relationship between all the participants in the financial system. The banking sector, the primary focus of this research, is only a subsector of the whole aggregate economy.

1.13 Contribution to Knowledge

Foremost, one of the unique strengths of this study is that it combined specialists' knowledge in various disciplines, including law, economics,

---

[119] Op. cit., P. Howells, and B. Keith, B. (n. 113)

[120] P. Alexander, 'Splitting Banks Divides Opinion in the EU' (The Banker, 2015)

[121] J. Brusden, 'European Commission Withdraws Bank Separation Proposal' (2017) https://www.ft.com/content/ddbedcd9-2dea-3b68-b8e2-2e1bc1eda13f

[122] Op. cit., (Howells and Keith (2007 (n. 113)

[123] S. Hefferman, 'Modern Banking in Theory and Practice' (John Wiley, 1996)

[124] Hupkes, E. 'Complicity in Complexity: What to do about the 'Too Big to fail' Problem' (2009) 9, 515, Journal of International Banking and Financial Law

business management, accountancy, banking, and finance, which helped in working through the study.

There are still gaps in our knowledge in this area of study. Even when the protagonists of structuralism and neo-liberalism agree on the need to have some reforms in the financial system, unending debates that stem from the thorny question of how banking regulators can achieve an optimal level of regulation remain. The difficulty is primarily due to the complex circumstances of various banks within the banking sector.[125] Thus, the second strength of the study is that it synthesised various views on the subject to enrich the literature in the study area.

Thirdly, as provided by this research, no previous definitive study has come up with a measured impact of the global financial crisis on the banks selected as case studies spanning the examination of accounting records for fifteen years, as was achieved by this study. At least none has come to this researcher's awareness. The outcome of this extensive data analysis is fundamentally the aim of this study and part of what this researcher hopes he has contributed to knowledge.

Fourthly, sets of comprehensive primary data comprising thirteen Key Performance Indicators, which covered fifteen years from 2004–2018, were built in connection with the case studies, the Royal Bank of Scotland, Barclays, Standard Chartered Bank, and HSBC Plc. The data thus constructed may serve as a starting or a reference point for other researchers in the future and which they can build upon in similar research activities as this study.

The new primary data compiled by this researcher include Table 5, on pages 204 - 205, relating to RBS. Table 6, on pages 231 - 232, relates to Barclays. Table 8, pages 264 - 265, relates to SCB and Table 9, pages 288 - 289, relates to HSBC Plc. These are tabulated extracts from the annual reports and consolidated accounts of the mentioned banks from 2004–2018.

Another contribution to knowledge derived from this study is that it helps us understand how and why RBS and Barclays ran into difficulties during and in the aftermath of the global financial crisis. In that regard, the study highlighted how the challenges faced by these banks affected their shareholders, staff members, and customers, as well as the impacts of the crisis on the UK economy generally. Finally, the study mapped out the banks' recovery journeys.

---

[125] M. Bagheri, and C Nakajima, 'Optimal Level of Financial Regulation under GATs' (2002) Vol. 5 (2) 507, Journal of International Economic Law

SCB, which was classified as one of the global systemically important banks, was not under any obligation to be ring-fencing compliant. This exemption is because most of SCB's core banking customers that the policy sought to protect are outside Europe. Overall, SCB had a good performance over the period evaluated, except in 2015, when the bank had an operating loss before tax of $1.5 billion.[126] Although HSBC also shared the burden of the global financial crisis, the bank thrived during and after it. On the other hand, the statistics in Tables 5 and 6 for RBS and Barclays indicate a downward trend in these banks' performance over the period evaluated.

Suppose other researchers picked up interest in this study area and keep under watch performance in the banking sector for the next 5–10 years following the implementation of the ring-fencing policy in 2019. The outcome of collective research endeavours may hopefully spearhead policy change on ring-fencing in the future, assuming it is desirable. Delanty and Strydom distinguish between knowledge, opinion, and common sense. According to these writers, what distinguishes knowledge from opinion and common sense is that knowledge should be supported with convincing evidence.[127]

This researcher supports the argument put forward by Delanty and Strydom that what constitutes acceptable knowledge would be a study that is based on evidence rather than mere opinions and assertions. The materials used in carrying out this study are robust, objective documentary evidence outside the influence of this researcher.

1.14 Content and Structure of the Book

The book comprises six generic chapters. Chapter 1 gives the content of the research. Chapter 2 contains the literature review. Chapter 3 is about methods and methodology; Chapter 4 is concerned with the presentation of data and analysis; Chapter 5 is a comparative evaluation of the results of RBS, Barclays, SCB and HSBC Plc; and Chapter 6 is a summary of findings and recommendations.

Broadly, the introductory chapter lays out the general background of the study. It states the aims and objectives of the study, setting out the research

---

[126] Please see Table 8 on page 264, column 3.
[127] G. Delanty, and P. Strydom, 'Philosophies of Social Sciences: The classic and Contemporary Readings' (Open University Press, 2003, p. 6)

questions, research hypothesis, rationale, and the importance of the study. It also locates the research within the context of the 2007–2009 global financial crisis and regulatory measures made in response to the crisis. The introductory chapter indicates that the Banking Reform Act 2013 is one of the prime laws under examination, being the legislative response to the financial crisis in the UK. Within the different components of the United Kingdom's financial system, the chapter distinguishes the banking sector as the focus of the study. The introductory chapter concludes by describing the contribution of the study to knowledge.

The second chapter is the literature review section of the book. The literature review comprises five sections marked A–E. In relationship to the first three objectives of the study stated earlier, each of these sections deals with the following topics in successive order: (A) the approach adopted in conducting the literature review; (B) the causes of the financial crisis in 2007–2009; (C) generic legal framework under which the banking sector operated before and in the aftermath of the global financial crisis; (D) the banking sector regulatory institutions concerned with the supervision, support, surveillance and enforcement of law and regulations in the banking sector. This section engaged with possible gaps in the existing legal framework and the supervisory institutions that may have warranted the adoption of the ring-fencing policy; and (E) the evolution of banking theories in the past one hundred years regarding structuralism and neo-liberalism, the drivers of economic policies. The section is also about a critique of the ring-fencing policy. This includes evaluating the effectiveness of ring-fencing as a measure capable of deterring financial crises in the future.

The third chapter relates to a report about the methods and methodology adopted for the research. This section focused on (i) the research design, (ii) the underpinning research philosophy, (iii) methods of data collection, and (iv) the justification for the approaches adopted.

The fourth chapter is concerned with the case studies group. The group members are Royal Bank of Scotland Plc, Standard Chartered Bank Plc, HSBC Plc, and Barclays Bank Plc. The chapter consists of four sections, each devoted to a member of the case study group. The chapter contains data built from the Annual Financial Reports and Financial Accounts for over 15 years from 2004–2018. It relates to the discussion and analysis of the consolidated data from the accounts of the group members.

The fifth chapter comprises a comparative analysis of the four case studies. The chapter evaluated shared characteristics among the case studies and contrasted their circumstances. These are related to issues such as the dominant markets where each bank operated and how the different risks exposure to the subprime financial instruments in the wake of the financial crisis in 2007–2009 affected the banks' performances differently. The chapter also discussed how the interactions between critical success factors, including leadership skills, asset quality, and managerial capabilities available within each bank, made the difference between success and failure. These are some of the prerequisites needed in managing the giant conglomerate banks during an unpredictable and acutely turbulent period as these banks have faced in the past ten years since the global financial crisis began in 2007–2009.

The sixth chapter concerns the research findings, conclusions, and comments regarding possible future research in the study area. Finally, the chapter reemphasised contributions to knowledge derived from this study by making a final pointer to the section containing the contributions to our understanding of the subject stated in Chapter 1 of this book.

Chapter 2
Literature Review: Literature Survey Strategies and Review Questions

Section A

2.1 Introduction

Broadly, the literature review section deals with the existing body of knowledge on banking sector regulations and allied theories surrounding the subject. However, it specifically concerns issues arising from general regulatory changes since 2009, including capital adequacy requirements, liquidity ratios, and the ring-fencing policy.

(i) This section states the aims and objectives of the literature review, (ii) it lays out theories on the literature review, (iii) it states sources consulted and subject leaders whose works were consulted, and (iv) it identifies steps taken to minimise incidences of bias and lack of rigour.

2.2 The Aims of Literature Review

The literature review aims to link the study with previous studies and the body of knowledge in this area of research. It is also to find answers to the theoretical questions in the research objectives in Chapter 1, pages 15 – 16.

In conducting the literature review, therefore, the following key areas were kept in mind:

(i)
- (a) as a background study, to undertake a review of extant literature to determine the causes of the global financial crisis in 2007–2009,
- (b) To review prevailing laws and regulations before the 2007–2009 financial crisis and determine whether gaps in the laws and supervisory regimes contributed to the crisis.

Also, to undertake a review of the changes to the laws after the global financial crisis, evaluating their impacts on the case studies, RBS, Barclays, Standard Chartered Bank, and HSBC Holdings Plc.

> (ii) to carry out a theoretical critique on the ring-fencing policy within the extant literature against the background of the UK's core competencies in the provision of financial services, a sphere in which the UK has comparative and competitive advantages,
>
> (iii) to critically evaluate the effectiveness of ring-fencing as a measure capable of deterring financial crises in the future.

2.3 The Objectives of the Literature Review

The objectives of this part of the book are concerned with how the research reported relates to previous studies conducted by others and, essentially, the issues that gave rise to the current research.[128] There are primarily two objectives for this literature review section. These include using the exercise to aid in the refinement of the research's overall aims and objectives stated in Chapter 1, pages 8 – 12, 15 – 16. It is also to engage with the existing literature to facilitate its critical evaluation.[129] In a nutshell, the study evaluated the desirability of retaining some of the aspects of the ring-fencing policy criticised in this book. Especially after implementing the additional regulatory changes following the GFC, such as capital adequacy requirement, enhanced liquidity and improvement in the banking supervisory regime. It also aims to determine the impact of the global financial crisis in 2007–2009 on the economic performances of some of the largest UK banks chosen as case studies from 2004 to 2018. In addition, the study evaluated regulatory responses designed to limit the effects of likely future crises on the banking sector.

The literature review section uses the historical reflexive method to present the report on the subject areas studied. For example, it highlights the state of banking regulations in the past. In addition, the review touches on the evolutionary development of banking regulations to what it is today. Finally, it

---

[128] M. Denscombe, 'The Good Research Guide 3rd Ed' (Open University Press, 2007, p. 325)

[129] J. Sharp, J. et al., 'The Management of a Student Research Project 3rd Ed.' (Gower, 2002)

identifies limitations within the current financial regulatory structure, and it gives considerations on what the likely position of financial services regulations should aim to be to secure the economic well-being of the UK banking sector into the foreseeable future.[130]

This rear mirror review approach is to see some of the financial services regulatory models adopted in the past, which either worked or failed. It also helps us know why some policy choices worked and others failed. In so doing, this may assist in identifying policies that worked for a season due to the economic circumstances of that time but which have changed with time. It is also to determine why a reversion to those models now may be harmful to the economy. For example, the prevailing circumstance during the Bretton Woods [131]era is far removed from what they are currently. The constantly changing business environment, innovations, technological advancement, and the world economy have become more globalised in the past thirty years.[132] One of the consequences of globalisation is that trade boundaries were largely eliminated. For example, due to the widely embraced deregulated economic policy, customs, exercise, and other artificial barriers to international trade were removed. Deregulation promoted free-market enterprise, strong private property rights, and free trade.[133, 134]

Gall *et al.* identified other reasons for conducting a literature review, including the opportunity to discover new research possibilities that were previously unnoticed, preventing a repetition of research that others have carried out and the prospect of gaining insight into research approaches and strategies.[135] Notably, there are abundant previous theoretical works on financial services regulations and critical reviews on the ring-fencing policy. However, the gap identified by this study concerns the uncharted area regarding measuring or quantifying the impact of GFC on the performance of the selected banks on a long-range basis as this study did (Examination of fifteen years of accounting

---

[130] A. Jankowicz, 'Business Research Project 4th Ed' (Thomson Learning, 2005, p 161)

[131] L. Rochon, and S. Olawoye, 'Monetary Policy and Central Banking: New Direction in Post-Keynesian Theory' (Edward Elgar, 2012)

[132] T. Friedman, 'The World is Flat: The Globalised World in the Twenty-first Century' (Penguin, 2006)

[133] Op. Cit., M. Friedman, 1962 (n. 14).

[134] D. Harvey, 'A Brief History of Neoliberalism' (Oxford University Press, 2005)

[135] M. Gall, et al., 'Educational Research: An Introduction 8th Ed.' (Longman, 2002)

records). Understandably, the reason for that gap is that the full implementation of the ring-fencing policy only became effective in January 2019. The ring-fencing policy was enacted into law in 2013 in the Financial Services (Banking Reform) Act 2013.

The following paragraph deals with sources of existing literature on the subject. It identifies contributors and established authorities/leaders in the areas consulted for this study.

2.4 Literature Sources Consulted and Some of the Subject Leaders

The literature sources consulted to gain insights on the subject area enabled this researcher to enter into the conversation around the issues discussed in this study. The materials used include academic journals such as the Journal of Financial Intermediation and Financial Regulation and Performance. It also includes the European Business Organisation Law Review and the International Banking and Financial Law Journal. In addition, there were Compliance, Law Review, the Institute of Economic Affairs Research, and publications from Parliament such as the Hansard. Others are textbooks, unpublished doctoral theses, conference papers, Government publications, and the Annual Financial Reports of the banks used as case studies for the research.

The list is by no means exhaustive, but to mention a few. Some of the identified prominent subject leaders in law and economics whose works were consulted include but are not limited to the following: law, economics, and finance professors, such as Arora, Haynes, Persaud, Cranston, Goodhart, Hudson, Ellinger et al., Tomasic, Grosse, Petitjean, Larosiere, Barth et al., Arthur, Booth, Friedman (Nobel laureate in Economics), Stiglitz (Nobel laureate in Economics), Howells, Bain, Blair (KC), Hadjiemmanuil (KC), Admati, and Cullen. Their works are listed among other people's works mentioned in the bibliography at the end of this report.

2.5 Approaches to Literature Review

Two main approaches to literature review have been identified: deductive and inductive. A deductive review uses existing literature to identify theories, which are then tested using collated data and an appropriate research design to determine whether the hypothesis tested is correct. On the other hand, the inductive approach involves exploring data to generate new theories.[136]

A deductive approach is considered more suitable when there is abundant literature to glean from and the time available for the study is limited. Meanwhile, with an inductive approach, there may be a paucity of literature on the subject, time is not a constraint, and risks are acceptable because a theory may not emerge at the end of the study.[137]

In the circumstances of this research, the hypothesis tested, as stated in Chapter 1, page 17, is,

"Notwithstanding the benefits that may accrue from the ring-fencing policy, the banking sector and by extension the economy in the UK may likely face long-term detriment arising from some aspects of the ring-fencing policy."

An abundance of wide-ranging literature is readily available in the field of study. This embraces financial law regulations and materials on banking and finance. Also, this study has a time constraint. It is a three-year research work. Under those circumstances, adopting a deductive approach in this study is considered justified.

Transfield *et al.* classified the presentation of the literature review into two categories, namely, traditional narrative style and systematic review.[138] These authors are concerned that the traditional narrative style in presenting a literature review is highly susceptible to lacking thoroughness and may suffer from bias and absence of rigour. In their opinion, a systematic review embraces the use of clear assessment criteria in the selection of articles to use, the development of clear aims and objectives for the literature review, a comprehensive search for all potentially relevant materials, and the presentation of the synthesised result in a balanced and impartial way.

In this literature review exercise, a reflexive historical narrative approach to research illustrated by Atkinson on creative writing was adopted in critically

---

[136] J. Wilson, 'Essentials of Business Research: A Guide to Doing Your Research Project', (Sage, 2010, p 7)

[137] R. Snieder and K. Larner, 'The Art of being Scientist: A Guide for Graduates Students and their Mentors' (Cambridge University Press, 2009, p. 16)

[138] D. Transfield et al., 'Towards Methodology for Developing Evidence informed Management Knowledge by Means of Systemic Review' (2003) Vol 14, (3) 207–222, British Journal of Management.

analysing theories on regulation.[139] This research tool was used to evaluate propositions made by an assorted range of professionals and academicians over the debate about finding a more favourable choice between **structuralist** and **neo-liberalism** theories. These are economic theories that inform the direction of policy decisions on regulation. For example, the debate relates to the arguments on the desirability or otherwise of foisting a restrictive concept of the ring-fencing policy on the banking sector in the prevailing circumstances of the UK economy.

A reflexive narrative approach is considered appropriate in legal doctrinal research, which essentially depends on documentary evidence, such as in this study. Moreover, as posited by Atkinson, a reflexive approach is particularly suitable in the case studies method, which was adopted for evaluating the annual accounts of selected banks included in the case study group.[140]

The nature of the research considered the historical and evolutionary development of financial market regulations in the UK, with a particular interest in socio-policy pathways to regulation from the late 1970s until the present (2023). Possible advantages of a reflexive narrative approach include its flexibility and spontaneity. Also, it allows for presenting originality of thinking creatively.[141] On the other hand, a possible drawback may be gravitation toward being overly subjective. For example, if the researcher has a blind spot to certain things and then exaggerates the importance of others, as may occur in any qualitative analysis.[142]

2.6 Steps Taken to Minimise Incidences of Bias and Lack of Academic Rigour

As pointed out by Transfield *et al.* referred to earlier, crucially, a vital part of a literature review that could be taken seriously begins with stating the devised

---

[139] T. N Atkinson, 'Using Creative Writing Technique to Enhance the Case Study Method in Research Integrity and Ethics Courses' (2008) Vol. 6 (1) 33–50 Journal of Academic Ethics

[140] Ibid (Atkinson, T. N. (2008))

[141] R. Sommer and B. Sommer, 'Practical Guide to Behavioural Research: Tools and Techniques' (Oxford University Press 2002, p. 59)

[142] Ibid.

aims and objectives of the literature review.[143] In addition to that, the standard of selection criteria would be used to determine articles that merit inclusion in the research.

The first three pages of this chapter state the literature review's aims and objectives. The chapter also identified opinion leaders of international repute in the subject areas consulted regarding this study. The materials used are peer-reviewed papers, mostly from five-star journals. This researcher made conscious efforts to avoid undue subjective views. The academic rigour employed and the quality and appropriateness of the structure and style adopted in presenting arguments in reporting the research are left for readers to judge.

In succession, the following four sections will deal with each of the identified financial services regulations and theories on regulation mentioned earlier.

Section B

A Review of the Causes of the Financial Crisis in 2007–2009 and the Estimate of the Extent of Losses Incurred by the Countries Mostly Affected by the Crisis.

2.7 Introduction

Based on the available literature on the subject, this section reviews the causes of the global financial crisis in 2007–2009. It provides a general overview of the losses incurred by the banking sector, using a sample of twenty-four countries among the leading industrialised nations hit hardest by the global financial crisis.

This section of the book is linked to objective (i) subsection (a) of the study concerning evaluating the causes of the global financial crisis in 2007–2009.

Since the ring-fencing policy is part of the government's responses to the 2007–2009 crisis, the starting point should be a review of the causes of the crisis to put into perspective what the ailments were relative to the medicine prescribed to cure the problem.

Secondly, a review of the causes of the crisis is considered vital because it is the only means by which we can start to appreciate the fault lines, facilitate

---

[143] Op. cit., Transfield, D., et al., 2003, (n. 138)

planning for financial crisis management and come up with suggestions on practical solutions.[144]

2.8 Some of the Causes of the Financial Crisis

It has been more than fifteen years since the crisis occurred. Quite a lot has been written about the causes of the global financial crisis since it happened. Doubtless, more is still going to be written about the crisis, which is reputed to be the worst of its kind in known economic history.[145] This would be more so as policymakers and regulators seek to tighten perceived loopholes within the financial system, making new regulations or modifying supervisory strategies to minimise instances of financial crises in the economy.

On 19th November 2012, five years after the global financial crisis started, Lord Adair Turner, the Chairman of the defunct Financial Services Authority, gave oral evidence before the Parliamentary Commission on Banking. In his testimony, he said the scale of the crisis and its impacts on the economy have only started to be appreciated much more than understood in 2009.[146] Writing in 2016, seven years after the crisis ended, Mamica and Tridico held that the negative impacts of the crisis were still being carried over by some advanced economies such as Greece, Spain, and Portugal.[147] The argument is that, even now, issues surrounding the causes of the crisis are still relevant, and they form part of the basis of this study.

A considerable number of reasons have been adduced as the causes of the global financial crisis, which had its origin in the USA but later spread globally with devastating consequences.[148,149,150]

---

[144] B Casu et al., 'Introduction to Banking 2nd Ed.' (Pearson Education, 2015, p. 251)

[145] Op. cit., D. Murphy, 2009, (n. 56)

[146] A. Turner, 'Oral Evidence given before Parliamentary Commission on Banking Standards on 19/11/2012'

[147] L. Mamica, and P. Tridico, 'Economic Policy and the Financial Crisis' (Routledge, 2016, p. 1)

[148] A. Turner, 'The Turner Review' (The Financial Services Authority, 2009)

[149] M. Baily, et al., 'The Origins of the Financial Crisis' (The Brookings Institution, 2008)

[150] I. MacNeil, 'The Trajectory of Regulatory Reform in the UK in the Wake of the Financial Crisis' (2011) Vol 11, pp 483–526, European Business Organisation Law Review.

Among several factors attributed as the causes of the financial crisis are failings arising from inadequate cross-border and unified international financial regulation, products and services that escaped the boundary of regulation and supervision, poor banking supervision,[151] securitisation of sub-prime mortgage assets, poor lending practices, failings in the administration/governance of financial institutions, general laxity in internal control mechanisms,[152] behavioural issues related to a corporate culture where there are tensions in power dynamics and internal politics, external socio-economic pressure leading to financial institutions intentionally circumventing rules[153] and less than acceptable standards of the activities of credit rating agencies.[154]

Other than the spillover of the causes of the crisis that emanated in America, in the particular circumstances of the UK, the trigger of the crisis was due to the loss of confidence in the banking sector. The lack of confidence led to a chain of events and reactions that started with the short-term money market freeze on 9th August 2007. The liquidity freeze prevented banks needing liquidity from accessing funds from the wholesale money market.[155] The problem for some of these banks was poor liquidity and inadequate capital. In addition, there was the problem of underlying weaknesses in assets/nonperforming loans. For example, as mentioned previously in Chapter 1, Northern Rock was the first casualty in September 2007. The underlying issue with Northern Rock was the precarious liquidity position of the distressed bank, inadequate operating capital, poor management decisions, weak assets and disproportionate nonperforming loan accounts. On top of that, from December 2007 to February 2008, major investment banks confessed that their structural credit assets were overstated and

---

[151] Op. cit., Arora, A. 2010, (n. 24)

[152] R. Grosse, 'Bank Regulation, Governance and the Crisis: A Behavioural Finance Review' (2012) Vol 20 (1) 4–25. Journal of Financial Regulation and Compliance.

[153] S. Ashby, 'The Turner Review on the Global Banking Crisis: A Response from the Financial Services Research Forum' (2009) Financial Services Research Forum
https://www.nottingham.ac.uk/business/who-we-are/centres-and-institutes/gcbfi/documents/researchreports/paper61.pdf

[154] Op. cit., G. Baber, 2013 (n. 22).

[155] Financial Services Authority, 'The Failure of the Royal Bank of Scotland: Financial Services Authority Board Report' (December 2011, pp 314–315)

needed to be written down.[156] Invariably, these write-downs led to the declaration of enormous losses, which caused RBS's share price to crash by 35%.[157]

2.9 Estimate of the Impact of the Global Financial Crisis on the Stock Market Capitalisation in the Banking System

In the period leading to the global financial crisis, banks in the USA aggressively marketed mortgage facilities to high-risk market segments. However, the bankers failed to verify the borrower's employment status and did not check whether the borrowers had other known means of income for the loan repayment. As a result, the transference of the inherent risks to investors globally through CDOs ultimately became the root cause of the 2007–2009 global financial crisis.

The traditional model whereby banks originated mortgages and held them down till they were fully discharged was replaced with a system of originating mortgages and then repackaging them into Collateralised Debt Obligations (CDOs), which were then sold to investors.[158] This model eroded bank lending standards as there were no incentives for the originator of the mortgages to bother about being circumspect regarding the quality of credits so advanced. The risks were passed on to investors in the ensuing securitised instruments. Thus, CDOs became a major factor that created the financial crisis of 2007–2009 following the housing market bubble burst.

---

[156] Ibid.

[157] Ibid.

[158] K. Pilbeam, 'International Finance' (Palgrave Macmillan, 2013, p. 503 4th Ed)

Table 1: The Impact of the Credit Crunch on the Stock Market Capitalisation of the Banking System Among Twenty-four foremost Industrialised Countries

Country	Bank Stock Market Capitalisation 1st Jan 2007 ($ Billions)	Bank Stock Market Capitalisation 31st March 2009 ($ Billions)	Estimated Reduction in Value over 2 Years *** ($ Billions)	Percentage of losses over two years ***
United States	1560.5	352.1	**1,208.4**	77%
United Kingdom	714.4	163.3	**551.1**	77%
China	667.4	525.3	**142.1**	21%
Japan	651.3	248.8	**402.5**	62%
France	372.8	97.8	**275.0**	74%
Hong Kong	345.8	131.5	**214.3**	62%
Italy	338.1	99.3	**238.8**	71%
Switzerland	281.9	81.3	**200.6**	71%
Spain	306.2	112.0	**194.2**	63%
Canada	236.7	135.1	**101.6**	43%
Australia	225.7	139.7	**86.0**	38%
Belgium	184.6	17.0	**167.6**	91%
Germany	151.6	37.0	**114.6**	76%
Russia	126.0	23.9	**102.1**	81%
Sweden	108.4	39.3	**69.1**	64%
Singapore	68.3	34.5	**33.8**	49%
India	60.4	41.1	**19.3**	32%
Ireland	53.9	1.2	**52.7**	98%
Poland	51.2	20.2	**31.0**	61%
South Africa	48.2	33.0	**15.2**	32%
Portugal	38.3	10.4	**27.9**	73%
Indonesia	30.9	24.8	**6.1**	20%
Netherlands	22.7	1.8	**20.9**	92%
Argentina	9.2	3.7	**5.5**	60%
			$ 4,280	

Source: Pilbeam, K. (2013, p 500) International Finance (4th Ed)
***–The 4th and 5th columns relating to the difference between banks' stock market values in 2007 and 2009 were calculated by this researcher.

The table indicates the level of the adverse impact the global financial crisis in 2007–2009 had on the banking sector related to the identified countries. These are countries where statistics are available regarding their Banks' Stock Market Capitalisation for the period stated. This is not necessarily the complete picture of the extent of damages caused by the global financial crisis in 2007–2009 because only twenty-four countries were sampled out of over 200 countries worldwide. Among the twenty-four countries identified, they lost nearly $4.3 trillion in their stock market value between 2007–2009. Also, the statistics do not measure the adverse ripple effects on all businesses generally, including companies that failed due to the financial crisis. However, the statistics give us a glimpse of the grim picture of the impact of the crisis on the banking sector in the countries hit hardest by the financial crisis.

As indicated in the table, America and European countries generally bore the brunt of the catastrophic event more than other parts of the world. Comparatively, Ireland, the Netherlands, and Belgium were the worst-off countries, with their banks' stock market value almost being wiped clean. In relative terms, China was the least affected country in this league table. The hardest affected was Ireland. China lost $142.1 billion. This was 21% of their banks' stock market capitalisation value.

Ireland had 98% of its banks' stock market capitalisation value wiped out in one clean swoop. Regarding the scale of losses, America suffered the largest in monetary value, having $1.2 trillion wiped off their banks' stock market capitalisation value. United Kingdom followed the USA regarding the scale of losses, having incurred a demurrage of $551 billion in the banking sector's stock market capitalisation value at the time. This is about a quarter of the average GDP of the UK.

A remarkable feature of the statistics is the spread of the adverse impact on the foremost industrialised nations worldwide.

2.10 The Contributions of Collateralised Debt Obligations to the Financial Crisis

While most of the reasons given earlier as the causes of the crisis may have contributed in some measures to worsen the global financial crisis in 2007–2009, it is argued that those reasons were almost secondary when compared with the scale of damages caused by the financial instrument, Collateralised Debt Obligations (CDOs). For example, this is because there have always been financial crises. There have always been incidences of poor or inadequate international financial regulation, and there have always been tensions in the organisational environment where there were boardroom disputes. None of these led to a catastrophic global financial crisis, as did the global financial crisis in 2007–2009. The impacts were localised if crises arose from these issues, not a global catastrophe.

Therefore, the causation of the global financial crisis arguably boils down to just one reason. This resulted from poor lending practices in America that had adverse spillover effects on the rest of the world. In addition, the financial crisis was fuelled by the weaknesses already on the ground in the banking sector in the UK, as explained on page 35, about the liquidity freeze and lack of confidence in the banking sector before the global financial crisis began in 2007–2009.

The origin of the crisis has been linked to the practice whereby, in America, expensive homes were sold to individuals who had no apparent means of repayment of the loans through earned income.[159] The properties were acquired with the bank's money under an assumed hope and premise that, with time, the property would significantly increase in value such that when repayment became due, it could be obtained through the sale of the property.

The crisis started to brew as a financial instrument called Collateralised Debt Obligations was designed to enable mortgage banks to relieve themselves of the burden of holding such mis-sold mortgages to their full term.

In the mortgage market context, the idea behind debt securitisation is an arrangement whereby a creditor (in this case, the bank) using a debt instrument referred to as 'Collateralised Debt Obligation', drawn in favour of a third party (an investor) or a bearer, sells the instrument at a discount or a premium value above the underlying property mortgaged to the banker by a group of homeowners (the debtors) over mortgaged properties (the security) to the third party whereby the third party takes over the position of the bank to claim the sum due on the property at the maturity of the instrument or when the mortgage becomes due for full repayment.[160] The additional feature of this instrument is that it could be traded as the investor wishes or when a buyer or seller exercises an option to buy or sell the financial instrument.[161]

---

[159] J. Goddard, and J. Wilson, 'Banking: A Very Short Introduction' (Oxford University Press, 2016, pp 91-92)

[160] A. Hudson, 'The Law of Finance 2nd Ed.' (Thomson, 2013, p. 1296)

[161] Bessis, J. 'Risk Management in Banking 2nd Ed.' (2007, p. 183)

With this ingenious device, the stage was set for the imminent catastrophe waiting to happen once the American banks doled out mortgage loans én-masse to people to buy houses regardless of their ability or inability to repay the loans.

What then followed was that the financial instruments (Collateralised Debt Obligations) were repackaged into large and very complex bundles according to their varying degrees of quality. The face values of these financial instruments were denominated in huge sums, which could be as high as $500 million. They are called **Collateralised Debt Obligations** backed by the underlying mortgages as the supporting security.[162] The credit rating agencies became complicit in supporting this arrangement. The problem was that since the **CDOs** were tied to the mortgaged properties, a fall in the housing market would invariably negatively affect the recoverable sum from any realised property. The additional problem was that valuation became extremely difficult and complex since the mortgages were held in large tranches.[163] The benefit is that there is always a realisable amount from the property, even if it does not cover the initial outlay. The other problem that could have surfaced was a situation where the underlying properties were unrealistically overvalued.

With the assistance of the **CDOs**, the original lenders did not have to hold the mortgages to their maturity as they could transfer the inherent risks to other investors who wanted to invest in the CDOs. This was how the American mistake and misfortune were offloaded and dispersed globally in what is now called subprime or toxic assets**.** Sadly, hapless institutions outside America got their fingers burnt by investing in what has been described as "mispriced, mis-rated, misunderstood and mis-sold instruments."[164]

It is not too difficult to see that those who invested in the CDOs had no way of seeing the underlying properties in America, their true worth and any other features of these properties, unlike the case in traditional mortgages such as we have in the UK. Investors in the CDOs could only trust the judgment of the Credit Rating Agencies concerning references given about the value and quality of the financial instruments.

---

[162] Op. cit., Pilbeam, K. (2013, p. 489) (n. 158)

[163] D. Coskun, 'Credit-rating Agencies in the Basel II Framework: Why the Standardised Approach is Inadequate for Regulatory Capital Purposes' (2010) Vol 25 (4), 157–169, Journal of International Banking Law and Regulation

[164] Op. cit., K. Pilbeam, (2013, p. 488) (n. 158)

An example of a tragedy in the USA and one of the foremost casualties is the collapse of Lehman Brothers Holding, an investment bank established in 1850, the fourth largest investment bank in the USA. Lehman Brothers reputedly had 28,600 staff worldwide. The bank's collapse was attributed mainly to exposure to Collateralised Debt Obligations.[165] Other major investment banks that were adversely affected by their involvement but managed to escape through reliance on bail-out funds and other support packages received from the Federal Reserve were Citigroup, Bank of America, Goldman Sachs, and Merrill Lynch.[166]

2.11 The Relevance and the Implications of the Causes of the Financial Crisis to this Study

First, it is remarkable that bankers in America would be so careless as to engage in the practice whereby huge mortgage loans were given so casually to borrowers, disregarding general lending practices.[167] This was so much so that, when giving out mortgages, they were less concerned about the evaluation of the ability of the borrowers to repay the amount owed. Instead, lending bankers relied on recovering the sums so lent, expecting that the property's value would continue to increase regardless.[168]

It is agreed that the United States of America and the United Kingdom have a lot in common. For example, they share a close association. They learn good practices from each other and have closely knitted economic ties.

The huge error in America in the years leading to the global financial crisis should now serve as an important lesson to bankers worldwide and a matter that regulators should pay close attention to. Even if considered a micro-prudential issue, preliminary evaluation of borrowers' ability to repay loans should always remain sacrosanct.

Secondly, this study is concerned with the extent of the regulation needed to support the banking sector in the UK and the long-term impact of the sector's restructuring.

The argument is not about disregarding needed banking reforms; the issue is, "What kind of overhaul is necessary for the banking sector?" Whilst there was a

---

[165] Op. cit., K. Pilbeam, (2013, p. 501) (n. 158).
[166] Op. cit., D. Murphy, 2009, (n. 56).
[167] Ibid
[168] Op. cit., K. Pilbeam. 2013, (n. 158).

need to restore confidence in the banking sector, the question remains whether the kind of restructuring inspired by the ring-fencing went far beyond what was necessary.

2.12 Summary of the Causes of the 2007-2009 Global Financial Crisis

Some of the factors that contributed to the 2007–2009 crisis are (i) inadequate unified international financial regulation,[169] (ii) devised financial products and services that escaped the radar of regulatory control,[170] (iii) poor lending practices,[171] (iv) failings in the governance/administration of financial institutions,[172] (v) external socio-economic pressure which led some financial institutions to deliberately flout the rules as was found in Barclays, RBS and HSBC especially and for which they were heavily penalised[173] (vi) untoward activities of credit rating agencies,[174] (vii) the contributions of Collateralised Debt Obligations to the global financial crisis and the prevalent weaknesses in the banking sector in the UK before the crisis began. The problem included poor liquidity, inadequate capital and deficiencies found in the underlying financial assets/nonperforming loans within the banking sector that suffered most from the global financial crisis and, very importantly, (viii) failings of supervisory institutions. These are extensively discussed later under Section D.

---

[169] Please see page 50.

[170] Please see page 50.

[171] Please see pages 50, 92, 108 and 324.

[172] Please see the examples of Northern Rock on pages 25, 50 and 152 and RBS on page 51.

[173] Please see pages 298 – 302, for HSBC, pages 220 and 310, for RBS, page 275, for SCB, pages 228, 233, 244 and 251 for Barclays.

[174] See pages 50, 55 and 324.

Section C

Law and Regulation of the Banking Sector Before the 2007–2009 Global Financial Crisis

2.13 Introduction

This Section C is linked to objective (i) subsection (b) of the study, which is concerned with a review of the literature,

"to determine whether there were gaps in the prevailing laws and regulations before the crisis, which may have contributed to the global financial crisis in 2007–2009."

Thus, the overall objective of this section is to expound on the prevalent legal environment under which the banking sector operated before the 2007–2009 global financial crisis. This exercise should aid the process of discovering answers to objective (i) subsection (b) of the study as to whether there were gaps in the law that may have contributed to the crisis.

While Section C deals with the regulatory aspect of the law, the following Section D deals with the supervisory element relating to how the banking sector was policed, supported, and supervised.

Section C starts by identifying the sources of banking laws and regulations applicable to the banking sector and the analysis of the legal framework under which the banking sector operated and how they impacted the banking sector before the global financial crisis in 2007–2009. The section concludes with arguments for justification for banking regulation.

2.14 Sources of Banking Law and Regulations Applicable to the Banking Sector

Until 2019, at least four primary sources of laws and regulatory frameworks were binding on the banking sector in the UK. These include (i) harmonised regulations and directives received from the European Union, (ii) statute law, (iii) regulations emanating from institutions with delegated authority such as the Bank of England and supervisory authorities, including the Financial Services Authority (latterly, the Financial Conduct Authority), Prudential Regulation

Authority[175] and, (iv) international accords and regulations from Basel Committee on Banking Supervision. From this came Basel I, Basel II, and Basel III. These accords are the underlying foundations of the current consolidated regulatory framework labelled: "A Global Regulatory Framework for More Resilient Banks and Banking System."[176]

As pointed out by Tattersall et al., it is the directives emanating from the EU to implement the principles contained in the Basel framework that are legally binding among the Member States in the European Economic Area, not necessarily the framework itself.[177] So, what makes the Basel Accords legally binding are the directives from the EU that support the Accords and regulatory frameworks emanating from the Basel Committee on Banking Supervision.

2.15 The Principal Laws and Regulations that Governed the Banking Sector Before the Global Financial Crisis in 2007–2009

In summary, the principal legal frameworks that were in force, regulating the banking sector prior to the 2007–2009 crisis are as follows:

- Banking Act 1979
- Company Act 1985 (The new Company Act 2006 came into force on the 1st of April 2010)
- Banking Act 1987 (This legislation is currently obsolete as the provisions contained therein have largely been consolidated into the Financial Services Markets Act 2000)
- Basel I 1988
- Financial Services and Markets Act 2000 (FSMA)
- Basel II 2004
- EU Directives

---

[175] C. Elliot, et al., 'English Legal System' 19th Ed. (Pearson, Longman 2018)
[176] The Basel Committee on Banking Supervision, Basel III: A Global Regulatory Framework for More Resilient Banks and Banking System (2010)
[177] J. Tattersall, et al., 'Basel II: A Briefing for Practitioners' (2004) Vol. 21 Compliance Officer Bulletin

This list may not contain all the laws and regulations that govern the banking sector. Still, this provides the main thrust of the regulatory framework applicable in the banking sector before the global financial crisis in 2007–2009.

2.16 Regulated Areas in the Banking Sector and Applicable Laws and Regulatory Framework Before the Global Financial Crisis in 2007–2009

This section deals with the scope of the regulated areas in the banking sector before the global financial crisis in 2007–2009. However, due to the breadth and immensity of the range of laws and regulations applicable to the banking sector at the period under review, examination of this huge area of the law runs the risk of making a report on it dull, like reading a telephone directory. Thus, this section only briefly highlights the principal governing legislation and sundry regulations applicable at the time.

Before the crisis in 2007–2009, banks were bound to operate within the boundaries of generic laws such as case law, company law, contract law, tort, land law, insolvency legislation, criminal law, EU regulations, and civil law generally.

Like other incorporated bodies, banks had to comply with consolidated provisions in the Company Acts of 1947,[178] 1948,[179] and 1985. This legislation, among other provisions, covers matters relating to the maintenance of capital, accounts and audits, issues around directors' duties, responsibilities, qualifications, and fiduciary relationship with the bank. In addition, the Financial Services Act 1986[180] was enacted to regulate investment banking activities. Apart from this legislation, there were others, such as the Banking Act 1979, which introduced the Deposit Protection Scheme and widened the scope of the regulatory powers of the Bank of England.[181]

The Banking Act 1987 (repealed but now consolidated into FSMA 2000) strengthened the position of the Bank of England as the general supervisor and regulator of deposit-taking institutions. It reflected the changing environment in which the banking sector operated, stressing a new approach that did not regulate

---

[178] Company Act 1947
[179] Company Act 1948
[180] Financial Service Act 1986
[181] Banking Act 1979, s. 21 and s. 22

every aspect of prudential regulation.[182] The Banking Act 1987 have been substantially incorporated into the Financial Services Markets Act 2000.

More specifically, financial regulation which affects the banking sector principally encompasses a broad range of activities including but not limited to the following: (i) setting up of accounting standards, (ii) bank capital requirements, (iii) insider dealing legislation, (iv) control on money laundering, and (v) rules on consumer protection and deposit insurance.[183]

While all these laws were there, they were not strictly adhered to.

2.16.1 Accounting Standards

It is considered very important to expound, even if briefly, on the impact of poor auditing and financial reporting services on financial institutions and how they can orchestrate failure in the banking sector. Therefore, this section also discusses the standards of auditing and financial reporting required of auditing firms when providing financial auditing services to financial institutions.

Regarding unified accounting standards identified as part of the legal framework under which banks are required to operate, globalisation has brought the need for standardised accounting reporting methods and financial reporting regulations styled International Reporting Financial Standards (IRFSs).[184] This plan is supported by the Company Act 2006. For example, s.399 imposes a duty to prepare group accounts, and s.406 stipulates that preparing the reports must follow International Accounting Standards.[185]

The benefit of that arrangement to this research is that all the annual financial accounts of the banks examined have common features and the same format of reporting, which facilitated comparison between the banks used as case studies.

Also, the importance of adopting impeachable accounting standards, transparency, and reliable auditing in the smooth running of the banking sector cannot be over-emphasised. For example, the collapse of Enron, a Houston-based energy company audited by Arthur Andersen but which failed in 2001, highlights a recognition that a decline in auditing standards of any financial institution could lead to irreparable damages and loss of confidence in the

---

[182] Banking Act 1987, s. 1 & s. 2
[183] S. Morris, 'Financial Services Regulation Practice' (Oxford University Press, 2016)
[184] A. Melville, 'International Financial Reporting 5th Ed.' (Pearson Education, 2015)
[185] Company Act 2006, s. 399 and s. 406

market. For example, in the case of Enron, there were reported examples of violations of accounting standards under the Generally Accepted Accounting Principles (GAAP). There were instances of manipulation of derivative accounts, irregularities in the off-balance sheet arrangements, and reported cases of outright fraudulent practices and collusion among the executive directors, which later exposed $43 billion out of the $74 billion profit reported to be fictitious.[186]

As a follow-up to the collapse of BCCI (Bank of Credit and Commerce International) in 1991, an inquiry into the causes of the bank's failure highlighted flaws in the auditing and financial reporting standards of that bank. In addition, the impact of Enron's experience on the corporate world in the early 2000s led to the introduction of stricter auditing requirements in the Company Acts 2006.

As a result, Company Acts 2006 s.503 (3) and s.507 (1) impose strict requirements on financial institutions' auditors concerning increased transparency, a requirement that senior statutory auditors must sign off the accounts of banks in their names. The Act also stipulates information that must be included in the financial reports, how they must be reported, and the commitment of a director of an accounting firm to be personally responsible for signing off the financial accounts of the financial institution.[187] It should be pointed out that the Company Act 2006 only came into effect in 2010, almost three years after the 2007–2009 global financial crisis began.

This researcher discovered that there were instances of grossly inflated derivative accounts in the financial accounts of some of the case studies in 2008. For example, the inflated Barclays' derivative accounts worryingly reached almost £1 trillion, but the external auditors failed to query the sudden rise in the derivative account. The concern is that escaping the auditors' scrutiny at that level of inflated figures is dangerous and is a potential time bomb that could cause difficulties in the banking sector. The impact of overblown derivative accounts on banks' performance in subsequent years is discussed in Chapter 4.

The next sub-paragraphs chronologically evaluate key legislation provided at both national and supranational levels. They formed the legal frameworks under which the banking sector operated from 2007 to 2009, the period leading to the global financial crisis.

---

[186] E. Lemus, 'The Financial Collapse of the Enron Corporation and Its Impact in the United States Capital Market' (2014) Vol. 14 (4) Global Journal of Management and Business Research: Accounting and Auditing

[187] Company Act 2006 s. 380, s. 503 (3) & s. 507 (1).

2.16.2 Basel Accords: Basel Committee on Banking Supervision

Under this heading, the background and the importance of the international collaborative efforts within the EU Member States in their work towards enhancing the stability of the financial services sector both in the EU and globally in the pre-global financial crisis era are evaluated. The section highlights the evolutionary development of the joint efforts which produced Basel I and II before the global financial crisis. This cross-border collaboration established the foundation for harmonized regulatory and supervisory legal frameworks. The legal frameworks are being refined on an ongoing basis.

The Basel Committee's name at its inception in 1975 was the "Committee on Banking Regulations and Supervisory Practices."[188] The body was formed in response to disturbances in the international currency and banking market, especially following the collapse of Bankhaus Herstatt in West Germany in 1974.

At the heart of establishing the Basel Committee at that time was recognising the need to, (i) foster international collaboration among governments by working through the central bank Governors of participating countries. This was with a view to harmonising regulations on banking supervision, (ii) ensuring that no bank escaped supervision, (iii) the need to suggest ways to encourage stability and efficiency in the banking system, and (iv) agreement on adaptable regulations in areas of concern such as solvency, liquidity and foreign exchange operations and positions of banks.[189]

The Basel Committee identified areas of weakness in the management of financial institutions that were internationally active and what could go wrong in a bank to destabilise the system as a whole. However, as reflected in the 1975 Concordat, the Committee also recognised the diversity of the circumstances of the participating countries, which, if not taken into account, could undermine the body's intentions. This assumes the Committee had insisted on a uniform rule at the onset. Thus, the pioneering Basel Concordat, dated 26ᵗʰ September 1975, saw

---

[188] Committee on Banking Regulations and Supervisory Practices (1975) Report to the Governors on the Supervision of Banks' Foreign Establishment
[189] Ibid, pp 1–4.

a need to work with the participating countries based on their unique local practices, considering local regulations.[190]

2.16.3 Basel I: The Basel Capital Accord

In 1988, the BCBS developed Basel I, the Basel Capital Accord. This Basel agreement rode on the back of the debt crisis in the early 1980s among some Latin American countries, including Brazil, Mexico, and Argentina. The debt crisis then highlighted the deterioration in the capital ratios of some banks, increasing international risks in the banking system.[191] This situation led to the BCSB focusing on the need to promote a drive for capital adequacy among banks doing international banking business, intending to boost soundness and stability in the international banking system.[192]

BCBS worked out a capital adequacy proposal, measured based on a weighted assets approach and suggested a minimum capital ratio with a benchmark of 8% to be implemented by the end of 1992.[193]

The importance of capital adequacy to a bank is that it protects depositors and other bank creditors, an adequate capital level reduces the risk of a bank's failure, it helps to lower the incentive for risk-taking, and it keeps the allocation of credit in check.[194] Therefore, apart from other risks that banks face, such as foreign exchange, interest rate, and operational risks, Basel 1 recognised credit risk that may arise from default or inability to repay a material level of loans and advances given to a customer or a group of customers.[195]

The prescribed minimum capital ratio of 8% of risk-weighted assets benchmark was an attempt to sensitise the banking sector to the need for financial discipline and to provide an easily understood means to enable banks to evaluate and compare capital adequacy within the industry. However, Basel 1 was roundly criticised for being rudimentary because the prescribed 8% capital ratio

---

[190] Ibid p. 3

[191] BCBS, 'History of Basel Committee' https://www.bis.org/bcbs/history.htm. Accessed 01/06/2020

[192] The Basel Committee on Banking Supervision, 'International Convergence of Capital Measurement and Capital Standards' (1988) BCBS

[193] ibid

[194] Op. cit., D. Coskun, (n. 163).

[195] Op. Cit., The Basel Committee on Banking Supervision (1988) (n. 192)

was considered arbitrary and static.[196] Besides, the methodology used to arrive at the 8% benchmark was considered inadequate as it failed to consider the maturity of exposure and the changing nature of default risks.[197]

The importance of Basel I to this research is that, following the emergence of widespread economic deregulation policy in the 1980s, and the exponential rate at which banks were merging, issues around capital adequacy and liquidity with the attendant risk-taking in the banking sector at the time became a topical issue. This was because concerns were raised about Basel I's fitness for purpose. An example of what this means to the banking sector was a disproportionate level of exposure of eight US commercial banks to Mexico, Argentina, and Brazil, which reached about $37 billion in 1982. As a result, when these countries defaulted on capital and interest repayment, they had to seek assistance from the International Monetary Fund (IMF).[198]

The issue then was that the exposure of the US Banks to these Latin American countries reached 147%[199] of the capital of the banks affected, such that if ultimately the countries mentioned had not been able to receive the desperately needed support from the IMF, those eight American commercial banks could have faced imminent insolvency.

Worse still, Chiu and Wilson pointed out that some banks that went down during the 2007–2009 global financial crisis reported capital ratios that were significantly above the prescribed ratios. For example, Lehman Brothers in the US claimed it had 16.1%, Northern Rock, a British bank, said it had 17.5%, and the Icelandic Bank Kaupthing also claimed it had 11.2%.[200]

The point is that the three banks claimed that they were Basel I compliant as they had a weighted capital ratio well above the stipulated 8%. However, doubts were later raised about the computation accuracy of the capital adequacy requirement reported.

In summary, this section suggests that, as far back as the 1970s, following the collapse of Bankhaus Herstatt in West Germany in 1974, the importance of

---

[196] Zufferey, J. 'Regulating Financial Markets in Times of Stress is a Fundamentally Human Undertaking' (2011) Vol. 8 (2) European Company and Financial Law

[197] Ibid

[198] I. Chiu, and J. Wilson, 'Banking Law and Regulation' (Oxford University Press, 2019, p. 333)

[199] Ibid.

[200] Ibid. (Chiu, I. and Wilson, J. (2019, p. 343)

sufficient liquidity and capital adequacy in internationally active banks was well recognised. However, in the early 1980s, some Latin American countries, including Brazil, Mexico, and Argentina, faced a debt burden and were at risk of default. The potential insolvency of these Latin American countries could have ruined some American banks that were over-exposed to those countries, except for the intervention of the IMF that bailed out those countries.

That scenario inspired the creation of Basel I in 1988. The criticism of that era has been that, though there was a recognition of the problems around insufficient liquidity and inadequate capital in major banks, the measures put in place then were very weak and inadequate at best.

2.16.4 Financial Services Markets Acts 2000

The context in which FSMA 2000 is evaluated under this heading concerns whether the provisions of the legislation and others before it were robust enough and capable of sustaining the banking sector against the financial crisis in the period leading to the global financial crisis 2007–2009. If not, determine the probable gaps.

This part of the study also seeks to evaluate the banking sector's and supervisory agencies' attitude towards compliance with the legal frameworks in force at the time, which may have contributed to failings in the banks engaged as case studies in this research. The case studies are the Royal Bank of Scotland, Barclays Bank, Standard Chartered Bank and HSBC.

As discussed under Section D of this Chapter (the next section), the incessant failure in the financial services sector in the 1980s and 1990s under the watch of the Bank of England fuelled the need to establish a strong, unified regulatory body that could have a general oversight on the financial services sector in the UK.

It may be helpful to mention that that same period was when the UK followed its European counterparts in embracing the universal banking model.[201] An important advantage of bringing together different facets of the financial services sector under one umbrella regulator was that it was considered efficient. In addition, having a unified regulator to regulate and supervise universal banks made sense, as did having multiple regulators supervising different segments

---

[201] Op cit., Ellinger, E. P et al 2011, p. 73, (n. 116).

within a universal bank comprising deposit takers, insurers, investment firms, providence, and mutual societies.[202]

By the same token, having an integrated body of law designed specifically for the financial services sector was also considered sensible. Accordingly, the FMSA 2000 became that integrated body of laws designed to govern the UK financial services sector. The Financial Services Authority was the regulator saddled with the responsibility to regulate, supervise, support and enforce the law within the financial services sector.

FSMA 2000 is comprehensive legislation that comprises 30 Parts and 22 Schedules (Sch. 22 has since been repealed) aimed at harmonising the regulatory structure of the financial services sector, as mentioned in the preceding paragraph.

The Act had six primary objectives: to boost public confidence in the financial system and to encourage stability in the financial markets. In addition, it promoted and increased public awareness about market information, thereby assisting interested stakeholders with market information that could aid decision-making processes. Finally, it is also to ensure consumers' protection and, as far as possible, to reduce financial crime.[203]

In response to the global financial crisis in 2007–2009, FMSA 2000 has been going through reviews and modifications.

FSMA 2000 is an all-embracing legislation that provides legal frameworks for the entire financial services sector. The financial sector includes Credit Unions, Insurance Companies, Building Societies, Friendly Societies and assorted Financial Market Operators, and the banking sector. Below are key legislation features related to the banking sector, which is this study's primary area of interest.

Before the crisis, Part I of FSMA 2000 identified the now-defunct Financial Services Authority as the official regulator of the financial services sector.[204] However, following the enormous losses sustained during the global financial crisis, the searchlight was focused on the performance and effectiveness of the FSA as the sole regulator of the financial services sector. [205] There ensued public

---

[202] The preamble to the FMSA 2000.

[203] FSMA 2000 Part 1 s.3 to 6A

[204] FSMA 2000 Part 1

[205] At the beginning, the pledge by the government to support the banking sector facing a financial crisis peaked at £1.162 trillion, but much later reduced to £456 billion as of

outrage at the attendant unprecedented support packages offered by the government at taxpayers' expense to forestall the total collapse of the Global Systemically Important Banks.

For example, in his testimony before the House of Common Parliamentary Committee that reviewed the report into the failure of RBS, Lord Turner, the then Chairman of the FSA, openly confessed that the supervisory model adopted by the FSA in the period leading to the global financial crisis was wrong and ineffective.[206] In a report named after Lord Turner published in 2009, the FSA Chairman also owned up to the fact that the supervision approach of the supervisory authority to the banking sector was fundamentally flawed. For example, the supervision of large complex banks such as the ones in the case studies should have been more intrusive and systemic, and more attention should have been paid to liquidity, capital adequacy and quality of the assets of these banks.[207]

Thus, under a new regime following the crisis, from the 1st of April 2013, Part 1A of the Act replaced the Financial Services Authority as the regulator of the financial services sector. In addition, a new simplified supervisory framework was designed comprising the Bank of England acting as the overall supervisory agent. At the same time, the Financial Conduct Authority and Prudential Regulation Authority each have clearly defined roles.[208]

S.1A provides the general duties of FCA, which include ensuring that the relevant markets function well to advance consumer protection and the duty to regulate the financial services sector. Also, formulate subsidiary rules supporting the Act's six broad objectives. In addition, the FCA had the mandate to promote competition, as far as possible, to reduce financial crime, a duty to consult

---

31st March 2011. RSB was the largest recipient of cash injection as they received £45.6 billion.
https://publications.parliament.uk/pa/cm201213/cmselect/cmtreasy/640/64007.htm (paragraphs 94–96).

[206] House of Commons, "The FSA's Report into the Failure of RBS–Treasury", (2012, para. 97)
https://publications.parliament.uk/pa/cm201213/cmselect/cmtreasy/640/64007.htm

[207] Op. cit., Turner Review 2009, (2009, pp. 86–91), (n. 148).

[208] FSMA 2000 Part 1A s.1A and s.2A

practitioners and consumers and generally, to see to the soundness, stability and resilience of the UK financial system.[209]

Until comparatively recently, with the enactment of the Banking Act 1987, which introduced a deposit protection scheme, consumer protection law was not in place for core banking customers.[210]

The issues about consumer protection were further consolidated through s.5 of the FSMA 2000, which required the Financial Services Authority to secure an appropriate degree of consumer protection in its supervisory role.[211]

Consumer protection, as it affects core banking customers, relates to transparency in the market products and ensuring that banks conduct their business appropriately.

Similarly, under s.2B, the PRA has the burden to promote soundness in the financial system and to see to it that authorised person carry out their business in ways that avoid adverse effects on the continuity of the provision of services in the UK. The PRA has the additional responsibility to ensure that ring-fenced banks carry out their business safely in a way that avoids adverse effects that could cause disruptions to the provision of their services in the UK. Additionally, they must ensure that the business of ring-fenced banks is protected from risks from within and outside the UK.[212]

Given the causes of the global financial crisis in 2007–2009 already discussed earlier under Section B and the extent of the damages caused to the global economy, the somewhat challenging and onerous responsibilities imposed on the regulatory institutions should be expected. This stringent regulatory control is necessary, especially in the face of supervisory failures of the BoE in the 1980s and 1990s, discussed in Section D.

Banking regulators and the financial sector, in general, learned lessons from the failure of the BCCI in 1991 as the official liquidators of the bank, Deloitte Touche Tohmatsu, attempted to shift the blame for the collapse of the bank on BoE based on assumed wilful negligence and malfeasance in the office on the part of the Bank of England.[213] Thus, a limitation clause was prudently inserted

---

[209] FSMA 2000 Part 1 section 1 b–d.

[210] R. Cranston, 'Principles of Banking Law 2nd Ed.' (Oxford University Press, 2002, p. 76)

[211] FSMA 2000 s.5

[212] FSMA 2000 Part 1A s.2B (ss.3) (c) i, ii & iii

[213] Three Rivers DC v Bank of England (No 3) (CA and HL) 2003 2 AC

under s.2G of FSMA 2000. The exclusion clause says, "Nothing in sections 2B–2D is to be regarded as requiring the PRA to ensure that no PRA-authorised person fails."

Simply, this clause serves as an express notice to other financial services operators who may, in the future, want to follow in the footsteps of the BCCI liquidators, blaming regulators for a failure in their bank that such claims would not stand. The clause also serves as a notice to the management of banks that they are primarily responsible for any failure in their banks and not regulatory/supervisory authorities.

Part II, IV, V and XXII of FSMA 2000 deal with regulated and prohibited activities, including controlling licenced persons carrying out banking business. These sections of the Act deal with authorisation to carry out banking business, conditions precedent to be licenced to carry out banking business and circumstances that could lead to the withdrawal of authorisation to practice. It also sets the rules prohibiting unauthorised persons from carrying out regulated activities. Part V deals explicitly with the qualification and vetting of senior employees or holders of specified sensitive duties by regulators and conducts expected from high-ranking officers holding sensitive offices in a financial institution. This part of FSMA 2000 was incorporated into Part IV of the Banking Reform Act 2013.

All these provisions of the Act are frontline defence mechanisms. They are put in place to ensure that members of the public are not conned by persons who may want to conduct banking business but have not been adequately assessed and certified as fit and capable of running a bank.

Part XIV is concerned with enforcing disciplinary measures against infringements by authorised persons, whilst Part XVI provides for Ombudsman Scheme meant to assist with informal dispute resolution between authorised persons and members of the public.

Part XXII relates to the appointment of auditors and their statutory duties. This part of the Act is without prejudice to Part 15 of the Company Act 2006 from sections 380–430. These sections of the Act provide in detail requirements about the nature of accounts to be prepared by the banking sector, how they should be presented, what should be included in the financial accounts and key officers' report and the timeframe within which the audit report must be prepared.

Although Insolvency Act 1986 generally applies to all corporate entities, Part XXIV of FSMA 2000 and Part 2, s.90–s.103 of the Banking Act 2009 provide 'customised legislation' for dealing with insolvency in the banking sector. The need for creating specialised legislation meant exclusively for the banking sector was heightened by a requirement to give effect to one of the objectives of FSMA 2000. This is concerned with the encouragement of stability in the banking sector. The purpose is that if a bank becomes insolvent, there would be a set of resolution plans. The options could be to either facilitate the taking over of the bank by another bank through merger/acquisition or that the winding up of the business of the stressed bank is conducted in such a way that it does not cause disruptions to the sector, especially the payment system.[214]

Part XXVII concerns offences relating to misleading statements, insider dealing and money laundry. In contrast, Part XXVIII is concerned with provisions giving powers to direct regulatory authorities to comply with UK international obligations.

In conclusion, FSMA 2000 is arguably a very 'rich' legislation. It benefited from cumulative knowledge gained over the years from issues identified from failures in some banks in the past, including the BCCI and JMB. Including provisions for consumer protection in the banking sector was also innovative. Similarly, clearly defining roles between the BoE, FCA and PRA is a welcome idea. So also, including an express disclaimer to the effect that regulatory and supervisory agents have no obligations for the failure of a financial institution is helpful.

The noticeable gap in the FSMA 2000 is its ominous silence on issues related to concerns about liquidity and inadequate capital in huge and complex major banks that were already strained by disproportionate debt/equity ratios. Apart from mentioning stability in the banks in general terms, FSMA 2000 is not specific about capital and liquidity adequacy. However, as discussed earlier, these areas are well under the control of international regulators that birthed Bases I, II, III and IV.

Banking regulation has come a full circle. Before the 1980s, subsectors within the financial system had distinctive regulations for each subsector in the narrow banking era. In the 2000s, umbrella legislation, FSMA 2000, combined regulations of the entire financial system. The Financial Services (Banking

---

[214] The Banking Act 2009, s.90.

Reform) Act 2013 was made specifically for the banking sector in response to the global financial crisis.

2.16.5 Basel II, 2004: The New Capital Framework

Basel II, released in June 2004, was a revision and a consolidation of the earlier Basel I accord, which aimed to strengthen further the soundness and stability of the international banking system.[215] The revised regulatory framework focused on three pillars: Pillar I—a minimum capital requirement that is risk-sensitive and hinged on categories of tiers of eligible capital, which took into account operational risks, market risks, and credit risks. Pillar II—is a supervision review process considering liquidity and systemic risks. Furthermore, Pillar III requires banks to provide reliable information about their market exposure.[216]

The question is whether Basel II, released in 2004 in addition to an array of other regulatory measures on the ground mentioned earlier, adequately prepared the world's banking system for the looming catastrophic global financial crisis in 2007–2009.

In 2005, just two years before the financial crisis began, Tanega mentioned the growing concern among regulators about banks' increasing exposure to securitised transactions (which ultimately led to the global financial crisis). Basel II, Pillar III sought to provide remedial protection against this risk by requiring banks to keep a capital reserve to hedge securitisation exposures.[217]

In 2010, practitioners, academics, and international governments still grappled with why, how and what broke down that needed fixing concerning the global financial crisis. Maxwell and Eichhorn contended that the best efforts and intentions of Basel I & Basel II failed to stop the global financial crisis. All the

---

[215] Basel Committee on Banking Supervision, 'International Convergence of Capital Measurement and Capital Standards: A Revised Framework Basel II' (BCBS, 2004)
[216] ibid
[217] J. Tanega, 'Securitisation Disclosures and Compliance under Basel II: A Risk Based Approach to Economic Substance Over Legal Form: Part I' (2005) Vol. 20 (12) 617–627 Journal of International Banking Law and Regulation

failed banks claimed to have complied with the regulatory requirements of the two prior Basel agreements on liquidity and capital ratios.[218]

Just as Admati also pointed out about the inadequate attention given by regulators to the problem of under-capitalisation in the banks, the overwhelming nature of the global financial crisis in 2007–2009 made mincemeat out of the regulatory 8% capital requirement as a mechanism created to provide soundness and stability in the international banking system. Whatever provisions the banks made as hedges against risks associated with securitisation exposure devised under Pillar III of Basel II was like a drop in a bucket of losses incurred from exposure to CDOs. As a result of the mishap, some banks are still counting their losses more than ten years after the crisis ended. Chapter 4 of this report will discuss issues around the subject using the case study financial accounts as illustrations.

2.16.6 Bank's Capital Adequacy Requirements Considering the Global Financial Crisis in 2007–2009

Regulations concerning the level of capital requirements in banks comprise two legs: (i) capital adequacy as a pre-requisite to starting a banking business, and (ii) capital adequacy concerning the relationship between owners' equity and the bank's exposure on loans and advances granted to bank customers on an ongoing basis.[219]

The first leg of capital adequacy requirements at the commencement of banking business stated under the old rule Schedule 3 criteria in the Banking Act 1987 [220] says that "the institution must have adequate capital." Provision about the level of resources required precedent to authorisation of licence is found under FMSA 2000 Part IV Permission. The detailed requirements are under Schedule 6 s. 4. What would be considered a minimum threshold would be determined from time to time by the relevant licencing authority and the nature of the banking business involved.

---

[218] A. Maxwell and M. Eichhorn 'Measuring Operational Risk in the Context of Basel II: Do Banks Move along the Spectrum of Available Approaches?' (2010) 25 (2) 83–88 Journal of International Banking Law and Regulation

[219] Op. cit., Cranston, R. 2002, p. 89, (n. 210).

[220] The Banking Act 1987 Sch 3

Meeting capital adequacy requirements at the inception of the banking business is hardly the problem. It is the second leg of capital adequacy that can be problematic. This is concerned with keeping up with capital adequacy on an ongoing basis. Then, capital adequacy is tied to the relationship between owners' equity and the loan exposure to the bank's customers.

Wadsley and Penn elaborate on the core capital characteristics that meet the capital adequacy rule. These include the ability to absorb losses and a requirement that it must have a certain degree of permanency.[221] Such would include fully paid-up ordinary share capital, general reserve, retained profit, and revaluation reserve, for example.[222]

Addressing concerns over liquidity and capital inadequacy among credit institutions is part of the agenda of the Basel I Accord, which tried to prescribe a benchmark ratio that should be the barest minimum applicable to all banks. This was stated as 7-8%.[223] However, the attempt to prescribe a benchmark for all banks has been subject to severe criticism on the grounds that the one-size-fits-all model would be ill-fitting for banks with varied circumstances.[224]

As a follow-up to the 1988 Basel I Accord, in 1989, the EU came up with an additional policy in support of the Accord styled 'Own Funds of Credit Institutions', which further stressed the importance of capital and liquidity adequacy as a necessity to strengthen the banking system within the Member States.

The Directive did not commit itself to prescribe the minimum threshold of liquidity and capital adequacy ratios apart from the recommended ratios specified by the Basel I Accord on the preamble page of the Directive. Instead, the policy allowed the Member States to adopt stringent self-determined provisions to safeguard the domestic banking sector. In addition, the Member States were encouraged to strive to achieve greater harmonisation within the community. It pointed out that when supervising huge and complex banks, standardised mechanisms should be adopted on how consolidated own funds are

---

[221] J. Wadsley, and G.A Penn, 'The Law Relating to Domestic Banking 2nd Ed.' (Sweet & Maxwell, 2000, p.39)

[222] Ibid.

[223] S. Schwerter, 'Basel III's Ability to Mitigate Systemic Risk' (2011) Vol 19 (4) 337–354 Journal of Financial Regulation and Compliance

[224] K. Pakravan, 'Bank Capital: The Case Against Basel' (2014) Vol. 22 (3) 208–218 Journal of Financial Regulation and Compliance

determined considering varied circumstances of the credit institutions involved and the local economy. Article 2 of the directive lists types of funds that should constitute own funds to determine liquidity and capital adequacy ratios.[225] These are paid-up capital, share premium accounts, balances on accumulated profit and loss accounts, revaluation reserves, contingent provision accounts for banking risks and fixed-term cumulative preferential shares accounts.[226]

In 2000, which was well before the global financial crisis, Wadsley and Penn and Basel I, in 1988, suggest that there was a recognition of the need for banks to maintain adequate liquidity and equity capital. Whether that requirement was followed is a different matter. Part of the difficulties in the pre-crisis era was the inadequate attention given by the banking sector's supervisors to these elements, which are vital to the survival of huge and complex financial institutions. For example, Johnson Matthey Bankers Ltd.'s (JMB) failure in 1984 was caused by poor risk management and excessive lending to a few creditors that defaulted. That case illustrates some of the dire consequences that could occur when bankers are lending in measures that are far disproportionate to the available equity support base.[227]

The failings in JMB later inspired law reforms which made it mandatory to report to regulators where a bank is exposed to a borrower or a connected group of borrowers of up to 10% of the financial institution's capital or where such lending would expose the bank to the risk of losing up to 25% of its capital. However, bankers were found to have often circumvented the rule.[228]

During the hearing before the House of Commons Committee commissioned to examine the Financial Services Authority's report into the failure of RBS, Lord Turner, in his own words, said,

"The basic fact that the capital and liquidity regimes were, to be blunt, rubbish, we knew already ... The supervisory approach was wrong...". [229]

---

[225] European Economic Community, "Own Funds of Credit Institutions", (1989) Directive 89/299/EEC

[226] Ibid.

[227] Op. cit., (Cranston, R. 2002, p. 63) n. 209

[228] The Banking Act 1987 s.38 (1a and 1b) and s.38 (2)

[229] House of Commons, "The FSA's Report into the Failure of RBS–Treasury", (2012, para. 117)
https://publications.parliament.uk/pa/cm201213/cmselect/cmtreasy/640/64007.htm

The argument is that, though bankers were primarily the architects of their misfortune and ultimately responsible for their losses, the banking sector supervisory authorities did little to help. This is if, all along, supervisory authorities were aware of gross irregularities in the banking sector's micro-prudential strategies and knew there was undue risk-taking in the banks. Moreover, it would be even worse if supervisory authorities were aware that Global Strategically Important Banks were operating under inadequate liquidity and capital ratios but did nothing to arrest the situation even when they had the power to do so.

The poor attention paid by supervisory agencies to issues around liquidity and capital adequacy ratios in the banking sector in the period leading to the global financial crisis invariably contributed to excessive risk-taking by banks. As a result, banks were notoriously using excessive debt capital to finance loans, overdrafts, mortgages, and other facilities to bank customers, thereby endangering financial stability in the economy.

The global financial crisis in 2007–2009 once again accentuated discussions around the importance of capital adequacy in the banking sector. Admati opined that adequate attention was not sufficiently paid to the importance of capital adequacy before and even after the global financial crisis. In the attempt to review the law, regulators were still not doing enough to put the need for capital adequacy in the prime position it deserved.[230] Much later, in 2019, Gurrea-Martinez and Remolina emphasised that capital adequacy is now increasingly recognised as one of the most important parts of international banking regulation. They suggested that banks with a sound capital base are more financially stable and less likely to take excessive risks.[231]

In recognition of the contributions of liquidity problems and inadequate capital to the global financial crisis in 2007–2009, part of Turner's review suggested that the overall quantity and quality of the capital and liquidity of the global banking system must be substantially increased. He further suggested that making provisions for counter-cyclical capital buffers should be a priority for banks exposed to other banks.[232]

---

[230] Op. Cit., A. R. Admati 2014, (n. 17).

[231] A. Gurrea-Martinez, et al. 'The Dark Side of Implementing Basel Capital Requirements: Theory, Evidence, and Policy' (2019) Vol 22 (1) Journal of International Economic Law

[232] Op. Cit., Turner, A. 2009, pgs. 53–68, (n. 148).

The conclusion under this heading is that, although in the pre-crisis era, there was a recognition that capital adequacy level in the banking sector is a *sine qua non* to stability in that sector, the principle was not put into practice as much as it should have been.

Secondly, the need for more regulations and associated costs could have been obviated where regulatory and supervisory architecture operated efficiently.

2.16.7 Argument for the Justification of Bank Regulation

Neo-liberalism ideology (discussed later under Drivers of Economic Regulation) suggests a laissez-faire approach to regulation and that economic activities should be unrestricted by law as far as possible.[233] Therefore, this section of the study deals with why banking regulation is imperative.

As pointed out earlier in this chapter, historically, it has been the case that whenever there is laxity in the supervision of the banking sector or some impediments stand in the way of adequate regulatory oversight of the financial sector, the result tends to be that eventually, financial crises occur.

The result of an earlier survey by Ramasastry and Slavova, which cuts across international boundaries, re-emphasised that lack of enforcement and effectiveness in the supervision of banks may lead to a situation where troubled financial institutions continue to operate even when insolvent or are no longer viable.[234, 235]

At the time of that study, which was in the late 1990s, the research of these authors suggested that financial institutions that ran into severe difficulties in the jurisdictions where the European Bank for Reconstruction and Development (EBRD) operated mostly had well-developed legal systems. However, there was laxity in the implementation strategy. According to these authors, there was inadequate trained regulatory personnel to conduct periodic supervision and failure to take remedial actions when such would have helped.[236]

---

[233] C. Colclough and J. Manor 'States or Market? Neo-liberalism and the Development Policy Debate' (Oxford University Press, 1993)

[234] A. Ramasastry, and S. Slavova 'European Bank for Reconstruction and Development (EBRD) Survey Result' (1999) (7) 297 Journal of International Banking and Financial Law

[235] Op. cit., L. Verril, 2008, (n. 25).

[236] Op. cit., Ramasastry, A. and Slavova, S. 1999, (n. 234)

At about the same time in 1997, the Ex- Solicitor General of England and Wales, Prof Cranston, observed that notwithstanding that the economy was in a period of financial liberalisation, legal regulation of banking and finance in the UK witnessed significant tightening given the aggressive marketing and increased risks which banks undertook.[237]

As pointed out earlier, meeting the level of capital requirement at the start of the banking business is hardly the problem. However, the minimum threshold for capital and liquidity ratios 'as a going concern' can be problematic.

Some of the most important monetary policy tools used during the Bretton Woods era to manage liquidity and control inflation in the economy included increasing or decreasing bank liquidity ratios as may be required. In addition, adjustments to the interest rates could assist with mopping up excess liquidity or inducing an increase in cash volume within the economy to dampen deflation effects.[238]

However, with the advent of liberalism and, with it, the adoption of the free market enterprise popularised by Friedman,[239] any attempt by regulatory authorities to arbitrarily influence the interest rate or banks' liquidity/capital ratios more than is necessary would be seen as an insidious reversion to the once rejected Keynesian protectionist/paternalism ideology. [240]

Protectionism is a notion that the government may wrongly adopt the position of an overprotective father enforcing rules on his children under the assumed protection of the children's best interests, even when the children are not welcoming of such intrusion. The tension concerns policy choices on how far the government should go to protect the economy. The importance of that tension to this research is that the adoption of the policy on ring-fencing also falls within this contentious area of law that generated a debate on whether it is appropriate to impose some aspects of the ring-fencing policy on the banking sector, as happened in January 2019. Another argument suggested in this study is that riskier investment banking should probably be carved out of the mainstream banks rather than creating a ring-fenced bank out of the universal

---

[237] Op. cit., R. Cranston, R. 2002, p. 63, (210).
[238] J. M. Keynes, 'The General Theory of Employment, Interest and Money' (Rinehart and Wilson, 1936)
[239] M. Friedman, 'Price Theory' (Aldine, 2007)
[240] J. S. Mill, 'On Liberty' (Penguin, 1974)

banking parent. What should no longer be in doubt is that public interest justifies government intervention in the economy when appropriate.[241]

In the case of the banking sector, as opposed to other institutions or business organisations, a bank's failure would likely have a much more adverse impact on the economy than would be the case with any other business organisation. This is because of the contagion effect a bank's failure can have on other facets of the economy. In addition, the results of bankruptcies in the banking sector would be more amplified because of the interconnectedness and dependency within the sector.[242]

For example, in the absence of a Deposit Insurance Guarantee Scheme, depositors could lose their life savings or a significant part of it, which would naturally lead to outrage and socioeconomic upheaval. Therefore, as a matter of prudence and the importance of the banking sector to the economy, it is considered necessary to regulate it.

For those who oppose ring-fencing, the question is not about resistance to the regulation of the banking sector. Instead, the issue is concerned with the type of regulation. The question is about what area the government should control. Are there better ways of dealing with the concern addressed by the ring-fencing policy? In the long run, would the cost of ring-fencing be disproportionate?

These issues will be revisited under the section on theories on structuralism and neo-liberalism.

2.16.8 Conclusion

The review highlighted the status of the general regulatory framework before the global financial crisis in 2007–2009.

The Banking Act of 1979 is a comprehensive piece of legislation enacted in response to the difficulties in the banking sector in the mid-1970s. The aim was to put on a statutory footing regulatory structure for the banking sector's activities and to firmly entrench the powers of the Bank of England in its supervisory role over the sector. In addition, the legislation was enacted in anticipation of potential difficulties that may surface following the emergence of banks that grew bigger due to the deregulation of the economy at the time.[243]

---

[241] Op. cit. L. Guiso, et al., 2006, (n. 11).

[242] A. Arora, 'Banking Law' (Pearson, 2014, p.168)

[243] Please see pages 60 – 61.

Similarly, at a supranational level, Basel I was introduced in 1988 to enhance resilience and stability among internationally active banks. Basel I was made in response to the debt crisis in some Latin American countries in the late 1980s. The aim was to restore confidence in the banking sector following the collapse of Bankhaus Herstatt in West Germany in 1974.[244]

FSMA 2000 created the new tripartite supervisory architecture comprising BoE, FCA and PRA. In addition, the legislation defined the differentiated roles of the regulatory/supervisory institutions.

Basel II, introduced in 2004, focused on the enhanced capital requirements, the need for banks to make special provisions against exposure to the risk of losses that might arise from the inter-connectedness among banks and the need to boost the supervision regime in the banking sector.[245]

Lessons were learned from issues arising from bank failures in the 1970s to the 1990s. As listed in this section, enhanced regulatory frameworks were developed in response to the problems identified in the banking sector since 1979. However, the big gap in the regulatory measures was the weak attention paid to insufficient liquidity, inadequate equity capital and excessive debt/equity ratios that plagued the banking sector over time. Although the regulatory authorities knew at that time that, there were deep-seated problems among global systemically important banks with complex needs, the effort was insufficient to adequately prepare for the looming financial crisis. As a result, the remedial measures did not go far enough to address issues that eventually formed part of the factors that led to the catastrophic global financial crisis in 2007–2009.

The following section evaluates the supervisory element of the regulatory framework on the ground in the banking sector before the global financial crisis. It also discusses a range of regulatory changes in response to the global financial crisis, including Basel III relating to the fortification of supervision framework, enhancement of the quality of capital, mitigation of pro-cyclicality, integration of micro and macro-prudential supervision and regulation of Liquidity Coverage Ratio.

---

[244] Please see pages 63 – 66.
[245] Please see pages 72 – 73.

Section: D

Banking Sector Regulatory Institutions: Supervision, Support, Surveillance and Enforcement

2.17 Introduction

The previous section evaluated the banking laws and regulations that imposed duties and obligations on the banking sector in the UK before the 2007–2009 global financial crisis.

This section evaluates the institutions responsible for policing, supporting and supervising the banking sector in the public's best interests. The primary role of these institutions is to ensure that banking laws and regulations are effectively enforced so that, ultimately, the banking sector maintains the confidence of the public and investors.[246]

This section is linked with objective (i) subsection (b) of the research, which seeks to establish whether there were gaps in the prevailing laws and regulations which may have contributed to the global financial crisis in 2007–2009. The section also evaluates regulatory changes at the supranational level on the quality of Capital and Liquidity Coverage Ratio (LCR).

This section is particularly important to this study because it discusses the failure of the regulatory institutions and the Financial Services Authority, the principal supervisory agency overseeing the banking sector, before the financial crisis. In Turner's review, the FSA was severely criticised for its failure in individual banks' prudential and micro supervision and in its failure to detect and warn the government of the impending crisis.

This supervisory failure has been cited as a large part of the contributory factors to the associated problems that came with the 2007–2009 financial crisis in the UK. That situation led to the disbandment of the FSA, which served as the supervisory authority in the period leading to the global financial crisis. In addition, it led to a policy change

---

[246] Financial Services and Market Act 2000 (the preamble)

encapsulated in the government policy statement, "A new approach to financial regulation: the blueprint for reform."[247, 248]

2.18 The Scope of Banking Supervision Activities

In context, supervisory activities refer to the exercise of close oversight of financial institutions without being overly intrusive in their affairs except where appropriate to prevent banking sector crises.[249] Support is concerned with providing help to a bank in times of distress by the supervising institutions so that instead of folding up, the supervising institution helps to stabilise the distressed bank by either nursing it back to life or assisting the bank with an orderly dissolution.[250] In the event of an inevitable winding up, the objective of the supervising institution is to avoid a contagion effect on the banking sector, bringing to the barest minimum the negative impact of the failed bank on the whole economy.[251] Surveillance activity includes a third party or secondary agents collaborating in the supervision process.[252] One example is auditors, who examine the bank's annual accounts and report fraud or irregularities directly to the supervising institutions.[253] This has become a vital part of the supervisory framework of the banking sector following the collapse of the Bank of Commerce and Credit International.[254] Enforcement refers to imposing sanctions on a defaulting financial institution for infringements of banking regulations and laws.[255]

---

[247] Op. cit., A. Turner 2009 (n. 148)

[248] HM Treasury, 'A New Approach to Financial Regulation: The Blueprint for Reform' (2011)

[249] A v. B (Bank of England Intervening) [1992] AII ER 778

[250] Banking Act 2009 Part 1 s.2 (a) Stabilisation Option (b) Insolvency procedure (c) Bank administration

[251] Banking Act 2009 Part 1, s.1

[252] Banking Act 1987 Part 1 s.41 (Investigation on behalf of the Bank) s.42 (Investigation of suspected infringement) s. 43 (Powers of entry in case of alleged contravention)

[253] Part 7, Banking Reform Act 2013, Banking Act 1987 Part 1 s.45, 46 & 47 Accounts and Auditors

[254] Price Waterhouse v BCCI Holdings [1992] BCLC 583

[255] The Financial Services (Banking Reform) Act 2013 s.71 (Compliance failure) s. 73 (Penalties)

Before deregulation in the 1970s, an essential part of the reasons for the exercise of control over the banking sector was the need to protect the economy from harmful external influences such as unhealthy practices and to enable policymakers to steer the economy toward a desired pathway by using monetary policy mechanisms such as interest rate and credit control measures.[256]

This section also surveys the banking sector's supervision regimes in the UK, the lessons learnt in the supervision of the banking sector over time, and the evolutionary developments of the banking supervision institutions and supervision policies in the UK. The section argues that banking supervision has come of age after the Bank of England Act 1946.

In so doing, Section D highlights instances in the 1990s when fundamental mistakes were made by taking the direct supervision of the banking sector away from the Bank of England and giving it to the Financial Services Authority. As well, key milestones were identified when innovative features were incorporated into the financial system supervision models in the UK through the Financial Services and Markets Act 2000 and the reinforcement of those features in the Financial Services (Banking Reform) Act 2013, as we witnessed lately after the 2007–2009 financial crisis. Finally, part of this section highlights what worked best and policies that failed woefully.

2.19 The Nature of Banking Supervision

It is not uncommon to wrongly assume that regulatory and supervisory activities relating to the banking sector are the same.[257] Some use the terms 'banking regulation' and 'banking supervision' together or interchangeably.[258]

Regulation and supervision are two distinctive roles, though, at times, the two roles may, to some extent, fuse. The regulatory role means devising the law, making the rules and determining the regulations that govern the banking sector's activities. The supervisory role concerns enforcement and compliance with the rules and regulations.[259]

---

[256] Hadjiemmanuil, C. (1996, p.1) Banking Regulation and the Bank of England

[257] Op. Cit., A. Arora, 2014, (n. 242).

[258] D. Singh, 'Banking Regulation of the UK and US Financial Markets' (Ashgate, 2007, p. 47)

[259] Op. Cit., E. P Ellinger, E. P et al, 2011, p. 27, (n. 116).

The institutions involved in making regulations include parliament through enacted statutes. Others include the Treasury, the European Union through directives, market makers through industry's self-imposed rules and the Bank of England, the apex bank, through directives to the financial system.

For example, parliament makes the law but does not exercise direct supervision over the banking sector, likewise the Treasury. The Treasury maintains oversight of the financial system (at a macro level) through the Bank of England. Although wholly owned by the Treasury on behalf of the government, through the Bank of England Act 1998, the bank became independent with autonomous powers to determine monetary policy through the Bank of England Act 1998.[260] The Bank of England can determine rules and regulations for the banking sector and exercise direct supervisory oversight over the financial system through the PRA and FCA.[261] So, in practice, the Bank of England and its subsidiaries combine 'regulating' and 'supervising' roles.

The misconception about the two roles can typically come to light when complaints are that the banking sector is unregulated. As pointed out earlier in Section C, there is a long history of the evolution of laws and regulations governing the affairs of the banking sector. Similarly, some agents are empowered to maintain supervisory oversight of the banking sector activities and to enforce the statutory laws and regulations imposed on the banking sector. Still, one must admit that the deregulation era ushered in the light touch regulation period. Before the global financial crisis, a subject often debated regarding the supervision of the banking sector concerned the effectiveness of the approaches to the supervision of the banking sector in the UK.[262] This section focuses on the role of the Bank of England and its newly constituted supervisory agents, the Prudential Regulatory Authority (PRA) and the Financial Conduct Authority (FCA), the twin-peaked model enunciated in the Banking Reform Act 2013.

As argued by Penn, a possible reason why some people assume that the banking sector was unregulated was that until the Banking Act of 1979, the duties which are now statutorily imposed on the banking sector were previously not

---

[260] Bank of England Act 1998 Part 1A Financial Stability s.9a–9g
[261] Ibid s.9h–9n, Directions by Financial Policy Committee
[262] J. Gray, and J. Hamilton, 'Implementing Financial Regulation' (John Wiley & Sons, 2006, p. 2)

placed on a statutory footing.[263] The previous stance on this was a general recognition that the characteristics of banking institutions falling within the regulation vary widely. As such, imposing rigid, uniform statutory requirements on the banking sector was considered imprudent.[264]

Therefore, previously, banking institutions generally yielded to the Bank of England's gentle or moral persuasion without requiring statutory regulations. This approach has been described as a 'command and control' or a 'soft touch' approach to banking regulation.[265] While this approach worked since 1946 after the Bank of England assumed the responsibility to supervise the banking sector, the circumstances that led to Johnson Matthey Bank's collapse in 1985 started to fuel discontent. Moreover, it increasingly caused concerns over the effectiveness of a soft-touch approach to the supervision of the banking sector.[266]

Rightly so, over time, the banking sector is seen to be one of the most regulated sectors of the economy, starting with meeting the licensing requirements to create a banking business.[267] The Financial Services and Markets Acts 2000 (FSMA) Part IV prohibits carrying out a regulated activity in the UK unless authorised or exempted.[268]

In the debate, one view was that the banking sector was not regulated sufficiently because demands on the banking sector were not spelt out in detail in statutory regulations. On the other hand, economists like Goodhart et al. argued that the financial sector was probably already over-regulated.[269] Similarly, renowned economics professors Arthur and Booth reject as utterly nonsensical any claim that the banking crisis in 2007–2009 resulted from the excesses of unregulated financial capitalism.[270] They also reject wholesale the popular notion that dislocations in financial and other markets were caused by too little regulation or that exercising more regulatory powers could have averted

---

[263] G. Penn, 'Banking Supervision: Regulation of the UK Banking Sector under Banking Act 1987' (Butterworts, 1989, p.10)

[264] Ibid (Penn, G 1989, p 17)

[265] Op. Cit., Gray, J and Hamilton, J. 2006, p. 2, (n. 262)

[266] Bank of England Act 1946

[267] Op. Cit., L. Guiso, et al., 2006, (n. 11)

[268] FSMA 2000 Part II s.19

[269] Op. Cit., C. Goodhart, et al., 1988, (n 19)

[270] Op. Cit., Arthur, T and Booth, P 2010 (n 21)

the crisis.²⁷¹ They reasoned that associating all regulatory activities with the state is a serious intellectual mistake. They argued that industry self-regulation, such as professional body self-imposed regulations, can be as effective as statutory regulations. Following the financial crisis, not many people would agree with these economists on this issue now.

Regulation of the banking sector is not limited to control mechanisms put in place by the national authorities but also includes regulation at the supranational level, such as the Basel Accords. For example, following the 1957 Treaty of Rome, the single market across the European Union required harmonisation of the regulatory systems among member states.²⁷² So, in addition to domestic laws and regulations, the banking sector was obliged to observe rules and regulations emanating from the European Union, as already pointed out in Section B.

As pointed out in Lord Turner's (the chair of the defunct FSA) report in the aftermath of the 2007–2009 financial crisis, what mostly failed was the system of supervision, not necessarily the legal framework.²⁷³,²⁷⁴ The conclusion was that FSA had to go. FSA was generally mocked for failing to do proper micro-supervision of the banks. At that time, the supervisory structure was called the 'Tripartite supervisory regime', comprising BoE, Treasury and FSA. The criticism was that there was no clear differentiation on what each of these bodies should be doing.

Whilst the distinctive regulatory and supervisory roles can sometimes overlap, as stated previously, the following section focuses on the supervisory element. That separation of roles would assist in determining the causes of the failure of the supervisory system in the period leading to the 2007–2009 global financial crisis. In addition, it would assist in identifying the lessons learnt, improvements made and whether there are still more things to do to bolster the strength of the supervisory agencies that have oversight over the affairs of the banking sector in the UK.

---

²⁷¹ ibid
²⁷² Op. Cit., P. Howells and B. Keith 2007, p. 381, (n. 113)
²⁷³ Op. Cit., A. Turner, A. 2009, (n. 148)
²⁷⁴ Op. Cit., C. Goodhart, et al., 1988, (n. 19)

2.20 The Hierarchy of Supervisory Institutions Overseeing the Banking

Sector in the UK

As mentioned in 2.19, the established principal supervisory bodies having direct oversight of the banking sector in the UK include the Treasury, the Central Bank (the Bank of England) and its subsidiaries, the Financial Conduct Authority and the Prudential Regulatory Authority.

The very fragile nature of the banking business and its high susceptibility to a real risk of collapsing, thereby creating instability in the economy, justify close monitoring of the sector.[275] Fragile in the sense that banks thrive when they enjoy public confidence. However, when that confidence is eroded, it can mean a 'run' on the bank, so depositors can start to queue up to withdraw their money before it becomes impossible to get their money back. Thus, even misplaced and needless bad press can all the same result in a disaster. The risk of market failure places enormous responsibility on the government to ensure that the banking sector is stable.

2.21 The Treasury

Recognition of the gaps and failings of the tripartite supervisory arrangements (the treasury, the Bank of England and the Financial Services Authority) during the crisis in 2007–2009 inspired the white paper 'A New Approach to Financial Regulation'. The document provided new policy guidelines that placed the responsibility for financial stability at macro and micro levels squarely on the shoulders of the Bank of England.[276] The problem with the old order of managing the financial system was that when the three different institutions mentioned were concurrently in charge of the financial system in the UK, no one was truly in charge of the 'fine detail' regarding focusing on individual banks at the micro level.

For example, this problem came to the fore when deficiencies were noted in the micro-prudential regulation of Northern Rock. As had previously happened

---

[275] Op. Cit., J. Wadsley, and G. Penn, 2000, (n 221)
[276] Op. Cit., HM Treasury 2011, (n. 248).

in the case of Johnson Matthey Bank's crisis in 1984,[277] the problem was repeated in Northern Rock because the bank continued to trade even when the bank was using short-term deposits to finance long-term loans. This continued for several years before the problem came into the open. As pointed out by Tomasic, the bank could continue trading because the bank was solvent, notwithstanding that it had liquidity problems.[278] The question was, "Who was supervising Northern Rock?" Why did no one spot the problem long before the crisis escalated?

This was one of the problems identified in the government White Paper, "A New Approach to Financial Regulation: The Blueprint for Reform." The then-proposed policy identified different levels of banking supervision, clearly specifying the roles to be given to each level of supervisory institutions and assigning the overall responsibility of managing the financial system to the Bank of England.

Therefore, the Financial Policy Committee became responsible for overall policy matters at the macro level. In addition, the Financial Conduct Authority now manages the supervision of the banking sector, while the Prudential Regulatory Authority micro-supervises individual banks.[279]

2.22 The Ascendance of the Bank of England to the Position of the Banking Sector Supervising Authority and a Review of Previous Remarkable Bank Failures

Historically, the Bank of England started with the intention to mobilise funds for the monarch to enable King William to prosecute the war against Louis XIV of France and to facilitate the military defence of England.[280] Following the defeat of the last Catholic King, James II, William inherited a poorly managed public finance that was in serious difficulty.[281] Thus, the primary aim of setting up the Bank of England in the first instance was to assist the King in sorting out

---

[277] Op Cit., R. Cranston, 2002, p 65, (n. 210)

[278] R. Tomasic, 'Corporate Rescue, Governance and Risk-taking in Northern Rock: Part 2' (2008) Vol 29 (11), 330–337 Company Lawyer

[279] Op. Cit., HM Treasury 2011, (n. 248)

[280] J Prager, 'Fundamentals of Money, Banking and Financial Institutions' (Princeton University Press, 1982, p.90)

[281] J. Kirk, and J. Ross, 'Modern Financial Regulation' (Jordan Publishing, 2013, p 5)

the debt crisis. The bank collected taxes and paid interest on loans on behalf of the King. In return for a loan of £1.2 million, the King granted a Royal Charter to the Bank's promoters styled "The Governors and the Company of the Bank of England."[282, 283]

At that initial stage, the Bank of England competed alongside other privately established banks on Lombard Street in London and other banks operating in the hinterland. As posited by Roseveare, at inception, the Bank of England was named the Bank of London, but at the time, it did little or nothing that could be called the function of a modern central bank.[284]

The Bank of England may not have performed the role of a modern central bank at its inception. This is more so because the aim of setting up the bank at that time was not necessarily to function as a central bank. This researcher, however, observed that the Bank of England maintained accounts for other private bankers-goldsmiths of that time due to the Bank of England's position of strength as the King's agent. The bank had a Royal Charter and physical protection, which the Bank of England could provide to the private banks by keeping in its vaults their precious metals, such as silver and gold, used as a medium of exchange at the time. In that sense, therefore, it could be argued that the Bank of England has, over centuries, acquired influence, which naturally led it to become a central bank. A recognised function of a modern central bank is serving in the role of a banker's bank. It is further argued that that function enables the central bank to quickly determine well-endowed banks and those showing early signs of liquidity problems.

In the 19th century, the Bank of England had an enhanced public service following the Bank Charter Act 1844, which granted the Bank the monopoly to issue banknotes.[285] This was a significant milestone in the economic history of the UK. It was a response to the growing need for commercial life. It encouraged reduced dependency on costly metals (gold and silver) as the instrument of exchange,[286] obviating the difficulties associated with transporting a large

---

[282] Op. Cit., n 248 (Pager, J. (1982))

[283] J. Rogers, 'The Early History of the Law of Bills and Notes: A Study of the Origins of Anglo-American Commercial Law', (Cambridge University Press, 1995, p.120)

[284] H. Roseveare, 'The Financial Revolution 1660–1760' (Longman, 1991, p.37)

[285] M. Howard, et al., 'Butterworths Banking Law' (Lexis Nexis, 2006, p.7)

[286] D. Richardson, 'Guide to Negotiable Instruments and the Bill of Exchange Acts 5th Ed.' (Butterworths, 1976, p. 14)

amount of money in silver and gold. McLoughlin also traced the history of negotiable instruments used to facilitate payments, of which the most common today include banknotes and cheques.[287]

Thus, the Bank of England gradually grew into a position of pre-eminence in the banking sector–*primus inter pares*, first among equals.

If this historical account is fast-tracked to the twentieth century, under the aegis of the Treasury (before the BOE became autonomous), the Bank of England became even more involved with assisting in formulating and implementing monetary policy after the Second World War. Thereby, the Bank of England acquired a significant influence in supervising financial institutions within the financial system following the Bank of England Act 1946.[288] Following the enactment of this Act, the Bank of England was entrenched as the supervising institution with a mandate to supervise the banking sector.[289] Section 4 (3) of the Act provides that, under the authorisation of the Treasury, the Bank of England, if they think it necessary and in the public interest, may issue directions to any bank.

The wording of this section of the Act was criticised much later by Lord Bingham[290] as being too loose, imprecise, and unclear as regards the extent of control the Bank of England should have over the banking sector.

The principal objectives of the Act are (i) to bring the capital stock of the Bank of England into public ownership, (ii) to bring the Bank of England under public control, and (iii) to set on a statutory footing the relationship between the Treasury, the Bank of England and other banks.[291] In addition, the Act empowers the Bank of England to seek information, give direction as necessary and give advice as it may deem fit.[292]

Although the Bank of England had the privileged position of being the government's banker, its governing body was in private hands.[293] The Bank of England's governors were traditionally drawn from the courts of the merchant

---

[287] J. McLoughlin, 'Introduction to Negotiable Instruments', (Butterworths, 1975)

[288] M.J Artis, 'Foundations of British Monetary Policy' (Basil Blackwell, 1965)

[289] The Bank of England Act 1946 s.4 (3)

[290] Bingham, Lord Justice, 'Inquiry into the Supervision of the Bank of Credit and Commerce International' (HMSO, 1992)

[291] The Bank of England Act 1946 s.1.

[292] The Bank of England Act 1946 s.4 (3)

[293] Op. Cit., Artis, M J 1965, (n. 288)

banking community in London.²⁹⁴ Nonetheless, the government still exerted considerable influence over the bank as the Bank of England had to subordinate its decisions to the government's economic policies. This went on through the Bretton Woods era from World War I to the 1970s, when the emergence of neo-liberalism caused the dismantling of structuralism ideology. Notwithstanding the deregulation in the 1970s through to the 1990s, regulation and supervision of banking activities still resided with the Bank of England.²⁹⁵

The Banking Act of 1979 widens even further the power given to the Bank of England to supervise deposit-taking Banks in the UK. The underlying assumption of the Banking Act 1979 was that prudential regulation would be the minimum regulatory benchmark that the banking sector had to comply with.²⁹⁶ Although the Banking Act 1979 was enacted in response to the first EC Directive, part of the motivation for passing the Act was to bring under the supervision of the Bank of England secondary banks that were hitherto unregulated.²⁹⁷

The specific aims of the Act were: (i) to regulate the acceptance of deposits. The objective was to safeguard the public from the activities of people of dubious character who may want to defraud the public by taking deposits from people for less than noble reasons. Moreover, vetting those licensed to accept deposits controlled entry into the banking market. (ii) to confer on the Bank of England the obligation to control institutions carrying out deposit-taking businesses; (iii) to afford protection to bank depositors; (iv) to regulate advertising and the invitation of the public to make deposits; (v) to restrict the use of names and descriptions associated with banks and banking. The word 'bank' or 'banking' presents an image of strength, hence the need to ensure that unscrupulous persons do not misuse the term bank as part of their business name to defraud the public and (vi) to prohibit fraudulent inducement to make a deposit.²⁹⁸

These are specific objectives concerning the supervision of the banking sector. It needs to be pointed out that this legislation followed closely after the economic deregulation of the 1970s to the 1990s. The assertion supports the view that, notwithstanding deregulation in the economy, the banking sector remained

---

[294] Ibid (Artis, M. J. (1965)

[295] Op. Cit., Ellinger, E. P. et al 2011, p. 30, (n. 116)

[296] Op. Cit., A. Arora, 2014, p. 180, (n. 242).

[297] Op. Cit., R. Cranston, 2002, p 65, (n. 210)

[298] The Banking Act 1979

one of the most regulated sectors of the economy.[299] It also goes without saying that a claim that the banking sector was unregulated is not entirely accurate. The aims of the Act regarding the position of prime importance attached to the protection of depositors are not in doubt, and the power given to the Bank of England to play that role could not have been more evident. Whether the Bank of England exercised that power and protected the interests of depositors at that time has been the subject of intense debate.

The crisis Johnson Matthey Bankers Ltd (JMB) faced in 1984 marked another important watershed in the UK's banking history.[300] JMB was an investment bank that ran into trouble, not because of speculative investment, the type against which the ring-fencing policy seeks to protect commercial banks. Instead, however, the bank became distressed because of poor risk management and deficient lending practices. Moreover, investigating what went wrong revealed significant shortcomings in how the Bank of England supervised the banking sector.

Hansard of 26th July 1985 demonstrates the outrage of the Honourable Members of Parliament at the shocking negligence of the Bank of England, particularly against Sir Robin Leigh-Pemberton, the governor of the Bank of England at the time. The MPs accused the Bank of England of negligence in its role as supervisor of a bank described as poorly managed (JMB). Part of the report states,

"…it ought to be the last day in public office of the governor of the Bank of England. His responsibility and culpability are awesome. He has presided over a fantasy so bizarre that it is believable only because it is true. He has supervised a bank that has financed fraud and provided money for the purposes of criminals."[301]

The issue with JMB was concerned with poor lending practices in that relatively few accounts accumulated bad debts of about £248 million.[302] Fraud was suspected. It needs to be pointed out that the problem JMB had was avoidable. It had nothing to do with the kind of risks that the ring-fencing policy

---

[299] Op. Cit. Cranston, R (2002, p 63 (n. 210)
[300] Ibid. R. Cranston, 2002, p. 65
[301] House of Common (1985) Debate 26/7/1985 Hansard vol. 83 cc 1442–50.
[302] Op. Cit., G. Penn, 1989, p 134, (n. 257)

seeks to address. Despite the ring-fencing policy, banks generally can still be affected by the type of problems JMB had, which was poor credit control.

The issues in JMB raised questions about the ability of the supervisory authority to monitor the financial sector effectively. However, the key issue was not concerned with whether the laws and regulations needed to control the banking sector activities were defective. It was rather the implementation strategy of the regulations that was problematic. For example, in JMB, the bank lent out money nine times above the limit the bank was authorised to lend. So the question is, "How did the bank expose itself to that extent, for that long, flouting prudential regulation without detection and redress before the situation spiralled out of control?"

The situation in JMB inspired major reforms in the way banks were supervised. As a result, the prevalent legal framework was revisited. The lessons learnt from the JMB debacle were incorporated into the Banking Act 1987. Since then, banks have been prohibited from lending beyond a proportion of their capital to a single entity or in addition to their corporate subsidiaries.[303]

One highlight of the significant causes of the crisis in JMB was that relatively few customers borrowed more than 10% of its capital.[304] Consolidating on the provisions of the Banking Act 1979, the Banking Act 1987 imposed a duty on the banking sector to (i) disclose to the Bank of England borrowing to any particular customer where the amount granted exceeded 10% of the bank's capital, [305] (ii) prohibition from lending more than 25% of their capital to one borrower[306] (iii) strengthened the role of auditors and relationships with banks' supervisors.[307]

Conversely, specific duties were imposed on the Bank of England to supervise authorised banking institutions proactively.[308] Furthermore, in recognition of that time's rapidly changing economic environment, the Act required the Bank of England, in its supervisory capacity, to flexibly take into account this changing environment.[309]

---

[303] The Banking Act 1987 s.38 (b)

[304] Op. Cit., G. Penn, G. 1989, p 134, (n. 263)

[305] The Banking Act 1987 s.38 (a)

[306] The Banking Act 1987 s.38 (b)

[307] The Banking Act 1987 Part II s.50 and s.51

[308] The Banking Act 1987 s.1 (1)

[309] The Banking Act 1987 s. 1 (2)

Finally, the Act also required the Bank of England to present reports annually about her activities under the Act to the Chancellor of the Exchequer, who would, in turn, table the same before Parliament for consideration.[310]

Notwithstanding all the powers given to the Bank of England in its supervisory role, the Bank of England still needed a comprehensive, accurate and timely rendition of information to enable it to function effectively.[311] Examples of such information are prudential returns and relevant statistical information that should enable the Bank of England to understand the financial position of any bank under its supervision.[312]

During the period leading to the enactment of the Banking Act 1987, this information was required to be supplied voluntarily by banks. However, to enhance the supervisory powers of the Bank of England, s.39 gave powers to the Bank of England to demand required information rather than expect banks to supply the required data voluntarily.[313]

These powers enabled the Bank of England to obtain information and to require the production of documents from banks to support the BoE's role as the supervisory authority. Moreover, s.40 of the Act gave the Bank of England the right to enter into a bank's premises to obtain information and documents.[314] This power is needed because an insolvent bank may continue trading by depending on short-term loans from the money market operations to sort out immediate liquidity problems but may not necessarily be able to resolve long-term liquidity issues.[315] With the powers given to the Bank of England, it was believed that a defaulting bank might run into hiding for a while, but not for too long.

This view is further strengthened by the outcome of decided cases such as *A v B (Bank of England Intervening)*[316], *Price Waterhouse v BCCI Holdings*[317] and *Bank of England v Riley*.[318] The Commercial Court in A v B held that the Bank

---

[310] The Banking Act 1987 s.1 (3)

[311] Op. Cit., A. Arora, 1997. P.44 (n. 106)

[312] W. Blair et al., 'Banking and the Financial Services Act 1998' (Butterworths, 1993, p 10)

[313] The Banking Act 1987 s.39

[314] The Banking Act 1987 s.40

[315] Op. Cit., L Verrill, 2008, (n 25)

[316] Op. Cit., A v B (Bank of England Intervening) [1992] (n. 249)

[317] Op. Cit., Price Waterhouse v BCCI Holdings [1992] (n. 254)

[318] Bank of England v Riley [1992] 1 All ER 769, CA

of England's statutory powers to order a banking sector institution to disclose documents that are reasonably required for the performance of its supervisory functions overrode a court order restraining the institution from disclosing the documents to a third party. The argument was that such a disclosure would breach the duty of confidence, but the court resolved the matter in favour of the Bank of England. Similarly, in the BCCI case, it was held that the accountants were entitled to disclose confidential banking information to the judicial enquiry investigating the BCCI's collapse on the grounds that an individual's interest in confidentiality is subordinated to the public interest in disclosure when necessary for its statutory functions. While in Riley, it was held that a defendant in a proceeding brought under the 1987 Act was not entitled to rely on the privilege against self-incrimination as a reason for not disclosing documents when required by the Bank of England, pursuant to its statutory powers.

These cases closely follow a seminal *Tournier* case, where it was held that a banker's duty of confidentiality to his customer is not absolute but qualified. It was held that the duty of confidentiality to its customers might be suspended under four circumstances: (a) where the customer gives express or implied consent to disclose, (b) where public duty requires disclosure, (c) disclosure under compulsion of law and (d) where the interest of the bank necessitates disclosure[319].

The foregoing demonstrates the powers given to the BoE to examine banks' books in detail. Under these circumstances, failure to provide documents or required statistical information by a financial institution to enable the Bank of England to exercise its supervisory function is hardly a justifiable argument in the light of the enumerated decided cases.

The argument is that up to this point, the Bank of England had all the powers it needed to supervise the banking sector effectively. The power includes the ability to demand the rendition of documents and physically enter a bank's premises to seek and obtain documents necessary for effective banking sector supervision.

In addition, given the powers contained under s.39 and s.40 of the Banking Act 1987, the Northern Rock supervisors had sufficient powers to monitor the bank but failed. The Banking Act 1987 s.39 and s.40 were later incorporated into FSMA 2000 Part VIII A, 89H–89J, power to call for information s.122D, and

---

[319] Tournier v. National Provincial and Union Bank of England: CA [1924] 1 KB 461

power to enter premises under warrant. For example, supervisors of Northern Rock and, in some other cases, failed to ask the right questions before the difficulties in the bank escalated beyond control. The failure to provide early intervention meant Northern Rock could continue to trade for years without the supervisors knowing at the time that severe problems were brewing beneath the surface.

Supervisory agents, auditors and compliant officers can only fully comprehend aspects of a bank's financial status if the agents can obtain a timely rendition of relevant documents about specific areas of the financial affairs of that bank. Banks' supervisors, compliant officers and auditors work with documents containing relevant information. Auditors and bank supervisors cannot do much without a rendition of honest and accurate returns.

Other than statutory documents that a bank is legally required to supply, the bank can do no more except the BoE specifically requests to be given prescribed documents to aid them in the diagnostic stage of problem-solving. This would ultimately contribute to effective supervision in the banking sector.

Secondly, in the face of other banks' failures in the 1990s and especially the 2007–2009 global financial crisis, arguably, the Bank of England may not have used to maximum effects the powers available to it to forestall banks' collapse after the enactment of the Banking Act 1987.

2.23 Banking Supervision Reforms in the 1990s–2000

Notwithstanding the widened scope of the statutory powers granted to the Bank of England through the Banking Act 1987 (which was later consolidated into the Financial Services Marketing Act 2000), four years after, in 1991, the collapse of the Bank of Credit and Commerce International (BCCI) further dented the credibility of the Bank of England's ability to identify and forestall difficulty in the banking sector. The crisis in BCCI was believed to be the worst mismanagement and fraud in the banking sector in the last century.[320]

The outcome of the Inquiry set up to investigate the supervision of BCCI under the Banking Act 1987 provided insight into deficiencies in the control of the banking sector in the UK. Lord Justice Bingham, the Chairman of the Inquiry set up for the purpose, pointed out that although s.4(3) of the Bank of England Act 1946 gave some generalised powers to the Bank of England to supervise the

---

[320] Op. Cit., A, Arora, 2014, p 171, (n. 242)

banking sector, the power was never exercised, and it was never understood to provide a statutory basis for the supervision of banks.[321] Instead, in Bingham's submission, from the 1900s to 1990, at best, there was a broad framework of rules, some of which were written and others unwritten, governing the banking sector. He went further to say that the supervision of the banking sector was essentially based on an informal approach, under an arrangement whereby supervision of banks was built on mutual trust and cooperation between the Bank of England and the banking sector.[322]

The Bingham report roundly criticised the Bank of England for not doing enough (if indeed it did anything) to follow up on the wrongdoing in BCCI. However, on the other hand, it is arguable that the huge difficulty in supervising BCCI was not wholly the fault of the Bank of England. This is because the case of BCCI's collapse presented a much more complex supervisory challenge to the Bank of England, in the sense that BCCI was an international organisation with a global spread and multiple supervisory agents. That challenge led to Bingham calling for international collaboration of bank supervisors.[323]

As if the BCCI crisis was not bad enough, in 1995, the Bank of England faced another round of criticism following the collapse of another investment bank, Barings Capital. The bank was brought down by the illegal feature trading of Nick Leeson in Singapore, where he accumulated losses in the total sum of about £830 million.[324]

The Inquiry found that Barings' management and the external auditors failed to spot the looming danger because of the elaborate method of concealment, falsification of reports to the Headquarters in London and misrepresentation of profit planned by the principal character who caused the downfall of the Bank.[325] The report noted a severe failure of the internal control mechanism at the management level. So also, the top-level management in charge did not know or understand the operation of their business. The report concluded that the failings

---

[321] Op. Cit., Bingham, Lord Justice 1992, (284) Ln. 4

[322] Ibid. (Bingham 1992)

[323] Ibid (Bingham 1992)

[324] E.A J George and A. Hardcastle, "Report of the Board of Banking Supervision Inquiry into the Collapse of Barings" (HMSO, 1995) https://assets.publishing.service.gov.uk/government/uploads/system/uploads/attachment_data/file/235622/0673.pdf (Ln. 5)

[325] Ibid (Report on Baring p. 232–232)

that led to the collapse of Barings were so elementary in nature. In the words of the report, it says,

> "Barings' collapse was due to the unauthorised and ultimately catastrophic activities of Leeson that went undetected as a consequence of a failure of management and other internal controls of **_the most basic kind_**."[326]

This researcher made the underlined and emphasised phrase.

The description of the failings in Barings as a kind that is so elementary was a very polite way of saying that the management staff members in the organisation were grossly incompetent. The bank's failure was not due to the complexity of any issue but because identified senior management failed woefully to carry out their responsibilities or, perhaps, did not know what to do.

Barings' case demonstrated how quickly a bank's ailing financial condition could deteriorate quickly if left unchecked. As of 31st December 1994, Leeson had accumulated losses of £208 million against his employers, and by 27th February 1995 (in just two months), the losses had escalated to £830 million. However, just like JMB, it was perhaps possible to save the bank if the losses had been spotted while still within the range of £208 million losses.

The lessons learnt from the Barings' debacle have been incorporated into subsequent legislation, including the Financial and Markets Services Act 2000 and the Financial Services (Banking Reform) Act 2013, relating to closer prudential oversights of the banking sector.

At about the same time, the Barings' difficulty was raging. In December 1996, it emerged that NatWest Bank lost £77 million in its investment banking arm caused by mispricing of derivatives. A former trader, Kyriacos Papouis, was held responsible for the loss caused by about two years of hidden unauthorised trading.[327]

This situation in the NatWest Bank would appear to be another case of poor internal control.

Notwithstanding the lessons learnt from Barings, another bank, Union Bank of Switzerland, almost failed due to the unchecked activities of a member of staff. Supervision of the bank rested with the BoE/FCA in collaboration with Switzerland. In September 2011, UBS faced a similar situation as in Barings

---

[326] ibid
[327] Op. Cit., A. Saunders, and M. Cornett, 2011, p. 476, (n. 112)

Capital. The bank narrowly escaped dissolution but ended with a staggering total loss of $2.3 billion.[328]

Like the facts in Barings' case and trader Kyriacos Papouis in NatWest Bank, Mr Kwaku Mawuli Adoboli, an employee of Union Bank of Switzerland, started fabricating fictitious trades without real counterparties, and he inflated the modest profits that he made. This started in October 2008. He concealed losses with elaborate but convincing lies. There was virtually no supervision by his managers. Other members of his team were unaware of his dubious activities. Although his trading limit was $100 million, he exposed his employers to a potential loss of $12 billion at one point.[329] His game ended on 14th September 2011 when he finally owned up to what he was doing. His four-year prison sentence was confirmed at the Court of Appeal on 4th June 2014.[330] The sentencing should serve as a deterrent to bankers generally.

The situation is troubling because Mr Adoboli evaded detection for three whole years. He was never caught until he reported himself, possibly because of a troubled conscience. It also means the external auditors saw nothing amiss for three consecutive years! Meanwhile, $2.3 billion went down the drain. If $2.3 billion could vanish like that, wiped clean out of the bank's books because of undetected activities of a single individual over three years, the security of depositors' funds in banks should indeed be a cause for concern to the government and the public. It is self-evident that the problem lies mostly with faults in the internal control system. Admittedly, it would have been near impossible for BoE to discover the irregularities while it was happening.

Arguably, giving powers to an individual to commit one's employers to exposure of $100 million without proper supervision should give real cause for concern to regulatory institutions and the public. As if that were not bad enough, the lack of oversight on the activities of Mr Adoboli, evidenced by his exposing his bank to a risk of a loss of up to $12 billion at a point, as reported in this case, is just mind-blowing. It is a mark of poor banking practice to allow an individual to commit his bank to such an extent for such a long period without adequate supervision.

The argument is that these are some of the weaknesses in the banking sector supervision that more efforts and attention could have been focused on.

---

[328] R v. Kwaku Mawuli Adoboli [2014] EWCA Crim 1204
[329] Ibid ([2014] EWCA Crim 1204)
[330] Ibid ([2014] EWCA Crim 1204)

However, it is agreed that it would have been challenging for the BoE to monitor every bank transaction to detect problems in the banking sector.

Although the cases of Adoboli and Nick Leeson may be raised as arguments to support the ring-fencing policy, the point is that if a bank's underlying poor internal control system remains unchecked, even a ring-fenced bank can run into difficulty. This is likely to be the case when wrong people are at the helm of a bank's affairs. When bank employees lack the skill, competence and integrity to be in charge of huge public funds, bank failure is inevitable.

As mentioned in the previous section, since these situations in JMB, BCCI and Barings Capital arose in the banking sector, lessons from the failures were incorporated into the law books. This includes a provision that employment of postholders of designated senior managerial functions in the bank now requires prior vetting, certification and approval of the postholders by regulators before a senior manager can assume the office.[331] This means one needs to have acceptable experience and relevant academic training to gain employment to perform a designated senior manager's role in a bank.[332]

An important question is whether the Bank of England was again complicit in the failures after JMB and BCCI. For example, the inquiry into the Barings disaster reported that whilst the Bank of England examined the overall consolidated group accounts of Barings, the group's investment subsidiary that caused the organisation's collapse escaped the scrutiny of the Bank of England.[333]

In a desperate attempt to improve its image, early in 1996, the Bank of England commissioned a consultancy firm, Arthur Andersen, to review its services 'Supervision and Surveillance' arm. The consultants were to consider the suitability and effectiveness of its operations and make recommendations for improving the methods, organisational structure and staffing of the supervision and surveillance arm of the Bank of England.[334]

Notwithstanding that the Bank of England expressed commitment to implementing all the recommendations for improvement of its supervision and surveillance recommended by Arthur Andersen Consulting, it appeared no one

---

[331] The Financial Services (Banking Reform) Act 2013 Part 4 s.18

[332] The Financial Services (Banking Reform) Act 2013 Part 4 s.19 & s.21

[333] Op. Cit., Bingham, Lord Justice, 1992, (n. 4)

[334] M.J.B Hall, 'UK Banking Supervision After the Arthur Andersen Report' (1996) Vol 11 (525) Journal of International Banking and Financial Law

was impressed.³³⁵ The government saw the Bank of England's efforts in that direction to be a little too late.

The collapse of Barings Capital in 1995 was considered one bank failure too many. The patience of the government and members of the public with the Bank of England had become so thin that it had worn out. So, there was a clamouring for reforms.

2.24 The Emergence of the Financial Services Authority (the 2000s)

In the period leading to May 1997, the New Labour Government under Tony Blair promised to overhaul the supervision structure of the entire financial system. The plan was to bring banks, insurance and investment services under the same umbrella with a supervision framework covering both prudential and how the financial sector conducted its businesses.³³⁶

The Labour government's manifesto and idea about changing the banking sector supervision landscape resonated well with the public, given the history of the difficulties in the banking sector narrated so far. Moreover, in one rare moment, the opposition party agreed with the ruling Labour government to create a statutory regulator that would take over the supervision of the banking sector away from the Bank of England.³³⁷

That promise gave birth to the Financial Service Authority in 2000 (The Security and Investment Board, established in 1985, metamorphosed into the Financial Services Authority). Whilst the Governor of the Bank of England welcomed the idea (expectedly, perhaps because it would be a relief from the apportionment of blame that had always come against the BoE each time a bank failed), the banking community was surprised and, at the same time irritated by the move.³³⁸ This was because it was an unusual move and unprecedented anywhere up until then.

---

[335] Arthur Andersen 'Findings and Recommendations of the Review of Supervision and Surveillance' (BoE, 1996)
[336] E. Lomnicka, 'Making the Financial Services Authority Accountable' (2000) Journal of Business Law Jan. 65–81
[337] Op. Cit., Morris, 2016 p. 6, (n. 183)
[338] Ibid. (Morris 2016. P 6)

The argument for putting supervision of all the financial services under one umbrella instead of several regulatory bodies was that financial services had become more integrated and globalised. As such, the UK needed a strong body to supervise global firms. Moreover, it was considered appropriate to merge supervisory agencies into one body since financial services were no longer segmented along the lines of insurance, banking and investment services. It was the era of universal banking. In any event, the Bank of England had not delivered the standard of supervision that could provide adequate protection to depositors and investors.

Others voiced concerns about the challenges of supervising such a hugely complex market in addition to retail banking in an era of fast-paced technological advancement and a globalised financial market.[339]

With the best intentions, while the government was planning to transfer regulatory and supervisory responsibilities to the newly created FSA[340], the Bank of England was being shored up, granted autonomy and given operational responsibility in the area of decision-making on monetary policy and to meet the government's inflation target.[341, 342]

Apart from being novel, Blair QC said taking direct supervision of banks away from the Bank of England took everyone by surprise.[343] The question is, "Why was it a surprise to remove supervision of the financial sector from the Bank of England?" Foremost, it was the first of its kind. It was unheard of in other developed economies. Traditionally, the Central Bank occupies a strategic position in the financial system, which enables it to be in a better position to supervise the financial sector. This is primarily because of the proximity between the BoE and commercial banks. As the banker's bank of last resort, BoE had the advantage of gathering market intelligence reports about each bank than the FSA would have been able to obtain. This is because the FSA did not keep accounts for banks as the BoE does.

For example, the Bank of England participates in the wholesale money market as a banker's bank of last resort, assisting in supplying funds when

---

[339] Ibid. (Morris 2016. P 6)

[340] Bank of England Act 1998 Part III s.21

[341] M. Blair et al., 'Blackstone's Guide to the Bank of England Act 1998' (Blackstone Press, 1998)

[342] Bank of England Act 1998 Part 2 s.10

[343] Op. cit., Blair, M. et al. (n. 341)

needed to enable participating banks to settle accounts among themselves.[344] The FSA was not a participant in the wholesale money market. The FSA did not control the wholesale money market, nor was it involved in the interbank settlement. Moreover, the FSA did not hold deposit/cash accounts for commercial banks as the BoE does.[345] The implication is that the BoE would be aware when a commercial bank struggles to honour interbank commitments.

For example, if too frequently a commercial bank approaches the BoE to borrow funds from it in its capacity as 'the bankers' bank of last resort', that scenario would make the BoE aware that the commercial bank is probably showing signs of liquidity problems. In that case, the situation presents an opportunity for the BoE to start to look more closely at the liquidity status of that bank. Except when it becomes inevitable, a bank would instead seek other ways of resolving liquidity problems than approach BoE for assistance. These were the advantages that FSA did not have.

The significance of this important strategic position, which the BoE occupies, is that it enables the BoE to be aware when a commercial bank faces an acute liquidity problem, whether temporary or endemic.

A practical example of this can be found in the Annual Financial Accounts of banks. We can use the Annual Report and Financial Accounts of RBS for 2010 to illustrate this.

On page 128, RBS reported the following extracts from their Assets and Liabilities accounts

Assets:

(i) Cash and balances at central banks £49.8 billion
(ii) Loans and Advances to banks £87.5 billion

Liabilities

(iii) Deposits by banks £85.2 billion
(iv) Settlement balances £8.5 billion

---

[344] Op. Cit., E. Ellinger, et al., 2011, (n. 116).
[345] The Royal Bank of Scotland, "Financial Report and Annual Financial Accounts", 2010, p. 128.

What do these figures mean? These are typical items that would be found on the balance sheet of any commercial bank. Item (i) is the aggregated sum of cash held in the vaults of RBS, including credit balances held with 'Central Banks' globally as of the balance sheet date. This is the most liquid part of RBS's 'Current Assets' on the balance sheet. Please note that the word 'Balances' and the term 'Central banks' are pluralised. This is because the report is a consolidated account of all the networks of branches in all the places that RBS operated globally as of the balance sheet date. Item (ii) is the consolidated debts owed by other banks to RBS as of 31st December 2010. Item (iii) represents the aggregated sum of deposits held by RBS on behalf of other banks. This is the extent of aggregated debt obligations that RBS owed other banks. Finally, item (iv) is the amount RBS owed, which is in the collection process by other banks.

Item (i) £49.8 billion included the credit balance BoE held for RBS in the UK on the balance sheet date. Although we are not given the specific part of that sum held with BoE, it is out of that amount held by BoE for the bank that RBS would be making payments and daily settlements relating to cheques presented for clearing against RBS. In addition, there are settlements of standing orders, direct debits, and other claims from other banks. Payments received from other financial institutions would be credited into the same account to increase the balance, while payments made out would deplete the balance daily. As long as the daily balances remain in a credit position, there are no problems. However, once this account starts to run into debit balances and RBS struggles to resolve the situation, BoE would have effective notice that RBS is beginning to have liquidity problems and may start to make formal enquiries, demanding an explanation from the bank. This is part of the advantages that BoE had over FSA as a supervisory agent.

In the BoE's capacity as the banker's bank of last resort, the Bank of England can monitor inter-bank borrowing and, from time to time, determine struggling banks. The BoE can also have first-hand information about a bank that can be rescued in times of distress and those that must be wound up or nationalised, as was the case with Northern Rock and BCCI. Northern Rock was nationalised under the Banking (Special Provision) Act 2008, while BCCI was allowed to dissolve. Bradford and Bingley Building Society went into public ownership.[346]

---

[346] Op. Cit., A. Arora, 2014, p 124, (n. 242)

As mentioned earlier, it should be noted that one of the criticisms Lord Bingham made against the Bank of England regarding the BCCI collapse was that the Bank of England did not respond in time **to the leads** it had. It was not the case that the Bank of England was unaware of the difficulty in the BCCI, but it failed to respond in time.[347]

So, when the Bank of England was replaced with another body that did not have those advantages that the BOE naturally possesses, banking practitioners knew that that move was a grave tactical mistake and that the travail in the banking sector was not about to end too quickly. That would appear to be why the policy announcement to replace BoE as the overall supervisory agent at that time was shocking.

Notwithstanding all the faults attributed to the Bank of England regarding the failed banks mentioned earlier, the government could have insisted that the Bank of England review their operational strategies. As stated earlier, and also in paragraph 2.26 below, the Bank of England occupies a strategic position within the financial system that places it at an advantage to supervise it. Although this vantage position does not guarantee absolute security, it does help in some practical ways, as explained previously.

The government should have made the Bank of England overhaul its systems and approach to banking supervision. In 1996, on its initiative, the Bank of England had already commissioned a consultancy firm Arthur Andersen, to review its banking supervision approach and proffer suggestions on improving its operational system, as mentioned on page 73. Arthur Andersen affirmed some of the methods engaged by BoE, whilst, in other areas, they suggested ways to improve, but sadly, the advice came too late. The politicians had promised the electorate that the banking sector's regulation and supervision authorities would be overhauled, and so it was.

2.25 The Financial Services Authority 2001-2009: How Did They Fare?

The Financial Services Markets Act 2000 that sets up FSA runs into 321 pages. Some of the primary aims of FSA were:—(a) to instil market confidence,

---

[347] Please refer to page 97, paragraph 2.

(b) to encourage public awareness, (c) to facilitate the protection of consumers, and (d) to bring about the reduction of financial crime.[348]

The FSA's policy was focused on creating an environment for financial stability; it planned to adopt a risk-based approach in its supervisory role. Thus, the aim was to imbibe a flexible and differentiated approach that reflected the general characteristics of each bank in terms of its size. This approach considered the quality of management and whether the bank is an investment or a retail bank. It held senior management accountable. It aimed to prioritise consumer protection and an operating ethos recognising the benefits of competition and innovation.[349]

At its inception, FSA merged nine supervisory agencies with oversight of different facets of operations in the financial system. The agencies' activities thus merged include the Security and Investment Board, the Building and Friendly Societies Commission, and the Insurance Directorate. In addition, the Supervision and Surveillance Department of the Bank of England, Self-Regulating Organisations, the Investment Management Regulatory Organisation, the Personal Investment Authority and Security, the Registry of Friendly Societies and the Features Authority are included.[350]

As pointed out earlier, the rationale for consolidating these regulators into one body was due to the prevalence of the universal banking model at the time. Having multiple supervisors overseeing different aspects of a bank would have appeared unwieldy. So, in some ways, it made sense that these organisations were merged.

This researcher argues that the FSA started on a promising note. There was a high expectation that the FSA would deliver. It started with a clear agenda of what the body wanted to achieve, as stated at the beginning of this section. The body had the support of a comprehensive statute, the Financial Services and Markets Act 2000. It had the resources it needed to function. However, crucially, it suffered from a lack of the advantages that the Bank of England had. These advantages stated earlier include the status of the BoE as a banker's bank of last resort, a position that enables the BoE to know first-hand when a bank has a liquidity problem. However, in the period leading to the global financial crisis in

---

[348] Financial Services Market Act 2000 s.2 (a) (b) (c) (d)
[349] Joint Committee on Financial Services and Market Report April 1999 https://publications.parliament.uk/pa/jt199899/jtselect/jtfinser/328/32802.htm
[350] Op. Cit., Morris, 2016 p. 7, (n. 183)

2007–2009, the FSA failed spectacularly in its supervisory role over the banking sector. Lord Turner's report heavily criticised the organisation for failing to detect and warn the appropriate authorities of the impending catastrophe.

This researcher contends that some reasons the FSA failed are not too difficult to see. The FSA would necessarily have to depend on reports filed by the banks within its purview of control. Expectedly, these reports may not reach the FSA in good time. As Hudson suggested, bankers cannot be relied upon to file adverse reports that would likely affect their business interests.[351] On the other hand, on account of the daily interbank positions that the Bank of England is aware of through the wholesale money market and the accounts held for banks, it can quickly determine whether a bank has liquidity problems. Thus, it is difficult to appreciate why the policymakers overlooked this significant point when supervision of the banking sector was removed from the Bank of England to the Financial Services Authority in 1998.

As explained previously, the BoE has the benefits of direct access to information about the liquidity positions of commercial banks by its status as the banker's bank of last resort and through its participation in the money market operations. That was part of the advantages FSA did not have, as illustrated in the example given earlier.

Based on the FSA report on the reasons for the collapse of RBS cited earlier, it is clear that the FSA did not pay due attention to capital adequacy and liquidity rules in the banks under its supervision. Neither did FSA concern itself with risks associated with the exponential growth in the banks through mergers and acquisitions, which almost ruined the banks. There was laxity in oversight on prudential matters, which led to cumulative weaknesses later found in the banks' assets. In summary, the layback type of banking supervision that prevailed in the wake of deregulation continued during the tenure in office of the FSA, which eventually proved disastrous to the banks and the economy.

2.26 Why Did the Bank of England and the Financial Services Authority Fail to Meet Expectations in their Roles as Supervisors of the Banking Sector?

The narrative so far has been that the Financial Services Authority partly failed because it lacked some strategic advantages that the Bank of England had.

---

[351] Op. Cit., A. Hudson, 2013, (n. 20).

So then the next question should be, "Why did the Bank of England, which had all the strategic advantages fail to effectively supervise the banking sector or at least failed to pre-empt the failings in the banking sector over the years?"

The Bank of England Act 1946 imposed a duty on the Bank of England to supervise the financial sector. [352] However, over the years, the crisis in JMB, BCCI, Barings, NatWest bank and Northern Rock et al. raised public outrage against the Bank of England for its failure to detect and prevent banking crises, notwithstanding the position of influence it occupied and its access to information concerning the banking sector.

This researcher posits that the lapses of the Bank of England and, latterly, the Financial Services Authority were not due to a lack of willpower to succeed or a lack of resources to function. Instead, the failings were purely about deficient implementation strategy.

To understand why the Bank of England and the Financial Services Authority failed in their supervisory roles over the banking sector, one has to look back at the reasons and how JMB, BCCI, Barings, NatWest, Union Bank of Switzerland and Northern Rock ran into troubled waters. This will enable us to determine if there was a common trend and emerging pattern as to why and how they failed.

To start with, the cause of JMB's failure was attributed to poor lending practices and flagrant flouting of prudential regulations. JMB lent nine times over the limit that the bank was allowed to lend. As a result, relatively few borrowers accumulated bad debt of £248 million.[353] The situation continued until the bank ran into serious difficulties, leading to its being rescued. However, unfortunately, the Bank of England was unaware of the problem, and even if it was aware, it did nothing to stop it.

In the case of BCCI, the problem had to do with a massive fraud that continued for over fifteen years.[354] Lord Bingham, in his comment, said that the Bank of England had leads about the problems in BCCI. Still, the BoE, as the supervising authority, did nothing until the matter escalated and went beyond any remedy. As a result, in the first of its kind at the time, the Bank of England was sued for £1 billion by the BCCI official liquidator Deloitte Touche Tohmatsu for wilful negligence and malfeasance in office in its supervisory role

---

[352] The Bank of England Act 1946 s.4 (3)

[353] Op. Cit., R. Cranston, 2002, p.65, (n. 210)

[354] Op. Cit., Three Rivers DC v Bank of England (No.3) 2003, (n.213)

over the BCCI.[355] The case eventually collapsed 12 years later, wherein BoE sought to reclaim costs from BCCI for about £80 million.

Regarding Barings Capital, the problem also had to do with unauthorised derivative offshore trading in Singapore by an unsupervised member of staff who posted false profits and rendered fictitious returns to the Headquarters of the bank. The internal auditors detected the irregularities and raised the issue, but it was not followed up properly. The problem in Barings highlighted how things could go wrong rapidly if not nipped in the bud quickly enough. The losses incurred as of December 1994 were about £208 million. By February 1995, the losses had escalated to over £830 million. There is no evidence that the Bank of England was aware of the situation even though the matter raged for a considerable time.

Similarly, in the case of Union Bank of Switzerland, over three consecutive years, an individual acting alone caused a colossal loss of $2.3 billion to his employer without it being detected by their external auditors.

This researcher would suggest that adequate banking sector supervision from 'outside' alone will always be a mirage, except there are enhanced internal control mechanisms within the individual banks.

To appreciate the scale of the volume of transactions undertaken by the banking sector and the enormous challenge that this can pose to supervising authorities, one needs to understand the statistics behind banking operations, the rapidity at which the operations take place and the fact that these processes are nowadays mostly paperless. For example, the Bank of England stated that daily interbank payments in the banking sector are valued at about £500 billion.[356] Monitoring a banking sector that operates a payment system on such an industrial scale can be a considerable challenge, even with the benefits of the tools available to the banking sector's supervisors.

The extent of the challenge is further demonstrated in the case of Union Bank of Switzerland, where UBZ incurred a loss of $2.3 billion over three years without the external auditors having the slightest clue that anything was wrong. The point is that it can take a considerable time for those working within the system of a big bank to fully understand how their bank functions and the interconnectedness of different departments, let alone an outsider. A further example that illustrates how this can work against a bank is demonstrated in the

---

[355] Ibid (Three Rivers DC v Bank of England)

[356] https://www.bankofengland.co.uk/about

case of Union Bank of Switzerland, wherein an individual's nefarious activities went undetected by his colleagues for three whole years. Had the internal control strategies been in good working order, those who were in a better position to discover the anomalies early enough were the colleagues working in that organisation.

It should be noted that the internal auditors spotted the irregularities early in Barings. They reported it, but it was not followed up at the management level. Typically, external auditors only examine the accounts annually, but the internal auditors are on the ground daily, monitoring the bank's operations.

Given the enormous challenges posed by the gigantic industrial-scale operations that banks undertake these days, it is suggested that the starting point of effective control and supervision of the banking sector can best begin with enhancing internal control mechanisms within individual banks. Acquisition of evolving sophisticated computing tools and the provision of specialised training to dedicated staff in each bank's internal audit and compliant departments would go a long way in enhancing stability in the banking sector. Similarly, regulators should consider a policy on incentivising whistleblowing in banks. Whistleblowing is not incentivised in the UK because of the risk of abuse. The rationale for such a position is understandable.

Under the Public Interest Disclosure Act 1998 (PIDA),[357] protection is available to workers in public service and private and voluntary sector organisations for acts of victimisation, unfair treatment or unfair dismissal by an employer against a worker arising from disclosure of wrongdoing at a workplace. PIDA works in tandem with the Employment Rights Act 1996.[358] Thus, potentially, uncapped compensation may be awarded at the Employment Tribunal to a worker who suffers from unfair dismissal following exposure of criminality, provided that the conditions stated under the protected disclosure s.43B to 43H are met. These conditions include provisions that a criminal offence has been or is being committed or is likely to be committed. A person has failed or is failing to comply with a legal obligation.

Regarding the financial services sector, the FCA and PRA have their policies on whistleblowing. As a matter of general policy, the FCA and PRA are not inclined to give financial awards to whistle-blowers owing to concerns that opportunists might be motivated by financial rewards to maliciously pass

---

[357] Public Interest Disclosure Act 1998, s.43B–s.43H

[358] Employment Rights Act 1996, s.43B–s.43H (The provisions are exactly as in PIDA)

misleading and speculative rumours which may needlessly damage other people's reputations.

On the other hand, Cynthia Cooper, a former internal auditor with the now defunct WorldCom in one of the most intriguing accounting record frauds ever, narrated how whistleblowing can be traumatic and become a life-changing experience for the whistle-blower, co-employees and investors. This is especially true when a multibillion-pound company crashes down irretrievably, as with WorldCom. At the time of its defunct, WorldCom employed over 100,000 people and had branches in 65 countries worldwide.[359]

This researcher considers that it would be a double-edged sword dilemma for most employees faced with a choice between exposing wrongdoing and then risks ending their career together with many other innocent professional colleagues. The alternative is to play safe and get along working in an environment where someone or a group within the organisation is defrauding or carrying on with some illicit activities. However, for others like Cynthia Cooper, regardless of the extent of personal costs to self and others, and whether there is a promise of a financial reward or no such promises, it would not present any difficulty coming forward to expose wrongdoing.

Arguably, there are no easy answers as this researcher equally identifies with the views of the FCA and PRA not to encourage frivolous allegations due to a promise of financial reward to whistle-blowers. Following the rigorous assessment criteria set out in PIDA s.43B–s43H, as stated in the previous page, this researcher argues for a system that favours compensating innocent people who may be affected by the exposure of criminal activities of others in the financial services sector.

This researcher admits that compensating everyone directly affected by whistleblowing exposure may not always be feasible. As may have been the case with WorldCom, which had about 100,000 employees and an unknown number of investors that lost out because of the scandal, the bank's supervisors should examine each case on its own merits.

If incentivising whistleblowing can help in some ways to prevent failure in a bank, this researcher considers that the need to set up such a structured reward system in the financial services sector is even more compelling. The need to consider creating a reward system for whistle-blowers is compelling because

---

[359] C. Cooper, "Extra-ordinary Circumstances: The Journey of a Corporate Whistle-blower." (2008), New Jersey: John Wiley & Sons

failure in the financial services sector can be far more damaging than in other corporate entities. This is due to the systemic risks that failure in the banking sector can cause the economy. This is only a suggestion, as it is understood that the supervisory agencies already have their whistleblowing policy.

The PRA laid out its operational strategies in a publication titled 'The Prudential Regulation Authority's Approach to Banking Supervision', wherein the PRA enunciates a three-pronged approach to how they plan to supervise the banking sector.

These are (i) judgement-based approaches—this is an approach whereby periodically, the PRA intends to holistically review risks undertaken by each bank and come to a decision where there are perceived risks that run against the objectives and policies of the PRA such that the bank concerned has to demonstrate how they intend to mitigate such identified risks and give their plan on how they intend to resolve shortcomings and problems highlighted in the PRA's review (ii) Forward-looking—each bank would be assessed based on current and foreseeable future risks and, (iii) Focus on key risks—attention will be given to banks that are more likely to cause harm to the economy in the event of their failure.[360]

Generally, the document's content is considered pragmatic and well thought out as it brought the work of PRA on a sound footing.

In particular, items 70–86 in the PRA regulatory book are concerned with rules applicable to capital adequacy. These are an expanded version of Basel III and the adjutant CRD IV buffer rules, which compel banks in the EU to comply. The difficulty that the UK banks face is that in addition to the requirements to comply with the UK ring-fencing policy, they are also required to follow other EU rules as their counterparts in the EU. However, their EU counterparts are not obliged to follow the ring-fencing policy. The concern, therefore, is that, given this scenario, the UK banks are in a disadvantageous position.

Generally, the ideas and resolutions in the PRA regulatory book are detailed and reasonable on paper. However, it remains to be seen how the strategic plan implementation will work out in the years ahead with the PRA and FCA in charge of the regulation and supervision of the banking sector.

---

[360] Bank of England, 'The Prudential Regulation Authority's Approach to Banking Supervision' (Bank of England, 2018)

2.27 Regulatory Changes in the Aftermath of the Global Financial Crisis

This section discusses various regulatory changes in response to the global financial crisis, primarily focusing on ring-fencing, an important aspect of the Financial Services (Banking Reform) Act 2013. The legislation is the UK's response to the global financial crisis of 2007–2009. This section also discusses Basel III, part of the regulatory responses at the supranational level to the financial crisis in 2007–2009. The final version of the policy was released in December 2017.[361]

In general, the focus of these regulatory changes embraced fortification of the supervision framework in the banking sector, enhancement of the quality of capital requirement (Basel III), mitigation of pro-cyclicality, integration of micro and macro-prudential supervision and regulation on Liquidity Coverage Ratio (LCR).[362] While micro supervision focuses on individual banks, macro supervision refers to mechanisms introduced to make the international banking system work and kept safe.[363]

The section starts by briefly highlighting the processes the Banking Reform Act 2013 went through before it became law. The reason for doing this is to point out the keen public interest and rigorous debate generated by the ring-fencing policy before it became a law. It also underscores the point that the ring-fencing policy was a major decision. Arguably, taking such a huge step was a major decision that was considered worthy of the attention of the Parliament.

The key features of the Financial Services (Banking Reform) Act 2013 were set out in Chapter 1. To avoid tedious repetition, references are only made to the sections containing aspects of the legislation discussed in this section. Kindly refer to paragraph 1.4, pages 13 - 15 in Chapter 1 concerning 'Ring-fencing in Brief' and paragraphs 1.11.1–1.11.9 on pages 29 – 33, which set out the benefits of the Banking Reform Act 2013 and identified concerns with the ring-fencing policy. Those issues are discussed in the next section, E, relating to the critique of the ring-fencing policy.

---

[361] Bank of International Settlement (2017) Basel III: Finalising Post Crisis Reform

[362] Op. cit., BIS (2017)

[363] A. Keller, 'De-biasing Macroprudential Policy Part 1: An Evidence-based Approach and the Precautionary Principle' (2019) 34 (1), 5–16, Journal of International Banking Law and Regulation.

2.28 The Background to the Ring-fencing Policy

The law imposes obligations to do as required by an Act of Parliament, or the law may enforce restrictions on members in a jurisdiction from doing a prohibited act. Arguably, laws are devised for the common good of the populace in a jurisdiction, but not everyone is bound to agree with the rationale for promulgating every law. However, once an issue becomes an Act of Parliament, there are no justifications not to comply with the law unless and until it is repealed.

Loveland expounds on the rigorous processes that policy initiatives of the cabinet introduced to the House of Commons and House of Lords typically go through before they receive the final royal assent of Her Majesty the Queen or the King, as the case may be, thus turning a Bill into law.[364] These processes include preparatory groundwork by civil servants on a proposed policy issue. Then, consultations with stakeholders at various levels, the introduction of the Bill in the Commons followed by debates at both the Commons and in the House of Lords, law drafting processes by specialists, and, when considered necessary, refinement and amendments are all considered. Finally, royal assent is obtained before the law is finally rolled out, and its implementation within the jurisdiction becomes mandatory.[365]

The point is that before the ring-fencing policy, an important part of this research, became law, it did not undergo any less rigorous processes than described earlier. There were elaborate consultations and debates [366]. The outcome of two principal commissions of enquiry led to the government's ring-fencing policy. Lord Turner headed the first commission[367], and Sir John Vickers led the second. [368]

Notwithstanding the high degree of consultation and the considerable time and debates invested in the process before the policy was enacted into law, the ring-fencing policy was roundly criticised by wide-ranging professionals,

---

[364] I. Loveland, 'Constitutional and Administrative law, and Human Rights 7th ed.' Oxford University Press, 2015, pp 131–136)

[365] Ibid.

[366] P. Sikka, 'Written Evidence Submitted to the Parliamentary Commission on Banking Standards' (Parliament, 2013).

[367] Op. Cit., A. Turner, 2009, (n. 148)

[368] J. Vickers, 'The Independent Commission on Banking: The Vickers' Report' (Parliament, 2011)

including academics, lawyers, and bankers, right after the publication of the Vickers' report.[369] These wide-ranging views on the ring-fencing policy are discussed in Section E.

2.29 Basel III: Responding to the 2007–2009 Financial Crisis at Supranational Level

Basel III agreement confronted head-on under-capitalisation, liquidity problems and issues with excessive leverage found in the banks in the period that led to the GFC. Distressed banks were found to have entered the GFC in a position of weakness, having high leverage, inadequate liquidity buffers, excessive credit growth, poor risk management and problems with governance.[370]

Basel III sought to address the weaknesses in the earlier Basel agreements, including the prescribed baseline capital requirements, which have been roundly criticised as inadequate.[371] The accord sought to improve banks' capacity to absorb shock in the system. In addition, it sought to improve risk management, governance, enhancement of banking supervisors' powers, improvements in market discipline and transparency in risk disclosure.[372]

Rather than replace Basel I, introduced in 1988, and Basel II, introduced in 2004, discussed earlier in this chapter, Basel III is a refinement and correction of the loopholes in Basel III's predecessors. Basel III: finalising post-crisis reform, released in December 2017, is the outcome of many years of cumulative learning and refinement processes on perceived loopholes in Basel I and II.[373]

The Basel III regulatory capital framework was initially released in 2010, but even that continued to be developed and refined until the integrated and consolidated version was released in 2017. The overarching aim of Basel III is to strengthen the resilience of the financial sector so that they can have the capacity to absorb losses should one occur and so that the banks can sustain their growth through sound economic activities.[374]

---

[369] J. Miller, 'Vickers' Report Slammed' (2011) 161 NLJ 1228 (2) New Law Journal

[370] Op. Cit., Bank for International Settlement (2017), n. 361

[371] Op. Cit., Adamati 2014, (n. 17).

[372] Op. Cit., Bank for International Settlement (2017), n. 361

[373] Ibid.

[374] Ibid. (p. 1)

Foremost, a matter of deep concern to the Basel Committee on the previous regulatory design was the wide variability in the methodologies adopted in the computation of Risk Weighted Assets (RWAs) among banks. As a result, some banks underestimated their assets' risk profiles, making their RWAs appear modest.[375] Additionally, while these banks reported strong risk-based capital ratios, they had already built up excessive on and off-balance sheet leverage.

The problem of variation in how RWAs were computed arose from the Basel II Accord. Then, banks were given some discretion to use their internally determined risk management model to calculate RWAs to determine the capital requirement level needed to back up their credit exposure. Sadly, the discretion granted to the banks to use an internal model to determine the riskiness of their assets was flagrantly abused. In addition, the banks that suffered the most during the crisis were found to have circumvented rules. Even when these banks claimed that they were compliant with the 8% baseline capital requirement specified in Basel I, the basis of their computation was later found to have failed to take into account the riskiness of their performing and non-performing credit exposures.[376]

Part of the corrective measures introduced by Basel III is a requirement for capital buffers to make banks meet a higher level of capital adequacy in addition to the baseline 8% risk asset ratio suggested in Basel I and followed in Basel II.[377]

Furthermore, micro-prudential regulations addressed procyclicality risks arising from interconnectedness and dependency within the banking sector so that additional capital requirements were made obligatory for counterparty credit risks.[378] Such buffer capital was required to be at least 2.5% of Risk Weighted Assets, but national regulators may wish to impose a higher percentage. These measures reconfigured capital requirements based on each bank's sensitivity to market risks. In addition, stricter regulations were made for Global Systematically Important Banks.

Banks are required to enhance their level of transparency and disclosure to investors. So also, the powers of banks' supervisors were increased to determine

---

[375] Ibid.

[376] P. Yeoh, 'Global Banking Reforms: Mission Accomplished?' (2018) Vol 33 (9), 305–313, Journal of International Banking Law and Regulation.

[377] Op. Cit., Chiu and Wilson 2019, p. 372, (n. 198)

[378] ibid

the leverage ratio buffer and the acceptable constituents of Common Equity Capital Tier 1 and 2 of banks under their supervision.[379]

Dealing with the leverage issues, the new regulatory measures under the Basel III accord seek to prevent banks from building up leverage in the banking sector to de-risk the banking sector and prevent damage to the economy. In addition, Basel III provided a specific and measurable formula to guide the banks and the banks' supervisors so that supervisors could use the tool as a measuring parameter to facilitate effective monitoring of the banks in this regard.[380]

The prescribed leverage ratio = $\dfrac{\text{Capital Measure}}{\text{Exposure Measure}}$

The minimum leverage ratio for banks is equal to 3%.

This index is expected to be calculated consistently at regular intervals, whether daily or at least once a month, subject to the bank supervisors' agreement.[381]

Another thorny issue faced by some GSIBs in the wake of the GFC was their parlous liquidity condition. The gravity of the problem came to the fore when the short-term funding facilities from the wholesale money markets dried up. As discussed in Chapter 4, RBS and Barclays were in the class of banks that were hit hardest. However, for the timely intervention of the UK government that supported RBS with a range of bail-out packages, RBS could have become history by now. Barclays was assisted with a cash infusion of £6.1 billion from the Qatar government.

The regulatory response from Basel to resolve the liquidity problem in the banking sector is encapsulated in the document "Basel III: The Liquidity Coverage Ratio (LCR) and Liquidity Risk Monitoring Tools."

The policy document aimed to promote resilience in the short-term liquidity requirements in the banking sector and to build the bank's capacity to meet customers' sudden cash withdrawal needs for up to 30 calendar days under stress scenarios.[382] This liquidity reserve will be kept in High-Quality Liquid Assets

---

[379] G. Thieffry, 'The Impact of the Latest Basel Accords on Commodity Trade Finance: An Update' (2019) Vol. 34 (7) 237–242 Journal of International Banking Law and Regulation

[380] Op. Cit., Bank for International Settlement (2017), page 140, (n. 361)

[381] Ibid. (BIS, 2017, page 140)

[382] Bank for International Settlement, 'Basel III: The Liquidity Coverage Ratio and Liquidity Risk Monitoring Tools, (2013) BIS.

(HQLA), the product of net cash outflows minus expected inflows in the next 30 calendar days. Examples of qualified HQLA include cash in stock, reserves held with zero-risk central banks, zero per cent risk-weighted securities issued or guaranteed by sovereigns, zero per cent risk-weighted assets, including those held with the Bank for International Settlement, and International Monetary Funds.[383] Keeping such reserve funds in zero-risk institutions and zero-risk assets is to meet liquidity needs without delay. However, zero risk-assets held in such institutions have costs because they hardly earn much, if at all they earn any income.

The preceding examples of Basel III requirements are some of the key regulatory and supervisory responses made to the financial crisis in 2007–2009. All these requirements were built up in 2010–2017 when there was a quest to find lasting solutions to some of the problems in the banking sector. In addition, as explained previously, Basel III addressed inadequate capital, poor liquidity, leverage and governance.

Although the impacts of the various regulatory measures that emanated from the EU on the banks induced pressure on the banks' profitability because the demand to increase their capital has cost implications, the imposed regulatory measures are considered proportionate and justifiable. Furthermore, the requirement to tie down HQLAs in zero-risk assets under the Liquidity Coverage Assets also reduces profitability because such assets held at zero-weighted risks earn little or nothing.

However, by every means possible, it is imperative that depositors' funds must be protected. This is because if a bank failed for whatever reason, whether due to fraud, risk-taking, mismanagement, or poor decisions, such that the owner's equity in the bank is unable to absorb the losses, depositors would be at the risk of incurring losses outside the provisions of depositors guarantee scheme. Therefore, the other alternative is for the government to come to the aid of the bank through a bailout. However, understandably, the government wants to avoid such an option by all means. This is why regulators are working assiduously to reduce such incidences to the barest minimum, even if they cannot outrightly stop it altogether.

In the particular instance of the UK banks and concerning this study, capital adequacy regulations are stricter in the UK than the Basel III requirements.

---

[383] Op. Cit., Chiu and Wilson (2019) (n. 198)

Arguably, the regulatory and supervisory environment has improved considerably since the GFC. So also, there has been considerable recovery from losses incurred from the nonperforming assets over the past ten years. There has been a huge divestment from risky investments in Barclays and RBS. Hopefully, the issue around mis-sold products and regulatory fines is now far behind these banks.

With all these developments, the regulator may hopefully consider easing the regulatory burden imposed on the UK banks regarding the ring-fencing policy in no distant future.

2.29.1 Conclusions

So far, this section of the research report has the following findings:

(i) Foremost, the wide-ranging laws and regulations, which increasingly widened the scope of supervisory powers given to the Bank of England, have failed to stop incidences of financial crises in the banking sector since the Bank of England Act 1946.[384] The Act empowered the Bank of England to seek information, give direction as necessary, and give advice as it may be deemed fit.[385]

(ii) Disturbingly, difficulties that arose in the banks that failed or ran into difficulties were not pre-empted by the Bank of England. With each bank failure, the Bank of England faced one embarrassing criticism after another.[386]

(iii) Worse still, the same error kept repeating itself, as was the case in Johnson Matthey Banks, BCCI, Baring Bank and Northern Rock.[387]

(iv) The Financial Services Authority created in the 2000s to take over as regulator/supervisor of the banking sector failed, just as the Bank of England did in its supervisory role because prudential micro-level supervision (focusing on individual banks) was grossly inadequate.[388]

---

[384] Pages 93 – 96. Bank of England Act 1946, Banking Act 1979, Bank of England Act 1987, Tournier (1924), A v B (1992), Price Waterhouse v BCCI Holdings (1992), Bank of England v Riley (1992)

[385] The Bank of England Act 1946 s.4 (3) Please see page 108

[386] Pages 92 - 93; House of Common Debate 26/7/1985 vol. 83 cc 1442–50.

[387] Pages 87, 95 and 105.

[388] Pages 105 – 106.

(v) The failure of both institutions in providing effective supervision to the financial sector was not borne out of a lack of willpower to succeed or adequate resources to carry out the task but due to ineffective implementation strategies. Micro-level supervision was grossly deficient. The Bank of England was empowered to enter (under warrant) and demand documents necessary to facilitate their supervision.[389, 390]

(vi) The fast pace of banking transactions, the fact that most of the transactions are paperless, and the massive volume of transactions in the banking sector, said to be worth about £500 billion daily, would ordinarily present enormous challenges for the banking sector's supervisors.[391]

(vii) As demonstrated by the failure in Barings, damaging losses could be incurred over a short period. In the case of Barings, the loss was £208 million in December 1994, but two months after that, in February 1995, the loss had escalated to £830 million.[392]

(viii) This Section (Section D) focuses on a critical evaluation of the effectiveness or otherwise of the Regulatory/Supervisory institutions saddled with the responsibility to supervise, support and enforce banking regulations. The objective is to evaluate the institutions responsible for maintaining stability in the banking sector. This is part of the study's objectives stated under objective (i) b. An array of banks that failed before the global financial crisis in 2007–2009 were examined. The conclusion was that, though the failure of BCCI and Baring Capital, for example, were not wholly the fault of the BoE, it is more likely that the supervisory institutions would have been able to assist the banks if the BoE had intervened early enough.

(ix) This researcher found that effective banking sector supervision will continue to be elusive without strengthening internal control mechanisms within the banks and providing ongoing training for dedicated staff within each bank's internal audit and compliance

---

[389] FSMA 2000 Part 8A, s.133 FB, The Banking Act 1987 s.40
[390] Pages 94 – 96.
[391] Page 109.
[392] Page 98.

departments. Basel III recognised and robustly addressed this gap, as discussed in paragraph 2.29. As well, if effectively implemented and adequately supervised, the policies in place to address openness and transparency in reporting, quality of capital requirement and liquidity ratios may help boost the capacity of banks to withstand stress in the event of future crises occurring.[393]

The document "The Prudential Regulation Authority's Approach to Banking Supervision, 2018," drafted by the BoE, provides a good starting point for the reforms to the supervision approach for the financial sector in the UK. However, what the outcome of the practical implementation of the approach would be is going to be self-evident in the years ahead.

It is also recognised that with the level of changes that have taken place since the GFC, the banking sector and the supervisory agencies are better equipped to deal with shocks in the UK financial system.

The empirical aspect of the study, which involved analysis of the Annual Reports and Financial Accounts of the case studies, is reported in Chapter 4.

Section: E

Evolutionary Development of Regulatory Theories from Structuralism to Neo-liberalism: The Impact on the Banking Sector

2.30 Introduction

The aspects of the literature review addressed in this section include (i) the business of banking, (ii) the classification of banks and other financial institutions, and (iii) the drivers of financial services regulatory policy and choices between structuralism and neoliberalism socio-economic ideologies.

There are some common grounds in the discussion in paragraphs 1.12, 2.31 and 2.32 relating to the description of 'Banking and the Classifications of Banks' evaluated under the topic, 'The UK Financial System', in Chapter 1 on pages 33 – 37. However, the materials in the paragraph emphasised different issues and served different purposes than those in 2.31 and 2.32, pages 125 – 131. For

---

[393] Pages 117 – 118.

example, paragraph 1.12 highlighted the exclusivity of the class of banks required by law to be ring-fenced compliant by 1st January 2019 and why the case studies in this research fit into that class of banks.

On the other hand, paragraphs 2.31 and 2.32 addressed the prerequisites for successfully incorporating a bank. In addition, it highlights the issues that led to the merger of various financial institutions, the previous supervision structure and the circumstances surrounding the new policy to de-merge core depositors' accounts from non-ring-fenced banks.

The overarching aims of this section are linked to objectives (ii) and (iii) of the study stated in Chapter 1, pages 15 - 16, relating to conducting a theoretical critique of the ring-fencing policy against the backdrop of the UK's core competencies in the provision of financial services. This is a sphere in which the UK arguably has comparative and competitive advantages.

The section also relates to the question about the efficacy or otherwise of the ring-fencing policy serving as a safeguarding measure capable of deterring future crises in the banking sector. Finally, it considers the costs of the ring-fencing policy to the banking sector and the economy vis a vis other methods available to deal with the difficulties in the banking sector in the period leading to the GFC. The problems identified include under-capitalisation in the banking sector, poor liquidity, and high leverage in the banks, which placed the economy at risk. In addition, issues with compliance, poor supervisory regime, risk-taking, governance, poor management decisions, and a host of unwholesome lending practices were part of the problems in the banking sector that were discussed previously.

Against that background is a discussion around banking regulation as a delicate balancing act between safeguarding the economy and encouraging creativity in the banking sector. The point is that where it becomes necessary for the government to intervene to correct anomalies in the financial sector, it behoves the government to do so in a sensible way that does not hurt the economy in a way that is not intended.

As pointed out earlier, before the 1980s, financial institutions were categorised under the type of services they provided. However, over time, the distinction between commercial banks and other financial institutions increasingly faded as some commercial banks became very large conglomerates providing an assorted range of financial services.[394] Thus, banks became all-round financial services providers rather than financial institutions providing specialist services. That banking model is commonly called universal banking, with banks having a wide network of branches and a vast geographical spread.[395]

Saunders and Walter gave four categories of universal banks: (i) banks whose core business includes accepting deposits, providing loans and other wide-ranging financial services through subsidiaries. Examples include the banks in the case studies: (ii) partially integrated universal banks that undertake commercial and investment banking under the same roof, which the ring-fencing policy opposes; (iii) a fully integrated bank providing all services within a single firm. The ring-fencing policy also rejects this class of universal banking: (iv) a holding company that controls separate subsidiaries set up to provide commercial banking, investment banking, and other financial services, such as Citigroup.[396]

This chapter attempts to distinguish the banking sector's general characteristics from other financial services providers, such as Insurance Businesses, Building Societies, Pension Funds, Money lenders, Post Office Saving Banks, National Savings Banks, Merchant/Investment Banks and Municipal Banks.

Until recently, when the regulations governing these institutions and their regulators were merged, the regulatory framework and supervisory bodies responsible for regulating each were separate.[397] For example, within a regime of industry-based Self-Regulating Organisations (SRO) and Recognised Professional Bodies (RPB), Investment Banking was overseen by the Securities and Investment Board (SIB).[398] The Bank of England had oversight of Commercial Banking, while the Building Societies Commission regulated the Building Societies.[399, 400]

---

[394] A. Saunders and I. Walter, 'Universal Banking in America: What Can We Gain? What Can We Lose?' (Oxford University Press, 1993)
[395] Op. Cit., Ellinger, et al 2011, p. 16, 73&75, (n. 116).
[396] Op. Cit., Saunders, A. and Walter, I. 1993, (n. 394)
[397] F. Mishkin, and S. Eakins, 'Financial Markets and Institutions 9th ed') Pearson, 2018
[398] Op. cit., Morris, S. 2016, p. 2, (n. 183)
[399] Op. cit., Arora, A. 1997, (n. 106)
[400] J Mills, 'Wurtzburg and Mills Building Society Law, 14th Ed', (Stevens & Sons, 1976)

This part of the literature review is a necessary precursor to the critique of the 'Ring-fencing policy', which relates to the study's second objective. In essence, this section aims to facilitate an understanding of the issues surrounding the evolutionary development of narrow banking into universal banking in the UK through the 1980s and into the 2000s. This situation also gave birth to the Financial Services Markets Act 2000, a unified umbrella regulatory instrument that governs the banking sector and other financial services providers listed earlier.[401, 402]

Against this background is the paradigm shift in the existing pattern of economic regulation to the free-market ideology, which emerged during the Margaret Thatcher era of the late 1970s to 1990s. While some considered the changes in the socio-economic policy of that era to be the factors that laid the foundations of a major economic breakthrough in the 1990s, others thought they were the reasons for the banking crisis in 2007–2009.[403] In turn, the crisis precipitated the policy on Ring-fencing encapsulated in the Financial Services (Banking Reform) Act 2013, a major part of this research.

The context in which structuralism and neoliberalism are used is more of an analytical tool engaged in evaluating shifting patterns in attitude towards socio-economic policy from the late 1970s/1980s to the global financial catastrophe in 2007–2009. The terms were used merely to segment and evaluate different periods in history. Segmentation of the period under appraisal assisted in evaluating the practical effects of the changes in policy decisions on the banking sector over time.

Structuralism is a term that has been used in different philosophical contexts, including, for example, in sociology styled 'Structuralism in Linguistics'. A Swiss theorist, Ferdinand de Saussure, popularised the concept. It was also discussed in the context of 'Cultural Anthropology', as expounded by Claude Levi-Strauss.[404] Structuralism and neoliberalism are paradigms that are also discussed in the contexts of political science, political economy, and regulation. For example, in their 1993 book, '**States or Markets? Neo-Liberalism and the**

---

[401] Financial Services Markets Act 2000

[402] K. Mwenda, 'Legal aspects of Financial Services Regulation and the Concept of a Unified Regulator' (The World Bank, 2006, p. 37)

[403] Op. cit., Arthur, T. and Booth, P. 2010, (n. 21)

[404] J. Ree and J. O. Urmson, 'The Concise Encyclopaedia of Western Philosophy' (Routledge, 2005, p. 346)

Development Policy Debate', Colclough and Mannor used the term 'Structuralism' to denote "Protectionism, interventionism and State controlled economy." These are the same ways they are used in this book.

Similarly, Ogus extensively discussed the concept of structuralism in the same tone in his book 'Regulation: Legal Form of Economic Theory' cited copiously in this book. Another book that discusses the subject is, 'A Brief History of Neoliberalism' by D. Harvey (Oxford University Press, 2005).

Structuralism and neo-liberalism are the ideologies that influenced government policy choices on economic and banking regulation from the aftermath of World War II to the period leading to the global financial crisis in 2007–2009. The importance of a review of these two ideological positions to this study is that they were the dominating schools of thought whose influences are the precursor to the events which cumulatively gave birth to the ring-fencing policy enshrined in the Financial Services (Banking Reform) Act 2013.

Concerning the literature review exercise, this section reinforces how societal values and views can change over time in the light of new understanding and how that may impact the making and remaking of laws.

The evaluation under this section also considers how global externalities, such as the influences resulting from dependency and interconnectedness of associated economies, led to the introduction of the ring-fencing policy in the UK.

2.31 The Business of Banking

As mentioned in paragraph 1.12, until the enactment of the Banking Act 1979 and the Banking Act 2009, the definition of 'Banker' and 'Banking Business' had always been problematic.[405, 406]

For example, the Bill of Exchange Act of 1882 describes a banker as

"a body of persons, whether incorporated or not who, carry on the business of banking."[407]

The legislation implies that an unincorporated body could carry on the banking business. While that legislation still exists in the law books, times have

---

[405] F. Perry, 'Law and Practice Relating to Banking 2nd Ed.' (Penguin, 1972, p.13)

[406] G. Penn and A. Arora, 'The Law Relating to Domestic Banking (Banking Law Volume 1) Sweet & Maxwell, 1987, p. 25)

[407] Bill of Exchange Act of 1882 s.2

changed. That provision of the law did not make it a legal requirement for an institution that aspires to carry on banking business to be incorporated. However, as pointed out below, in the Banking Act 2009, any institution that carries on banking business is now expected to be an incorporated body.

The Banking Act 2009 defines a bank as a UK institution having permission under Part 4 of the Financial Services and Markets Act 2000 to carry out the regulated activity of accepting deposits.[408] However, as discussed below, not all institutions that take deposits are banks.

This implies that the institution must be a UK institution to conduct banking business in the UK. That provision requires the banking institution to be incorporated in the UK.[409] Passporting enabled any incorporated body from the EU countries to trade freely in the UK[410]. The privileges attached to Passporting will now be subject to the outcome of the agreements post-Brexit. Also, for other incorporated bodies outside of the EU, the implication is that a foreign bank that wishes to carry on banking business in the UK must comply with the requirement to register in the UK. The institution must be licenced before it can commence banking business. The Act makes the point that the banking business in the UK is regulated and that unless an institution is authorised, it cannot accept deposits from the public.

This initial vetting of incorporated bodies licenced to carry on the banking business is part of the protective measures to safeguard the public from dishonest practices.

Earlier legislation, the Banking Act 1979, stipulates the minimum criteria for a 'Recognised bank' to be licenced. In addition, the institution must have enjoyed a high reputation and good standing in the financial community for a reasonable period.[411] This means that the prerequisite qualification for a bank to be licenced is "A high reputation and good standing in the financial community." Suppose the institution has not traded long enough to acquire the reputation demanded. In that case, allowance is given to such an institution to practice, assuming the bank's control lies with another institution of appropriate standing in the UK.[412]

---

[408] Banking Act 2009 Part 1, s.2 (1)
[409] Banking Act 2009 Part 1, s.2 (3)
[410] P. Craig, and G. De Burca, 'EU Law' (Oxford University Press, 2008, p. 725)
[411] Banking Act 1979 Schedule 2 s.1
[412] Banking Act 1979 Schedule 2 s.2 (b)

However, this exception provides that the controlling institution must be a bank in its own right.

These legal requirements aim to afford greater protection to bank customers so that unauthorised organisations do not defraud the public. Examples of such banks include Barclays Bank, Lloyds Bank, HSBC Plc, Royal Bank of Scotland, Santander Plc and Standard Chartered Bank Plc. Within this range of classes of banks, some are chosen as case studies for this research.

Part of the unique distinguishing feature of a bank in this category is that it accepts deposits from customers withdrawable by cheque.[413] Of course, there are other means of withdrawing funds from an account. However, withdrawals from an account by cheque are unique to commercial banks, as expounded by Lord Denning and Lord Diplock in United Dominion Trust mentioned earlier under 1.12.[414] The Banking Act 1979 s. 7 makes accepting deposits from the public without authorisation an indictable offence. If convicted, an offender is liable to a term of imprisonment, a fine, or both.[415]

It should be mentioned that there is an important exception regarding other institutions that can accept deposits even when they are not categorised as banks within the meaning of banking business as defined in the Banking Act 1979 and Banking Act 2009. The list of those granted that exemption includes the Bank of England, the National Savings Bank, the Post Office, Credit Unions, Building Societies (within the meaning of the Building Society Act 1962), Stockbrokers and Stock Jobbers.[416] It also needs to be noted that even though some of these institutions have 'Bank' as part of their names, they are not categorised as banking businesses within the meaning of the Banking Act 1979, and the Banking Act 2009 stated earlier. The importance of this distinction is that this category of financial institutions does not fall within the ambit of the Ring-fencing banking operation policy.

An apt description of the fundamental nature of the banking business is also derived from Foley v Hill.[417] In that case, the House of Lords stated that the relationship between a banker and a customer is not that of a banker holding deposits on trust for the customer. Instead, the relationship is contractual,

---

[413] Op. Cit., P. Fidler 1982, p 33, (n. 109)

[414] Op. Cit., United Dominion Trust v Kirkwood (n. 117)

[415] Banking Act 1979 s.7

[416] Banking Act 1979 Schedule 1

[417] Foley v Hill (1848) 2 HLC 28

whereby the bank is obliged to give back on demand 'the equivalent amount of money deposited' to the banker. Thus, the bank receives deposits from their customers to an account, which could be a current or another type of deposit account. The bank is obliged to repay the equivalent of the amount deposited on demand, not the actual notes previously deposited.

That suggests the bank can trade with such deposits by lending them to other customers at a profit. The bank is not answerable to its customers for the profit thus generated. Also, Foley v Hill's case implies that the nature of the contract between a banker and the customer is not a 'Custodian of funds' or bailment relationship that requires the bank to return exactly the money kept with the bank. For example, this is a situation wherein the banker would be keeping monies deposited for safekeeping as in the bailee and bailor relationship. The depositor of an item (the bailor) delivers an item to another (the bailee) on terms which normally require the bailee to hold the item and ultimately redeliver it to the bailor or according to his directives.[418]

Again, the relevance of the distinction between a bank and other financial institutions is to enable readers to appreciate the banking institutions affected by the Financial Services (Banking Reform) Act 2013 and those excluded from the policy on ring-fencing and the reasons why they are excluded. Those excluded generally do not have an extensive clientele and asset base as those covered by the ring-fencing policy. The banks that fall within the ambit of the ring-fencing policy are considered to be of systemic importance. This is because they are internationally active and have a core deposit base well above the minimum threshold of £25 billion, the benchmark at the point which regulation about ring-fencing applies.[419]

It also helps readers appreciate the inherent credit risks associated with banks trading with their customers' money. Finally, it is meant to assist in appreciating the colossal impact a bank can have on its customers when it runs into difficulties and cannot refund the money deposited by bank customers because borrowers defaulted.

In order to strengthen and safeguard the position of customers against the excesses of banks that already occupy a position of power, there are other laws and regulations made to protect the interests of bank customers. This regulatory framework was discussed previously in Section D.

---

[418] P. Atiyah, et al., 'The Sale of Goods 11th ed' (Pearson, 2005, p. 13)
[419] Op. Cit., Financial Conduct Authority, 2015, (n. 40)

2.32 Other Financial Institutions

Suffice it to acknowledge other financial institutions mentioned under this heading. Issues relating to them are not considered at any length because they are not the primary focus of this study. As mentioned in Chapter 1, the study focused more on deposit-taking banks.

Other financial institutions within the financial system include but are not limited to the following: Pension Funds, Unit Trust Businesses, Building Societies, Savings Banks, Credit Card Providers, National Loans Funds and Mortgage Services Providers.

One way to classify the financial sector is by a framework provided by the Wilson Committee Report that categorises financial intermediaries into three groups: Investing Institutions, Deposit-taking Institutions and Specialist Financing Agencies.[420]

An Investment Bank is defined as an institution which has permission under Part 4 of the Financial Services and Markets Act 2000 to carry on the regulated activity of (a) safeguarding and administering investments, (b) dealing in investments as principal, or (c) dealing in investments as agents.[421]

This Act's provisions cover merchant banking activities, including stock market activities, financing of long-term venture capital, export finance, factoring and leasing capital-intensive equipment. In addition, unit and Investment Trusts involve pulling together funds from investors under a long-term contractual arrangement and investing such funds in a highly diversified investment portfolio to reduce risks.[422] Some activities related to investment banking also include high-risk speculative derivative options, features and swaps, which primarily caused the financial crisis in 2007–2009.

Within the meaning of the Banking Acts 1979 and 2009, the unique features of deposit-taking institutions were discussed previously.

The third category mentioned by the Wilson Committee is the Specialist Financing Agencies. This class of financial intermediaries includes developmental banks such as the Industrial and Commercial Finance Corporation, which specialises in providing venture capital and long-term

---

[420] Wilson Committee Report, 'The Functioning of the Financial Institutions' (HMSO, 1980)

[421] Banking Act 2009 s. 232

[422] Op. Cit., A. Arora, 2014, p. 11 (n. 242)

finances for up to 20 years.[423] As a result of the short-term nature of the deposits usually held by commercial banks, typically, they are wary of lending long-term so as not to create a deposit/loan term mismatch. Such disparity happened in Northern Rock, which ran into liquidity difficulties in the years leading to the financial crisis in 2007–2009. This was because the bank gave long-term facilities against short-term deposits.[424] Developmental banks bridge the gap in the provision of loans by commercial banks and the long-range finances needed by industrial concerns.[425]

2.33 The Driver of Economic Regulation: Structuralism and Neo-Liberalism Socio-Economic Ideologies

This part of the study considers socio-economic ideologies that influenced policy direction on banking regulation, especially in the aftermath of World War II.

The idea of making choices between a free market economy (Neo-liberalism) and a government interventionist approach (also called Structuralism) has a long history dating back to the days of Adam Smith, the renowned eighteenth-century Scottish economist. He described market forces as an invisible hand that should be left alone to regulate the market.[426] Adam Smith is renowned for having popularised the concept of division of labour, the law of comparative advantages, and the theory of the law of demand and supply. Although he is a Scotsman (not an American), he is often called the father of capitalism.

The importance of evaluating these ideologies in this study is that they help us to understand the background of the evolutionary development of the banking sector from narrow banking to a universal banking model. Universal banking embraces various specialist banks (listed in Chapter 1 under paragraph 1.12, pages 23–26), gradually started to merge and grew to become the huge banks that now pose a systemic risk to the economy. In the years before and after World War II till the 1970s, when the structuralism model prevailed, there was a strict separation between investment banking services and commercial banking

---

[423] M. Collins, 'Money and Banking in the UK: A History' (Routledge, 1988, p. 446)

[424] Op. Cit., Tomasic, 2008, (n. 278)

[425] Op. Cit., M Collins, M. 1988, p. 446, (n. 423)

[426] A. Smith, '*An Enquiry into the Nature and Causes of the Wealth of Nations*' Dent edn 1933 Cited in G. Davies *A History of Money (University of Wales Press, 1996)*

operations. However, following the era of deregulation in the late 1970s, the restrictions were lifted, giving rise to enormous banks. Since the global financial crisis in 2007–2009, these super big banks have taxed governments, regulators and banking sector supervisors in no small measure.

A review of the circumstances that led to the merger of these various classified banks is also considered necessary, as the global financial crisis of 2007–2009 was partly blamed on the lifting of the lid on the Glass-Steagall Act of 1933 (legislation in America) that imposed strict separation between commercial and investment banking.[427]

2.34 Structuralism

Structuralism is a protectionist ideology that advocates centralised economic planning and government intervention in economic activities to influence the general direction the financial sector and the economy should follow.[428]

Structuralism has also been defined as a sustained and focused control exercised by a public agency over the activities valued by a community.[429] This approach to regulation is associated with economist John Maynard Keynes. Structuralism was popular after World War II. This was a period usually referred to as the Bretton Woods era.[430] This approach to regulation prevailed until the 1970s. Then, Keynesian theory emphasised government establishing mechanisms to determine interest rates, exercising control over foreign exchange and capital movement, retaining administrative control over export and import and generally using licences to regulate the economy.[431]

The presumed advantages of protectionist ideology include predictability, stability, safety and facilitation of economic protection. Whilst these qualities may appear generally appealing, the downside of structuralism is that it unduly hindered entry into the market, caused inefficiency in resource allocation,

---

[427] Op. Cit., R. Nattrass, (n. 68).

[428] Op. Cit., C. Colclough, C. and J. Manor, J. 1993, (n. 233)

[429] A. I Ogus, 'Regulation: Legal Form of Economic Theory' (Oxford Clarendon Press, 1994)

[430] Op. Cit., L. Rochon and S. Olawoye 2012 (n. 131).

[431] Ibid.

bureaucratic, distorted prices and placed undue reliance on the government to provide a subsidy when rendering public services.[432]

Until the late 1970s, in the UK, the economy and, by extension, regulation and supervision of the banking sector were motivated by protectionist ideology. At the time, it was believed that the philosophy served the public interest better, as this approach to regulation enabled the government to step in where necessary to maintain stability in the financial sector.[433] Moreover, interventionism was viewed as advancing the nation's common good and promoting the collective determination of all. Ordinarily, such idealism appears faultless.

However, structuralism fell out of favour as this regulation approach was considered inflexible and too burdensome.[434] Reflecting on the harsh economic environment of that era may have prompted Cappie to ask rhetorically whether the interventionists' regulation approach was 'a cure worse than the problem'.[435]

2.35 Neo-liberalism

In the early 1970s, economist Milton Friedman, a Nobel Laureate in Economics, resurrected the notion of liberalism.[436] Liberalism is a theory first popularised by Scottish economist Adam Smith, who raised the idea in his book 'Inquiry into the Wealth of Nations', published in 1776.[437] Friedman's idea of liberalism is usually referred to as Neo-liberalism. However, the Oxford Advanced Learner's Dictionary defines '*Neo*' as a new, modern or 'a latter form'.[438] So, neo-liberalism promoted by Friedman is regarded as a new form, modern or a later form of liberalism in the same genre as Adam Smith's theory.

In contrast to the structuralism approach to regulation, neo-liberalism economic ideology favours a laissez-faire approach to regulation. It advocates

---

[432] Op. Cit., S. Hefferman, 1996, (n. 123).

[433] I. Johnson, and W. Roberts, 'Money and Banking: A Market-oriented Approach' (CBS College Publishing, 1982)

[434] S. Picciotto, 'Globalisation, Liberalisation and Regulation' (1998) Conference Paper Sussex University

[435] F. Cappie, 'Capital Controls: A Cure Worse than the Problem?' (The Institute of Economic Affairs, 2002)

[436] Op. Cit., M. Friedman, 2007, (n. 239).

[437] Op. Cit., Smith, A. 1776, (n. 426).

[438] A. S Hornby 'Oxford Advanced Learner's Dictionary' (Oxford University Press, 1998)

removing barriers to commerce, suggesting active encouragement of the free enterprise model.[439] Neo-liberalism favours deregulation, advocating privatisation, free movement of capital, goods and services, market-determined rules and that, as far as possible, market activities should be unrestricted by law.[440]

This means that, to a large extent, in the developed economies, there was a removal of barriers to the limit of foreign currencies that could be bought or sold, thus facilitating the free movement of capital, goods and services. In addition, the free-market enterprise lifted restrictions on cross-border ownership of interest in foreign securities. This allowed the entrance of foreign investors and corporate entities seeking to widen their sources of additional capital outside their domains to expand their businesses.[441]

The importance of all these in the context of the UK's economy is that the deregulation policy met a well-prepared and sophisticated City of London, adequately equipped for global leadership in banking and finance. Moreover, with the support of an evolving legal framework devised to regulate financial activities for centuries, the banking business in the UK has increasingly become more and more sophisticated. Arguably, this rich legacy of financial regulation may have paved the way and oiled the wheels of the famed British Industrial Revolution in 1700–1914, which paved the way to turn the UK into a world economic capital.[442]

In addition, the UK has a long history and a solid foundation regarding the development of shrewdness in commerce generally. These include the shipping industry, aviation, banking, insurance, and the associated legal environment that has become a model for many parts of the world that have embraced the English Common law system and the notion of the Rule of Law.[443] So also, for over two hundred years, the UK has spread its tentacles to different parts of the world. For example, the UK extended its reach to a large part of Asia (Indo-China), Africa, Australia, the USA, Arabia, Canada, the Caribbean Islands, New Zealand, the

---

[439] Op. cit. M. Friedman, 2007, (n. 239)

[440] Op cit., Colclough & Manor, 1993, (n. 233).

[441] K. Matthews, and J. Thompson, 'The Economics of Banking 2nd Ed' John Wiley, 2008, p. 61

[442] Op. Cit., P. Mathias, 2001, (n. 70).

[443] A Carroll, 'Constitutional and Administrative Law 3rd Ed' (Pearson, 2003)

Middle East and Europe. This led to different alliances, culminating in forming the League of the Commonwealth Nations, which the UK leads.

In addition, the outward drive and engagement with the outside world have meant that the English language became widely used as a medium of communication and even adopted as the official lingua franca in many parts of the world. The argument is that this socio-political influence is not without its long-term benefits to the UK. One is that the forged alliances and bilateral relationships naturally attracted the governments and the people of these nations to the UK.

Thus, with the lifting of frontier barriers and the resulting globalisation, the UK naturally became a haven where international governments may wish to invest their external reserves. As of 2019, the Bank of England kept accounts for about two-thirds of nations' central banks worldwide.[444] As well, encouraged by a very strong and stable pound sterling, wealthy individuals worldwide can hope to benefit from private wealth management facilities widely available in the legal and financial sector in the UK.

There are three important reasons for considering these broader issues in this research. Foremost, this historical background explains part of the UK's many attributes, which gave her unique *Competitive Advantages*. Competitive advantages are attributes, extraordinary resources and capabilities that allow an entity to rise above its rivals in the same industry to generate exceptional long-run rates of return on its investments.[445] The factors enumerated are unique to the circumstances of the UK and make the UK stand out among developed economies of comparable status. The combination of these factors gave the UK an edge in attracting more investors to London.

Secondly, it is argued that the banking business is one of the UK's core competencies and an area of business in which the UK has comparative advantages. Core competencies refer to cultivated or learnt specialist skills, knowledge, expertise, capabilities and attributes that can become a critical success factor in managing an organisation in a rapidly changing business environment.[446] The phrase 'Core Competence' is rooted in human resources management but borrowed to describe banking and finance acumen, including

---

[444] https://www.bankofengland.co.uk/about Accessed 15/4/2019

[445] T. Hannagan, 'Management: Concepts and Practices' (Pearson, 2008, p. 150)

[446] Op. Cit., L. J Mullins, 2016, (n. 52)

the high reputation that the UK as a nation has cultivated over several centuries, which arguably makes London stand out as a leading world financial centre.

The law of Comparative Advantage finds usage in economics. The principle argues that output will increase if a nation specialises in producing goods or services in areas with leverage so that the nation can produce the goods or services at a lower opportunity cost than others.[447] As indicated later in **Fig. 2 on page 147,** in the UK, the financial sector was the sixth largest contributor to the Gross Domestic Product (GDP) in 2015. Hence a need to encourage the banking sector's expansion rather than shrinking the sector. The argument is that the UK particularly has both comparative and competitive advantages in banking and finance due to its history, the legal environment, the relative stability of the pound sterling and the ambient political climate in the country, which naturally attracts investors to the UK. Therefore, the point is that it makes sense to exploit these outstanding advantages to the fullest in the economy's best interests.

The third reason all these broader issues are important in this research is that it is considered necessary to highlight the burden shared by structuralism and neo-liberalism theorists on policy options that would serve the best interest of the UK economy.

2.36 Argument for and against Structuralism (Protectionism) and Neo-liberalism (Deregulation/Free Market Economy)

Although both schools of thought have the same objectives, seeking the best interest of the UK economy, they share different views on how to achieve common goals.

Depending on the position one adopts in the argument a structuralism supporter may want to say the points about the history, reputation and implicit trust imposed by the investing world on the financial system in the UK makes a compelling argument as to why it is incumbent upon the UK government to retain that trust. If considered necessary, the UK government should ensure that it intervenes through legal restraints on the banking sector as may be deemed appropriate to maintain the position of trust and confidence the investing world has in the UK banking sector.

---

[447] A. V. Deardorff, 'The General Validity of the Law of Comparative Advantage', (1980) Vol. 88 (5) 941–957 The Journal of Political Economy.

Thus, an interventionist (protectionism) supporter would hail the ring-fencing policy as a sensible proposal because it would safeguard banks' depositors' interest and, importantly, prevent the need for the government to provide an expensive bailout to banks in the event of another crisis. An interventionist would cite the cases of Adoboli of UBS and Nick Leeson of Barings to support the argument that, with the ring-fencing policy, core banking customers would be protected from the effect of huge potential losses that may be incurred through speculative trading. This happened in UBS and Barings Capital, as explained in the previous section.

Furthermore, Hudson, a supporter of the ring-fencing policy, pointed out that, before the 2007–2009 crisis, Citigroup comprised 2,000 entities. A newly created subsidiary ultimately caused the organisation's insolvency before the US taxpayer rescued it.[448] One may conclude that breaking up the super big banks into smaller manageable ones would be safer.

A protectionist may wish to add that, but for the economic deregulation in the 1980s, which enabled banks to venture into risky proprietary trading and hedge fund speculative businesses, the financial crisis would not have happened. To support such an argument, a protectionist would claim that the whole cataclysmic financial crisis of 2007–2009 had its roots in President Clinton's regime's creation of the Financial Services Modernisation Act 1999. The legislation removed the legal divisions between investment and commercial banking entrenched in the Glass-Steagall Act of 1933.[449]

Conversely, a neo-liberalism enthusiast (A Free Market Economist) could also say, yes, by all means, the position of trust enjoyed by the UK's financial system should be protected. However, there are better ways of placing a rein on the bankers without hurting or hampering their financial intermediation capabilities.

Such measures could, for example, include improving the quality of corporate governance so that the boards in charge of banks are made to comprise competent hands [450] and invest in the training and development of compliance officers of banks. Also, empowerment of internal auditors; enhanced incentives

---

[448] Op. Cit., Hudson, 2013, (n. 20).

[449] Financial Service Modernization Act 1999; Glass-Steagall Act 1933

[450] K. J Hopt, 'Corporate Governance of Banks and Other Financial Institutions After the Financial Crisis' (2013) Vol. 13 (2) 219–253 Journal of Corporate Law.

and protection of 'whistle-blowers' as provided for in the Dodd-Frank Model[451]; keeping abreast with up-to-date technology as tools in the banking sector; enforcement of capital adequacy requirements and liquidity ratios as expressed in the Basel III accord to minimise propensity for taking undue risks[452, 453] and a rigorous supervision regime by the regulatory authorities as opposed to the restrictions exemplified by the ring-fencing policy.

Furthermore, a supporter of the Free-Market Economy may accept that the economic deregulation of the 1980s–2000s opened the door to vast opportunities in the banking sector. As pointed out earlier, eventually, some of the fallouts allegedly caused the 2007–2009 global financial crisis. However, the point is that being given economic freedom to exercise choices on how best to invest banks' funds does not include a licence to be reckless. It could be argued that antiquated, restrictive regulations curtail entrepreneurial initiatives, and fragmented banks will be ill-equipped to effectively meet the needs of modern-day conglomerate organisations that require the support of well-resourced banks.[454, 455]

A neoliberalism supporter would, for example, point to **Table 2 on page 148 and Fig 1 on page 147** of this report, which indicates a phenomenal growth in the UK's Gross Domestic Product (GDP) from £860 billion in 1980 to £1.923 trillion in 2016. The point is that the free-market policy tremendously favoured the economy over that period, notwithstanding the financial crisis that followed in 2007–2009. Arguably, the free-market paradigm ushered in a period of unmatched prosperity in the UK. Therefore, throwing away the bathwater with the baby does not make sense. Instead, we should learn from past failures rather than revert to imposing greater restrictions on the banks that are more than necessary to grow the economy, as is the case with the ring-fencing policy. At least not in the current way that the ring-fencing policy operates. The suggestion is that risky investment services, such as proprietary trading, should be excluded from mainstream banking, not core deposits.

---

[451] R. Garson and C. Fladgate, 'Whistleblowing: The Dodd-Frank Model–A Brief Primer and is it Replicable Elsewhere?' (2018) Vol. 33 (11), 705–707 Butterworth Journal of International Banking and Financial Law

[452] Op. Cit., S. Schwerter, 2011, (n. 223).

[453] Op. Cit., K. Pakravan, 2014, (n. 224).

[454] M. Steger and R. Roy, 'Neoliberalism: A Very Short Introduction' (Oxford University Press, 2010)

[455] Op. cit., R. Nattrass, 2010, (n. 68).

To cap it all, a neo-liberalism theorist might point to the example of other jurisdictions, such as America, which shares the same values and economic ties with the UK. For example, America had a similar large-scale financial crisis in 1929, and there were concerns similar to those in the UK following the 2007–2009 financial crisis. They responded by enacting the Glass-Steagall Act of 1933, with objectives similar to those of the ring-fencing policy.[456] However, it took 66 years for America to repeal the Act, recognising that the policy created gaps for unregulated shadow banking businesses to take over and exploit the resultant arbitrage position in the market.[457] From 1980, when deregulation took hold, to 2007, when the crisis occurred is 27 years. From 1999, when the Glass-Steagall Act was repealed, to 2007, when the crisis occurred, there was a gap of about eight years.

Following the financial crisis in 2007–2009, there was a loud outcry in which it was alleged that repealing the Glass-Steagall Act brought about the calamity of the 2007–2009 financial crisis.[458] Thereupon, the Barack Obama administration responded by rolling out the Dodd-Frank Act in July 2010, which was, in effect, a resuscitation of the character of the Glass-Steagall Act. The Dodd-Frank Act covered areas of concern about systemic risks. For example, the Volcker rule sought to protect core depositor accounts by prohibiting bankers from engaging in risky speculative investment banking such as derivatives and swaps. Importantly, its provisions include consumer protection.[459]

Although America was affected by the 2007–2009 financial crisis more than any other nation, only about eight years after the Dodd-Frank Act 2010, the Donald Trump administration substantially repealed the Dodd-Frank Act through the Choice Act 2017, granting exceptions to dozens of financial institutions.[460, 461]

In the Financial Times of 24th October 2017, under the heading 'European Commission Withdraws Bank Separation Proposal', it was reported that the Members of the European Parliament could not secure a consensus over the

---

[456] The Glass-Stealgall Act 1933

[457] Op. Cit., J. Larosiere, 2015, (n. 90)

[458] Op. Cit., M. Steger and R. Roy, 2010, (n. 454).

[459] The Wall Street Amendment and Transparency Act 2010

[460] The Financial Choice Act 2017

[461] M. Islam et al 'After Wrangling in the Financial Sector Following the Great Recession' (2019) 40 (3), 81–87 Company Lawyer

proposal to separate investment and commercial banking. Moreso because France and Germany were not particularly interested in the proposal.[462]

In an earlier recommendation submitted in 2012 by the EU's Expert Group led by Erkki Liikanen, the Finland central bank governor, the group suggested that the core banking operation should be separated from investment banking, just as the Vickers' report did in the UK.[463] In addition, the EU's expert group assessed the way forward for European financial stability. However, reviewing Liikanen's report in 2015, Gunnar Hokmark, the Repateur to the European Parliament on banks' structural reform, refused to support the recommendation but opted for an EU growth agenda.

He said,

"We cannot proceed with a discussion about regulation of our main financial institutions without considering what sort of effect it will have on the European economy." [464]

If the EU had adopted the ring-fencing policy, the number of banks in Europe that could have fallen within the ambits of the ring-fencing policy would have been almost the same as those caught up with the policy in the UK. Besides, as pointed out by Ellinger et al., for more than one hundred years, France and Germany have had universal banks that included investment banking within the fold of their operations without having the kind of difficulties that came with the global financial crisis in 2007–2009. As such, these two principal partners in the EU project were arguably not keen on adopting the ring-fencing policy in the way the UK embraced it.[465] The argument in this study is not about including risky investment businesses in providing core banking services in the UK.

Prior to the adoption of the ring-fencing policy, the largest concentration of big banks was in the UK, which is not surprising. The argument in this study has been that the provision of financial services is one of the core competencies of the UK. However, except for a well-resourced HSBC, following the ring-fencing policy, the smaller UK banks (RBS and Barclays) will now compete on an uneven playing field with the big European banks not subject to the same

---

[462] Op. Cit., J Brunsden, J, 2017, (n. 121).
[463] Op. Cit., Alexander, P. 2015, (n. 120).
[464] Ibid
[465] Op. Cit., Ellinger et al., 2011, (n. 116)

stringent rules as the banks in the UK. This is more so that these European banks have access to the cheap core deposits, which could have been ring-fenced if they had adopted the ring-fencing policy in the way it was adopted in the UK.

The conclusion is that the EU did not refuse to adopt the ring-fencing policy merely because only a small number of banks would have been affected if it had been adopted in Europe. Instead, their decision was based on a well-considered analysis of the overall implications of the policy to their banks and economy.

This conclusion is partly premised on the statement by Gunnar Hokmark, the Repateur to the European Parliament, on banks' structural reform. As stated earlier, he refused to support the proposal by the commission led by Erkki Liikanen that suggested adopting the ring-fencing policy. Instead, Hokmark said the EU could not adopt the policy until they fully understood the sort of effects the policy would have on the European economy.

Given that position statement, it may be argued that the EU gave a well-thought-out consideration to the possible overall effects of the ring-fencing policy on their banks and the European economy. However, in the end, the EU rejected the policy. The outcome of this research calls for more careful consideration of the broader implications of the ring-fencing policy on the UK's big banks and the economy.

The consequence was that Brussels chose to look for alternative ways to manage systemic risks posed by Global Systemically Important Banks as opposed to the ring-fencing policy adopted by the UK.

Thus, a possible argument is that if other large European economies such as Germany and France refused to restructure their banks by structurally separating their investment and commercial banking, does that not amount to putting the UK's big banks at a disadvantage? The UK banks would be operating in an uneven playing field, considering that these banks built up clientele and assets globally over centuries of hard work. Would the UK banks not be at a disadvantage against their competitors from Europe and elsewhere, where they are not supportive of restructuring their large banks into a bank with core deposits and a mainstream bank? Is the UK not unwittingly putting itself at a disadvantage by embarking on a project that has the potential to hurt its economy more than any other European country?

Apart from Switzerland, which held offshore customers' accounts and assets in their private banks valued at $2 trillion in 2008,[466] arguably not many other European countries had extensive global outreach as much as the UK did in the period leading to the crisis.

In the case of Switzerland, it was not the case that Swiss banks opened extensive branches globally fishing for customers, but other nations and high net-worth people brought their wealth to Switzerland as a haven. The Swiss private banking system has often been subjected to scathed criticism because it allegedly provides secretive services for some clients who are criminals, tax evaders and people avoiding divorce settlement. There are also instances of corrupt politicians who looted the treasury of their countries and took the proceeds of crime to Switzerland (especially in some third-world countries).[467]

While it is agreed that the excesses of the bankers and their propensity for taking risks ought to be checked, the question remains whether the banking regulatory environment in the UK has not increased and needlessly become too hostile to the banking industry.

A better approach could have been to use legislative powers to stop the banks from engaging in speculative investment trading. Then, on application, licences could be given to qualified banks wishing to open separate entities that could engage in speculative proprietary and commodity trading. Such newly licenced banks would need to source fresh capital for speculative trading. In effect, the risky investment banking elements should be removed from mainstream banks. That way, core depositors' accounts would be protected in the same way that the ring-fencing policy would.

The added advantages are that the cheap core deposits would be available for traditional corporate lending, enabling banks to meet the financial needs of huge multinational corporate customers. Also, the UK universal banks would have retained their competitiveness in relationships with the other European counterparts that did not adopt the ring-fencing policy.

Notwithstanding the UK's regulatory response to the 2007–2009 global financial crisis and the issues surrounding Brexit since 2016, as indicated by the Global Financial Centres Index, as of September 2017, London still maintained

---

[466] J. Goddard, et al., 'The Financial Crisis in Europe: Evolution, Policy Responses and Lessons for the Future'(2009) Vol. 17 (4), 362–380 Journal of Financial Regulation and Compliance.

[467] Ibid.

its position as a world-leading financial centre.[468] The Global Financial Centres Index is a commercial think-tank publication that specialises in studying the competitiveness of financial centres worldwide. The publication is widely cited in the International Banking & Financial Law Journal. The body has consistently rated London as the leader of the world's financial centres since 1997.

Arguably, the benefits of deregulation are undeniable. These include promoting efficiency and competition, boosting productivity and enhancing innovations and technological advancement.[469] In addition, the ideals of the free-market model encourage new entrepreneurial ventures, promote the proliferation of small and medium-sized enterprises, boost employment, attract foreign investors, and generally improve people's standard of living.[470]

China is an example of a recipient of the benefits accruable from the free-market enterprise model. Although China has a very long history dating back to about 3000 years, they have always remained an agricultural economy and were hardly better than most third-world countries until the 1970s reformation after the death of Chairman Mao, their leader. Then, China jettisoned communism and embraced free-market principles. The result is there for all to see today. China is now one of the leading world economies.

From the late 1970s to the 1980s, there was a change in policy toward state intervention (structuralism) in Britain under Margaret Thatcher, the prime minister at that time.[471] A free market model was embraced, leading to the deregulation and privatisation of state-owned assets.[472] The government sold State-owned institutions to private investors to increase efficiency.

In tune with neo-liberalism ideology, the choice to deregulate the economy may have been a giant leap from strict regulation and protectionist ideology to the free-market model. However, adopting neo-liberalism was not without initial pains in the UK. Foremost, there were issues about negative equity with homeowners and confrontation with workers' unions arising from resistance to de-unionising workers following the deregulation of the labour market.[473]

---

[468] Op. Cit., Z/Yen, 2017, (n. 69).

[469] Op. cit., D. Harvey, 2005, (n. 134).

[470] J. Morrison, 'International Business: Challenges in a Changing World' (Palgrave Macmillan, 2009)

[471] Op. cit., D. Harvey, 2005, (n. 134).

[472] Op. cit., G. Arnold, 2005, (n. 31).

[473] I. T. Smith and G. H. Thomas, 'Industrial Law 8th Ed)' (Lexis Nexis, 2003 pp 39-40)

The Employment Act 1980 sought to restrict the unions' powers, as there was growing discontent against the trade unions throughout 1978–79 when widespread industrial strikes almost brought the nation to a halt.[474] The previously prevalent collective bargaining standards, whereby agreements were reached through collective negotiations between employers or groups of employers on the one hand and the trade unions on the other,[475] were supplanted by Employment Protection Regulations, which focused more on individual protection than group rights.[476, 477]

Notwithstanding the difficulties at that time, with the benefit of hindsight, neo-liberalism ushered in a period of prosperity in the UK, as mentioned earlier. According to Booth, even those who oppose the free-market model agree that adopting it has been very beneficial to the UK's economy.[478]

Doubtless, the free-market model has disadvantages. However, the model is often criticised and challenged as a policy that only serves the interests of capitalists instead of the nation's collective interest.[479] Stiglitz pointed out that a perfect market that can regulate itself is illusory and that the free-market model imposes a real burden on developing economies that cannot favourably compete against developed economies in the global market.[480]

2.37 The impact of Neo-liberalism on the Banking Sector

Adopting a neo-liberalism ideology in the UK in the late 1970s also meant a great deal to the financial institutions, as that policy choice altered the size and character of the banking sector in the UK. This led to restrictive regulations being removed, allowing financial institutions to gain more freedom than ever

---

[474] ibid

[475] S. Deakin and G. Morris, 'Labour law 4th Ed' (Hart Publishing, 2005 pp 17–35)

[476] Employment Protection Act 1975

[477] Employment Rights Acts 1996

[478] P. Booth 'Were 364 Economists all Wrong?' (The Institute of Economic Affairs, 2006)

[479] Op. cit., Brink, 2000, (n. 86).

[480] J. Stiglitz, 'Stiglitz Report: Report of the Commission of Experts to the President of the UN on Reforms of the International Monetary Fund and Financial System' (The United Nations, 2009, p.132)

before.[481] The overall effect of deregulation on the banking sector from the 1980s through to the 2000s was that some banks grew phenomenally to become large conglomerates.

For example, during this period, the concept of universal banking services started to emerge in the UK. As mentioned previously, universal banking is an approach wherein a bank provides different types of specialist financial services to customers under the same umbrella.[482] These banks were previously classified as retail/commercial banking, mortgages and investment banking/merchant banking services. They are services previously provided by specialist financial institutions before adopting the deregulation model.

The scenario that led to removing the lid on strict banking regulation created an environment that eventually led to the merger of banks, such as the creation of the Lloyds/TSB Group. It also led to the Royal Bank of Scotland Group acquiring more financial institutions.

For example, they purchased ABN AMRO in 2007 (in conjunction with Santander Group and Fortis), which sadly led to the RBS running into serious liquidity problems that could have ruined the bank but for the government intervention.[483] The four banks evaluated had a long history of mergers and acquisitions. Sometimes, it went well, and when it went badly, it was very bad. The combination of different services into a group offered these banks the opportunity to provide wide-ranging banking services. Some of the services provided include commercial banking, mortgage, insurance, and investment banking services, which were all previously regarded as distinctive areas of banking services that should be offered only by specialist institutions.[484] However, given the vastness of their assets that developed over time and the systemic risk they pose to the economy, these banks are now considered "too big to fail and too big to rescue without government intervention."[485]

While the large size has advantages, it also presents several other worrying challenges and complications. For example, the large size makes the banks to be highly vulnerable. Along with that is the attendant dire consequences that could follow in the event of their failure. Moreover, there can be immense

---

[481] M. Kohn, 'Financial Institutions and Market'(McGraw-Hills, 1994)
[482] Op. Cit., Arnold, 2005, (n. 31).
[483] Royal Bank of Scotland, 'Annual Report and Financial Accounts' (RBS, 2008)
[484] Op. Cit., K. Matthews, and J. Thompson, 2008, (n. 441).
[485] Op. Cit., C. Hofmann, 2017, (n. 32).

complications in supervising such banks at home and across international frontiers, as was in the case of the failed BCCI mentioned earlier in this chapter.[486] Sometimes, due to the immensity of the level of operations of an internationally active bank, there is a risk of management losing internal control of the organisation.

As mentioned in paragraph 2.36, this was the case with Citigroup, which had about 2000 separate entities within the group before the global financial crisis hit. As a result, a newly established part of the group brought the organisation to its knees.[487] So, the complexity arising from managing jumbo-sized organisations, the operational risks attached, and the need to secure adequate capital and liquidity levels necessary to keep the banks sound and safe gave rise to the government's concern. This concern inspired a need to enact the Banking Reform Act 2013. The legislation primarily aimed to promote soundness in the country's financial system and to make situations that could give rise to a need for the government to provide an expensive bailout less likely, as was the case during the 2007–2009 global financial crisis.

On the other hand, universal banking benefited the economy in several ways. Foremost, the banks benefited from the effects of synergy. With improved wide-ranging sources of deposits and investment outlets, the banks had a better cost of capital, and they derived profits from the ensuing economies of scale, as suggested by Barth *et al.*[488] Ultimately, all these factors led to the provision of cheaper banking services to customers and, in some ways, contributed to bringing about low interest rates. Moreover, in the past 40 years of universal banking, small and medium-sized enterprises benefited more through increased access to banking facilities. Arguably, as banks prospered, that also meant more corporate tax contributions. Furthermore, as the banks flourished, this also led to improved indirect and direct employment within the economy.

As mentioned, China, a once die-hard communist and agricultural-dependent economy, embraced the free-market model's tenets, leading to phenomenal economic growth.[489] As of 2018/2019, the four biggest banks in the world were in China.[490] On page 113 is **Table 3,** which contains the list of the ten biggest

---

[486] Please see pages 108 – 109.

[487] Please see the comment on this on pages 136, paragraph 2.36

[488] Op. Cit., Barth, J., *et al.* 2004, (n. 65).

[489] Op. Cit., J. Stiglitz, 2009, (n. 480).

[490] https://fxssi.com/top-20-largest-world-banks-in-current-year

banks in the world, including Barclays, which ranks 20. The number one position among the biggest banks in the world is the Industrial Commercial Bank of China, with assets worth $4 trillion and 450,000 employees. Another of the biggest Chinese banks, holding the third position, had assets worth $3.3 trillion and 470,000 employees. None of the UK banks comes anywhere close to these. The largest UK bank, HSBC Plc, is in a distant 7th position. HSBC Plc had $2.5 trillion in assets and employed 235,000 staff members. Further down the line, the next bank to HSBC in the UK is Barclays Plc, which held the 20th spot globally. Barclays had assets worth $1.4 trillion and a total of 84,000 employees.

Not only did China become highly successful due to adopting the free market model, but from the late 1970s through to the 1990s, the free-market model was also embraced in other parts of the world, such as New Zealand, the USA, Sweden, fragmented Soviet Union States and post-apartheid South Africa, leading to improvements in their economy.[491]

Specifically relating to the UK, **Figure 1** on the next page is a trend series in connection with the gross domestic product from 1948–2016, which succinctly elucidates the positive impact of adopting the free market model at home in the UK.

A statement to the effect that the free-market model has been beneficial and remarkably improved the economy in the UK is amply supported by economists cited earlier. Over time, the national GDP/Per capita income has been widely accepted as one of the most popular standards for measuring national economic growth or lack of it. For example, the International Monetary Fund accepts performance measurement standards in evaluating growth in countries globally. Moreover, that performance measurement yardstick usually forms part of the basis on which needy countries are assessed and can obtain assistance from the IMF.[492]

Major work on the GDP as a yardstick for measuring growth or lack of it was carried out by Prof Coyle of the University of Manchester. That work is referred to in the next chapter on methods and methodology.

---

[491] Op. cit., J. Stiglitz 2009, (n. 480).
[492] Ibid.

Figure 1: Gross Domestic Product: Claimed Volume Measures Seasonally Adjusted 1948–2016

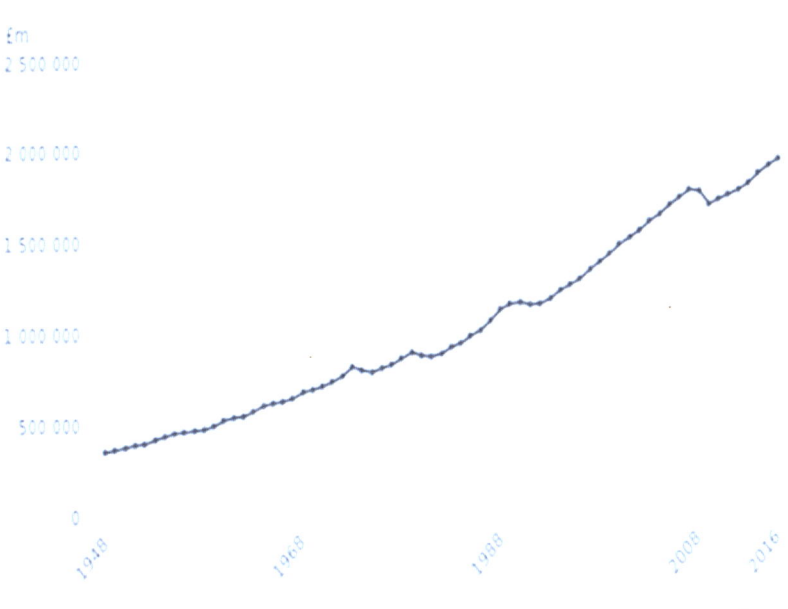

→ Gross Domestic Product: chained volume measures: Seasonally adjusted £m

Source:

Office for National Statistics GB

https://www.ons.gov.uk/economy/grossdomesticproductgdp/timeseries/abmi/pgdp

Construction of the actual figures relating to the values of the x and y axes of the graph is stated below in **Table 2**

As the heading of the graph suggests, the variables have been adjusted to incorporate the time value of money. Generally, the time series indicates a fairly consistent growth in the GDP over the years since 1948, when the GPD was, in relative terms, a mere £345 billion. Except for 1980/1981, there was a dip in the GDP from £877 billion in 1979 to £853 billion in 1981. The reduction in the GDP may be associated with the effects of the crippling industrial unrest at that time, and possibly the situation may have been fuelled by debt-led expansion.

The construction of actual figures related to the values of the x and y axes of the graph is tabled below.

Table 2: Gross Domestic Product Chained Volume Measures Seasonally Adjusted £ (m) 1948–2016

Year	GDP £m	Year	GDP £m	Year	GDP £m
1948	345,311	1985	966,495	2003	1,588,019
1968	665,784	1986	996,691	2004	1,625,567
1969	678,594	1987	1,049,581	2005	1,675,896
1970	696,970	1988	1,109,907	2006	1,717,055
1971	721,255	1989	1,138,425	2007	1,757,521
1972	752,283	1990	1,146,756	2008	1,749,216
1973	801,247	1991	1,134,296	2009	1,675,963
1974	781,509	1992	1,138,538	2010	1,704,364
1975	769,950	1993	1,167,308	2011	1,729,121
1976	792,356	1994	1,212,600	2012	1,754,736
1977	811,714	1995	1,242,548	2013	1,790,750
1978	845,821	1996	1,274,093	2014	1,845,444
1979	877,467	1997	1,325,543	2015	1,888,737
1980	859,674	1998	1,367,136	2016	1,922,626
1981	853,046	1999	1,411,112		
1982	870,197	2000	1,462,818		
1983	906,936	2001	1,500,034		
1984	927,580	2002	1,536,903		

Source: Office of National Statistics (Data based on the link below)
https://www.ons.gov.uk/economy/grossdomesticproductgdp/timeseries/abmi/pgdp

However, there was a full recovery by 1983, when the GDP reached £907 billion.

By 1987, when the free-market model had been fully adopted, the GDP had hit a trillion-pound mark at £1,050 billion. Ten years later, GDP continued to increase, hitting £1,757 billion in 2007, when the financial crisis began. The GDP recovered by 2012 as it rose to £1,755 billion. In 2016, the GDP had reached £1,923 billion, more than double the GDP of £856 billion in 1978, just at the tail end of the structuralism regime.

As indicated in the heading of the above statistics, the time value of money has been taken into account. Overall, the argument is that the free-market model has remarkably improved the UK economy.

Figure 2: Breakdown of Gross Value Added at Basic Prices by Industry 2015 UK

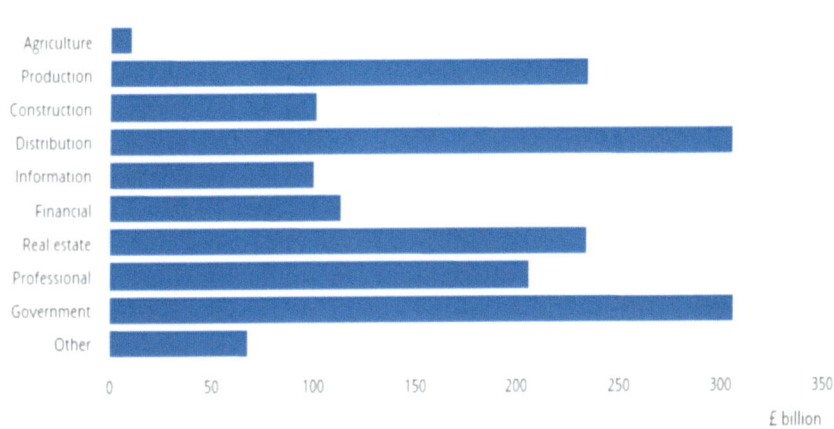

Source: Office for National Statistics

Fig. 2 indicates that the financial sector was the sixth largest contributor to the economy in 2015, contributing £114 billion.

Figure 3: Compensation of Employees by Industry 2015

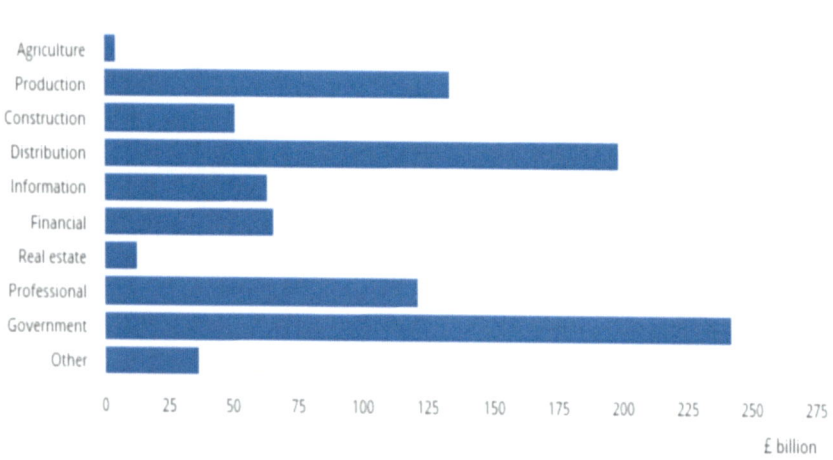

Source: Office for National Statistics

Fig. 3 places the financial sector in the fifth position on the table of compensation of employees in 2015, having expended £66 billion on employees.

Figures 2 and 3 demonstrate the importance of the financial sector to the economy. They also indicate why policymakers should seek ways to consolidate past achievements instead of adopting policies that could reverse them.

Table 3: The World's Biggest Banks 2018/2019

Rank	Bank	Year of Establishment	Country	Assets $	No of employee
1	Industrial & Commercial Bank of China	1984	China	$4.027 trillion	450,000
2.	China Construction Bank Corporation	1954	China	$3.377 trillion	372,000
3.	Agricultural Bank of China	1951	China	$3.287 trillion	470,000
4.	Bank of China Ltd	1912	China	$3.092 trillion	311,000
5.	Mitsubishi UFJ Financial Group	2005	Japan	$3.069 trillion	106,000
6.	JP Morgan Chase	2000	America	$2.727 trillion	250,000
7.	HSBC	1865	UK	$2.558 trillion	235,000
8.	Bank of America	1998	America	$2.354 trillion	204,000
9.	BNP Paribas	1848	France	$2.336 trillion	203,000
10.	Credit Agricole	1894	France	$2.123 trillion	142,000
20.	Barclays Plc	1690	UK	$1.444 trillion	84,000

Source: https://fxssi.com/top-20-largest-world-banks-in-current-year Accessed 22/4/2020

In this league table, HSBC, a UK bank, is 7th in the queue. The next British bank on the list is Barclays, which is ranked 20th globally.

2.38 Would the Ring-fencing Policy Established in the Banking Reform Act 2013 Prevent future Occurrence of Financial Crises in the Banking Sector?

This section deals with research objective number (iii), which concerns evaluating the effectiveness or otherwise of the ring-fencing policy as a measure capable of deterring future financial crises.

Depending on the cause of the crisis, the ring-fencing policy cannot by itself stop all financial crises. Apart from the risk factors in investment banking that can induce crises, several other factors can cause turmoil in the banking sector. Nevertheless, it is accepted that the ring-fencing policy can stop potential crises in investment banking from spreading to the ring-fenced bank. The ring-fencing policy can also minimise the impact of financial crises on core banking customers and obviate the need for the government to provide bailouts if the crises were induced by recklessness in the investment arm of the banking sector.

For example, some of the banks that failed in the past, including Northern Rock Plc and Bradford & Bingley Plc, failed because of poor management and not because they were big or because they had anything to do with the provision of investment banking services.[493] So, notwithstanding the application of ring-fencing, any bank, regardless of its size and whether it operates narrow or the wider universal banking model, runs the risk of failing if it is poorly managed.

However, this researcher accepts that in the foreseeable future, the Banking Reform Act 2013, especially Parts 1, 4, and 7, will go a long way to help curb avoidable financial crises. This is because these sections of the Act robustly address pertinent issues regarding moral hazards among bankers, it deals with identified gaps in the functions of supervisory organs, and it seeks solutions to the lapses found in the corporate governance within the banking sector prior to the financial crisis of 2007–2009. Part 1 of the Act identifies the class of banks that falls within the ambit of the ring-fencing policy, and it specifically gives PRA the responsibility for the smooth transition and implementation of the ring-fencing policy.

Another commendable aspect of the Banking Reform Act 2013 is Part 4, which deals with regulating and vetting those taking up senior management roles

---

[493] Please see pages 50, 88, 97 – 98 and 104 – 105; on Northern Rock, JMB, please see pages 75, 92 - 93, For BCCI, please see pages 62, 97 – 98 and 104 – 105; For Barings Capital, Please see pages 4, 97 – 98 and 100; Bradford & Bingley 104 – 105.

in the banking sector.[494] By involving supervisory agencies in scrutinising those holding key roles in the bank, this researcher accepts that this necessary step will ensure that the most capable people are given the roles of gatekeepers on financial issues of grave consequences that are of immediate concern to the public. This part of the Banking Reform Act 2013 particularly seeks to make individuals personally accountable for decisions and dereliction of duty that could put the bank at risk of losses. Such a responsible senior manager risks serving a custodial sentence of up to seven years with a heavy fine should there be a system failure under his watch. This measure can serve as a deterrent to recklessness by such officers, thereby leading to fewer incidences of needless financial crises in the UK.

Similarly, Part 7 addresses the enhanced powers and differentiated roles of regulatory authorities, the PRA, the FCA and the Bank of England. Unlike the tripartite supervisory arrangement in the period leading to the financial crisis, when there was no clear strategy on how individual banks' books were to be scrutinised at the micro-level, those issues have been addressed under the new regime. This researcher is of the considered opinion that resolving where responsibilities lie and specifying a clear demarcation in the responsibilities between the PRA, FCA, and the BoE will go a long way to rectify the kind of rudderless supervisory regime which was in place during the period leading to the financial crisis in 2007–2008.

Part 7 emphasises that it is particularly important for banks' auditors to collaborate with their supervisory agents by directly reporting matters of concern to them in their audit role. For example, suppose this policy had been in place at the time leading to the collapse of Barings. The failure of the bank may have probably been avoided. This is because, at that time, the auditors spotted anomalies in the bank's books and pointed them out to the bank's management, but they failed to pick up the issues until the bank had run aground.

While this researcher acknowledges the importance of the provisions of the Banking Reform Act 2013 Part 1, 4 & 7 as elaborated hitherto, it is contended that restructuring the banks in the UK and the ensuing dissipation of the benefits of synergy in the universal banking models was unnecessary. As indicated earlier, the four biggest banks in China are far bigger than the biggest banks in

---

[494] These Parts of the Banking Reform Act 2013 were discussed on pages 28 - 33, paragraphs 1.11.1–1.11.9

the UK. The Chinese adopted the best of the free-market model and put aside aspects that they considered unhelpful to their economy.

It may be argued that RBS was the world's biggest bank before the crisis, but later, it encountered difficulties. RBS did not have to be in trouble but for the poor management and bad decisions. Before the crisis, the foundation RBS was standing on was already severely compromised. HSBC was huge before and after the crisis. HSBC remained strong. With their eyes wide open, RBS walked right into the eye of the storm when, in conjunction with other banks, they purchased the Dutch Bank ABN AMRO in a cash deal. As pointed out in Chapter 4 of the book, if RBS had settled for a cash/share deal to purchase ABN AMRO, their situation may not have been so precarious.

There are examples of other equally big banks that did not suffer the same fate as RBS in the period leading to the global financial crisis, especially HSBC in the UK. Even though the Chinese banks were huge in the period leading to the global financial crisis, they did not fall casualties of the crisis. Instead, they even grew bigger, creating more employment for their people. In the case of the UK banks, tens of thousands of people lost their jobs in the process.

In the same way, America, one of the closest allies of the UK, did not wait for another 70 years before repealing a significant part of the Dodd-Frank Act 2010 in 2017, as pointed out earlier. The Donald Trump administration began to rethink the propriety of the inhibitive reforms in the Dodd-Frank Act 2010, now repealed in the Financial Choice Act 2017.[495]

By separating the investment arm of a bank structurally, it is held that it would insulate depositors' funds in the retail banking arm in the same banking group from the consequences of a fallout that may arise from crises emanating from the investment arm.[496]

Undoubtedly, investment banking presents a real systemic risk which can be challenging to hedge. The objective of the Banking Act 2013 is that if the investment arm of a banking group runs into difficulties needing rescue, such a bank either survives or is allowed to wound up. That action would remove the

---

[495] Please see page 138 on the partial repeal of the Dodd-Frank Act 2010

[496] Banking Reform Act 2013, Part 1 (2), (i) & (ii); Please see paragraph 1.4, pages 13–15 on 'Ring-fencing in Brief'.

adverse impact on the depositors' funds in the commercial banking side of the group's business and the economy.[497]

Therefore, with the ring-fencing policy, only the non-ring-fenced subsidiary within a group will be affected should a failure like the Barings Capital mentioned earlier occur in a banking group with an investment bank.[498] Thus, the public is safeguarded under such circumstances.

Ring-fencing cannot hedge against the class of difficulty Northern Rock ran into in 2007, resulting in its nationalisation. Northern Rock's long period of poor credit management resulted in liquidity problems. The bank pursued a business model that used short-term deposits to finance long-term assets, resulting in a maturity mismatch.[499] Neither will ring-fencing be of much use with the nature of problems the Royal Bank of Scotland had that necessitated a bailout of £45 billion. The issue with the bank was also poor management-related. The bank regulators did not provide adequate oversight of the bank.

The bank's capital was inadequate, with poor liquidity and huge nonperforming loans. In addition, there was an error of judgment in the management's decision to purchase a rival Dutch bank, ABN AMRO, in 2007, and an accusation regarding building an extravagant Headquarters for the bank at the cost of £350 million, while the bank reported an annual loss of £40.7 billion for 2008. This loss was the highest ever in UK corporate history.[500] The CEO of the bank, Sir Fred Goodwin, subsequently had his knighthood annulled.

In previous research, Petitjean argued that rule-based regulation could not, on its own, prevent bank failures. Instead, he suggested that effective regulation must be holistic and risk-based, emphasising efficient monitoring, supervision, and quick intervention with solid international coordination.[501]

2.39 Summary of Findings and Conclusions

---

[497] Banking Act 2009 Part 1 s.2 (a) Stabilisation Option (b) Insolvency procedure (c) Bank administration; Please see pages 30 – 31, 32, 71 and 82 on the aims of the Banking Act 2009.

[498] Please see pages 5, 98 and 101, regarding Barings Capital's difficulties.

[499] Op. Cit., R. Tomasic, 2008, (n. 278)

[500] The Guardian 'RBS Collapse: Timeline https://www.theguardian.com/business/2011/dec/12/rbs-collapse-timeline' (2011)

[501] M. Petitjean, 'Bank Failures and Regulation: A Critical Review' (2013) Vol 21 (1) 16–38 Journal of Financial Regulation & Compliance

Very importantly, as discussed in Chapters 4 and 5, it should be noted that banks within the banking sector in the UK vary widely in many ways. For example, some banks are better managed and more resilient than others. In addition, banks of different sizes in the UK felt the impact of the financial crisis differently. Many banks in the UK went through the financial crisis without the need to accept the government's bailout packages. Notably, the banks that benefited from the rescue packages are Royal Bank of Scotland, Lloyds Banking Group, Northern Rock Plc and Bradford and Bingley.[502, 503, 504] Although banks such as Barclays Bank Plc and Standard Chartered Bank Plc, for example, did not use the government bailout packages to varying degrees, they were also affected by the global financial crisis.[505]

The extent to which RBS, Barclays Plc, HSBC Plc and Standard Chartered Bank were affected individually is discussed in Chapters 4 and 5 of this report.

This section came up with the following findings from the literature:

- First, the overall effect of deregulation on the banking sector from the 1980s through to the 2000s was that some banks grew phenomenally to become large conglomerates.[506]
- The empirical literature review exemplified by **Fig. 1** (on p. 147) and **Table 2** (on page 148) abundantly demonstrate that the emergence of neo-liberalism, the free-market model, ushered in a period of unprecedented prosperity in the UK.[507]
- While large size has advantages, huge banks also present several other worrying challenges and complications. These include increased vulnerability as the banks are more susceptible to failing. In addition, supervising complex multinational banking groups can be very challenging.[508]

---

[502] HM Treasury 'The Comptroller and Auditor General's Report on Accounts to the House of Commons: The Financial Stability Interventions' (HMSO, 2011)

[503] HM Treasury, 'The First Sale of Shares in Lloyds Banking Group' (HMSO, 2013)

[504] HM Treasury, 'The First Sale of Shares in Royal Bank of Scotland' (HMSO, 2017)

[505] Discussed under Chapters 4 and 5

[506] Please see pages 37, 122 – 123, and 144.

[507] Page 7, 137 and 143

[508] Please see pages 37, 131 and 137.

- The 2007–2009 crisis justifiably called for concerns and reforms in some ways. This mainly includes regulatory control over capital adequacy and liquidity to improve banking sector stability.
- A better approach to ring-fencing could have been to use legislative powers to stop the banks from engaging in speculative investment trading. Then, on application, licences could be given to qualified banks wishing to open separate entities that could engage in speculative proprietary trading, hedges, swap and derivative activities. In effect, it is the risky investment banking elements that should have been removed from mainstream banks. That way, core depositors' accounts could have been protected in the same way that the ring-fencing policy would.[509]

The added advantages are that the cheap core deposits would be available for traditional corporate lending, where banks could cater to huge multinational corporate customers' financial needs. Also, the UK universal banks would have retained their competitiveness with the other European counterparts that did not adopt the ring-fencing policy.

---

[509] Please see page 141.

Chapter 3
Research Design: Methods and Methodology

3.1 Introduction

This Chapter is concerned with identifying and developing the research procedures engaged in this study. It states recognised underpinning principles of research design and the variety of philosophical positions that stand behind academic research.

More importantly, within that broad range of frameworks, this section evaluates how this research sits within these general theories on research design and philosophies of knowledge. Finally, the section provides justifications for the choice of methods adopted in collating the data used for this research and why the philosophical approaches engaged in analysing the data thus collected are considered the most appropriate for this piece of work.

Except for the specific methods and methodology used for this research, most other approaches and strategies are only developed briefly. Not much emphasis is placed on writing about those approaches since they are not employed in this research. However, even though those methods, philosophies and strategies were not used, they could arguably apply and may have been adopted. That is why, to some extent, they are mentioned. This only demonstrates awareness of their importance and the fact that they were taken into account before making choices on the methods and strategies considered the most suitable and used for this research.

3.2 Research Design

Research design is a structured plan and strategy used to elicit answers to the research questions.[510] This part of the book states how the researcher carried out this research from start to finish. Thus, the aim of the research design explained in this section is to provide outlines of what this researcher did to achieve the research goals.

Lincoln and Guba point out that research design entails a convincing presentation of an action plan that would persuade readers that the researcher is competent to undertake the research and capable of employing a range of methods to complete the study successfully.[511] This plan also demonstrates that the research is worth doing, is well-planned, and can be successfully executed.[512]

Bearing all these in mind, this part of the book provides the narrative behind the procedural approaches adopted in the study. In addition, it gives the rationale for the choice of methods and strategies designed by this researcher to find valid, objective, and accurate answers to the stated aims and objectives of the research indicated in Chapter 1 of this book, which are:

3.2.1 Aims of the Study

Following the turbulent global financial crisis from 2007–2009 and as the dust settled, the study, with the benefit of hindsight, evaluated the varied long-term impacts of the crisis on the performance of four of the largest UK banks to highlight what went wrong during and after the Global Financial Crisis. The study reviewed various legislative responses to the crisis.

The study evaluated whether to retain the ring-fencing policy after the global financial crisis (GFC) or grant more concessions to banks to cushion the policy's effect. This was more so in the circumstances of the Global Systemically Important Banks in the UK.

It has been about fifteen years since the GFC occurred in 2007–2009. Through evaluation of the financial accounts of the case studies from 2004 to 2018, the research aimed to determine the varied long-term impacts of the GFC

---

[510] F. Kerlinger, 'Foundations of Behavioural Research 3rd ed', (Rinehart and Winston, 1986, p 279)
[511] Y. Lincoln and E. Guba 'Naturalistic Inquiry' (Sage Publications, 2016, p.66)
[512] C. Marshall and G. Rossman 'Designing Qualitative Research 6th ed.' (Sage Publications, 2016, p. 66)

on the performance of some of the largest UK banks. In addition, the study evaluated the regulatory responses designed to limit the future effects of likely financial crises on the banking sector. The years 2004–2006 were the good years before the crisis began, 2007–2009 was in the heat of the crisis, 2010–2012 was when multiple regulatory responses started to take effect, 2013–2018 represented the recovery period, including the time of moratorium granted to the banks to prepare for the implementation of the ring-fencing policy.

The stated aim acknowledges that the global financial crisis had some long-term detrimental impacts on the financial performance of the banking sector. It also underscores the importance of the long-term effects of regulatory responses designed to reduce the consequences of likely future financial crises in the banking sector. The banks selected as case studies are the Royal Bank of Scotland (RSB), Barclays Group, Standard Chartered Bank Group (SCB) and HSBC Holdings Plc.

3.2.2 Research Objectives

(a) as a background to the study, a review of the extant literature was undertaken to ascertain the causes of the global financial crisis in 2007–2009,

(b) a review of the prevailing laws and regulations before the financial crisis in 2007–2009 was undertaken to determine whether gaps in the laws and supervisory regimes contributed to the crisis. Also, a review of the newly introduced changes to the laws after the global financial crisis was conducted, evaluating their impact on the banking sector,

(c) a theoretical critique of ring-fencing policy was conducted as it applies to the UK banking sector and against the backdrop of the UK's core competencies in providing financial services, a sphere in which the UK has comparative and competitive advantages.

Core competence is a term borrowed from business management which refers to cultivated or learnt specialist's skills, knowledge, expertise, capabilities and attributes that can become a critical success factor in the management of an organisation in a rapidly changing business environment, as happened in the aftermath of the global financial crisis,[513]

> (d) an evaluation was conducted of the effectiveness or otherwise of the ring-fencing policy as measures that are capable of deterring financial crises in the future and
>
> (e) Using the case studies approach, the annual financial accounts of RBS, Barclays, SCB, and HSBC Plc between 2004 and 2018 were evaluated to determine the impact of the global financial crisis on the banks' varied performances over the period stated. This exercise aids our understanding of some of the direct costs of these banks' downward journey and the difficult road back to recovery as a recorded lesson for the future.

Research objectives (a)–(d) are essentially a literature review exercise. The first four objectives have been accomplished under Chapters 1 and 2 of this report. Activities related to objective (v) are extensively carried out in chapters 4 and 5 of this report.

According to Kerlinger, there should be two objectives in designing a research plan: (i) the identification and development of procedures and (ii) the importance of quality and adequacy in the procedure to obtain a valid result.[514] The procedures adopted are stated in the succeeding paragraphs.

3.3 Guiding Research Philosophies

This section evaluates alternative research philosophies, emphasising the choice of research philosophies underpinning this study and justifying why that may be the case.

Guba and Lincoln defined research philosophies as worldviews or belief systems guiding researchers about knowledge development.[515] Easterby-Smith *et al.* identified three important uses of philosophical issues in research, namely: (i) to clarify research design, (ii) to help to see in advance design that will work

---

[513] Op. Cit., L. J Mullins, 2016, (n. 52).

[514] Op. cit., Kerlinger 1986, p 280, (n. 510)

[515] E. Guba, and Y. Lincoln, 'Competing Paradigms in qualitative Research'(Sage, 1994, pp 105–107)

or not work, and (iii) potentially to help to suggest how to adapt research designs within the limitations of different subjects.[516]

The third point raised by Easterby-Smith et al. acknowledges the need to adapt the research design within the context of the areas of the subject covered. Although the study is primarily law-related, it sits within multiple disciplines, including law, socio-economic policy, and business management. In addition, it covers banking and finance, engaging key financial accounting tools required to analyse the annual reports and financial accounts of the case study banks chosen for the research.

Different authors use different classifications and terminologies when grouping research philosophies. Blaikie, for instance, lists seven of such, which he labelled 'Approaches'. These are *positivism, realism, interpretivism, critical theory, structuration theory, feminism and critical rationalism*.[517] Tesch lists 28 approaches classified into four branches in a flow chart specifying options that may appeal to different researchers.[518]

Saunders *et al.* chose four in the same class, which they termed 'Philosophy'. These are *positivism, realism, interpretivism,* and *pragmatism*.[519] These relate to how collected research data should be analysed. They argued that individuals have preferences and assumptions about human knowledge (epistemological assumptions), the nature of realities as individuals see it (ontology) and the extent to which individuals' values influence their research process (axiological assumptions).[520]

What Blaikie called 'Approaches' Saunders *et al.* labelled 'Philosophy', and instead, Saunders *et al.* used the term 'Approaches' differently to classify the notion of 'deduction, abduction and induction'.[521] Ritchie and Lewis have a list called 'Paradigms' or 'Research Traditions'.[522] In some cases, there are overlaps in the meanings adduced to these concepts. Moreover, emphases are placed on

---

[516] M. Easterby-Smith, *et al.,* 'Management Research 3rd Ed'(Sage Publications, 2008, p 56)

[517] N. Blaikie, 'Approaches to Social Enquiry' (Polity Press, 1993, pp 93–100)

[518] R. Tesch 'Qualitative Research: Analysis Types and Software tools', (Falmer Press, 1990)

[519] M. Saunders, et al., 'Research Methods for Business Students 7th ed.' (Pearson, 2016)

[520] ibid

[521] Ibid.

[522] J. Ritchie and J. Lewis, 'Qualitative Research Practice' (Sage Publications, 2003)

some terms more than others. In other instances, 'Approach' and 'Philosophy' are used interchangeably. For example, Guba and Lincoln observed that the phrase 'Approaches to qualitative research' implies that qualitative or quantitative are umbrella terms that may suggest superiority to 'Paradigm', but their position is that the terms qualitative and quantitative should be reserved for methods.[523]

This assortment of classifications and use of terminologies within the domain of philosophy in social sciences research can appear somewhat unwieldy. It becomes a treacherous terrain that must be navigated carefully.

Therefore, for consistency and clarity, the 'onion' metaphoric model popularised by Saunders *et al.* is preferred and adopted for this work.

---

[523] E. Guba and Y. Lincoln, 'Competing Paradigms in Qualitative Research'(Oxford University Press, 2004, p 17) In Hesse-Biber, S and Leavy, P (eds)

3.4 Fig. 4 Research Philosophy in the 'Research Onion Model'.

Figure 4: Research Philosophy in the Research Onion Model

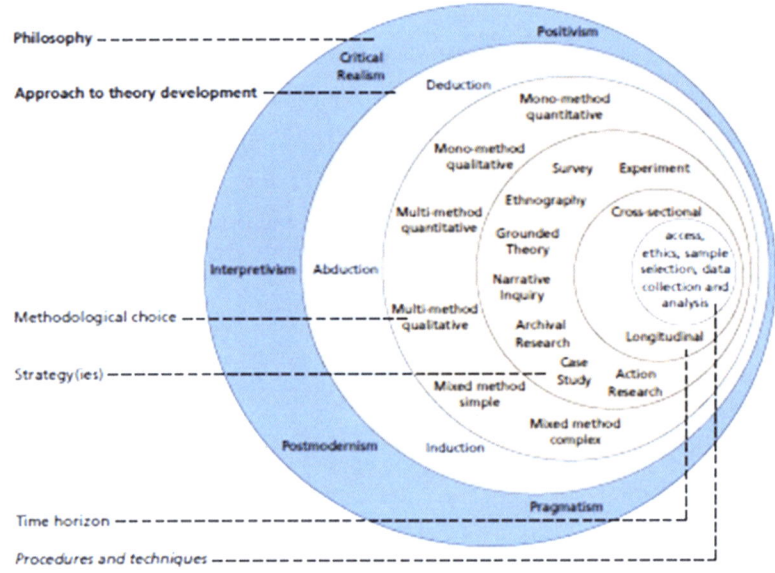

Figure 4.1 The 'research onion'
Source: © 2022 Mark NK Saunders; developed from Saunders et al. 2019

"Source: Saunders MNK, Lewis P and Thornhill A (2023) *Research methods for Business Students* (9th edition) Harlow: Pearson: p 131.

The research onion is ©2022 Mark NK Saunders and reproduced with their permission."

Looking at the diagram from the innermost circle, what the structure implies for this study is illustrated in Table 4.

Research 'Onion' Model Adapted and Applied for this Study

Table 4: Analysis of the Research Onion Model

No	Category	Options	Approaches Applied in the Study
1.	Technique & Procedure	Assorted Ways of Gathering Research Data: • Questionnaire • Interview • Experiment • Observation • Documents	The documentary method is chosen for the collection of data for the research. This includes banks' annual accounts and government white papers on policy relating to ring-fencing. The choice of method presents the best means of gathering reliable evidence to measure the performance of banks in the case study.
2.	Time Horizon	• Longitudinal • Cross-sectional	The Longitudinal The research is longitudinal because it focuses on a few selected banks as case studies, and it evaluates the banks' performances over a long period spanning 15 years from 2004–2018
3	Strategy	• Experiment • Survey • Archival Research • Case Study • Ethnography • Action Research • Grounded Theory • Narrative Inquiry	Case Study A case study strategy is adopted involving an in-depth investigation of the performances of four banks over 15 years using multiple sources of evidence.
4.	Methodological Choice	• Mono Method Quantitative • Mono Method Qualitative	Mixed Method Simple A mixed method is preferred because the research engages with qualitative and

		• Multi-Method Quantitative • Multi-Method Qualitative • Mixed Method Simple • Mixed Method Complex	quantitative analysis of available numerical data.
5.	Approach	• Deduction • Abduction • Induction	Deductive A deductive approach is adopted to test the validity of the hypothesis proposed in Chapter 1
6.	Philosophy	• Positivism • Realism • Interpretivism • Pragmatism	Interpretivism This study is essentially a qualitative approach that takes into account the evaluation of the complex nature and interaction of phenomena in organisations to draw conclusions about the research questions faced by this researcher.

3.5 Philosophical Positions

Saunders *et al.* summed up research philosophy as "a system of beliefs and assumptions about the development of knowledge."[524]

The word 'Ontology' has its roots in Greek, meaning "theory of the nature of reality."[525] Ontology seeks to answer the question of the nature of reality, whether reality is objective and independent of our perception, whether it is constructed by those who experience it and whether it exists apart from our experience.[526] Objectivism is an ontological position implying that social phenomena are external facts outside our influence. On the other hand,

---

[524] Op. cit., Saunders et al., (2016, (n. 519).
[525] Op. Cit., G. Delanty, and P. Strydom, 2003, p. 6, (n. 127).
[526] N. Blaikie, 'Approaches to Social Enquiry 2nd' (Polity Press, 2007)

constructivism suggests that phenomena and their meaning are socially constructed.[527]

Epistemology is about the kind of knowledge that is possible, what can be known, its limitations, and validity–the means of ascertaining whether a declared knowledge can be considered adequate and acceptable.[528] Delanty and Strydom distinguish between knowledge, opinion and common sense. According to these writers, what distinguishes knowledge from opinion and common sense is that knowledge has to be supported with convincing evidence.[529]

What all these mean to this study is that this researcher needs to avoid generalised assertions that are not evidence-based.

3.5.1 Positivism/Empiricism

Positivism, also called logical positivism, is an epistemological position typically associated with the scientific approach to research. Data collection employs objective reality, usually numeric, producing a law-like generalisation.[530]

The central claim of positivism is the view that only authentic scientific knowledge emerges from the positive confirmation of theory through the application of rigorous scientific methods.[531] Positivism assumes that science separates facts from values, so invisible theoretical entities are rejected.[532] It emphasises that reality has to be experiential and observable through the human senses.[533]

Positivism holds that inquiry should be value-free, time and context-free, generalisations are possible, there is a single reality, and there should be a separation between the investigator and the subject of investigation.[534] Positivism assumes that there is order or structure to reality. It rejects metaphysical and value judgments from scientific knowledge.[535] The assumption

---

[527] A. Bryman, 'Social Research Method 5th Ed' (Oxford University Press, 2016)

[528] M. Crotty, 'The Foundations of Social Research' (Sage Publications, 1998)

[529] Op. cit., Delanty, and Strydom, 2003, p. 6, (n 127).

[530] Op. cit., Bryman, 2016, p. 20, (n. 527).

[531] R. Wacks, 'Understanding Jurisprudence 5th ed.' (Oxford University Press, 2017)

[532] C. Robson, 'Real World Research 2nd ed' (Blackwell Publishing, 2002, p. 20)

[533] N J. Blaikie, 'Designing Social Research 2nd ed' (Polity Press, 2010, p. 97)

[534] Op. cit., Lincoln and Guba, 1985, (n. 511).

[535] Op. cit., Blaikie, 2010, p. 97, (n. 533).

is that since the data collection process is value-free, the research outcome should be objective.

A positivist research approach implies that data should be collected using observable reality. When analysed, it should identify a causal relationship within the data and produce law-like generalisation.[536] It is a process of gaining objective knowledge from analysing statistical data obtained under strict rules and procedures. The data may be collected through a survey or questionnaire.[537]

David Hume (1711–76) is the founding father of the empirical research tradition.[538] This study's approach emphasises that only experiential knowledge gained through unbiased observation using physical senses is acceptable.[539]

The criticism of positivist-based methodology is that the questionnaire typically uses closed-end questions, leading to limited outcomes. In addition, the approach can be costly and time-consuming. Finally, the data used may be outdated and challenging to analyse for researchers with no prior statistical training or background.[540]

Although numerical data was used in this research to evaluate the circumstances of the case studies, the study was supported more by qualitative/interpretivism analysis.

3.5.2 Realism

Realism is also part of the scientific approach genre, which studies the natural world through the prism of causation, intending to identify structures that led to the generation of the world.[541] Robson suggests that part of the worldview of a realist is an approach that sees the task of scientists as inventing theories to explain the natural world and to test these theories by rational criteria, explaining how and why a natural phenomenon occurred.[542]

---

[536] J. Gill and P. Johnson 'Research Methods for Managers' 4th Ed. (Sage Publications, 2010)

[537] K. McCartan, and C. Robson, 'Real World Research 4th Ed' (John Wiley, 2017, p. 21)

[538] Op. Cit., J. Ritchie, et al., 2014, p. 9, (n. 522)

[539] Op. cit., Bryman, 2016, (n. 527).

[540] A. Tashakkori, and C. Teddlie 'Mixed Methodology: Combining Qualitative and Quantitative Approaches' (Sage Publications, 1998)

[541] Op. cit., Bryman, 2016, p. 20, (n. 527).

[542] Op. cit., Robson, 2002, p. 20, (n. 532).

As in 3.5.1, the approach adopted in this study depended more on interpretivism rather than realism.

3.5.3 Interpretivism

Social constructivism is often combined with interpretivism.[543] Ontology under qualitative philosophy believes that there are multiple constructed realities; the relationship between the researcher and those being investigated is inseparable, and value-bound and generalisation are not always possible.[544] Lincoln and Guba humorously said, "The only generalisation is: there is no generalisation."[545]

A quantitative methodology is often given more respect, which may be because numbers tend to give the impression of factual accuracy.[546] It may also reflect the general tendency to regard science as related to numbers and implying precision.[547] However, Dabbs argues that a qualitative approach should not be considered inferior since numeric data do not always tell the whole story.[548]

An interpretivism approach has notable advantages. It interprets outcomes based on a deep familiarisation with typical life situations.[549] The worldview is that a qualitative approach provides a holistic understanding of a phenomenon, the factors involved, and how they interrelate, identifying the less noticeable issues and those that initially attract attention.[550]

Some of the advantages of qualitative methods include the richness of the study, the detailed data generated, and the tolerance for ambiguity and contradictions.[551]

---

[543] D. Mertens, 'Mixed Methods and the Politics of Human Research: The Transformative-Emancipatory Perspective' (Sage Publications, 2003, pp 135-164)

[544] Op. cit., Lincoln and Guba 1985, (n. 511).

[545] Ibid

[546] B. Berg, 'Qualitative Research Methods for the Social Sciences' (Pearson, 2001)

[547] Ibid

[548] J. Dabbs, 'Making things visible' (Sage Publications, 1982)

[549] M. Miles, and A. Huberman, 'Qualitative Data Analysis: An Expanded Sourcebook' (Sage Publications, 1994)

[550] Ibid

[551] M. Denscombe, 'The Good Research Guide for Small-Scale Social Research Projects 3rd Ed' (OAU, 2011)

The criticism of an interpretivism approach to research stems from its subjectivity, leading to the assumption that it is generally unreliable. In addition, generalisations based on a qualitative approach may be called into question.[552] Qualitative methods are usually considered overly descriptive, with large amounts of data needing contextualising, and the outcome can be hard to sell to others.[553] On the other hand, the importance of a qualitative approach in social research is appreciated because numeric data (as in quantitative study) can be meaningless unless interpreted or well explained.

In light of this study's objectives, it is considered appropriate to use mixed methods. One part of the research objectives concerns textual evaluation, while the other concerns numerical data analysis.

3.5.4 Pragmatism

Part of the methods of a qualitative paradigm is an observation of participants. This method requires the researcher to be directly involved with those being studied. The researcher's involvement would enable him to understand what is occurring in the group or organisation being studied and facilitate the collection of current data.[554] This relationship and interaction with participants birthed the idea of '***Interactionism*** or ***Pragmatism***', popularised by Dewy and Mead in the early part of the twentieth century.[555, 556] This researcher suggests that pragmatism philosophy will be invaluable to ethnographic and action research strategies but not applicable in the circumstances of this research because the events researched happened in the past.

---

[552] Ibid

[553] J. Mason, 'Qualitative Researching' (Sage Publications, 1997, p. 145)

[554] A. Bryman, 'Quantity and Quality in Social Research' (Routledge, 1998, p. 45)

[555] J. Dewey 'Creative Intelligence: Essays on the Pragmatic Attitude' (Henry Holt, 1917)

[556] G. Mead 'Scientific Method and the Individual Thinker'(Henry Holt, 1917, pp. 176–227)

3.6 General Features and Debates Around Qualitative and Quantitative Approaches to Doing Research and What that Means to this Study

Research methodology could be positioned within quantitative/positivism or qualitative/phenomenological paradigms.[557]

Methodology refers to the systematic processes adopted in data analysis and the philosophies underpinning the variety of philosophies evaluated previously.[558] O'Leary suggests that methodological design embraces the philosophies underpinning the research, the methods/techniques used to collect data, and the tools used to interpret the data, i.e., questionnaires, interviews, inferential statistics, and interpretivism.[559]

Creswell points out that a research design that adopts a quantitative or qualitative research methodology infers that the researcher implicitly accepts the philosophical assumptions related to that approach to studying phenomena.[560]

As pointed out earlier, interpretivism philosophy and a mixed-method approach are engaged to achieve the study's aims and objectives. The choice of approach reflects the fact that the study combines relevant features of quantitative and qualitative paradigms. Apart from the numeric data evaluation, aspects of the research objectives relate to a critical textual evaluation of secondary documentary data. Essentially, though, the qualitative approach played the dominant role.

Tashakkori and Teddlie contended that applying mixed methods, combining qualitative and quantitative approaches, is compatible and enriches the research experience.[561]

The study employed a deductive approach in the sense that the data focused on testing the validity of the hypothesis stated in Chapter 1. The hypothesis is, "Notwithstanding some benefits that may accrue from the ring-fencing policy, the banking sector and, by extension, the economy in the UK may likely face

---

[557] Op. cit., Denscombe, 2011, (n. 551).

[558] D. Silverman, 'Doing Qualitative Research' 4th Ed. (Sage Publication, 2010).

[559] Z. O'Leary, 'The Essential Guide to Doing Research' (Sage Publications, 2009, p. 85)

[560] J. W. Creswell, 'Qualitative Inquiry & Research Design: Choosing Among Five Approaches 2nd Ed' (Sage Publications, 2007, p. 16)

[561] Op. cit., Tashakkori, and Teddlie, 1998, (n. 540).

long-term detriments arising from the implementation of the ring-fencing policy."

In the past hundred years until the 1980s, a debated pertinent question has been whether enquiries in social sciences such as anthropology, social psychology, economics, law and sociology could apply methods and methodology in the natural sciences such as biology, chemistry and physics.[562] There has not been a straightforward yes or no answer. For example, it has been argued that evaluating chemical structure through statistical inferences differs from studying social structures or issues about human thought, feeling and behaviour.[563]

That said, rating questions that allow respondents to indicate how strongly they agree or disagree with a statement and coding using the Likert scale model have made it possible for social science research to benefit from the advantages of using quantitative tools.[564]

Writing in the mid-2000s, in the context of social enquiries, Manicas suggested that if subjectivity is avoided so that objective functioning systems and methods are engaged to identify 'Social facts', the assumption is that there is no critical difference between natural and social sciences.[565] The point emphasised by Manicas is that the methodology applied in science can be used in social research.

After World War II, there has been increasing discontent and contention against logical positivism.[566,567] The argument is that the social world is far too complex to lend itself to theorising by definite laws in the same way as in the natural sciences.[568]

---

[562] A. Chalmers, 'What is this thing called science? 4th ed' (Open University Press McGraw-Hill, 2013)

[563] Op. cit., Blaikie, 1993, p.12, (n. 517).

[564] Op. cit., Saunders, M. et al., 2016, (n. 519).

[565] P. Manicas, 'The Social Sciences Since World War II: The Rise and Fall of Scientism' (Sage Publications, 2007)

[566] C. Reichardt, and S. Rallis, (Jossey-Bass, 1994, pp 85-92) Qualitative and Quantitative Inquiries are not Incompatible

[567] K. Howe, 'Against the Quantitative–Qualitative Incompatibility thesis or Dogmas Die Hard' (1988) Vol 17, 10–17

[568] Op. cit., Saunders, 2016 et al., n. (519).

The argument is that both qualitative and quantitative methodologies can be used in the circumstances of this study.

3.7 Methods

Methods refer to tools and various ways of collecting data to carry out research objectives, whilst methodology is the systematic process adopted in analysing the data.[569]

Creswell suggested that the ideal number should not exceed four in multiple case studies, as planned for this study. Otherwise, there is a risk of a dilution of the analysis.[570] On the other hand, Glesne and Peshkin point out that there is always a desire to include more cases to satisfy the notion of 'generalisation', a term which they suggest holds little meaning for qualitative researchers.[571]

A case study strategy is becoming increasingly popular and widely used in business management and organisational behaviour.[572] study has four case studies, the maximum number suggested by Creswell.

3.8 The Variety of Data Gathering Options Available to the Researcher

Creswell suggests five data collection methods available to the qualitative researcher, including observations, interviews, questionnaires, documents and audio-visual materials.[573] Other authors classify audio-visual materials as part of documentary data.[574, 575]

---

[569] Op. cit., Silverman, 2013, (n. 558).

[570] Op. cit., Creswell, 2007, (n. 560).

[571] C. Glesne and A. Peshkin, 'Becoming Qualitative Researchers: An Introduction' (Longman, 1992)

[572] A. Mumford 'When to use the Case Study Method' (1997) European Case Clearing House, Autumn pp 16–17.

[573] Op. cit., J Creswell, 2007 p. 130, (n. 560).

[574] Op. cit., M. Denscombe, 2011, (n. 551).

[575] Op. cit., Saunders, M. et al. 2016, (n. 519).

3.8.1 Observation

Observation as a primary means of obtaining data involves systematic watching and taking notes of related activities of participants in a study.[576] The observation could entail a combination of sensations, including sound, touch, smell, taste and perception.[577] The researcher could be involved as a participant, watch from the sidelines as an outsider, or alternate both positions.[578] Observing as a participant may have the added advantage of developing rapport with others, enhancing the prospect of success. This data collection method would be particularly suitable for ethnography, case studies, and action research.

Part of the observation method's benefits includes generating reliable data. The data are collected as the event occurs. In addition, it allows the collection of data that participants may not see as relevant or essential. The direct experience can give useful insight. It is straightforward, and it only requires a bit of common sense.[579, 580] The disadvantages include the researcher having to be at the site, only overt actions can be observed while inferences have to be made, and it may be time-consuming.[581]

The observation method is not applicable in the study's context because the current research concerns matters that have already occurred.

3.8.2 Interview

An interview as a method of primary data collection is a purposeful conversation between the interviewer and interviewee(s), which could be one-on-one or a focus group of participants in which the person(s) being interviewed is/are able and willing to respond to questions from the interviewer.[582] The interview could be structured, semi-structured or unstructured.[583] This method could be useful in exploratory, descriptive, explanatory and evaluative

---

[576] D. Gray, 'Doing Research in the Real-World 2nd Ed' (Sage Publications, 2009, p 396)
[577] Ibid
[578] Op. cit., J. Creswell, 2007, n 560
[579] N. Moore, 'How to Do Research 2nd ed' (Library Association Publishing, 1987)
[580] Op. cit., K. Howe, 1988, (n. 567).
[581] ibid
[582] Op., cit., Saunders, M. et al., 2016, (n. 519).
[583] Kvale, S. and Brinkmann, S. (2009) Interviews: Learning the craft of Qualitative Research Interviewing (2nd ed)

research.[584] Marshall and Rossman suggest that the interview method may be the overall strategy or one of several methods.[585] While many benefits could be derived from this method, it is essential to have a clear plan so that the session does not go adrift or lose focus.[586]

One of the advantages of the interview method is its flexibility. For example, it could be tailored to fit a study. It allows inventive strategies. It can yield a large quantity of data very quickly; follow-up and clarification are possible; it enables interviewers to understand the meaning that everyday activities hold for people, and it could be therapeutic and rewarding to the person giving the information.[587] The disadvantages are: it could be time-consuming; responses are non-standard; inhibitions on the part of the interviewee; the interviewee may not be entirely truthful; sometimes, the interview method may involve invasion of privacy; it may go adrift losing focus; it can be costly in terms of time to both the interviewer and the interviewee.[588]

Interview methods could be invaluable to most research on society, culture and business management. However, in this study, while interviewing key stakeholders may have some value, it is not one of the critical success factors for the research. This is because (i) the empirical part of the research took a rear mirror view of events that happened in the banks more than seventeen years ago. Even if it is possible to recollect some of the events, a detailed memory of matters that occurred during that period would, at best, be very hazy. (ii) Moreover, most people currently working in the banks selected as case studies may not have worked in those banks back then (iii) the subject of the empirical research is concerned with 'Performance' in the banks. It is thus considered that a better means of gathering data about performance in the banks would be the banks' annual reports and financial accounts for the period under review, evaluated in light of other relevant literature materials.

---

[584] Op. Cit., D. Gray, 2009, p 396, (n. 576).
[585] Op. cit., Marshall and Rossman, 2016, p 147, (n. 512).
[586] Ibid
[587] Op. cit., M. Denscombe, 2007, pp 202–203, (n. 128).
[588] Ibid

3.8.3 Questionnaires

The questionnaire method consists of a written list of questions designed to collect information by asking people about issues related to the research. Moore argues that a questionnaire survey is perhaps the most commonly used research method, which could be relevant in a small or large-scale study.[589] The advantages of the questionnaire method include: they give room for scaling (Likert scale model); they can be flexible; low-cost written questionnaires can be mailed out; avoidance of potential interviewer's bias; they place less pressure for immediate answers; they give respondents a greater feeling of anonymity.[590]

One of the disadvantages of the questionnaire method is low response rates, especially if the questionnaire is too long. In addition, the accuracy and completeness of responses to questions may be an issue. There may be no room to correct errors or misconceptions of a question; there is no control over the context in which the questions are answered; lack of qualitative depth to the answers, thereby leading to superficiality.[591] Nevertheless, the questionnaire method can be helpful in both qualitative and quantitative methods, and they can be valuable and relevant in the context of this study. However, as mentioned under the interview method, it is considered more appropriate to use documentary evidence obtainable from the annual reports and financial accounts of the banks selected as case studies.

3.8.4 Documents (Secondary Data Sources)

The documentary data collection method uses written sources but may include audio-visual sources.[592] Written documents include government publications, white papers/reports of inquiries, official statistics from the Office of National Statistics, newspapers and magazines. In addition, records of meetings, letters and memos, emails, diaries, books, journals, annual financial accounts of companies, website pages and the internet, court records, church

---

[589] Op. cit., Moore, 1987, (n. 579).
[590] L. Kidder, and C. Judd, 'Research Methods in Social Relations 5th Ed' (CBS Publishing, 1986 pp 221–222)
[591] Ibid
[592] Op. cit. Denscombe, M. 2011, (n. 551)

records and welfare office records, to mention a few.[593] Using documents in research requires specialist analytic skills referred to as content analysis.[594]

Some of the advantages of secondary data sources include saving time and money. Documents can be obtained more quickly than compiling primary data, which can lead to unforeseen discoveries. Since they are permanent records, they can be rechecked.[595] Part of the benefits of using documents for research is that they are unobtrusive and do not disturb the location.[596]

Some important considerations in using documents as data collection sources are authenticity, whether the documents are genuine and credible, and whether they are dependable, representative, and comprehensible.[597] The researcher would need to be satisfied that the documents relied on are genuine and not of questionable origin, that they are free from error, that they are typical of their kind and that their presentation is clear.[598]

Part of the disadvantages of documentary sources of data collection is that sometimes the necessary documents are unavailable, inaccessible, or lost. In addition, it could sometimes be an issue with gatekeepers who may enforce restrictions.[599] On the other hand, accessibility is one of the most important advantages of the documentary data collection method.[600]

3.9 The Documentary Data Sources in the Context of this Study

This researcher used documentary sources to generate data for the research. Financial accounts and annual reports of four major UK banks considered systemically relevant were collated for the research. These banks have core deposits above the minimum threshold of £25 billion, the ring-fencing

---

[593] U. Flick, 'An Introduction to Qualitative Research 4th Ed' (Sage Publications, 2009)

[594] Op. cit., Marshall and Rossman 2016, (n. 508).

[595] Op. cit., Saunders, 2016, p. 331 (n.519)

[596] Op. cit., U. Flick, 2009, (n. 593).

[597] J. Scott, 'A Matter of Record: Documentary Sources in Social Research' (Polity Press, 1990)

[598] Op. cit., U. Flick, 2009, (n. 593).

[599] ibid

[600] Op. cit., M. Denscombe, 2011, (n. 551).

regulation's benchmark. The annual bank accounts evaluated are the Royal Bank of Scotland, Barclays Bank, Standard Chartered Bank and HSBC Holdings Plc.

The analysis of these accounts helped to determine the extent of the global financial crisis's impact on the evaluated banks. In addition, the analysis of the financial statements and annual reports considered the likely costs of regulatory changes to the banks and the market environment under which each bank operated.

The annual financial accounts serve multiple purposes and have different users. Corporate yearly financial statements and reports are primarily addressed to the company's shareholders.[601] The annual financial accounts and the Chairman/CEO's reports are typically embodied in the same document, which must be tabled before the shareholders for consideration at the company's Annual General Meetings. It reflects the performance of the company over the accounting period.

Also, it indicates the bank's response to the challenges encountered during the accounting year and its plans for the future. Typically, in the annual report section of the document, the Chairman and the Chief Executive Officer of the banks would narrate the socioeconomic and legal environment under which their banks operated. This would include the bank's plan and how the organisation intends to respond to those issues. The CEOs will also address how the bank plans to achieve its organisational goals in the foreseeable future.

Stakeholders who may be interested in a bank's financial accounts include shareholders, the tax authority, workers' unions (if there are any), investors, the Companies House, and bank regulators, especially the BoE, PRA, and FCA.[602]

Part of the disadvantages of the annual financial accounts as a source of gathering information on the performance of the banks is that it is historical and does not necessarily represent the current status of the company and, thus, may not even reflect what the future holds.[603] For example, some may argue that the annual financial accounts of a bank are susceptible to manipulation and may not reflect the actual financial standing of the bank. This is probable, especially in light of what happened in the case of BCCI, which was extensively discussed in the literature review. After that incident, banks' auditors are now required to be

---

[601] Op. Cit., G. Arnold, 2013, p. 17, (n. 31)
[602] F. Wood, and A. Sangster 'Business Accounting 2, 11th Ed' (Prentice-Hall, 2007)
[603] D. Cotter, 'Advanced Financial Reporting' (Prentice-Hall, 2012)

more vigilant and could be held liable for gross negligence concerning flawed and inaccurate auditor reports.[604]

The prime advantage of annual reports and financial accounts as a veritable source of data collection is their comprehensiveness. They contain information far above what could be generated from any other data collection method. For example, the Royal Bank of Scotland's annual financial accounts for the year ended 2016 are 463 pages, 2015s are 430 pages, and 2014s are 516 pages. This presents a huge opportunity to extract relevant information for the study.

In order to access the annual accounts of the banks, some of which dated as far back as 2004, this researcher directly contacted the banks. Part of the backup plan was to contact the Companies House to get the old accounts if the banks were unwilling to cooperate. At the beginning of the research, part of the immediate concern then related to difficulties that may arise in getting the annual financial accounts of banks. There was also a concern that paying for copies of bulky financial accounts that run into over 500 pages and accounts over ten years old may be very expensive.

However, accessing the electronic copies of the banks' financial accounts was not difficult at all. Bank officials helped, and the researcher did not have to pay for the electronic documents. The annual financial reports of the banks and the policy statements on ring-fencing obtained were over 40 volumes with more than 20,000 pages.

Handling such voluminous documents requires significant skill and knowledge of what one is searching for and where to look for it in the annual accounts.

Government white papers on the causes of the 2007–2009 financial crisis (Lord Turner's report), Vickers' report on 'Ring-fencing', the report on the collapse of Barings Capital (an investment bank), journals, press reports, textbooks, case law, the Banking Reform Act 2013, and information about the UK's GDP were also required for this research. These documents were readily available as they were mainly within the public domain.

---

[604] Company Act 2006 s.507 Offences in connection with auditor's report

3.10 How the Objectives Stated in Chapter 1 Were Achieved

This section briefly outlines the action taken to achieve each stated objective.

At the beginning of this study, this researcher planned to collate data from a large number of banks in the UK using inferential statistics to determine the impact of the global financial crisis and changes in banking regulations on the performance of the banking sector generally.

However, after further consideration, the researcher changed his mind on the basis that analysis of the combined data of all the banks or a significant part of the banks would result in averaging outcomes, where the strength of some banks would compensate for the weaknesses of other banks. This would not have served the objectives of the research. Eventually, the approach adopted evolved over time.

Secondly, although all four banks evaluated have some common denominators in the sense that they are all UK-regulated banks, they have varied markets and other factors that distinguish each of the banks. For example, HSBC and Standard Chartered Bank's operational bases are more rooted in Asia, while Barclays and RBS focus more on Europe and America.

Thirdly, the impact of the global financial crisis on each of the banks evaluated is more pronounced on some banks than others. This is because of their different circumstances. For example, Standard Chartered Bank did not have to ring-fence because their core deposit customers that the ring-fencing policy sought to protect were outside the UK and the EU. However, the other three case studies (RSB, Barclays and HSBC) are under obligation to be ring-fencing compliant. Therefore, evaluating the banks separately and comparing where appropriate served the study's objectives.

The threshold of core deposits a bank needs to hold and at which the ring-fencing policy kicks in is £25 billion and above. However, many banks did not fall within this criterion. As such, they were not affected at all by the ring-fencing policy. Thus, the study focused on four of the biggest UK banks that are considered globally systemically important. These are banks whose failure could cause severe damage to the UK economy and even beyond the UK borders.

To achieve the study's aims and objectives, a longitudinal multiple case studies strategy was proposed, engaging both quantitative and qualitative methodologies in the data analysis.

The study used a longitudinal approach because it focuses on a few selected banks as case studies. The research takes a rear-view approach by evaluating the banks' performance over fifteen years spanning 2004–2018. Although it took a considerable time to extract the Key Economic Performance Indicators of the banks selected as case studies and to evaluate the statistical data, the exercise was rewarding.

The empirical data collected on the financial accounts of the case studies did not cover 2019 when the ring-fencing policy started and after that date.

At the time of the research, the available empirical data regarding the financial activities of all the banks examined as case studies only extended to the 31st of December 2018. Although the Banking Reform Act 2013, which contains the ring-fencing policy, became law in December 2013, the full implementation of the ring-fencing policy only took effect on 1st January 2019.

We can analyse the ring-fencing policy in light of the abundance of other materials, including that (i) we now know the causes of the global financial crisis. Suppose we know the associated problems that caused the global financial crisis. We can then gather up the bits and pieces of available information together and reasonably determine the most viable solutions to fix the problem. We can reasonably determine how and why the ring-fencing policy can fit in or not fit in among the range of solutions designed to address the issues.

We can reasonably work out what can and what cannot work (ii) what we do not have now is not too important than all that we already have. We have the benefit of the output of at least two Panels of Inquiry specifically set up to investigate the causes of the crisis (Lord Turner Panel) and the white papers produced by the Vickers' Panel that came up with the idea about ring-fencing. We also benefit from the FSA's voluminous report on the causes of the RBS' near collapse in 2008. There are others, including the report on failed Barring Capital and BCCI.

In addition to all these, since the crisis began in 2007, many journal articles and books have been written on various facets of the ring-fencing policy. These materials were copiously cited in this report. This research is an addition to the works of several other scholars. The financial data produced and analysed in this book can serve as a foundation for further study in the future, say, in another five to ten years' time, when additional data would be available for more analysis on the subject.

The research design for this study embraced multiple data and mixed strategy, which involved evaluating the data using both numeric and qualitative data. By engaging qualitative and quantitative methodology in the analysis, each approach supported the other to arrive at the conclusions.

The qualitative approach took pre-eminence in the study, while the quantitative side of the evaluation only played a secondary role. This was considered imperative to the achievement of the objectives of the study because objectives (i) a & b, (ii), and (iii) required a qualitative approach as they were matters related to textual evaluation. Objective (iv) required quantitative tools for the numeric evaluation of data and a qualitative approach to review in the 'round', contextualising all the information gathered on the subject.

The choice of a mixed methods approach reflects the fact that the study combined relevant features of quantitative and qualitative paradigms. Apart from the numeric data evaluation, aspects of the research objectives related to a critical textual evaluation of secondary documentary data. Carrying out mixed methods in this way supports the view of Tashakkori and Teddlie, who contended that applying mixed methods, combining qualitative and quantitative approaches, is not only compatible but enriches the research experience.[605]

Objectives

(i) (a) as a background to the study, the researcher reviewed the literature on the causes of the financial crisis in 2007–2009.

To achieve this objective, materials related to the 2007–2009 financial crisis were consulted. As a result, there is an increasingly wide range of publications on this subject, starting with Lord Turner's report on the financial crisis, journal articles, publications, textbooks, and other materials.

(b) To review the prevailing law and regulations before the financial crisis in 2007–2009 and to determine whether there were gaps in the law and supervisory regime then that contributed to the crisis. Also, the researcher reviewed the newly introduced changes to the law after the global financial crisis, evaluating their impact on the case studies.

---

[605] Op. cit., Tashakkori, and Teddlie, 1998, n 511.

To determine whether there were inadequacies in the legal framework that may have given room for the crisis to occur, key legislation before the crisis was reviewed. The legislation reviewed includes but is not limited to the Banking Act 1979, the Company Act 1985 & 2006, the Banking Act 1987 and regulations at supranational levels. These are Basel I (1988), Basel II (2004) and FMSA 2000. In addition, post-crisis legal responses such as Basel III (2010 & (2017) and Banking Act 2009 focused on Global Systemically Important Banks. Policy documents issued through the HM Treasury (2011) styled "A New Approach to Financial Regulation: Blueprint for Reforms and the Financial Services (Banking Reform) Act 2013 were evaluated."

(ii) *To conduct a theoretical critique of the Ring-fencing policy against the backdrop of the UK's core competencies in providing financial services, a sphere in which the UK has comparative and competitive advantages.*

Critiquing ring-fencing involved a descriptive critical analysis of the literature on the subject. Evidence on this aspect was taken from literature materials, including Journals, Articles, Textbooks, Government whitepapers, and evidence from other jurisdictions such as America and Europe. In addition, secondary statistics from the Office of National Statistics were used, including those on Fig 1, page 109, and Table 2, page 109.

(iii) *To evaluate the effectiveness or otherwise of the ring-fencing policy as a measure capable of deterring future financial crises.*

This objective also evaluates the literature, drawing on resources from journals and other publications.

(iv) *Using the case studies approach, the annual financial accounts of RBS, Barclays, SCB, and HSBC Plc between 2004–2018 were evaluated to determine the impact of the global financial crisis and regulatory changes on the performance of the banks over the period stated. This exercise aids our understanding of some of the direct costs of the downward journey of these banks and the difficult road back to recovery as a lesson on record for the future.*

This is an empirical aspect of the research, which evaluated the annual reports and financial accounts of chosen banks. This aimed to highlight the extent of the global financial crisis's long-term impact on the case studies' performance. Statistical data was extracted from the banks'

Annual Reports and Financial Accounts. This was evaluated in light of the market environment and regulatory changes under which the banks operated each year of the review. In addition, journals, articles, the banks' websites, news reports and textbooks were consulted to contextualise the evaluation's findings.

Thirteen key performance indicators were extracted from the annual accounts of the banks selected as case studies. The KPIs are Total Annual Income, Operating Profit Before Tax, Total Assets, Impairment Charges, Number of Branches, Employees, Earnings Per Share, Dividend Per Share, Total Deposit, Total Loans, Investment Banking Contributions, Insurance Income and Income from Wealth Management. These indices were used to draw a profile of each of the banks' performance over fifteen years, from 2004 to 2018. This is related to the evaluation of numeric data. This data evaluation agrees with positivists' claim and follows empiricists' ideology about objective reality, obtaining evidence outside the researcher's influence and being value-free.

The first three years' accounts from 2004 to 2006 represented the good years immediately preceding the global financial crisis. This was when the banks declared huge profits.

The next three years, from 2007 to 2009, were when the crisis occurred. After that, the next three years, 2010 to 2012, were the period of the planned government's response to the financial crisis. Then the next six years, from 2013 to 2018, was the period of moratorium granted to the banking sector to fully prepare to implement the ring-fencing policy contained in the Banking Reform Act 2013, which was the embodiment of the UK's legal response to the global financial crisis. A trend analysis was constructed around the Profitability ratios using charts to illustrate and analyse the numerical data generated.

Reliance was placed on the balance sheet, income statement, notes to the accounts and the comments in the director's report section of the annual financial accounts of each of the banks to help draw pictures of each bank's performance yearly. A notable difference between the statement of financial position or balance sheet and the income statement is that the balance sheet is a 'snapshot' of the variables comprising the assets and liabilities as of the last day of the accounting year.

This was 31ˢᵗ December annually for the banks evaluated. On the other hand, the income statement shows the income stream earned (for example, commission, interest on loans and overdraft, exchange and insurance premium) between two dates, usually 12 months apart.[606] The balance sheet is very fluid. It does not remain the same as the value changes daily. As such, the income statement proved to be a rich source of information for analysing the accounts.

3.11 Profitability Models as Performance Measurement

Profitability ratios, including Return On Capital Employed, Earnings Per Share, Dividend Per Share, Profit Before Tax, Profit After Tax and Operating Income, indicate whether an entity performed satisfactorily. Indices on income generation on an annual basis can be compared with the previous years' performance or against a benchmark to determine whether there had been quarterly or annual growth. Returns earned on the total capital employed are measured in percentages and can facilitate comparison in the organisation with a predetermined level of annual growth. ROCE determines whether the income earned is commensurate with the cost of resources expended to generate profit.

EPS measures the profit attributed to each ordinary share, typically denominated in pence. Importantly, the part of the earnings per share distributed to shareholders in the company is the DPS. The difference between EPS and DPS (the proportion distributed to the shareholders from the EPS) is the income retained by the business. So in the years that the company's EPS is significantly high, other things being equal, the shareholders will benefit from an increase in the dividend paid out. At the same time, the bank would have a significant amount left as retained earnings to grow the business organically.

Correspondingly, when the income level is not particularly good, the shareholders will have little or no earnings for the year. Where there is little, or nothing left to distribute as dividends to shareholders from the income generated during an accounting year, there would likely be little or nothing to retain in the business. As such, the bank would suffer a decline or stunted growth. This was

---

[606] J. Berk, and P. DeMarzo, 'Corporate Finance 3ʳᵈ Ed' (Pearson, 2014, p 29)

sadly the case on many occasions with the banks evaluated as case studies, especially RBS.

Using profitability ratios in the way described has shortcomings: (i) it takes a retrospective view of profitability, (ii) the ratios are only meaningful when compared against a benchmark, and it assumes that the benchmark chosen is suitable, (iii) it relies on the balance sheet assets which, typically is book value at historical cost (this can be grossly undervalued), and (iv) profitability ratios are based on the balance sheet figures, ignoring economic factors.[607]

While the disadvantages of a profitability model as a performance yardstick are important, they are not considered fatal to the research. This is because (i) the study itself looks backwards to see what happened in the past, and (ii) it is generally recognised that grossly understated assets could be made to give an overly impressive performance of the bank when desired. This can easily be picked up if it is the case that the company revalues its assets too frequently or retains the historical value for too long, say for over ten years, depending on the policy of each bank.

Under ISA 545, 'Auditing, Fair Value Measurements and Disclosures', a company is required to declare a fair value for their assets.[608] However, in a manipulative accounting method usually called 'accounting cushioning', a bank may want to grossly understate its fixed assets in the good years when profit is high. This will have the effect of lowering profit and reducing tax bills for that period. Much later in the 'bad years' when profit is low, the situation allows the bank to overstate the relevance of an upward revaluation of the assets to cushion the effects of the poor performance in the bad years, thereby giving shareholders a false impression of stability.

The critical issue here is that the increased value attributed to fixed assets such as land and buildings is not revenue generated in the ordinary course of business operations for that period but a windfall from the property market. The upward review of the value of the assets has nothing to do with the good business acumen of the bank managers. Part of the incentives that could motivate the bank management to engage in such activities is that it would help to boost stock prices in the stock market in the years when operational performance is poor. In addition, it could enhance investors' confidence in that bank and help the directors claim bonuses in the year when operational performance is poor.

---

[607] G. Arnold, 'Corporate Financial Management' (Prentice-Hall, 2013, p 615).
[608] G. Cosserat, "Modern Auditing 2nd ed' (John Wiley, 2006, p 319)

To reduce the effects of incidents like this and to help external auditors, tax authorities, and financial analysts determine the accurate picture of the profitability status of the bank, one of the key measures available to examiners is to request the company's policy on assets revaluation. This would assist the evaluator in determining how often the bank should professionally revalue its assets and whether it is consistent in carrying out asset revaluation when it should. In the case of this research, reliance is placed on the auditors' doing their professional duty, that they took cognisance of this factor and fulfilled their obligations to the highest professional standards.

Notwithstanding the shortcomings of profitability ratios as a performance measurement, other researchers have used the model successfully in performance measurement-related research.[609, 610]

3.12 Analysis, Interpretation and Written Presentation

Wolcott suggests three components of data analysis in qualitative research: description, analysis and interpretation.[611] A description is concerned with summarising, presenting, and narrating the data, including activities related to transcribing tape recordings of interviews.[612] Analysis requires coding, while interpretation is about making sense of the data.

Three widely used approaches to interpreting data are content analysis, grounded theory and narrative analysis.[613] There are others, such as conversation analysis, discourse analysis, hermeneutics and deconstruction. Content analysis could be defined as a systematic evaluation of the characteristics found in a data set, including the frequency of words and recurrent patterns of phrases and themes within the data. This ultimately enables the researcher to construct extant or emergent outcomes.[614] In the context of these case studies, content analysis

---

[609] J W Wilcox, 'The P/B–ROE Valuation Model', (1984) Jan–Feb, 58–66, Financial Analysis Journal.

[610] J. Karr, 'Performance Measurement in Banking: Beyond ROE' (2005) Vol 18 (2) 56–70, Journal of Performance Measurement.

[611] H. Wolcott, 'Transforming Qualitative Data: Description, Analysis and Interpretation'(Sage Publications, 1994)

[612] D. Silverman, 'Interpreting Qualitative Data 5th Ed' (Sage Publications, 2014)

[613] Ibid

[614] Op. Cit., Easterby-Smith, M. et al., 2008, (n. 516).

was used to produce emerging themes from the trend analysis extensively discussed regarding each of the banks in the case studies in Chapter 4.

Neuendorf suggests that content analysis could be imported into quantitative methods using SSPS software.[615] As mentioned previously under the documentary data sources, Neuendorf's suggestion supports this researcher's plan to use content analysis in evaluating secondary data sources in the context of the quantitative method in the research.

Glaser and Strauss' grounded theory is a three-stage approach which involves developing categories within data sets, a saturation of the categories to demonstrate relevance and the development of the categories into more general analytical frameworks with relevance outside the setting.[616] The Grounded theory aims to generate or discover theory from the data or the life experiences of social actors.[617] Saunders et al. suggest that grounded theory could be used in different contexts, including a class of study in this book.[618]

3.13 Limitations and Justification of the Choice of Method Adopted

The concern usually raised when documentary data sources such as companies' annual financial accounts and the national GDP are mentioned as the principal sources of data collection for major research is that annual accounts of organisations do not always reflect reality. As mentioned in the case of 'Accounting Cushioning' earlier, a company's account may be highly susceptible to manipulations to accommodate how organisations manipulating their accounts want them to be seen by others.

During this study, the researcher's attention was drawn to the bloating of the derivative accounts of the case studies in the year 2008. However, the undue increase in the derivative accounts was reversed in 2009. In the case of Barclays, the inflated derivative accounts increased by almost a trillion pounds, yet the Auditors signed off the audited reports. The worrying bit was that when the anomaly was rectified, nothing or not much was said about the error. The account was just corrected, and that was it. The possibility of inflating a bank's assets by

---

[615] K. Neuendorf, 'The Content Analysis Guidebook' (Sage Publications, 2002)
[616] B. Glaser and A. Strauss, 'The Discovery of Grounded Theory' (Aldine, 1967)
[617] Op. cit., Saunders, M. et al., 2016, (n. 519)
[618] Ibid

a trillion pounds should be a genuine concern. Such instances are capable of causing instability in the banking sector and potentially causing a bank to fail. This issue is discussed in Chapter 4.

The effect of the new regulatory control after the crisis may make it more difficult for the banks and Auditors to get away lightly with such practice.

Also, regarding the GDP, there are claims that government agencies' statistics can be biased and influenced by political considerations.

A major work on such criticism came from Harvard-trained economist Prof Diane Coyle of Manchester University in her work, "GDP: A Brief but Affectionate History."[619] Coyle gave an anecdotal reference to the case of Greece, where the government arraigned Greece's Head Statistician before the court for the offence of Treasonable Felony. Greece's government alleged that the Head Statistician understated Greece's GDP, putting the inflow of financial support from the International Monetary Fund at risk. It is as though the figures stated as the GDP by the Head Statistician of Greece were subject to his mood or personal control. Coyle also raised doubts about the factual accuracy of the constituents of the GDP.

First, this researcher accepts that the computation of GDP is not an exact science. Second, the risks of account manipulation do exist. However, one of the important lessons learnt from the failed Bank of Credit and Commerce International (BCCI) in the 1990s was the ability of the bank's Official Liquidator to sue the BCCI auditors for misrepresentation and gross negligence. This was because the auditors signed off on the bank's audited accounts, even when the bank was obviously in turmoil.[620]

The banks under study are all publicly listed companies. However, following the BCCI incident and especially in light of the financial crisis of 2007–2009, greater transparency and scrutiny are now demanded from the banks in the UK. The auditors are made accountable and required to report key elements of the banks' operations directly to the banks' regulators.[621]

For example, Company Act 2006 s. 503 (3) requires that,

> "...the report (Audited Accounts) must be signed by the senior statutory auditor in his own name, for and on behalf of the auditors."

---

[619] D. Coyle 'GDP: A Brief but Affectionate History' (Princeton University Press, 2014)
[620] BCCI (Overseas) Ltd v Price Waterhouse (No 2) [1998] PNLR 564
[621] Royal Bank of Scotland (2017) Annual Financial Accounts for 2016 on page 49

This provision commits a senior partner in a firm to certify that the audited account is an accurate and fair representation of the account audited.

Company Act 2006 s.507 (1) makes it an indictable offence if the auditor knowingly or recklessly allows a report to include any misleading, false or deceptive material in the annual financial report.

A pertinent question is whether external analysts have other credible means of determining the performance trend of banks apart from using their annual financial accounts. The answer is straightforward: no.

In the context of this study, annual reports and financial accounts of the banks are considered to be the most suitable sources of data for this study because these documents contain consolidated accounts of the groups in the banks. In addition, the annual financial accounts and reports have information that cannot be obtained elsewhere. Typically, the annual report contains the chairman's statement, Business Review, Governance, Capital and Risk Management, and Strategic Report given by the Chief Executive Officer of the bank. At the same time, the financial accounts provide information about the independent auditor's report, consolidated income statement, consolidated balance sheet, consolidated cashflow, accounting policies and notes to the accounts.[622]

Company Act 2006 stipulates the information the annual reports and financial accounts must contain and how it must be presented. It makes it obligatory for the directors to prepare a report.[623] The point is that these documents have the backing of the law and are so comprehensive that it is not feasible to obtain the information they contain through any other means. As such, they are the most suitable sources for this study's primary data.

Saunders *et al.* point out that, unlike national governments, non-governmental agencies and corporate bodies with huge resources, individual researchers do not have the resources and the time to collect detailed data sets as could be funded by the government and corporate bodies.[624] For example, some banks in the case studies operate in over fifty countries worldwide. It would be unrealistic to expect a researcher to travel around the globe to collect data in those places solely to conduct a study of this kind.

---

[622] G. Morris, 'UK Accounting Practice'(Lexis Nexis Butterworths, 2005, pages 62–66)
[623] Company Act 2006 s. 380 concerning Accounts and Reports and s.415 Duty to Prepare Director's Report
[624] Op. cit., Saunders, M. et al., 2016, p 316, (n. 519)

Using published accounts and statistics on GDP in the way proposed has drawbacks. Notwithstanding, it is arguably the best evidence available to generate the most comprehensive and near-accurate data for the research undertaken.

Denscombe points out the benefits of official statistics and publications from government agencies as important sources of information for social scientists in the Western world.[625] Denscombe is not in the least suggesting that government reports and publications in Western nations are error-free. However, in the current research, it is not considered that such risks are excessively out of proportion or that the risks are so high as to unduly impede an objective outcome for the study.

An added advantage of using the annual accounts of the banks in the case studies is that the effect of globalisation has brought to the fore the need to have standardised accounting reporting methods and financial reporting regulations styled International Reporting Financial Standards (IRFSs).[626] The benefit of that arrangement to this research is that all the annual financial statements of the banks examined have common features. Also, the accounts share the same format of reporting, which facilitates comparison.

Analysing corporate financial accounts requires distinctive abilities. For example, banks' annual accounts/reports can be voluminous and complex. Banks' financial accounts also have some distinctive features that differentiate them from conventional corporate accounts. For example, the extensive components and layout of the banks' financial statements are strictly regulated, as stated earlier.

This researcher has a strong background in accountancy and financial management at a higher education level, which aided in collating the data and analysing the accounts.

---

[625] Op. cit., M. Denscombe, 2011, n. 551.
[626] Op. cit., Melville, 2015, n. 184.

3.14 Training, Qualifications and Practical Work Experience of the Researcher in Law, Business Management, Economics, Accountancy and Banking & Finance

In addition to being a barrister at law and a corporate lawyer, the researcher has a strong academic background in banking and finance, economics, accountancy and financial management, coupled with about twenty years of work experience in the banking sector.

He is a Fellow of the Chartered Institute of Bankers. He has a PhD and also has a couple of years of legal practice behind him. In addition, the researcher has two master's degrees, one in business management received at the University of Liverpool and the other in law obtained at Manchester Metropolitan University. The additional advantages of conducting this research are the benefit of 'insider's knowledge' on how commercial banks' operations work, supervision within the bank, internal auditing and control mechanisms in the banking system. The experience has been invaluable to this research.

3.15 Ethical Consideration

This research did not require the collection of individuals' personal data, so most of the required data is already in the public domain.

In social investigations, especially concerning health issues, it is recognised that, increasingly, attention is paid to protecting participants in studies by ensuring that suitable measures are in place to safeguard their privacy.[627] This study does not fall within that category of research.

This researcher is mindful of maintaining anonymity and confidentiality as appropriate. He also considered the importance of maintaining an up-to-date reference list to avoid accusations of plagiarism.

3.16 Conclusion

The importance of presenting the enumerated theories to this study is that (i) foremost, they provided a 'shopping list' of arrays of approaches to doing research that this researcher could choose from, (ii) they enabled the researcher to consider what approach might be fit for purpose or not in the context of the

---

[627] Op. cit., M. Denscombe, 2011, (n. 551).

study, (iii) the theories emphasised the need to pay the most careful attention to the research design, that it ensured that the design is suitable for the study, (iv) also, they encouraged the researcher to justify the methods and methodology engaged in data collection, presentation, analysis and their interpretation. This is so that the research product could be impeachable and the study is worth presenting to the academic community and banks' regulators.

Chapter 4
Presentation and Analysis of Data Collated from Banks Selected as Case Studies

4.1 Introduction

This chapter presents data collated from the Annual Reports and Financial Accounts of the four UK banks chosen as case studies. The banks include (i) the Royal Bank of Scotland Plc, (ii) Barclays Plc, (iii) Standard Chartered Bank Plc and (iv) HSBC Plc.

These are banks identified as Global Systemically Important Banks by the Financial Stability Board (FSB).[628] Although the Royal Bank of Scotland made it into the list in 2011, due to the massive reconstruction in RBS, it was excluded in 2019, as well as Lloyds Banking Group.[629] However, given the enormous size of these banks, the collapse of any of them is recognised to be capable of causing systemic catastrophe not only in the UK but the ripple effect potentially spreading globally.

The background issues raised in this chapter's introductory part apply to all four banks chosen as case studies. As such, except where there is a good reason for it, these matters are not repeated when evaluating the financial accounts of the other banks in the separate sections allocated to each of the case studies within this chapter.

First, this researcher considers it a great privilege to access the annual reports and financial accounts of the four banks chosen as case studies. This also serves to emphasise that the products of the examination conducted and comments made about the financial accounts of these banks, whether positive or negative, are purely outputs of an academic exercise to illustrate what, how and why things

---

[628] Op. Cit., Financial Stability Board 2019 list, n. 34.
[629] OP. Cit., Financial Stability Board 2011 list, n. 33.

could go well or go wrong in a huge bank that is internationally active and in light of the aims of this research.

This researcher was not acting as a front for the tax authority, nor did he investigate the bank's books of account as a team member of the UK banking regulators. The intention was not to criticise the banks nor to put doubts in readers' minds about the integrity of the bank, its staff members, and the accounts evaluated, including the auditors.

As such, the comments should not be taken beyond an inquisitive analyst's licence to evaluate how figures stated in one section of the financial statement in the annual financial report corroborated another section. On the other hand, if it was the case, where the data failed to hang together correctly in another area.

This researcher has never been an employee of any of the banks in the case studies. Furthermore, the researcher does not claim to have exhausted all the elements in the financial reports that could be considered relevant to this research.

The data collated and its analysis is integrated within this chapter. This approach was adopted to allow the data and its analysis to flow seamlessly to avoid disruptive forward and backward movements in-between chapters to connect data with the analysis thereof. The annual reports and financial accounts evaluated cover a period of fifteen years, from 2004 to 2018.

The previous chapter explains that over three hundred banks operate in the UK. However, most of the banks are excluded from the ring-fencing policy due to their small size, status as Building Societies, or private banks.

The four banks were selected as case studies because they fall within the range of global systemically important banks and have the level of core deposits that make it mandatory for them to be ring-fencing compliant by 1st January 2019. These banks have aggregate core deposits above £25 billion. They are considered to be in the category of banks that could pose a systemic risk to the economy in the event of their failure.

It should be recognised that some of the banks that fall within the ambit of the ring-fencing policy carry more risks than others. For example, three of the four banks chosen as case studies, the Royal Bank of Scotland, Barclays Plc and HSBC, had assets close to or over two trillion pounds within the period evaluated. Thus, the £25 billion core deposits threshold for those banks is a relatively 'small amount'. The super big banks are the banks that are of immediate concern to the regulatory authorities. These are the banks where their failures could be more difficult to absorb in the economy. They are classified as banks that are too big to fail and too big to rescue in a crisis. These are the kind of banks that the government felt compelled to rescue during the 2007–2009 global financial crisis. Concerns about risks associated with these banks are the reasons that gave birth to the ring-fencing policy in the first instance.

Thus, these are the same reasons that motivated the selection of these banks in the case studies group. The third bank, Standard Chartered Bank, is a middle-level bank in the sense that it is not a small bank considering that it has assets above £500 billion but not close to a trillion pounds as did each of the bigger players. That mid-range size is chosen as part of the case studies to represent that class of banks in the banking sector.

This chapter is divided into four sections, A–D, with each section dealing with information relating to one bank at a time.

The aim is to present the following data in a simple chart form and a digestible narrative format so that even non-expert readers can easily follow the argument and appreciate the significance of the numerical data presented in light of the aims and objectives of the study.

This chapter concerns the fourth objective of the study stated in Chapter 1, pages 8 – 9.

"The study aimed to determine the long-term impacts of the Global Financial Crisis on the performance of some of the largest UK banks up until 2018 and evaluated the financial impact of the regulatory response designed to limit the effects of likely financial crises on the banking sector in the future."

Thus, the financial accounts of the banks were evaluated from 2004–2018. The years 2004–2006 were the good years when huge profits were declared, the period 2007–2009 was in the heat of the crisis, 2010–2012 was when multiple regulatory responses started, 2013–2018 represented the recovery period, and the period of moratorium granted to the banks to prepare for compliance with the ring-fencing policy.

It should be noted that there are occasional instances in the financial accounts of the case studies where, after the balance sheet date, events necessitated the banks to make further reviews, revaluations, reclassifications, and amendments to assets in their financial accounts.

Banks are obliged to present accurate reports about their financial status, which reflect a fair value of their assets, especially when an adverse market environment or new regulation causes impairment to their assets.[630] In the case studies where such changes resulted in a significant adjustment to the financial accounts in the following year, this is taken into account.

For the benefit of external users and investors, Paragraph 27 of International Financial Reporting Standard 5 (IFRS) requires a new measurement basis to be applicable when an asset ceases to be classified as assets held on a 'going concern' basis or when the asset's value is adversely affected by some other circumstances. In this case, the basis of that measurement would be at the lower of the book value or the amount recoverable on the asset.[631] For example, this situation would be applicable where there is an indication of impairment on the assets because of a fall in the assets' market value or new regulations that bring about adverse changes.[632]

The preceding position was adopted in relation to all the banks chosen as case studies.

One clear example concerns the Royal Bank of Scotland's financial accounts for 2017. The financial accounts for that year were significantly altered in a review made in 2018. On that occasion, the recorded **Operating Loss** Before Tax for the 2017 financial year was £1.2 billion[633], and the total assets were stated as £726 billion[634]. In contrast, when the accounts were redrafted the following year, the Operating Loss Before Tax became **Operating Profit** Before Tax of £2.2 billion.[635] That is a change of £3.4 billion.

Similarly, total assets, which were £726 billion in 2017 accounts, increased to £738 billion after adjustments were made to the accounts.[636] This is an increase of £12 billion. This level of change is considered significant enough to warrant

---

[630] R. Ball, 'International Financial Reporting Standards (IFRS): Pros and Cons for Investors' (2006) Vol 36: 5–27 Accounting and Business Research

[631] International Accounting Standards Board (IAS) 'Financial Accounting Foundation: Conceptual Framework for Financial Reporting' (IAS, 2010)

[632] B. Elliott, and J. Elliott, 'Financial Accounting and Reporting 18th Ed' (Pearson, 2017, p. 424)

[633] The Royal Bank Scotland, 'Annual Report and Financial Accounts' (2017, p.82)

[634] Ibid (2017, p. 84)

[635] The Royal Bank of Scotland, 'Annual Report and Financial Accounts' (2018, p.176)

[636] Ibid (2018, p. 178)

being taken into account when evaluating the financial accounts of RBS for those two years. This is referred to in the body of the subsequent analysis. Another reason it is important to consider that level of amendments is that the bank's corporate tax for the 2017 financial year was based on the revised operating profit and not the operating loss previously recorded in the Financial Accounts prepared in 2017.

The same principle was adopted in the extraction of statistics and analysis regarding Barclays Plc in 2012 when the total income, profit before tax and earnings per share were significantly restated for the same reasons. In other instances, where insignificant adjustments were made due to events after the balance sheet date and thus the changed variables were stated differently in the following accounting period, the previously reported figures were left undisturbed in the statistics used. Suppose the changed figures are considered not so significant as to distort the analysis. In that event, it is considered unnecessary to overcomplicate issues moving forward and backwards, adjusting and readjusting data on trivial amendments, more so that the restated figure will inevitably even out itself in the next accounting year.

The general reason behind the approach adopted is to stick with figures that reflect the underlying economic performance of the bank annually while separately dealing with extraordinary items or one-off events that are not typical of the business operation of the bank. This is to avoid distorting or beclouding the bank's actual economic performance in each year under review. An example of that approach is reflected in the fact that this researcher worked more with Operating Profit Before Tax rather than Profit After Tax. Of course, this does not understate the importance of Profit After Tax as a key performance indicator. It only demonstrates due recognition of a wide variety of factors that could influence the computation of company tax, which may not all apply yearly.

Section A — The Royal Bank of Scotland Group

4.2 The Background of the Royal Bank of Scotland Group and the Nature of its Business Model Over Time

The RBS was established in Edinburgh, Scotland, almost 300 years ago in 1727.[637] Ever since the Group Headquarters has remained in Scotland.

RBS's financial year starts on 1 January and ends on 31 December annually. The accounts are denominated in pound sterling. The independent external auditors were Deloitte & Touche LL P, Chartered Accountants and Registered Auditors, Edinburgh. The firm audited RBS accounts for the financial years 2004 to 2015. Also, Ernst & Young LL P, Chartered Accountants and Registered Auditors based in London, served as the independent external auditors for RBS from 2016 to 2018.

It is worth mentioning that following the global financial crisis in 2007–2009 and the subsequent enhanced regulatory requirements, a more onerous burden was imposed on the independent external auditors. As a result, the auditors are to provide a more comprehensive report from their audit on wide-ranging issues. These include specific reports on the financial statement, the accounting report standard used, liquidity and insolvency risks, loan impairment provisions, valuation of complex or illiquid financial instruments, the estimate of future profitability and the audit scope.[638]

These were general weakness areas in the bank's business that nearly led to the total collapse of the bank in the autumn of 2008. Unlike in previous years, when the auditor's report was limited to just about a page or two, the auditor's report in 2016 covered twelve pages. For the period evaluated, there was no adverse report from the auditors.

From the inception of RBS to 1900, the bank grew to 130 branches, though only one branch was opened in London by 1900.[639]

However, the bank's presence became more pronounced in England in the 1920s—1930s, as RBS purchased Glenn, Mills, and William Deacons, an established major commercial bank in England with a vast network of branches.

---

[637] The Royal Bank of Scotland 'Annual Report and Financial Accounts' (RBS, 2005)

[638] The Royal Bank of Scotland 'Annual Report and Financial Accounts' (RBS, 2016, p. 278–289)

[639] Op. Cit., n 608 (RBS, 2005)

Then, in 1970, RBS merged with the National Commercial Bank of Scotland. This strategic acquisition enabled RBS to become the largest bank in Scotland, with over 700 branches in the 1970s.[640]

In the 1980s through to the 1990s, the free-market model and deregulation policy adopted during the Margret Thatcher era allowed RBS to grow even bigger, venturing into the insurance business. For example, in 1985, RBS established Direct Line, a motor vehicle insurance subsidiary.[641] During the famed free markets era, RBS also foraged into the global platform by acquiring Citizen Bank of Rhode Island. In addition, RBS also purchased Charter One and Mellon Bank, which are all in the USA.[642] As the literature review chapter pointed out, this was when the universal banking model started gaining ground in the UK.

From the 1990s to the early 2000s, the business could not have been better for RBS. With the ever-increasing number of branches and customers resulting from organic growth and the acquisition of other financial businesses at home and abroad, RBS took advantage of the giant leap in technological advancement in the 1990s to upgrade their operating systems to a comprehensive Internet banking service by 1997.[643]

In 2000, RBS took the bold step to acquire NatWest Bank in a mega deal of £21 billion, the biggest takeover of its kind in banking history in the UK up to that time. Profitability was at an all-time high in 2005 when the bank recorded an increase in the Group's operating profit by 16% to £8.3 billion from £7.1 billion in the preceding year. In 2005, the group had a total income of £26 billion. Earnings per ordinary share rose by 175.9p. For RBS, the early part of the 2000s were the good years. It was the boom era.

At that time, the unprecedented growth in the number of branches reached 2,278 in 2007,[644] and the numerical strength of their customer base clocked 44 million in 53 countries worldwide.[645] The growth necessitated changes in their banking operating systems. This included re-engineering RBS retail banking

---

[640] ibid

[641] ibid

[642] ibid

[643] Ibid

[644] The Royal Bank of Scotland, 'Annual Report and Financial Accounts' (RBS, 2007, p.15)

[645] Ibid (2007, p.11)

operating procedures and replacing branch handling processes with a preferred centralised business operation. The objective was to strengthen coordination and manage the delivery of efficient services to the widening scope of their clientele. In addition, customers were segmented to facilitate tailor-made services to meet personalised needs.

Apart from the strong organic growth (meaning ploughing the profit made by the Group back into the business), RBS followed a culture of exploiting the benefits of merger and acquisition of other financial businesses for its expansion strategy. This view is strengthened by the earlier purchase of Glenn, Mills and William Deacons in the 1920s, the merger with National Commercial Bank of Scotland in 1970 and entrance into the USA market through the purchase of Citizen Bank of Rhode Island in 1980. Further purchases of other financial businesses in 1990–2000 include Mellon Bank and Charter One, venturing into the insurance business by establishing Direct Line in 1985, as mentioned previously, and subsequent acquisition of Churchill Insurance in 2003 and then Privilege Insurance. For RBS, the icing on the cake was the purchase of NatWest Bank in 2000.

The ever-increasing appetite and aggressive mergers and acquisitions of other financial institutions later proved to be the undoing of RBS. Moreover, some of the institutions purchased were later seen to be overpriced, including ABN AMRO, which had very weak underlying assets.

4.3 Constituents of RSB Group Prior to the Financial Crisis

RBS Group operated a universal banking model comprising the following members:

4.3.1 Insurance Brand (RBS Insurance)

The insurance arm of the business included Direct Line, Churchill, Privilege, Green Flag and NIG.

By 2005, RBS Insurance's policies had increased from 1.6 million to 25.9 million.[646] The RBS insurance arm was the market leader in car insurance, with

---

[646] The Royal Bank of Scotland, 'Financial Accounts' 2005, p. 39.

8.7 million policies, and held the second position in home insurance, with 4.6 million policies.[647]

4.3.2 Wealth Management/Private Banking

This arm of RBS comprised:

(i) Coutts & Co
(ii) Adam & Company

Coutts & Co. was the market leader in providing wealth management and private banking services in the UK, with about 11,000 customers globally.[648] The bank maintained a strong presence in specially selected locations such as Dubai, Monaco, Switzerland, Singapore and Hong Kong, with twenty-three offices.[649,650] Similarly, Adam & Co had relatively few offices. They had only five branches in the UK.

It needs to be emphasised that this niche market focuses on few but exceptionally rich institutions and wealthy individuals globally. This arm of the bank derived its income from managing the wealth of highly valued customers. In relative terms, that arm of the bank does not require extensive branches, a large number of employees or large office spaces, thus reducing overhead costs.

4.3.3 Banks Within the Group

The financial institutions within RBS Group were:

NatWest Bank
RBS Holding (ABN AMRO)
Citizens (USA)
Charter One (USA)
Ulster Bank Group (Ireland)

---

[647] ibid
[648] The Royal Bank of Scotland, 'Financial Accounts', 2007, p. 16.
[649] The Royal Bank of Scotland, 'Financial Account Accounts', 2006, p. 23
[650] The Royal Bank of Scotland, 'Financial Accounts', 2005, p. 76

As pointed out earlier, NatWest was purchased by RBS Group in 2000. ABN Amro was a Dutch bank purchased in 2007.

Charter One and Citizen Bank have a combined corporate and retail banking network that covers about forty states in the USA, including Delaware, Massachusetts, Pennsylvania, Illinois, and Rhode Island.[651]

Through integration, the combination of these two banks made the bank the eighth-largest commercial organisation in the USA in terms of the deposit base. The bank had its 13th consecutive year of record profits in 2004.[652]

Bearing in mind that these banks in the USA were only part of the subsidiaries of RBS stresses the size of RBS and its influence globally at that time.

4.3.4 Strategic Divisions within the RBS Group

For administrative purposes, the RBS had seven divisions before the global crisis. This includes the Corporate Markets, Retail Banking/Commercial Banking, Wealth Management, Citizens and Capital One, Manufacturing, RBS Insurance and Ulster Bank.

The Corporate Markets Division of the bank carried out financial market operations and investment banking roles.

In that role, the Division undertook the following functions:

- Structural finance and financial market products and services
- Acquisition Finance
- Trade Finance
- Leasing
- Factoring
- Treasury services
- Money markets
- Foreign exchange
- Derivatives
- Bond origination and trading
- Sovereign debt trading

---

[651] Ibid (RBS, 2005, p.33)
[652] ibid (RBS, 2005, p. 33)

- Futures brokerage
- Interest rate risk management services

The foregoing is the general background and business model of the RBS Group.

Table 5: Tabulated Data Extracted from the Annual Reports and Consolidated Financial Accounts of the Royal Bank of Scotland Group From 2004–2018 (Financial Year Ending on 31st December Annually)

Year	Total Income £ (b)	Operating Profit Before Tax £ (b)	Total Assets £ (b)	Impairment Charges £ (b)	Branches in the UK	Number of Employees	Earnings Per Share
1	2	3	4	5	6	7	8
2004	23.4	7.3	588	1.5	-	136,600	157.4p
2005	25.9	7.9	777	1.7	2,274	137,000	175.9p
2006	28.0	9.2	871	1.9	2,250	135,000	194.7p
2007	31.1	9.9	1,901	2.1	2,278	226,400	78.7p
2008	25.9	(40.7)	2,402	8.0	-	199,800	-
2009	38.7	(2.6)	1,696	14.0	-	184,500	-
2010	23.7	(0.2)	1,307	9.4	-	113,600	-
2011	21.8	(0.9)	1,433	7.2	-	113,700	-
2012	17.9	(5.6)	1,312	5.3	-	137,200	-
2013	19.8	(6.8)	1,020	8.4	-	106,100	-
2014	15.2	(2.7)	1,051	1.4*	-	110,027	-
2015	12.9	(2.7)	815	0.8*	-	93,659	-
2016	12.6	(4.0)	799	0.5	-	77,900	-
2017	13.1	2.2	738	0.5	-	69,700	6.3p
2018	13.4	3.4	694	0.4	-	65,400	13.5p

Dividend Per Share	Total Deposit £ (b)	Total Loan £ (b)	Contribution Corporate Market £ (b)	Contribution Insurance £ (b)	Contribution Wealth Management £ (b)
9	10	11	12	13	14
52.5p	383	408	4.2	0.9	0.3
72.5p	453	488	5.2	1.0	0.4
77.3p	516	549	6.1	1.0	0.3
33.2p	995	1,049	5.6	0.9	0.4
-	898	1,013	(8.7)	0.8	0.4
-	756	820	5.7	0.06	0.4
-	558	606	3.2	-	0.3
-	581	587	1.5	-	0.3
-	623	564	1.5		0.3
-	537	506	0.7		0.3
-	452	421	-	-	-
-	408	364	-	-	-
-	420	382	-	-	-
-	392	322	-	-	-
13p	384	318	-	-	-

4.4 The Constituents of Table 5

Table 5 is the tabulated data extracted from the Annual Reports and Financial Accounts of RBS Group for fifteen years, from 2004 to 2018. **Appendix 1,** at the back of this report, references the page numbers in each year's Annual Report and Financial Accounts of RBS Group, indicating where the numerical data were extracted.

While some columns on the Table provide complete data on the variables, others do not. The 'incomplete' information regarding such columns is mainly due to structural readjustment in the methods of operation of the Group's businesses over the years, which necessitated merging some of the Divisions within the Group that previously existed independently and whose accounts were reported separately. In other instances, the provision of the data stopped, including, for example, information on the number of branches. A fuller explanation is provided in the section that provides written explanations of the significance of the data collated. It specifies what the numbers on the Table mean or represent, their relationships with one another (if there is any relationship) and how the data answers the study's objectives.

Meanwhile, **Figures 5–10** below are graphical presentations in Chart forms relating to the same information contained within Table 5. The Charts are designed to provide a visual aid indicating a visible trend of developments or lack thereof regarding the defined variables for fifteen years.

Beneath each chart is a summary of the information contained in the chart. They are aids to see at a glance what the charts illustrate. The scales of the **'x and y'** axes are listed in Appendices 5 to 10 at the back of this report.

Figure 5: RBS Group: The Relationship Between Income and Profit Before Tax 2004–2018

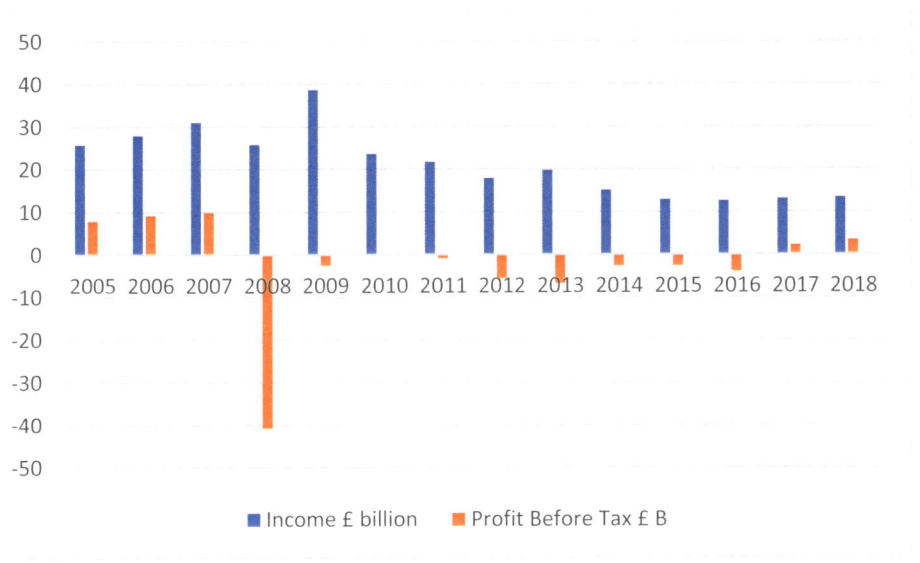

Fig 5 relates to columns 2 and 3 of Table 5. Income peaked at about £39 billion in 2009. After that, it started to decline to an average of about £13 billion from 2015 to 2018. Similarly, from 2004 to 2007, RBS recorded a PBT of about £8 billion. From 2008, RBS continued to declare operating losses for nine consecutive years until it broke even in 2017 and 2018. The highest operating profit was about £10 billion in 2007, immediately followed by the largest operating loss of £40 billion in 2008.

Figure 6: RBS Group: The Relationship Between Assets, Deposits and Loans 2004–2018

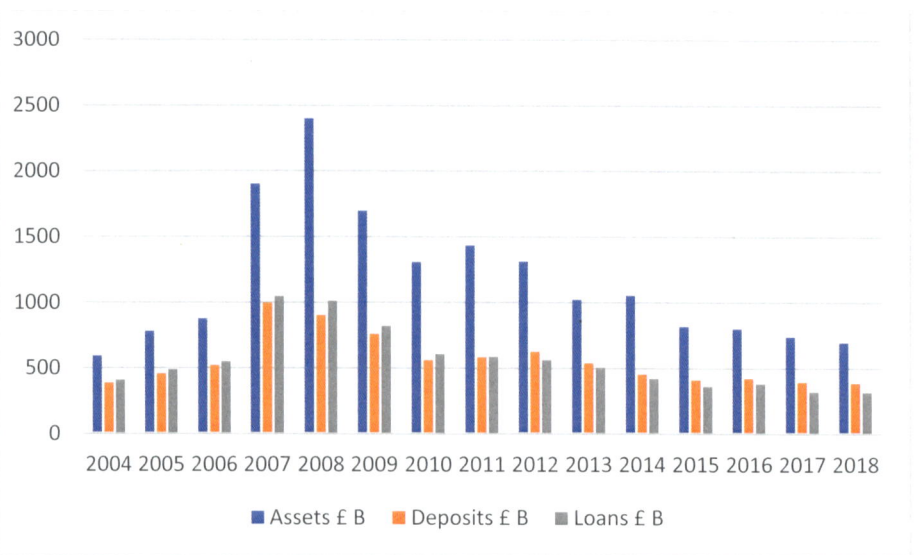

Figure 6 is concerned with columns 4 (Assets), column 10 (Deposits) and column 11 (loans) on Table 5. The assets grew rapidly from a modest £588 billion in 2004 to £2.4 trillion in only four years to 2008. Subsequently, from 2009 onward, the assets declined almost steadily until they reduced to just about £700 billion in 2018. This was due to divestment and a downward review of overstated derivative assets between 2008 and 2009. From 2004 to 2010, Loans exceeded Deposits, indicating poor liquidity. Liquidity only started to improve in 2011.

Figure 7: RBS Group: Trend of Growth/Decline in the Total Assets 2004–2018

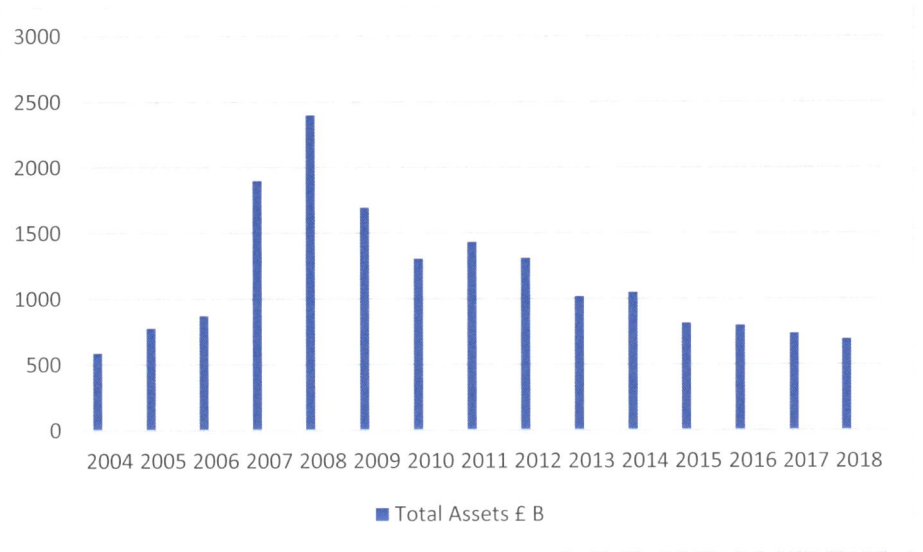

Figure 7 is concerned with column 4, relating to the growth and decline of assets. Total assets climaxed at £2.4 trillion in 2008 but continued downward as the bank began restructuring and divesting.

Figure 8: RBS Group: The Percentage of Contribution of Earnings From the Investment Banking to the Profit Before Tax 2004–2013

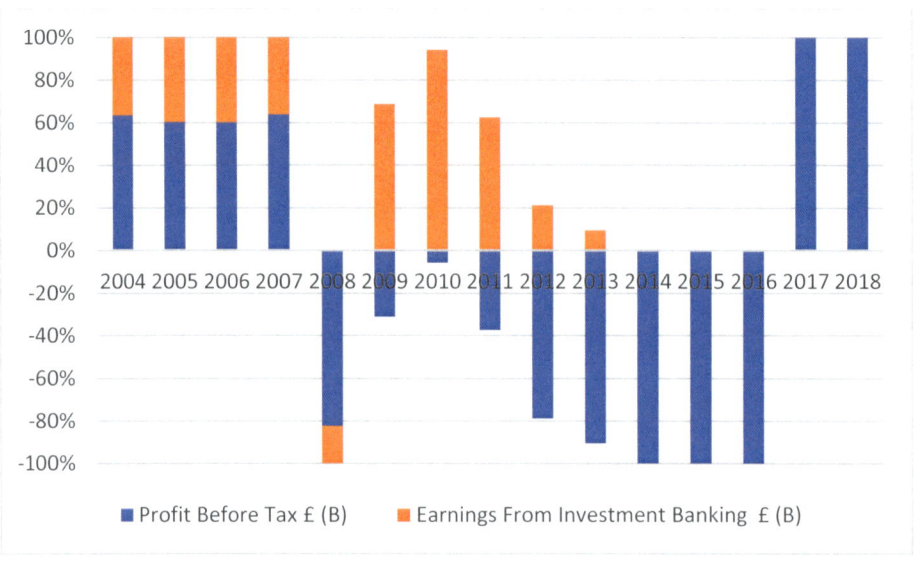

Figure 8 is concerned with PBT column 3 and column 12 relating to contributions from investment banking to the PBT. Except in 2008, when the Corporate Market made a loss, from 2004 to 2013, the Division contributed more than half of the PBT earned by the Group.

Figure 9: RBS Group: Impairment Charges 2004–2018

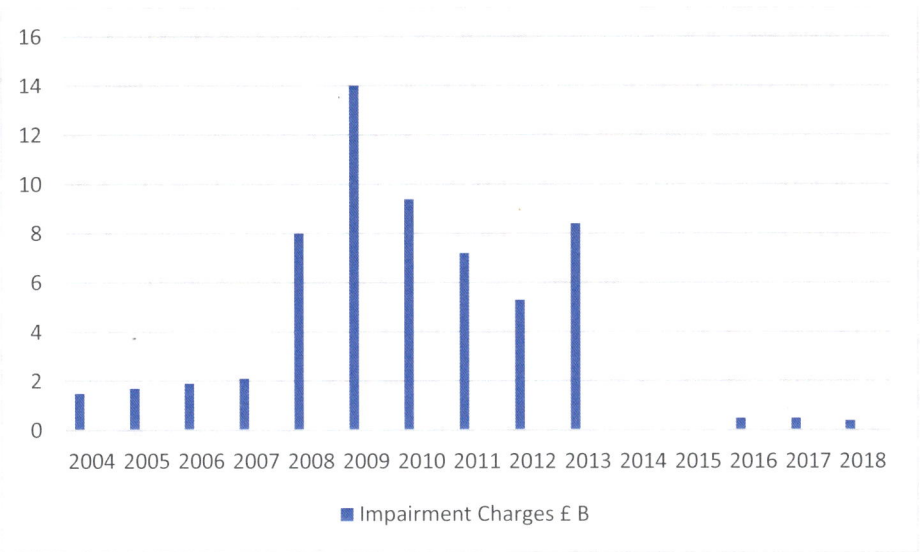

Figure 9 is about column 5 on the Table relating to impairment charges. Impairment charges are the amounts set aside from the annual profit of RBS to defray potential losses or demurrage that may arise from assets held by the bank. In addition to that are non-performing loans and overdraft accounts. While such charges were fairly consistent and moderate from 2004–2007 and 2016–2018, the sum charged to the Profit and Loss account in 2008–2013 was remarkably high, reflecting the turbulent time that RBS faced in those years and due to the poor quality of its assets/nonperforming loans.

Figure 10: RBS Group: Trend of Growth/Decline in the Employees' Profile from 2005–2018.

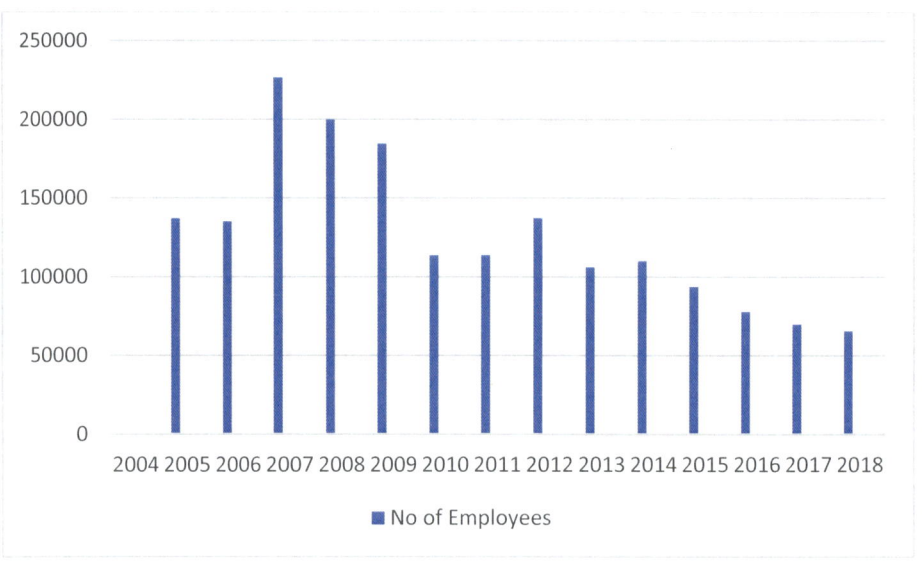

Figure 10 concerns the number of staff employed globally by RBS from 2005 to 2018. In 2007 the number of staff employed globally was at its highest when the bank engaged about 227,000 people, but by 2018, the number had reduced to a mere 66,000 staff members.

4.5 Analysis and Interpretation of Extracted Information Collated from the Annual Financial Accounts of the Royal Bank of Scotland in the Light of the Aim and Objectives of the Study

Table 5 comprises fourteen columns, with the characteristics of each column defined in the headings. The Table is a numeric extract of key indices about the annual performance of the Royal Bank of Scotland Group for fifteen years, from 2004 to 2018, as indicated in the first column.

2004–2006 Accounts

In 2004–2006, operating income grew moderately; in relative terms, it was proportionate to the increase in the assets. The operating income of £23.4 billion in 2004 increased to £25.9 billion in 2005 (11% increase) and subsequently increased to £28 billion in 2006 (8% growth). The Profit Before Tax in that same period maintained a similar growth pattern, the bank having made £7.3 billion, £7.9 billion and £9.2 billion in 2004, 2005 and 2006, respectively. After that, however, the asset level started showing signs of galloping increase, rising from £588 billion in 2004 to £871 billion in 2006 (48% increase).

The number of employees at an average of 136 000 for the three years remained within the bank's usual business range. As a result, DPS and EPS were consistent in the three years. Moreover, except that total loans exceeded the deposit balance in the three years under review, generally the period's statistics remained reasonable compared with what later happened in the accounts.

2007–2009 Accounts

This was when the global financial crisis took place. As a result, although the bank declared increasing income, which rose from £28 billion in 2006 to £31.1 billion in 2007 and to £38.7 billion in 2009, total costs eroded all the gains. As a result, 2008 ended up with an operating loss before tax of £40.7 billion, the UK's highest declared loss in corporate history.

From 2006 to 2008, the asset increased by almost 300% to £2.4 trillion. In 2009, impairment charges climbed to a phenomenal proportion at £14 billion against £1.9 billion charge in 2006, £2.1 billion in 2007 and £8 billion in 2008. The number of employees reached its highest level of 226,400 in 2007. As the bank rolled in losses from 2008 to 2016, the bank could not pay dividends for nine consecutive years. Signs of liquidity problems persisted till 2012, when the deposits' account balances only started to exceed the loan aggregate. Part of the reasons for the unprecedented operating loss in 2008 was the exposed weaknesses in the banks' assets and the writing down of goodwill (intangible assets) by about £33 billion.[653] Obligations under IFRS 5 require RBS to state its assets at fair value. The inclement economic environment, the all-time low

---

[653] The Royal Bank of Scotland, 'Annual Report and Financial Accounts' (2008, p.174)

interest rate and the artificial bloating of the derivative assets necessitated the downward revaluation of the assets, especially the goodwill.

In the particular instance of RBS, the bank's strength in its centuries of banking business operation was its policy of buying up other financial businesses for its growth through mergers and acquisitions.[654] Unfortunately, this also proved to be the bank's greatest undoing in the years leading to the 2007–2009 global financial crisis after RBS, in conjunction with Fortis and Santander, purchased ABN Amro for about $98.3 billion. The transaction's timing could not have been worse, and the price and payment method were criticised as complicit in the ruinous deal.[655]

After RBS ran into difficulties in 2008 and bailed out with taxpayers' funds, questions were asked as to why such a huge commitment to buy up ABN Amro in a consortium with others was not subjected to the scrutiny and approval of the bank's supervisors and independent assessors. Part of the lessons learnt from the crisis is that a deal at that level would now necessarily be brought to the attention of the bank's supervisors and independent assessors. As a result, they must pay close attention to the prudential risks involved before agreeing to such acquisitions going through in the future.[656]

The weaknesses of the underlying nonperforming assets in RBS reflect the exorbitant provisions made for impairment charges in 2009. In addition, the derivative assets were exaggerated due to distortions in the market prices at the time.

In August 2008, following an announcement of a half-year pre-tax loss of £691 million by RBS, the company also owned up to the fact that due to some error in the pricing of their derivative assets, the balance on the account was overstated and required a write-down.[657] Consequently, in 2009, the derivative asset was eventually written down by a staggering sum of about £600 billion. This declaration led to widespread indignation and a general public mistrust against RBS.

The group's asset of £2.4 trillion as of 2008 has since been criticised as grossly exaggerated through the group's derivative account.

---

[654] The Royal Bank of Scotland, 'Annual Report and Financial Accounts' (2007)
[655] Op. Cit., (Financial Services Authority, December 2011, p 159, (n. 155)
[656] Ibid. (Financial Services Authority, December 2011, p 264)
[657] Op. cit., Financial Services Authority, December 2011, pp 318–319, (n. 149)

The positions of the Derivatives Account Balances for five years are as stated below:

2006 £117 billion P. 140 RBS Group Accounts
2007 £337 billion p. 121
2008 £992 billion p. 175
2009 £441 billion p. 243
2010 £429 billion P. 128

Looking, at the figures, it is very disturbing that a conservative balance of £117 billion in 2006 suddenly grew to almost one trillion pounds in assets in 2008. This is more so because auditors did not pick up issues with it.

Also, part of the difficulties RBS Group faced from 2009 to 2016 arose from the stringent conditions attached to the financial support package the bank received from the government during the crisis. These incidents did not only affect RBS Group's performance adversely, they almost crippled the bank altogether.

In October 2008, RBS received a lifeline capital injection of £20 billion from the UK government and an additional £19 billion equity stake.[658] As a prerequisite for taking the bailout package, the European Commission imposed a four-year divestment programme on RBS Group, starting from November 2009. The requirement to dismantle RBS subsidiaries had a limited timeframe of only four years, starting from 2009. This led to selling some of RBS's branch networks worldwide, including in England, Wales and Scotland.[659] Apart from the requirement to divest, RBS did not meet the new regulatory capital requirements. As such, RBS had to divest to recapitalise.

The divestment programme led to the sale of Citizens Financial Group, the US arm of the RBS Group. It also led to the downsizing of the RBS global market, resulting in the group's decimation from a £2.4 trillion business group to a mere £700 billion company by 2018.

2010–2013 Accounts

Following the downsizing of RBS, operating income continued to slide from £38.7 billion in 2009 to £23.7 billion in 2010 and subsequently to £21.8 billion,

---

[658] Op. Cit., J Goddard et al., 2009, (n. 466).
[659] The Royal Bank of Scotland, 'Annual Report and Financial Accounts' (2009, p. 4)

£17.9 billion and £19.8 billion in 2011, 2012 and 2013, respectively. The operating loss before tax continued to remain a cause for concern. It was getting worse, with losses rolling over from 2010–2013 and subsequent years till 2016. There was a £200 million loss in 2010, £900 million in 2011, £5.6 billion in 2012 and worse still, £6.8 billion in 2013. Notwithstanding, as reflected by the financial accounts for 2012, core banking operations remained profitable, making £6.3 billion OPBT, and commercial banking also yielded £5.3 billion. Sadly, all these profits were wiped out by other costs.

Given the huge amount of impairment provisions made between 2008 to 2013, it may be fair to say that this reflected the poor quality of the assets, including subprime assets and other non-performing facilities. Some of the difficulties that the RBS faced then included the inclement business environment of that time and the poor quality of the assets that gave rise to colossal impairment charges and divestments that resulted in substantial losses. So in addition, there were charges, penalties, and an all-time low interest rate, especially the low-income generation on mortgages in the period under review.

The adverse impact of low mortgage rates was hugely reflected in the poor economic performance of banks when related to a widespread hike in commercial banks' investments in the expansion of mortgage lending during the property boom era in the pre-crisis period. The investment in mortgage facilities later became a burden as they were not earning a commensurate yield on the level of banks' commitment to the mortgage assets.[660]

By 2013, the RBS's assets had come down to £1.020 trillion through downward asset revaluation and asset disposals. The total number of employees decreased by over half to 106,000 as of 2013. There was a slight improvement in the relationship between deposits and loan accounts as deposits increased to £623 billion against a reduction in loans to £564 billion.

Due to the massive public fund of about £45 billion injected into the RBS, there was public outrage and agitation to redress the problems in RBS. This was a top priority at that time. As a result, from 2008 to 2013, RBS witnessed some changes in their management. However, the bank continued to remain under the keen attention of the regulators.

---

[660] J. Cullen, 'Securitisation, Ring-fencing, and Housing Bubbles: Financial Stability Implications of UK and EU Bank Reforms, (2018) Vol, 4 (473–118) Journal of Financial Regulation.

In a 452-page report produced by the defunct Financial Services Authority in December 2011, the then banking sector regulator summarised their findings on the causes of the failure of RBS to six major issues. These include a string of poor management decisions made by an ineffective governing body of the RBS. Second, the global regulatory capital framework tolerated an inadequate capital level before the crisis. Third, there were issues with the excessive reliance on short-term wholesale funding, which covered up for the insufficient liquidity in the bank. Poor asset quality was not previously subjected to any analysis by the supervisory authority. The last straw was the ruinous acquisition of ABN Amro without the exercise of due diligence and the flawed or absence of an effective supervision approach adopted by the regulatory authority at that time.[661]

2014–2018

In this period, operating income came to its all-time low at £12.9 billion in 2015, £12.6 billion in 2016, £13.1 billion in 2017 and £13.4 billion in 2018. The reason for this is not farfetched. There has been considerable restructuring through demergers and substantial divestments. There were relatively poor earnings from the assets due to non-performing loans, and the interest rate was also very low. In addition, there was pressure on the banks on the need to increase their capital and boost their liquidity position.

On a positive note, since 2007, the bank had a positive PBT of £2.2 billion in 2017 and £3.4 billion in 2018. In addition, impairment charges came down to about £500 million annually from 2016 to 2018, whilst the bank had a reprieve and managed to recoup £1.4 billion in 2014 and £800 million in 2015 out of some of the previously written-off bad debts. The total number of employees came down to 65,400 from a peak of 226,400. For the first time since 2007, the bank managed to declare dividends of 13p.

From 2016 to 2018, RBS became a very 'lean' organisation, with the balance sheet value massively reduced from £2.4 trillion to a 'mere' £700 billion business.

RBS Group reached a point in 2017/2018 when the company decided to retire some of the state aid previously given to boost the equity capital of RBS. As stated earlier, in these two years, RBS recorded a positive operating profit of £2.2

---

[661]Op. Cit., Financial Services Authority, December 2011, pp 21–22, (n. 155).

billion and £3.4 billion, respectively. This was the first time RBS had a bottom-line net profit in ten years. Bottom-line net profit in this context means net profit after taking into account all charges, deductions, appropriations, amortisation and taxes. Thus, in June 2018, the bank redeemed 925 million Class B ordinary shares worth £2.5 billion, which the government held through the Her Majesty's Treasury.[662]

Column 6 on Table 5 relates to the number of branches of the RBS Group in the UK. Only in three years was the numerical strength of the branches of RBS Group featured in the financial reports. From 2005 to 2007, the Group had about 2,300 branches locally. At that time, the large number of branches was a mark of the success and strength of the bank. However, the requirement to downsize and sell off some of the branches of RBS Group due to the bank obtaining state assistance and other business exigencies, including the need to improve liquidity, necessitated some branches' disposal. Scaling down its branches for these reasons de-emphasised the importance of an extensive branch network in the bank's financial reports.

Also, technology improved so that many banking transactions could be carried out using online facilities and mobile telephone applications, dispensing with the need to attend bank branches physically. So, the importance of a large number of branches declined. In order to indicate the widespread usage of internet-based and online services, RBS reported that about three-quarters of active RBS customers are regular digital users, and the digital lending platform allows customers to apply digitally for secured and unsecured loans of £750,000, subject to eligibility criteria.[663]

Column 12 is related to investment banking contribution. Corporate market consistently contributed to the PBT at an average of £5 billion for about five years. However, the division also sustained a massive loss of £8.7 billion in 2008.

Under the new regulations, RBS was under intense pressure to improve its liquidity and equity capital, just like other banks. Other than making efforts to raise capital from new issues, which RBS attempted, but to improve liquidity and equity capital at the RBS, a rational thing would be to fall back on the non-core banking assets. This required selling off as appropriate and using the proceeds from such disposal to support liquidity and prop up the capital base. Taking such

---

[662] The Royal Bank of Scotland, 'Annual Report and Financial Accounts' (2018, p. 6)
[663] Ibid, RBS Financial Accounts' (2018, p. 9)

a strategic route is in addition to the requirement to divest as part of the conditions for taking State aid.

In March 2015, citing the Financial Times, an Australian Business tabloid, Business Insider, reported RBS's plan to massively scale down its investment banking arm by laying off 14,000 of its 18,000 investment banking jobs.[664]

Column 13 contains the available statistics on the insurance division's contributions. For six years, the division generated an average of £0.8 billion annually.

Column fourteen is concerned with private banking services provided to super-rich customers. At first sight, an annual contribution of £400 million may appear small in the grand scheme of a bank with assets of about £700 billion. However, the significance of this £400 million net contribution can be appreciated more when considering that this bank division involves a relatively small group of customers. This niche market does not require an elaborate branch network, huge operating capital and large numbers of staff. This arm of the banking operation did not close but merged with the retail banking/commercial banking division of RBS.

4.6 Conclusions: Final Review on the Performance of RBS in the Light of the Aim of the Study

Evaluating the annual reports and financial accounts of RBS for fifteen years (2004–2018) reveals a taste of the sweetness of success when banking operations were going well. However, it also demonstrates all that could possibly go wrong in a mega bank, the crippling price of failure and the long hard road to recovery.

At the pinnacle of RBS's success in 2007 (if it could be called that), RBS Group served about 44 million customers worldwide.[665] This is more than double the number of customers RBS had in 2005. RBS' business operations extended to fifty-three countries across Asia-Pacific, Europe and America, with a combined population of about 3.4 billion people and a total regional GDP of

---

[664] L. Brinded, 'RBS Plans to Cut a Shocking Amount of Investment Banking Jobs' Business Insider, (2015)
https://www.businessinsider.com.au/rbs-plans-to-cut-a-shocking-amount-of-its-investment-bank-jobs-2015-3

[665] The Royal Bank of Scotland, 'Annual Report and Financial Accounts' (2007, p. 11)

about $28 trillion.[666] In 2008, RBS' assets hit £2.4 trillion, with employees reaching over 220,000 worldwide. Such was RBS' status that the bank became the focus of serious attention by the UK government and the European authorities. This was more so because RBS' assets were only £588 billion four years earlier but rapidly grew to £2.4 trillion in a short time. It could be argued that perhaps RBS took on itself too much too quickly.

In hindsight, Fred Goodwin's tenure of office from 2000 to 2008 was characterised by an aggressive drive for mergers and acquisitions, some of which were unprofitable. Moreover, the CEO was accused of adopting an overbearing leadership style that saw rational questioning of some of his positions on management issues as an unwanted opposition. In addition, he was accused of having an inordinate pursuit of global influence, desirous of RBS competing at the highest level with giant global banks.

Ultimately, this drive made RBS grow big too quickly and temporarily become the world's largest bank in 2007.[667] However, the bank crashed badly almost before it reached the top. Worse still, the erstwhile CEO was accused of actively encouraging and handsomely rewarding aggressive development, promoting sales of financial products. Some of these products were later considered dubious, such as the PPI insurance that added virtually nothing in real value to the customers.[668] Although the immediate reward of those activities brought the share price of RBS from £4 in 2000 when Fred Goodwin took over to £18 at the height of his popularity, by the time he left, the share price had tumbled down to 67p and with it, bundles of unending litigation costs, penalties and fines which in 2014 alone gulped £9 billion.[669]

As stated in the literature review chapter, Admati thought that Basel's generally prevalent prescribed equity capital level was the major issue with the high-impact banks during the period leading to the crisis and its aftermath. The FSA's report on RBS' failure amply demonstrated that Basel I and Basel II on capital requirements were deeply flawed and inadequate for high-impact banks.

The FSA admitted its failure as it paid little or no attention to evaluating the equity capital levels among globally relevant banks before the crisis. Neither was

---

[666] ibid

[667] L. Brinded, 'The Sorry History of the Near-destruction of Investment Banking at RBS (2015)

[668] Ibid.

[669] The Royal Bank of Scotland, 'Annual Report and Financial Accounts' (2014, p.7)

FSA mindful of subjecting the quality of the bank's assets to any critical review. In this wise, the fault line in RBS' accounts only started to emerge following the financial meltdown in the autumn of 2008 when RSB faced liquidity pressure and had to be rescued by the State through a bailout financial package.

Huge impairment expenses on nonperforming loans also started to emerge in staggering proportion from 2008–2013, when the annual cost of impairment charges peaked at £14 billion, as indicated in Table 5 column 5. Similarly, regarding a benchmark of an acceptable liquidity level, even in the so-called good years when RBS was making a substantial profit, total loans always exceeded deposits, as indicated in columns 10 and 11 in Table 5. This situation led to RBS' dependency on wholesale market funds to cover its back for liquidity needs until that source suddenly dried up, exposing RBS' years of dangerous walking on edge.

The immediate cause of the bank's near failure in October 2008 was that RBS ran out of direly needed cash resources to continue in business. Nevertheless, in the reaction of the wholesale funding market to the large-scale accumulated losses incurred by the bank, there was a growing concern as to whether the bank had the capacity to continue to bear the growing losses.[670] As a result, there were doubts about RBS's ability to remain in business. So, in a chain of events starting with the short-term money market freeze on 9 August 2007 and ending with the freefall of the share price of RBS by 35% between 12 May and 2 June 2008, the wholesale funding providers generally became reticent to provide further assistance to RBS.

The case for RBS worsened following an announcement of a half-year pre-tax loss of £691 million on 8th August 2008. This was due to a credit market write-down of £5.9 billion. By the 7th of October 2008, the situation had reached a critical emergency, direly needing immediate cash resources to continue in the business.[671]

Under these desperate circumstances, the UK government intervened by requiring Fred Goodwin to step down as the bank's CEO.

In 2005, Sir George Matthewson, the then Group Chairman, said the bank had no further plans for large acquisitions. However, according to him, the bank remained open to evaluating such opportunities if and when they arose.[672]

---

[670] Op. Cit., Financial Services Authority, December 2011, (n. 155)

[671] Op. Cit., Financial Services Authority, December 2011, pp 318–319, (n. 155)

[672] The Royal Bank of Scotland, 'Annual Report and Financial Accounts' (2005, p.4)

In the late 1990s and early 2000s, before their situation deteriorated, RBS maintained a high level of efficiency across the group, reaping the benefits of economies of scale from acquisitions and integration of the financial institutions acquired by the group. This invariably yielded much more profit for the group than anticipated at acquisitions of the financial institutions.[673] However, RBS indeed made many mistakes, and the FSA acquiesced to those mistakes because the FSA failed to follow up on any of the key areas of banking supervision as they should have. This is attested to by their report on the failure of the RBS.

The FSA did not pay well-deserved attention to the bank's governance. They did not handle issues around equity capital and liquidity. They paid little or no attention to prudential issues and matters around asset quality.

The argument is that these failings did not happen overnight or have to happen. Arguably, the leadership of RBS at the time of the crisis was wholly responsible for the near collapse of the bank and no one else. Moreover, many other banks did not encounter the difficulties that RBS encountered. One such bank is Standard Chartered Bank. Notwithstanding the size and spread of HSBC, the bank also stood the test of time during the crisis. It is not the case that they were not affected by the GFC, and it is not that they did not have their record of failings, but they did not take a government bailout.

On a positive note, the implication of the changes in the circumstances of RBS is that the ring-fencing policy and newly introduced capital and liquidity regulations, coupled with the new supervisory architecture, would most likely make RBS safer. However, the bank may still witness more contractions in their business activities due to taking the ring-fenced bank out of the mainstream non-ring-fenced bank. This would invariably adversely affect the bank's profitability because of the forfeiture of the benefits of economies of scale that would naturally arise due to the ring-fencing policy.

The ring-fenced bank carved out of RBS may be able to carry out corporate financing. However, it is doubtful whether both organisations, as separate entities, would be able to meet the enormous needs of big conglomerate customers as RBS did in its prime.

As pointed out earlier, the risky part of investment banking should be removed from the mainstream/non-ring-fenced bank rather than the core depositors' accounts.

---

[673] Ibid (The Royal Bank of Scotland, 2005, p 4)

Before the global financial crisis set in, an example of the benefits of a large-scale operation to the bank, which greatly enhanced the profitability of RBS and provided a host of add-on benefits to the economy, is found in the Group's annual accounts for 2006.

In a consortium arrangement, RBS collaborated with other financiers to grant £750 million facilities to Pendragon, a national motor retailer group in Birmingham. In the same period, a £450 million revolving facility was granted to a Yorkshire company, Croda, towards the acquisition of Uniquema. Mitchells & Butlers, a pub and restaurant operator, benefited from a £2 billion facility to fund strategic acquisitions. In addition, RBS provided Barchester Healthcare with a structured facility of £1 billion. Similarly, a £300 million revolving credit facility was granted to Manchester Airport and £30 million to SBS Marine to acquire about six vessels. WA Developments Group, which includes the UK's largest haulage company, Eddie Stobart, benefited from invoice finance and refinancing packages to assist the group's growth.[674]

These are just a few examples of business organisations that got massive funding from the RBS Group with an aggregate sum of about £4.5 billion in just one year. In light of the evidence presented from the RBS Group accounts, this researcher posits that a restriction from accessing core retail deposit accounts as it is currently is unhelpful to RBS, its customers and the economy, notwithstanding that ring-fenced banks can perform corporate lending.

Even if ring-fenced banks can carry out corporate lending involving invoice financing, consortium lending and leases to facilitate the acquisition of capital-intensive assets such as vessels and aircraft, the resources available to a ring-fenced bank may still not be adequate to meet these demanding services. Where ring-fenced banks are allowed to carry out corporate banking, as pointed out in the literature review, like other banks, it would need to build up adequate equity capital and liquidity sufficient to meet the demands of multinational companies in need of substantial financial support.

The argument is that without the benefit of gaining access to retail deposits, it would not be feasible to provide such high-level assistance to those organisations mentioned. The multiplier effects of the large-scale support to those organisations can be estimated by calculating the number of people who gained employment in those

---

[674] The Royal Bank of Scotland, 'Annual Report and Financial Accounts' (2006, p 17)

organisations, taxes paid at various levels, the improved scale of operations and the potential increase in profitability across those organisations in addition to the resultant growth in the economy.

It is not the case that Manchester Airport, Pendragon, etc., cannot get alternative funding sources, but the question is, at what cost? A possible alternative to sourcing huge finance is to approach the capital market. However, this could be much more expensive and arguably more complex, involving underwriters, accountants, specialist legal services, and other onerous requirements at the primary stock market.

On the other hand, with access to retail banking deposits, the cost of capital would understandably be cheaper. These benefits would, in turn, be passed on to the borrower, leading to cheaper and possibly better services to the end users. Losing out on that benefit is part of the costs of the ring-fencing policy.

It may be argued that the operation of universal banking that included multifaceted financial services was not the only cause of the crisis in 2007–2009. Poor supervision of the banking sector and defective regulation hugely contributed to the problems. Universal banking has been practised successfully in France and Germany for over a hundred years.[675]

Although following the global financial crisis in 2007–2009, the USA enacted the Dodd-Frank Act in 2010, which has similar characteristics to the Glass-Steagall Act 1933, a significant part of the Dodd-Frank Act was repealed in 2017 with the coming into force of the Financial Choice Act 2017. Moreover, the European Union neighbours refused to adopt the ring-fencing policy in the same way as the UK. That means that the foremost banks in the UK would be at a disadvantage competing with the banks in Europe and America that are not subject to the ring-fencing policy. Worse still, at additional costs, multinational corporations in the UK with huge financial needs may have to seek financial assistance from multiple sources instead of dealing with just one or relatively few banks where complications arising from perfecting security against loans and advances can be minimised.

---

[675] Op. Cit., R. Cranston, 2002, n. 210.

Section B: Barclays Plc (Group Accounts)

4.7 Barclays Plc: Historical Background, Size and Structure of the Bank

Barclays Group is a public limited liability company registered in England and Wales. Its registered office is 1 Churchill Place, London E14 5HP.

The bank's financial year starts on 1 January and ends on 31 December annually. The accounts are denominated in pound sterling. The external auditors were PricewaterhouseCoopers LL P, Chartered Accountants, London, UK, and KPMG LL P, Chartered Accountants, 15 Canada Square, London E14 5GL.

By assets, Barclays Plc is the second-largest bank in the UK and the 20th-biggest bank worldwide as of 2018/2019.[676] Due to its huge size, Barclays was considered one of the financial institutions that posed a systemic risk to the economy if it collapsed.[677, 678] At the bank's zenith in 2008, Barclays Plc's assets stood at £2.1 trillion.[679] The bank had about 160,000[680] employees globally, and in 2008, the bank had 1,733 branches across the UK. By 2009,[681] it served about 48 million customers globally.[682]

Barclays had a very humble beginning. Barclay's highly inspiring and rich history began in April 1690 when a 21-year-old man, John Freame of Cirencester in Gloucestershire, veered from his family's textile merchant occupation venturing into the goldsmith/banking business on Lombard Street, London.[683] In the formative years of the bank, the original partners were Quakers whose uppermost business pursuit and ethos were then focused on gaining and protecting the trust of the English merchants of their time.[684]

---

[676] Please see Table 3 on page 113, https://fxssi.com/top-20-largest-world-banks-in-current-year Accessed 22/4/2020

[677] Barclays Bank Plc, 'Annual Report and Financial Accounts' (2006, p. 8)

[678] Op. Cit., Financial Stability Board, 2019, (n. 34).

[679] Barclays Plc, 'Annual Report and Financial Accounts' (2008, p. 205)

[680] Ibid (2008, p.23)

[681] Barclays Plc, 'Annual Report and Financial Accounts' (2009, p.4)

[682] Barclays Plc, 'Annual Report and Financial Accounts' (2008, p.4)

[683] M. Ackrell, and L. Hannah, 'Barclays the Business of Banking: 1690–1996' (Cambridge University Press, 2001)

[684] Barclays Plc, 'Annual Report and Financial Accounts' (2015, p.6)

Over time, Barclays went through different registration status and name change phases. The bank was named Barclays & Company Ltd when it was first incorporated as a company limited by shares on the 20th of July 1896 in England and Wales under the Companies Act 1862 to 1890.[685] However, the bank changed its name to Barclays Bank Plc on 1st January 1985 when it acquired public limited liability (Plc) status pursuant to the Barclays Bank Act 1984.[686]

Since 2018, the bank's new structure comprised a newly incorporated Barclays Bank UK Plc, the ring-fenced bank formed due to the Banking Reform Act 2013. Barclays Bank Plc comprised its International Division, the Head Office and the Treasury Functions Division. The ring-fenced bank, Barclays Bank UK Plc and Barclays Bank Plc operate alongside each other, but they are independent in line with the ring-fencing policy. Barclays Bank UK Plc, Barclays Services Ltd and Barclays Bank Plc are all subsidiaries of Barclays Plc.[687]

The ring-fenced bank, Barclays Bank UK Plc, was incorporated on 19th August 2015 with registration number 09740322. The implication is that, though the ring-fenced bank is part of the Group, it is economically independent, so the group members cannot rely on the funds in the ring-fenced bank. It has a separate board independent of the group. The ring-fenced bank, as a separately incorporated entity, is legally obligated to file its separate returns to the Company House in addition to the returns filed along with the consolidated group accounts of the group members.[688]

4.8 The Nature of Barclays' Business Model and International Outreach

Before the global financial crisis in 2007–2009, Barclays provided wide-ranging generic and specialist financial services, including wealth management, credit card facilities, mortgage services, retail and commercial banking, insurance services, investment banking and investment management services.[689] As of 2006, by market capitalisation, Barclays was known to be one of the

---

[685] Barclays Bank Plc, 'Annual Report and Financial Accounts' (2006, p. 148)

[686] Ibid (2006, p. 148).

[687] Barclays Plc, 'Annual Report and Financial Accounts' (2017, p. 134)

[688] Barclays Bank UK Plc, 'Annual Accounts' (2020)

[689] Barclays Bank Plc, 'Annual Report and Financial Accounts'(2005, p.1)

biggest financial services providers in the world, operating in over fifty countries worldwide.[690] In addition, Barclays Bank is the first financial institution to pioneer elaborate branch banking, the first to operate Automated Teller Machines (ATM) and the first financial institution that helped to shape modern international trade finance.[691]

Barclays Bank operated the universal banking model with wide global outreach in many countries in Asia, Africa, Europe, the United States of America and South America. Barclays is mostly involved in these businesses as joint ventures or wholly owned subsidiaries. As of 31st December 2005, Barclays had twenty-eight principal subsidiaries, of which sixteen were in the UK, with the other twelve spread worldwide.[692] Before the global financial crisis in 2007–2009, Barclays followed a business model that embraced expansion through organic growth by ploughing profits into the business. The bank has a long history of growing its businesses through mergers and acquisitions. Growing its business through mergers and acquisitions is not new to the bank. For over one hundred years, mergers and acquisition strategies served the bank's interest, especially when such activities were limited to takeovers of commercial banking institutions. However, the increased appetite for far and wide-ranging acquisition of other financial institutions eventually proved to be the bank's undoing in the past twenty years.

For example, in 1896, Goslings Bank, Gurney's Bank and Backhouses Bank came together in a merger to join Barclays Bank under the name Barclays and Co. Similarly, in 1918, Barclays acquired London Provincial and South Western Bank. In 1919, British Linen Bank joined Barclays. Also, in 1925, the National Bank of South Africa, the Colonial Bank and the Anglo-Egyptian Bank came together under Barclays (Dominion Colonial and Overseas, (Barclays DCO). In 1975, Mercantile Credit joined Barclays,[693] and in 2000, Woolwich became part of Barclays and Lehman Brothers in 2008.

These are just a few of the many mergers and acquisitions Barclays has been involved in in the past 100 years. There could not have been fewer than 100 in different parts of the world. Unfortunately, after the deregulation of the 1980s,

---

[690] Op. Cit., Barclays Plc 2006, p. 148, (n. 681).
[691] Op. Cit., Ackrell, M. and Hannah, L. 2001, (n. 683).
[692] Barclays Plc, 'Annual Reports and Financial Accounts' (2005, p.209)
[693] Op. Cit., M. Ackrell and L. Hannah, 2001, (n. 679).

mergers and acquisitions became too frequent and widely diversified into businesses that had little or nothing in common with the core banking business.

In 2012, Barclays was embroiled in the London Inter-Bank Offered Rate (LIBOR) manipulation scandal, severely damaging the bank's credibility and attracting huge fines. However, for some of these broader issues, including investment banking transactions that went sour, complicity in manipulating LIBOR rates and exchange rates fixing scandal, the 330-year-old bank would have easily passed as one of the oldest and finest financial institutions in the UK and worldwide.[694] In addition, some other problems Barclays had included accusations of money laundering, illegal tax avoidance schemes and the sale of questionable financial instruments. The financial analysis section discusses the impact of the fines on the bank's poor economic performance.

During its very long existence spanning over three centuries, Barclays did not only weather the storms of several financial crises detailed in the literature review, but the bank also survived the impact of two World Wars. Moreover, the bank thrived in those difficult years.

Barclays was also adversely affected by the 2007–2009 global financial crisis, just as other banks and financial institutions in the UK were. However, unlike the RBS, which took the UK government's bailout packages with the attendant adverse consequences expounded on in Section A, Barclays sought a different route for assistance by seeking external cash ingestion of £6.1 billion from Qatar's government. Barclays also sold several businesses to resolve the liquidity crisis and compensate for inadequate capital status.

Although Barclays maintained some marginal growth in its income-generation capacity during the crisis, most of its profits were eroded by huge impairment charges caused by the poor quality of its financial assets. Moreover, low interest rates, fines for infringements, and losses incurred on the sale of assets contributed significantly to Barclays' financial difficulties. As a result, as indicated below in Table 6, page 232, column 9, the bank could only pay modest dividends to shareholders throughout the global financial crisis and beyond.

As mentioned previously, in the heat of the crisis, whilst RBS accepted a government bailout option, which turned out to be like the proverbial poisoned chalice, shrewdly, Barclays rejected the offer of a bailout package from the UK

---

[694] Op. Cit., A. Salz and R. Collins, 2013, (n. 55)

government. Instead, Barclays sought and negotiated for cash ingestion from Qatar's government, which yielded a loan package of £6.1 billion to Barclays.[695]

About ten years after that, in 2017, the UK Serious Fraud Office (SFO) brought up a criminal case against the bank and four former directors for unlawfully obtaining financial assistance from a foreign government. The FSA also accused the bank of inadequate disclosure of fees paid for arranging the capital infusion from Qatar's government. Southwark Crown Court in London promptly dismissed the case against Barclays. However, the UK's anti-fraud agency further attempted to reinstate the case in the High Court on account of an alleged loan of £2.3 billion granted by Barclays to Qatar, which Qatar reinvested in Barclays.[696] This is concerned with allegations of illegal assistance to buy own shares. That case against Barclays was also promptly dismissed.

It is not too difficult to see why these cases failed. Foremost, two legal tests must be met for a criminal indictment to validly lead to a conviction. This concerns satisfying the court about the (i) *Actus Reus* and (ii) the *Mens Rea* of the case.[697] The first leg concerns the fact that the accused committed an offence known to the law (indictable offence). The second leg, which is the mental element, is that, in so doing, the defendant had a 'guilty mind'; that is, the accused either had the 'intention' to commit the crime or that the accused negligently or recklessly committed the offence.[698]

It may be difficult to persuade the court that the bank committed an offence by seeking a loan for its own survival from another country that is not an enemy nation. First, it would have been difficult to persuade the court about criminal intent if there were no corrupt personal gains in the transaction. If the first leg of the prerequisite conditions for a guilty verdict failed, the second leg had very few chances of leading to a conviction except if a case of corrupt enrichment was established against those who arranged the finance. In such an event, the individuals behind the crime would bear the consequences, not Barclays.

---

[695] R. Davies, 'Barclays Avoids Trial Over £6 billion Qatar Rescue package' (The Guardian 26/10/2018)
https://www.theguardian.com/business/2018/oct/26/barclays-avoids-trial-over-6bn-qatar-rescue-package

[696] Ibid

[697] D. Ormerod and K. Laird, 'Smith, Hogan & Ormerod Criminal Law 15th ed' (Oxford University Press, 2018)

[698] M. Jefferson, 'Criminal Law 12th Ed' (Pearson Education, 2015)

Secondly, in the case of providing financial assistance to buy their shares, though there is a general prohibition against public companies giving financial assistance to purchase their shares, it is not an absolute rule.

There are some exceptions to the general rule. One such exemption is found in the Company Act 2006 s.678 (2) b, which says,

"...the giving of the assistance for that purpose is only an incidental part of some larger purpose of the company, and the assistance is given in good faith in the interest of the company."

This legal provision was available to Barclays to defend itself against the litigation brought against Barclays.

Then, Barclays was under precarious financial circumstances. Moreover, in a private arrangement, the bank secured some cash ingestion of £6.1 billion from Qatar's government. Much later, after the storm, Barclays granted a loan of £2.3 billion to the Qatar government's nominee company to purchase shares in Barclays on behalf of the Qatar government.

So, the circumstances under which the loan was given differ from the usual conditions that apply when approaching the capital market to buy stocks. The loan to purchase the shares was given in good faith, and it was in the best interest of Barclays to grant the loan as it did. Barclays benefited more and owed its survival to the £6.1 billion given to support Barclays by the Qatar government at a crucial time. It is, therefore, unsurprising if, based on the provisions of the Company Act 2006, s.678 (2) b, the court dismissed the cases against Barclays. The reasons for the dismissal of both cases are not too complicated. Obtaining legal advice from appropriate professionals may have obviated the need to take the matter to court.

Given the onerous preconditions imposed on RBS by the European Commission before RBS could take the much-needed bailout financial packages, the argument is that it made more commercial sense for Barclays to seek alternative ways of dealing with the liquidity problems. Moreover, as pointed out in Section A of this chapter, RBS faced a rapid consequential decimation of the Group following its adoption of the conditionality attached to the bailout package it received from the UK's government. Therefore, it was shrewd on the part of Barclays to seek external sources of finance rather than follow the disastrous path taken by RBS.

In conclusion, Barclays' longevity, which spans over three hundred years, should be seen as a remarkable achievement. That durability is a testimony to the ruggedness of this extraordinary British-branded iconic global financial institution, which has been out of favour in the eyes of the public in recent times due to Barclays management's contributions to the global financial crisis.

Table 6: Tabulated Data Extracted from the Annual Reports and Consolidated Financial Accounts of the Barclays Group From 2004 to 2018 (Financial Year Ending on 31st December Annually)

Year	Total Income £ (b)	Operating Profit Before Tax £ (b)	Total Assets £ (b)	Impairment Charges £ (b)	Branches	Employees 000	Earnings Per Share (pence)
1	2	3	4	5	6	7	8
2004	14	4.6	538	1	2,891	83	51.0p
2005	17	5.2	924	2	3,545	120	54.4p
2006	22	7.1	997	2	3,627	132	71.9p
2007	23	7	1,227	3	1733UK	135	68.9p
2008	23	6	2,053	5	-	156	59.3p
2009	29	4.6	1,379	8	1700 UK	144	86.2p
2010	31	6	1,490	6	-	148	30.4p
2011	32	5.9	1,564	6	-	141	25.1p
2012	29*	7*	1,490	4	-	139	34.5p
2013	28	5.1	1,312	3	-	140	16.7p
2014	25	5.5	1,358	2	-	132	17.3p
2015	25	5.4	1,120	2	-	129	16.6p
2016	21	3.2	1,213	2	-	119	10.4p
2017	21	3.1	1,129	2	-	80	-
2018	21	3.5	1,133	2	-	84	9.4p

Dividend Per Share (pence) 9	Total Deposit £ (b) 10	Total Loan £ (b) 11	Investment Banking £ (b) 12	Contribution Insurance £ (000) 13	Contribution Wealth Management £ (000) 14
24.0p	330	343	1		0.1
26.6p	316	300	1.3	0.6	0.2
31.0p	339	313	2.2	0.6	0.2
34.0p	386	386	2.3	0.5	0.3
11.5p	450	510	1.3	0.2	0.7
2.5p	399	461	2.5	-	0.1
5.5p	424	466	4.8	-	0.2
6.0p	458	479	3	-	0.2
6.5p	464	466	4	-	0.3
6.5p	483	468	2.5	-	(0.1)
6.5p	486	470	1.4	-	-
6.5p	465	441	1.6	-	-
3.0p	471	436	2.7	-	-
-	467	402	2	-	-
6.5p	395	326	2.6	-	-

Note: The asterisk ** in column 2, the Year 2012, concerning £29 billion total income and Column 3, regarding £7 billion Operating Profit Before Tax, are receipts which were not part of the ordinary trading income but proceeds of the sale of non-core assets. This is explained further in the analysis.

4.9 The Constituents of Table 6

Table 6 above contains the tabulated data regarding the financial summaries extracted from the Annual Reports and Financial Accounts of Barclays Bank over 15 years, starting from 2004 to 2018. The first three years' accounts from 2004 to 2006 represent the good years immediately preceding the global financial crisis. The next three years, from 2007 to 2009, were when the crisis occurred. After that, the next three years 2010 to 2012, was the period of planned government's response to the financial crisis, while the next six years, from 2013 to 2018, was the period of moratorium granted to the banking sector to prepare for the full implementation of the ring-fencing policy within the Banking Reform Act 2013. The legislation embodied the UK government's response and intervention agenda regarding the global financial crisis.

Appendix 2, at the back of this report, contains page reference numbers indicating the pages in the Annual Reports and Financial Accounts where the financial summaries were extracted.

The Table comprises fourteen vertical columns with self-explanatory headings indicating the variables contained in each column. The horizontal rows are the Key Performance Indicators (KPI) values recorded annually.

Figures 11–18 below are the graphical presentation of the variables in Table 6 in chart form to illustrate visually the relationships between the variables indicated on the headings of each chart. In addition, beneath each chart is a summary providing at a glance the result generated from the chart.

Appendices 11 to 17, at the back of this report, present the numerical values of each chart's 'X' and 'Y' axes.

Figure 11: Barclays Group: The Relationship Between Income and Operating Profit Before Tax from 2004–2018

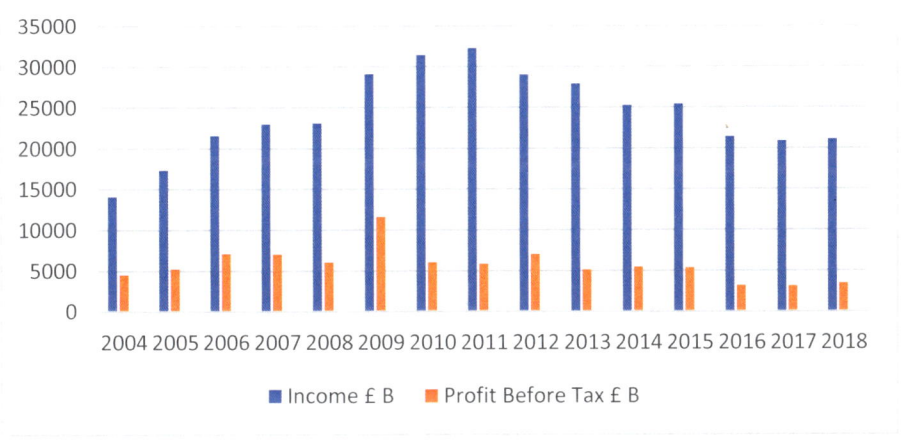

Fig 11 shows the relationship between the Barclay Group's annual income and annual Operating Profit Before Tax listed in columns 2 & 3 of Table 6. Generally, the chart indicates a steady growth in the annual income peaked at £32 billion in 2011. After that, from 2012, income began to slide and did not recover significantly before 2018. Remarkably, PBT did not grow in proportion to the increase in annual income. This is because overhead costs, fines, levies, and other charges keep increasing faster than annual income. As well, the interest rate was low. The underlying assets were overblown in 2008. There were weaknesses in the assets, including Non-Performing Loans.

Figure 12: Barclays Group: The Relationship Between Assets, Deposits, and Loans from 2004–2018

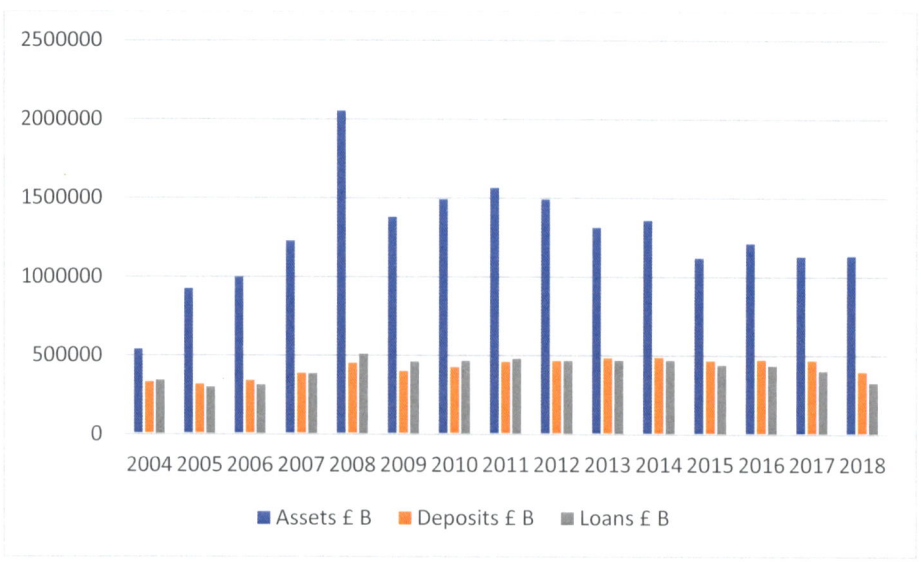

Fig. 12 is the chart relating to Barclays Group's assets, deposits and loan profile as they stood on the balance sheet date, 31st December annually listed in columns 4, 10 & 11. The total assets grew rapidly from a modest £538 billion in 2004 to a peak of £2.1 trillion in 2008. The bank struggled from 2008 to 2011 to keep deposits above the aggregate loan profile. The total loans should not have exceeded the total deposits. This is indicative of a poor liquidity position. However, from 2013 to 2018, there was a recovery in which deposits exceeded loans for five consecutive years.

Figure 13: Barclays Group: Trend of Growth/Decline in the Total Assets from 2004–2018

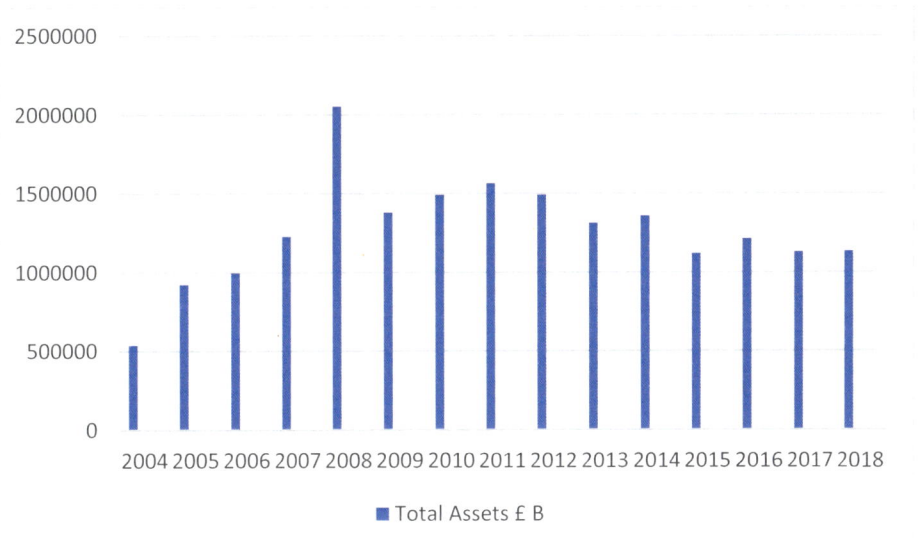

Fig. 13 displays graphic movements in the Barclays Group's total assets annually, as listed in Table 6, column 4. After a dip in the bank's assets by £700 billion in 2009, the subsequent undulating movements in the value of the assets remained well-controlled from 2010–2018. The substantial dip by about £700 billion was due to the revaluation of derivative assets, which was previously overstated.

Figure 14: Barclays Group: Trend of Growth/Decline in Impairment Charges from 2004–2018

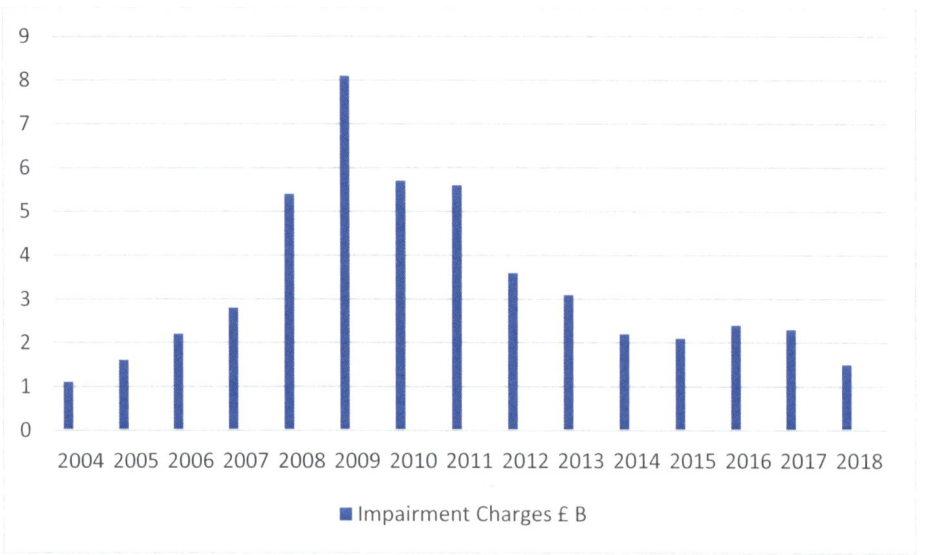

Fig. 14 concerns Barclays Group's provisions for impairment charges annually over 15 years, as listed under column 5. The worst tide of impairment charges was between 2008 and 2011 when the bank made a provision of £8.1 billion in impairment charges in 2009. This indicates an expectation of a significant fall in the bank's assets due to a downward revaluation of assets. It also includes an expectation of an increase in the non-performing loan facilities.

Figure 15: Barclays Group: The Percentage of Contributions of the Investment Banking to the Profit Before Tax from 2004–2018

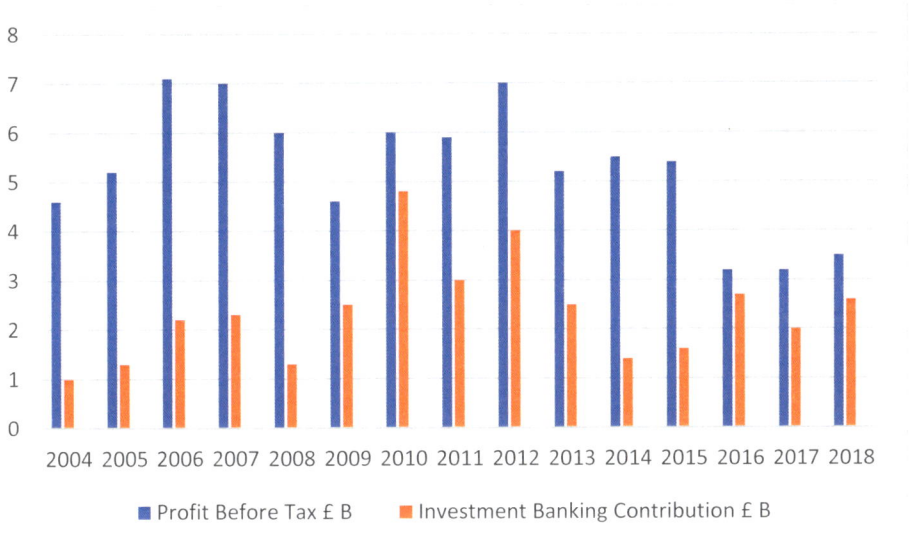

Fig. 15 is a chart on the contribution of investment banking income to the PBT of Barclay Group from 2004 to 2018, as stated in column 12 in Table 6. Remarkably, investment banking contributed 79% to the PBT of Barclays in 2010, 82% in 2016, 65% in 2017 & 74% in 2018. These statistics underscore the importance of the investment banking division of the bank to the profitability of the bank. However, whilst that arm of the bank's business was initially profitable, through mismanagement and exponential growth beyond what Barclays was prepared to handle and several scandals that Barclays was embroiled in, that bank division was substantially reduced from 2015.

Figure 16: Barclays Group: Trend of Growth/Decline in the Employees' Profile from 2004–2018

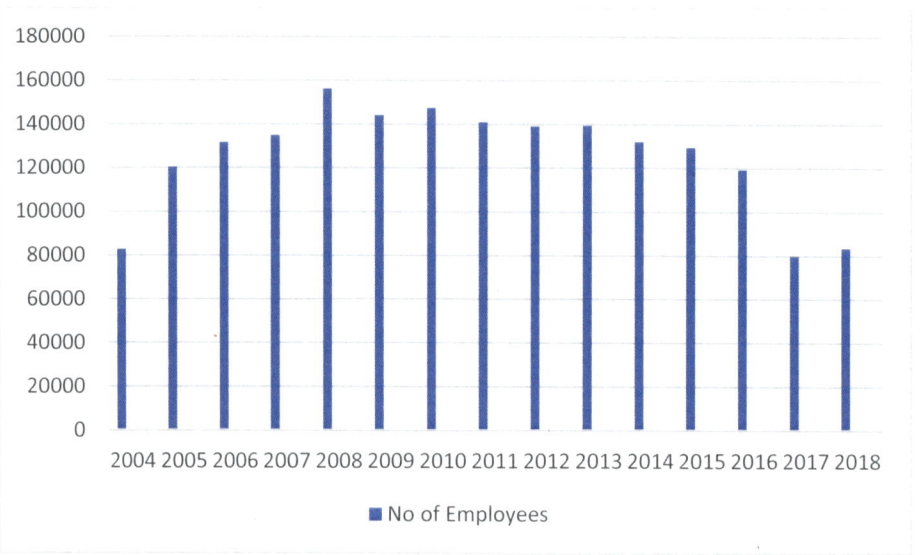

Figure 16 is a graphical presentation of Barclays Group employees' annual growth and decline, as listed in column 7. Barclays Group had about 153,000 staff members, which was its highest number but reduced to 83,000 by 2018. The decline followed a massive divestment and discontinued operations of several of the bank's businesses across the globe.

Figure 17: Barclays Group: Trend of Growth/Decline in Earnings Per Share and Dividend Per Share from 2004–2018

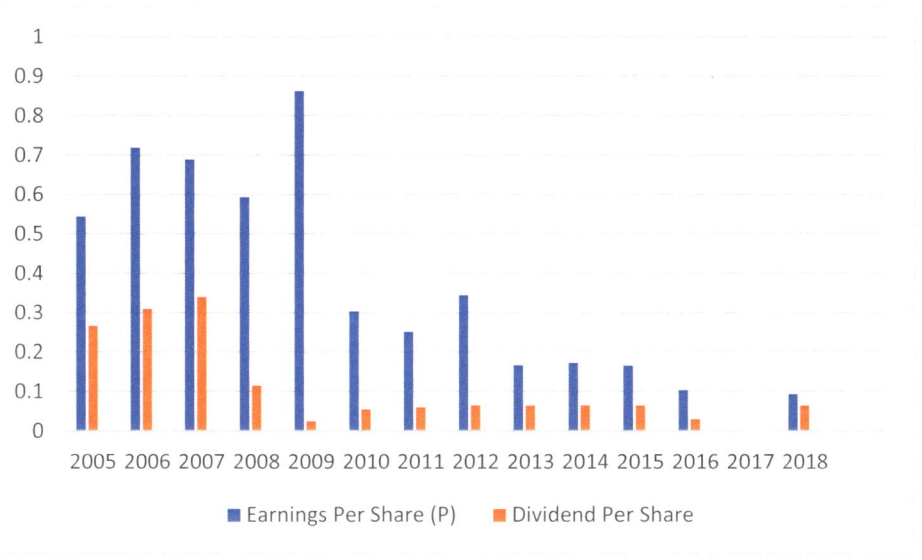

Figure 17 shows the decline in earnings per share over the years under study and the relatively low dividend paid per share over the same period. Barclays did not pay dividends in 2017.

4.10 Analysis and Interpretation of the Extracted Information Collated from the Annual Financial Accounts of Barclays Bank Plc in the light of the Aim and Objectives of the Study

Some of the Key Performance Indicators (KPI) examined to draw conclusions from the data include the income generation capacity of the business, operating profit before tax, changes in asset level, impairment charges, earnings per share, dividend per share, deposit held in relationship to loans and advances, and a summarised contribution to income received from the investment banking, insurance and wealth management services divisions of the Barclays Group.

Income and profit could be mistakenly considered synonymous terms, but they are not.[699] In the context of this study, income is differentiated from profit. Income is the combination of revenue received as interest on loan accounts, advances, fees and commissions received for services provided, earnings from insurance premiums less direct costs and impairment charges.[700] On the other hand, Profit Before Tax is the aggregated income less total operating expenses (associated direct and indirect costs) before tax.

The trend in the income level generated by a business is an important performance indicator that enables assessors to see whether the company is gaining or losing its hold on its market share. More importantly, this performance marker enables managers to assess whether their assets are being effectively deployed to generate a sufficient income level that meets the bank's budget and whether costs are justified by the level of income the organisation generates.[701]

4.10.1 Analysis for 2004–2006

In Barclays Group's case, steady income growth was maintained from 2004 to 2006. In 2005, the bank experienced a 23% increase in its income level, above 2004, and about a 25% increase in 2006. As of 2004, the annual income was £14.1 billion, which increased to £17.3 billion in 2005 and £21.6 billion in 2006. This growth in the income level reflects the corresponding substantial increase in Barclay's assets, which increased by 72% between 2004 and 2005.[702]

The asset increase was largely due to the purchase of 57% controlling shares in a top South African bank, Absa Group Ltd, in 2005.[703] A significant feature in the financial accounts of Barclays Plc in the period before the crisis shows that the bank exploited opportunities to acquire interests in other financial institutions. Other examples besides the purchase of Absa Group include EquiFirst Corporation, which was purchased for about US$225m in 2006, Indexchange Investment AG, which was purchased for about €240m on 8th

---

[699] D. Alexander et al., 'International Financial Reporting and Analysis' (Cengage Learning, 2014, p.62)
[700] Barclays Plc, 'Annual Report and Financial Accounts' (2007, p. 176)
[701] E. McLaney and P. Atrill, 'Accounting and Finance 8th Ed' (Pearson, 2016, p. 70)
[702] See Table 6, page 231 Column 4
[703] Barclays Plc, 'Annual Report and Financial Accounts' (2005, p. 6)

February 2007,[704] and the purchase of part of Lehman Brothers' businesses in North America.[705]

These purchases explained the significant jump in the assets of Barclays from £996 billion to £1,227 billion in 2007. The subsequent increase from £1.2 trillion to £2.1 trillion in 2008, as indicated in Table 6, has been criticised as an inflated value. This is fully discussed in the 2007–2009 review. The sudden increase in the derivative account from £120 billion in 2007 to £968 billion in 2008 was mostly due to a jump in the revaluation of derivative accounts.[706] This was a difference of £848 billion.

The operating profit before tax also grew commensurately, with the income level having had a PBT of £4.6 billion in 2004, which increased to £5.2 billion in 2005 and £7.1 billion in 2006, respectively. This positive performance is further demonstrated by the growth in the earnings per share and dividend paid out in that period.

Other performance indicators in Table 6 for 2004–2006, including earnings per share and dividend per share, indicate overall growth in 2004–2006. For example, EPS in 2004 was 51.0p. It increased to 54.4p in 2005 and 71.9p in 2006. These years of good harvest enabled a dividend of 24.0p, 26.6p and 31.0p to be paid to shareholders in 2004–2006. Now, with the benefit of hindsight, in 2004–2006, impairment charges were under control. Impairment charge relates to a provisional amount set aside to defray possible future demurrage in assets and provision for non-performing accounts and unsecured loans that may run into difficulty.

If provisions for impairment charges are growing too quickly, it will give bank management and supervisors cause for concern. Increased impairment charges mean more financial assets face devaluation or more loans and advances accounts become non-performing. Thus, provisions are made for those accounts against risks of possible losses.

With the widespread use of mobile phone banking apps and online real-time access to bank accounts, an increase in bank branches is no longer seen as a particular bank strength. However, in 2004–2006, an increase in the number of bank branches was considered an important parameter for measuring the growth and achievements of a bank. In 2004, the number of Barclays branches globally

---

[704] Barclays Plc, 'Annual Report and Financial Accounts' (2006, p. 225)
[705] Barclays Plc, 'Annual Report and Financial Accounts' (2008, p.12)
[706] Ibid (2008, p.9)

grew from 2,891 to 3,627 by 2006. However, after 2009, only a passing reference was made to the number of Barclays branches in the UK, which was stated to be above 1,700.

Moreover, from 2010 to 2018, Barclays stopped mentioning the size of the bank's network of branches. The aggregate number of employees in 2004 increased from 82,700 to 131,700 in 2006.

As indicated in columns 10 and 11 of Table 6, from 2004 to 2012, total loans and advances were more than the deposit accounts. This implies stress in the bank's liquidity ratio and increased risk level. It is a marker of Barclays' struggle to control the increasing loan and advance accounts relative to the total deposit accounts. The aggregate loans and advances are not expected to exceed the total deposit accounts. The liquidity problem in Barclays was at its worst in 2008 when loans and advances exceeded deposits by £60 billion and in 2009 when loans exceeded deposits by £62 billion.

This precarious liquidity position and the requirement to bolster capital requirements under Basel III led to massive divestment from non-core banking businesses in America, Europe and South Africa. A whole division, Barclays Global Investors, was sold. In 2012, Barclay started regaining liquidity control over the next six years. In 2018, depositors' accounts were more than loans and advances by £69 billion.

2004–2006 were good years for Barclays' banking operations before the global financial crisis of 2007–2009 set in.

4.10.2 Analysis for 2007–2009

During the global financial crisis in 2007–2009, the intense decline in the economic performance of Barclays was remarkably palpable. A casual look at the income level shows only a slight increase of 7% in 2007, achieving an income level of £23 billion. Then there was only 0.5% growth in income in 2008 when the income level increased to £23.1 billion and a further increase of 26% in 2009 when the income level attained £29.1 billion. However, within the £29.1 billion income in 2009 was an income of £6.3 billion made from the sale of Barclays Global Investors, a bank division.[707] Thus, this income was not derived from the bank's ordinary day-to-day business. Instead, it was an income derived by disposing of some of the bank's assets.

---

[707] Barclays Plc, 'Annual Report and Financial Accounts' (2009, p. 3)

Therefore, the increase in income recorded between 2007 and 2009 for Barclays is only small and pales into insignificance when viewed against the backdrop of the fact that the assets of the bank increased from £997 billion in 2006 to £2.1 trillion in 2008. The point is that if £997 billion in assets in 2006 generated £21.6 billion in income and PBT of £7.1 billion, ordinarily, assets of £2.1 trillion would be expected to generate an income level that is about twice the amount earned in 2006. Instead, £2.1 trillion assets generated a relatively small sum of £23.1 billion in income and £6 billion PBT in 2008.

The reasons for the disparity in the income level and the lacklustre profit before tax earned in the period under review are not farfetched.

There was a substantial increase in the balance sheet figures from £997 billion in 2006 to £2.1 trillion by the end of 2008. That large increase was due to overstated derivative accounts and the purchase of Lehman Brothers, which was then burdened with subprime assets. Included in the huge balance sheet figure is a considerable jump in the derivative accounts, which was only £120 billion in 2007 but astronomically increased to £968 billion by 2008, a difference of about £848 billion. The historical balances on the derivative accounts revealed the following on the balance sheet dates from 2006–2011.

2006—Derivative Financial Instruments-£141 billion on page 12, 2006 Accounts

2007—Derivative Financial Instruments-£120 billion on page 177, 2007 Accounts

2008—Derivative Financial Instruments-£968 billion on page 205, 2008 Accounts

2009—Derivative Financial Instruments-£417 billion on page 206, 2009 Accounts

2010—Derivative Financial Instruments-£420 billion on page 74, 2010 Accounts

2011—Derivative Financial Instruments-£539 billion on page 177, 2011 Accounts

First, distortions and inflated prices caused the bulk of the overstated value of the derivative instruments. Second, the ballooned balance sheet figures and derivatives were also largely due to Barclays' mergers and acquisition of some financial institutions in 2007–2008, especially the takeover of the investment trading arm of Lehman Brothers. Lehman Brothers had a large swathe of derivatives valued in hundreds of billion pounds in 2008.[708]

As stated earlier, some other financial institutions acquired during that period, which caused the expansion of Barclays assets, included Absa Group Ltd in South Africa, Equifirst Corporation and Indexchange Investment AG. At that time, Barclays took an over-optimistic view of the value of these companies. However, within a year after that, in 2009, reality settled in. As a result, the derivative assets were revalued downward, leading to a massive write-down from £968 billion to £417 billion in 2009, making a difference of about £551 billion net of trading on that account for that year. In essence, the revaluation cleaned out £551 billion from the balance sheet as of 31st December 2009.

The overall effect is that the income in 2008 was not commensurate with the huge balance sheet figure of £2.1 trillion. At the same time, a generally low interest rate caused a reduction in the yield on the assets held. Growing non-performing accounts induced large impairment provisions that peaked at £8 billion in 2008. There was also an inclement business environment caused by the overheated economy brought about by the global financial crisis. There were fines for regulatory breaches and remediation for mis-sold financial products. The cumulative effects of all these took its toll on the bank's profitability in that period.

In September 2008, Barclays took over several of Lehman Brothers' businesses, including the skyscraper headquarters of Lehman Brothers in New York at the cost of almost £1 billion, Lehman Brothers Canada Inc., Sudamerica, Uruguay and New Jersey data centres. In addition, Barclays took over Lehman Brothers' investment banking division and trading operations. In the process, the securities, trading liabilities, private investment management business and responsibility of over 9000 former employees of Lehman Brothers were all taken over by Barclays.[709, 710]

Barclays also needed some time to settle in as the new owners of Lehman Brothers' business operations and all other businesses purchased at that time. The bank required sufficient time to turn around the companies acquired by

---

[708] Op. Cit., B. Casu, et al., 2015, p. 267, (n. 144).

[709] Ibid. B. Casu, et al., Pearson, 2015, p. 267, (n. 144)

[710] D. Teather et al., 'Barclays to Buy Lehman Brothers' Assets' (The Guardian, London 17/09/2008)

Barclays, assuming they could do so, especially given the inclement business environment at the time and the fact that Lehman Brothers was overpriced.

Acquisition costs under various headings, such as legal fees, arrangement fees, valuation fees, commissions, charges, taxes, etc., on several financial institutions purchased at that time, including a huge institution like Lehman Brothers, can be expected to be very high.[711] However, the details of these costs are not explicitly specified in the minute details of Barclays's accounts. Also, the company's policy on how Barclays treated such costs was not specifically indicated in the annual report.

However, there are two broad methods to deal with such costs. (i) The total costs of mergers and acquisitions under different subheadings may be fully absorbed into the profit and loss account in the year costs were incurred. (ii) Alternatively, Barclays may opt to use the amortisation method.[712] Under that method, the costs may be spread equally on a straight-line basis over five years or more so that the total costs would be written down gradually and defrayed by the end of the 5th year or at the end of a predetermined number of years. Barclays may also use a method by which deduction may start low, and then subsequent annual charges get higher until the costs are fully amortised at the end of the fifth year or a predetermined number of years. The amortisation could also begin with large amounts and gradually reduce the annual contributions towards the expenses over five years or more until the costs are fully defrayed.

The relevance of this analysis to the study is a consideration of the cost implications and how they affected the bank's profitability in the period under evaluation. For example, if Barclays had adopted the first method, this might have significantly impacted the income and profit before tax for the year. That would have meant that the total costs for all the financial institutions acquired in that period were charged to the profit and loss account for the year. This could have resulted in a significant reduction in the profit for the year.

In addition to all of these, there was a general dislocation in the market during the global financial crisis, which no doubt affected the general performance of Barclays in those years as much as it affected other financial institutions. This is

---

[711] A. Docherty and F. Viort, 'Better Banking: Understanding and Addressing the Failures in Risks Management, Governance and Regulations' (John Wiley, 2014, p.125). These authors cited examples relating to high transaction costs of £366 million paid by Barclay's for raising £7 billion capital in 2008.

[712] Op. cit., G.D. Morris, 2005, p. 468, (n. 622).

more so with the credit crunch, the burden of reduced interest income from mortgage accounts as a result of low-interest rates on mortgages and the pressure on banks to meet capital and liquidity requirements.

In 2009, Profit before tax crashed to £4.6 billion from £7.1 billion in 2006. Moreover, if not for the income of £6.3 billion made from the sale of Barclays Global Investors in 2009, Barclays would have had a negative PBT in 2009. Impairment charges rose to an all-time high of £8.1 billion against £2.2 billion in 2006 before the crisis began. It may well be the case that a large part of the costs of acquisitions mentioned earlier came through in 2009, leading to the very low PBT in 2009.

As mentioned previously, the expectation is that at least the aggregate loans and advances should not exceed the level of deposits. However, from 2008 to 2012, Barclays could not control the disparity for five consecutive years. This is indicative of Barclays' poor liquidity position at that time.

These statistics further demonstrate the inclement environment under which Barclays operated during the global financial crisis. The dividends paid to shareholders in 2009 were a mere 2.5p, compared to 11.5p paid in 2008 and 34.0p in 2007.

4.10.3 Analysis 2010–2012

The background to 2010–2012 marked a time of intense debate regarding considerations over the appropriate government regulatory response to the 2007–2009 crisis. This is exemplified by the work of the following scholars: Grosse, R. (2012), Hudson, A. (2013), MacNeil, I. (2011), Moosa, I. (2010), Arora, A. (2010) and Persaud, A. (2010). All these works were referred to in the literature review. It was also the period that the Vickers' Independent Commission on Banking report was published.

In addition to the burden of the global financial crisis on Barclays, there was the damaging allegation of criminal manipulation of the London Interbank Offered Rate (LIBOR), in which some employees of Barclays were deeply enmeshed.[713, 714] In June 2012, it came to light that in collaboration with others, some employees of Barclays were involved in manipulating the all-important

---

[713] G. Baber, 'Interbank Offered Rates: HM Treasury's Decisive Act' (2013) Vol 20 (2), 237–252, Company Lawyer

[714] Op. Cit., A. Salz and R. Collins, 2013, (n. 55).

LIBOR, which served as the benchmark interest rates used in the determination of interest rates for derivatives, mortgages, overdrafts and other complex financial instruments.[715, 716] It later came to light that this unethical practice was far more widespread than initially envisaged as the scandal extended to the EURO Interbank Offered Rate (EURIBOR) and Tokyo Interbank Offered Rate (TIBOR).[717]

The damaging impact of the fines imposed on the bank for this misdeed is discussed later in this section. At that time, Barclays appointed consultants to assist the bank in evaluating its business ethos and practices.[718]

By 2012, the draft Bill, which accepted Vickers' recommendations and would be the basis for new legislation on banking law, the Banking Reform Act 2013, had reached an advanced stage. By then, it had become clear that government policy favoured removing core deposits from the investment arm of banking operations. Well before the Bill was enacted into law in 2013, Barclays was committed to restructuring as far back as 2010 when it reported restructuring charges of £330 million.[719]

In 2010 and 2011, income picked up slowly, increasing by 8% in 2010 (£31.5 billion) and a further 3% in 2011, leading to £32.2 billion income earned in 2011. This was the highest revenue generation recorded by the bank. However, that growth was not sustained. As of 2012, income levels started to dwindle, coming down to £29 billion in 2012. The low interest rate was biting hard. As a result, there was also pressure on the bank to improve liquidity and equity capital. In addition, the cost of the non-performing accounts was hard on the bank.

While income increased in 2011 and 2012, albeit only mildly, PBT did not respond to that growth. This was due to relatively high impairment charges and the burden of a penalty of £850 million imposed against the bank for interest rate hedging products and a £1.6 billion fine for mis-sold PPI.[720] This situation and other events in the bank at the time led to the Chairman of the bank, Marcus

---

[715] M. McKee, 'The Implications of Moving to SONIA' (2020) Vol 35 (6), 223–230, Journal of International Banking Law and Regulation

[716] O. McDonald, 'Should LIBOR Come to an End?' (2019) Vol 40 (8), 237–238, Company Lawyer

[717] Op cit., Baber, G. 2013, (n. 715).

[718] Op. cit., Salz, A. and Collins, R. 2013, (n. 55).

[719] Barclays Plc, 'Annual Report and Financial Accounts' (2010, p.6)

[720] Barclays Plc, 'Annual Report and Financial Accounts' (2012, p.9)

Agius, and the CEO, Bob Diamond, stepping down from leading the bank. The bank only managed to keep up with paying a static 5.5p, 6.0p and 6.5p dividends to shareholders in 2010, 2011 and 2012.

4.10.4 Analysis for 2013–2018

Since 2011, assets have started dropping from £1.6 trillion to £1.3 trillion by 31st December 2013 due to the disposal of assets, as stated previously. This was achieved through divestment, de-risking and de-leveraging of the bank. For example, Barclays reduced legacy assets in Exit Quadrant portfolios by £40 billion, Investment Bank legacy assets were reduced by £17 billion, and similarly, there was a write-down in the derivatives account, which had a deficit of £23 billion.[721]

In January 2013, ring-fencing became law, though there was another six-year moratorium before the full effect of that law was to take place. However, the bank had to work towards meeting the demand for stricter capital requirements. Thus, Barclays went forward in restructuring and de-risking its activities.[722] The bank recognised the need to work towards compliance with both the ring-fencing policy and the US Dodd-Frank Act relating to its investments in the USA. Barclays set a target for full compliance with the ring-fencing policy by the spring of 2018 instead of the 1st January 2019 set by law.[723] In a plan to achieve this goal and the need for a general overhaul of the bank's image and business strategy, the bank then launched a new strategic business plan termed 'Transform Programme'. This project had an initial cost of £1.2 billion.[724]

In 2013, income fell by about 4%, from £29 billion in 2012 to £28 billion. Also, PBT decreased by 25%, from £7 billion in 20012 to £5 billion in 2013.

Further to the Transformation Programme started in 2013 under the leadership of David Walker, the Chairman, and Anthony Jenkins, the Group Chief Executive, in 2014, Barclays went through what John McFarlane, the subsequent Chairman of Barclays, described as one of the largest restructurings in history.[725] In promoting a vision of a safer banking model in keeping with the

---

[721] Barclays Plc 'Annual Report and Financial Accounts' (2012, p.9)
[722] Barclays Plc, 'Annual Report and Financial Accounts' (2013, p.4)
[723] Barclays Plc 'Annual Report and Financial Accounts' (2014, p.2)
[724] Barclays Plc, 'Annual Report and Financial Accounts' (2013, p. 12)
[725] Barclays Plc 'Annual Report and Financial Accounts (2016, p. 2)

new thinking then, Barclays engaged in wholly-owned subsidiaries as of 31st December 2015, numbered 564 business entities, out of which joint venture companies numbered 288.[726]

These wholly-owned and subsidiary companies provided specialist financial services, including, but not limited to, investment banking, leasing, security realisation outfits, assets management services, trusteeship, holding companies, nominee services, capital margin financing, capital security services, export financing services, industrial development services, and investment trust.

The names of the companies, percentages of Barclays Plc's stake in each of the companies and their locations worldwide are listed on pages 341–347 of the Annual Report and Financial Accounts for the year 2015.[727]

The explanation given by the bank for this level of unprecedented spread of investments in 2014, hitherto not seen in its history of over three hundred years, was that they intended to deliver the divestment of non-strategic assets and businesses. This was meant to release capital to support core banking growth and to strengthen the Group's capital position.[728] However, ultimately, the bank incurred total losses of £12 billion in the disposal of Barclays's classified non-core business arm.[729]

The obvious intention of the management of the bank in promoting this level of vast diversification was to keep Barclays in a position of strength and safety, as required by Basel III. It was also Barclays' leadership's proposed solution to dealing with the nagging problem of what Moosa called the mythical 'Too big to fail and too big to rescue' banking model.[730, 731]

By creating almost six hundred subsidiaries and joint ventures worldwide in this way, the question remains whether the bank spread itself too thinly, putting its fingers in too many pies and thus becoming less effective. It also raises the question of whether this unprecedented level of diversification was in the best interests of the bank and shareholders. Before this new initiative, Barclays had only five operational divisions, namely Barclays Capital, Barclays Global Investors, Barclays Wealth Management, UK Banking and International Retail

---

[726] Barclays Plc 'Annual Report and Financial Accounts (2015, pp.341–347)
[727] ibid (2015, p.341–347)
[728] Barclays Plc 'Annual Report and Financial Accounts' (2017, p.3)
[729] Barclays 'Annual Report and Financial Accounts' (2018, p.2)
[730] Op. Cit., I. Moosa, 2010, (n. 67).
[731] Barclays, 'Annual Report and Financial Accounts' (2014, p.2)

and Commercial Banking. Within this framework, as of 2010, it had only about twenty-three subsidiaries worldwide.[732]

Not surprisingly, as of 31st December 2015, out of the 564 businesses, fifty-two of the wholly owned subsidiaries were in the process of liquidation. In the first quarter of 2016, forty-six wholly-owned companies were already sold. Similarly, seventeen of the 288 joint venture companies were undergoing a liquidation process.[733] Therefore, it is also not surprising that the Chairman and the Group Chief Executive Officer, under whose tenure this initiative took place, were allowed to go.

With all the de-merger, divestment and restructuring taking place, the income generation capacity of the bank continued to deteriorate steadily from 2013 to 2018, as can be observed from Table 6 Column 2. Barclays sold its International private banking businesses other than those in the UK, Monaco and Geneva. Investment banking withdrew from nine countries, using the proceeds to boost capital requirements.[734] Also, Barclays sold a significant interest in Barclays Africa Group Ltd to enable Barclays to take Barclays Africa Group out of the consolidated accounts.[735] This move was partly to enable the bank to meet its Common Equity Tier 1 Ratio.

Scaling down operations and walking away from most businesses built around the world over the years was a significant issue that affected Barclays Bank and, by extension, the economy. Although Barclays did not provide statistics on the proportion of its income from nations outside the UK, RBS declared that in the year ended 2006, it earned 42% of its income abroad.[736]

Similarly, PBT suffered a similar fate, crashing from £5.1 billion in 2013 to £3.5 billion in 2018, which was a reduction of 31%. Assets had reduced from £2.1 trillion in 2008 to almost half at £1.1 trillion in 2018.

In the Chairman's report in 2016, John McFarlane commented that shareholders' equity had increased from £36.6 billion in 2008 to £58.4 billion, up by 60%. He concluded that although the group had grown smaller, it had become safer, more focused, better capitalised, less leveraged and very liquid.[737]

---

[732] Barclays Plc, 'Annual Report and Financial Accounts' (2010, p.130)

[733] Barclays Plc, 'Annual Report and Financial Accounts' (2015, p. 341–347)

[734] Ibid (2015, p.2)

[735] Ibid (2016, p.3)

[736] Royal Bank of Scotland, 'Annual Report and Financial Accounts'(2006)

[737] Barclays Plc, 'Annual Report and Financial Accounts' (2016, p.3)

This is what is seen as a desirable position in which a healthy bank should be. Moreover, this outcome is what the regulators would want to see across the banking sector.

McFarlane was not dishonest or trying to paint an inaccurate picture when he said the Group had become smaller, safer, more focused, less leveraged, better capitalised and highly liquid, with the customers at the centre of the business.

The context in which he gave the report was that of a steward reporting about his stewardship and how he had made the most of an adverse situation he would wish did not happen. He was paid to make things work for the benefit of the shareholders, regardless of the economic environment and the challenges he faced, and not to complain about the laws and regulations imposed on the sector.

Although McFarlane said progress had been made because the bank had become compliant with the new regulations, the problem remains that the company could still not generate sufficient bottom-line profit that yielded returns above the cost of capital. As a result, the dividend per share and payout ratio remained static and very low, varying from 2.5p–6.5p for 11 years from 2009 to 2018, as opposed to the 34p dividend paid when the bank made healthy profits (see column 9 of Table 6).

In 2015, Barclays complained about what they termed a disproportionate fine and the incalculable damaging consequences to society.[738] To worsen the situation for the bank, in 2014, it paid a penalty of £1.5 billion regarding misconduct matters and another £1.3 billion for remediation on mis-sold PPI.[739] In addition, a £4 billion litigation expense was incurred in 2015, further eroding Barclays' profit.[740]

Barclays paid a total sum of £15.1 billion in litigation costs, £2.4 billion as bank levies, incurred £10.1 billion in losses from the sale of their non-core business (which grew to £12 billion[741] in 2018), and suffered £2.5 billion losses as a result of selling their interest in the Africa arm of the business, totalling the sum of £34.8 billion.[742] In addition, there is a separate £17 billion cost on legacy

---

[738] Barclays Plc, 'Annual Report and Financial Accounts' (2015, p.3)

[739] Barclays Plc, 'Annual Report and Financial Accounts' (2014, p.15)

[740] Barclays Plc, 'Annual Report and Financial Accounts' (2015, p.4)

[741] Barclays Plc, 'Annual Report and Financial Accounts' (2018, p. 2)

[742] Barclays Plc, 'Annual Report and Financial Accounts' (2017, p.2)

issues relating to the operation in America.[743] Altogether these amounted to about £49 billion in losses by 2018 (Excluding £2.4 billion bank levy).

With all this in the background, it is hardly surprising why Barclays floundered under intense pressure, could barely meet the cost of capital and could only deliver less-than-desirable dividends to shareholders.

McFarlane admitted that the fines levied against the bank were justified based on Barclay's contribution to the global financial crisis. He pointed out that the bank was working hard to address conduct issues.

For example, the then Chairman of Barclays Group pointed out that a fine of £50 million is the equivalent of a reduction of employees by 1000, the closing down of one hundred regional branches and forgoing the capacity to lend £500 million to customers.[744] As indicated in the previous paragraphs, the fines and remediation payments were in billions of pounds. It could be argued that the pain and the impact of the enormous fines on the banks affected would be a deterrent to the bankers, giving them a strong warning that any untoward behaviour in the future will not be visited with just a slap on the wrist. Such strong warnings may curb the excesses of bankers in the future.

4.11 Contributions to the Operating Income Before Tax by the Investment Banking Division of Barclays Group

In general, this section examines the annual contributions from the bank's investment banking division to the common purse in Barclays Group over a period of fifteen years to emphasise the division's relative importance and over-reliance on investment banking's contribution to income generation in Barclays.

---

[743] Barclays Plc, 'Annual Report and Financial Accounts' (2018, p. 2)
[744] Barclays Plc, 'Annual Report and Financial Accounts' (2015, p.3)

Table 7: Contributions of the Investment Banking to the Profit Before Tax Relative to Other Divisions: Barclays Group

Year	Profit Before Tax £ million	Contributions of Investment Banking to The PBT £ million	Contributions Of all others To the PBT £ million	% Contributions Of Investment Banking	% Contributions Of all other Divisions
2004	4,580	1,020	3,560	22%	78%
2005	5,280	1,272	4,008	24%	76%
2006	7,136	2,216	4,920	31%	69%
2007	7,076	2,335	4,741	33%	67%
2008	6,077	1,302	4,775	21%	79%
2009	4,585	2,464	2,121	54%	46%
2010	6,079	4,780	1,299	79%	21%
2011	5,879	2,965	2,914	51%	49%
2012	7,048	4,063	2,985	58%	42%
2013	5,167	2,523	2,644	49%	51%
2014	5,502	1,377	4,125	25%	75%
2015	5,403	1,611	3,792	30%	70%
2016	3,230	2,650	580	82%	18%
2017	3,166	2,056	1,110	65%	35%
2018	3,494	2,593	901	74%	26%

It should be noted that this aspect of the evaluation suffers from one crucial disadvantage. This is because there are no available statistics to let us know pound for pound in weighted averages, the amount invested in each division which generated the amount contributed to the common purse. Such statistics would enable us to accurately say that £1,000 invested in the Investment Banking Division generated 'x' value. In contrast, the same £1,000 invested in the other divisions generated 'y' value.

Notwithstanding this gap, the available statistics underscore the investment banking division's capacity to generate income. **Table 7** indicates that for the fifteen years under review, the investment banking division contributed more than 50% to the PBT in seven years. Out of those seven years, on three occasions, in 2010, 2016 and 2018, the investment banking division contributed more than 70% to the PBT. This summary emphasises the investment banking division's substantial importance to Barclay's profitability. With the removal of the core banking arm of the bank arising from the ring-fencing policy, the contention is that the synergy that had hitherto existed would be dissipated, and predictably, the level of profitability in Barclays after this separation is more likely than not to be adversely affected.

In 2006, Barclays declared that,

"The group provides banking services to its associates, joint ventures and the group pension funds…providing loans, overdrafts, interest and non-interest-bearing deposit and current accounts to these entities as well as other services."[745]

A ring-fenced member in a group may provide intra-bank services to members within the group, such as current account and deposit account agency services. However, the ring-fenced bank is prohibited from exposing itself to other group members. This is a cardinal principle of the ring-fencing policy.

Drawing on the provisions under s.142 D (2) Banking Reform Act 2013 Part 9 B (Ring-fenced banks excluded activities), the Guidance Consultation paper 15/5 at paragraph 1.6 reiterates the policy on intra-dealing activities within a group. Accordingly, ring-fenced banks are generally prohibited from engaging in investment banking as principals or commodity trading. They are also prohibited from being exposed to financial institutions, branches (within the group) and subsidiaries outside the EEA.

The idea behind this is to prevent situations where exposure by a ring-fenced bank to a member of the group results in the ring-fenced bank's inability to continue in business should the group member be exposed to insolvency. In the same way, the non-ring-fenced bank cannot rely on the ring-fenced bank for support should the mainstream non-ring-fenced bank run into financial difficulty.

This researcher proposes that only the riskier elements of investment banking should be removed from the mainstream bank. These include proprietary trading, which ruined Baring Capital and brought considerable losses to Union Bank of Switzerland. Other parts, such as core banking services, corporate banking, and less-risky wholesale banking, should be properly supervised and allowed to continue to operate together. That way, the big UK banks would have remained

---

[745] Barclays Annual Accounts p. 218

competitive with their European counterparts that did not adopt the ring-fencing policy.

4.12 Insurance Services Contributions to the Operating Profit Before Tax

Before the 2007–2009 global financial crisis, universal banking status allowed Barclays to engage in insurance services as a part of its other financial services provisions. This remained the case until 2008 when the bank closed some Life Assurance businesses with a disposal profit of £326 million.[746]

Notwithstanding, Barclays collaborates with other insurance companies as commissioned agents and intermediaries acting as introducers. For example, Barclays works with Legal & General to provide insurance services for mortgage holders. The bank also works with Allianz Insurance Plc and Simply Business regarding business insurance; Gresham Insurance Company Ltd does Homes Insurance, Aviva Insurance and RAC provide travel packs and breakdown covers.[747]

The statistics available for insurance contributions to the PBT are only for four years, from 2005 to 2008.

For the period in which statistics are available, the average annual contribution to the PBT was over half a billion pounds.[748] Given that the company's insurance arm is a 'service' based operation with its income mainly derived from earned insurance premiums and commissions, huge capital and asset investments are not a requirement for its success. This is because the service, for example, does not need huge office space or an overly large number of employees. In addition, the bank benefited from using frontline staff in their local branches to sell insurance services as an add-on work to the core banking business. Thus, contributions to PBT, which reached over half a billion pounds annually for this auxiliary service, can reasonably be considered a highly profitable business.

---

[746] Barclays Plc, 'Annual Report and Financial Accounts' (2008, p. 17)

[747] https://www.barclays.co.uk/insurance/travel-insurance/

[748] Please see Table 6, page 205 column 13.

4.13 Wealth Management's Contributions to the Operating Profit Before Tax

In Barclays, Wealth Management services are a niche market, allowing the bank to provide private and investment management services to wealthy individuals and corporate bodies. This service is operated through a few dedicated branch offices and subsidiaries of Barclays in the UK and overseas.[749]

In 2015 accounts, Barclays disclosed that international private banking businesses other than those in the UK region, Monaco and Geneva, were disposed of with the sum realised from the sale used to boost capital requirements. Meanwhile, Barclays continued to provide this lucrative service in the few selected places listed above.

We have access to ten years of statistics on the contributions of the Wealth Management division to the PBT from 2004–2013.[750] However, in 2014, there was a restructuring that led to the merging of the wealth management arm with other divisions of the bank. Thus, there was no separate rendition of the Wealth Management division statistics from that time forward.

4.14 Findings and Conclusions Regarding Barclays Group in the Light of the Aim of the Study

(i) Barclays Bank was founded about 330 years ago. Over time, it grew into a vast and highly successful universal bank with a global reach extending to over fifty countries. About 160,000 employees serve 48 million customers worldwide.[751]

(ii) Following Margaret Thatcher's government's adoption of the trade liberalisation model in the late 1970s, Barclays operated within the universal banking model, which initially benefited the bank. However, mergers and acquisitions went out of control, which led to disastrous outcomes. Nevertheless, the bank grew phenomenally, with its assets reaching over £2 trillion. The asset was later criticised for being overinflated through the derivative accounts.[752]

---

[749] Barclays Plc, 'Annual Report and Financial Accounts' (2008, p. 155)
[750] Please see Table 6, page 205, column 14.
[751] Please see page 225.
[752] Please see pages 227, 243 – 244.

(iii) The global financial crisis affected Barclays, as huge losses were incurred due to its exposure to the subprime credit market, especially through its acquisition of Lehman Brothers' businesses in the USA. This resulted in demurrage on the derivative accounts and consequently led to high impairment provisions made against the bank's high-risk assets. As a result, Barclays struggled to keep up with the acceptable liquidity requirement in six of the fifteen years evaluated.[753]

Barclays sought alternative means to resolve the acute liquidity problem and meet the new regulatory requirements on capital. The bank avoided taking a government bailout package but took a £6.1 billion loan from Qatar.[754] Although this led to the bank being taken to court on an allegation of obtaining unlawful assistance from a foreign government, the charges were dismissed at the Crown Court and the High Court.[755]

In addition to Barclays' quest to meet the new capital and liquidity requirements imposed by the new regulatory changes embedded in Basel III, Barclays had to dispose of Barclays Global Investors, Absa Group in South Africa, and other non-core banking businesses in Europe and America.[756]

(iv) Barclays planned to be ring-fencing compliant by the first quarter of 2018, which the bank succeeded in doing.[757]

(v) Under Basel III and the Capital Requirements Directive Regulations (CRD3), which require banks to hold more buffer capital against market risks, Barclays complied with the directive by 31st December 2011. However, due to several scandals that emerged in Barclays' business operations and the need to source funds to meet new regulatory requirements regarding liquidity and capital, the management decided it was time to shut down a substantial part of its non-core banking services.[758]

---

[753] Please see pages 243 – 244.
[754] Please see pages 229 – 230.
[755] Please see pages 229 – 230.
[756] Please see page 242.
[757] Please see page 248.
[758] Please see page 250.

	Barclays was found wanting in its involvement in LIBOR manipulation, mis-sold insurance products and other irregularities in the investment arm of its banking operations.
(vi)	The global divestment occurred when the economy was only recovering from recession. A pertinent question is whether Barclays got the best value available for the businesses sold at that period and whether the bank could have received more for its assets if the bank had the opportunity to differ sale of the asset to a more auspicious time. Barclays incurred losses of about £12 billion from selling its non-core assets.[759]
(vii)	Part of the consequences of low-level profitability was that from 2013, Barclays only managed to sustain a modest profit and had modest dividend payouts to shareholders with the worst-case situation in 2017 when the bank could not make any dividend payment whatsoever.[760] Another fallout of this poor performance was that the profit level did not meet the cost of capital.[761] Worse still, if shareholders are not getting returns on their investments that are competitive enough with the income from alternative investment outlets elsewhere, there may be a shift in the number of people willing to hold to their shareholding in Barclays. This may also create additional difficulties when attempting to raise new capital from the stock market in the future, arising from poor historical dividend payout.[762]
(viii)	Based on income level and distributable profit, it could be argued that Barclays has not fully returned to its status in the pre-crisis period when earnings per share were 71.9p, and dividend per share was 31.0p. This was against the company's performance in 2018 when earnings per share were 9.4p, and dividend per share remained at 6.5p.[763]
(x)	On a positive note, as of April 2018, Barclays had fully restructured and became compliant with the ring-fencing policy. As a result, the

---

[759] Please see page 249
[760] Please See pages 231 – 232, Table 6.
[761] Barclays (2016, p.3) Annual Report and Financial Accounts
[762] Please page 232, Table 6, column 9.
[763] Please see pages 231 – 232, Table 6, column 9.

enormous restructuring costs are unlikely to be repeated. Hopefully, issues about huge fines, huge litigation expenses and costs on mis-sold PPI would also be put behind the bank. Thus, the bank can have a new beginning free from the shackles of the past so that in no distant future, the bank may hopefully be able to generate a sufficient profit margin which will yield returns above the cost of capital.

(xi) **Table 7** on page 253 indicates that for the fifteen years under review, the investment banking division contributed more than 50% to the PBT in seven years. Out of these seven years, on three occasions in 2010, 2016 and 2018, the investment banking division contributed more than 70% to the PBT.[764] With the removal of the core deposit accounts of the bank arising from the ring-fencing policy, the contention is that the synergy that had hitherto existed would be dissipated, and predictably, the level of profitability in Barclays after this restructuring is more likely than not to be adversely affected.

(xii) Barclay's provision of insurance services as an auxiliary work of the bank was hugely successful and profitable to Barclays because this secondary service provision worked well by using its existing vast branch network and front desk staff of the bank to sell insurance services to many existing bank customers.[765]

In light of the preceding statements and the study's aim, the analysis of the data extracted from Barclays's Annual Reports and Financial Accounts led to the hard conclusion that Barclays sustained huge losses through the sale of non-core financial assets at a time when the economy was only recovering from recession. In addition, Barclays was also hit with enormous fines for breach of conduct, which eroded the company's profits.

---

[764] Please see page page 253, Table 7.
[765] Please see pages 255.

Section C: Standard Chartered Bank (Group Accounts)

4.15 Introduction

At the planning stages of this study, SCB was not part of the banks earmarked as a case study. Instead, the original plan was to examine some of the biggest global systematically important banks in the UK that are most likely to be affected by the ring-fencing policy and whose risks of possible collapse could pose significant harm to the economy more than others. These are banks with assets over a trillion pounds and whose possible collapse could seriously affect the real economy, endangering the availability of credits and jeopardising employment security on a massive scale.

However, during a review, it was considered expedient to also include a mid-range bank with total assets below a trillion pounds. That was how SCB came into focus. SCB is a UK bank and should ordinarily be ring-fencing compliant because its core deposits far exceeded the £25 billion minimum threshold required to fall within the range of banks required to comply with the ring-fencing policy.

However, in evaluating SCB's accounts, it was discovered that though the bank's total core deposits far exceeded the £25 billion minimum threshold, it escaped because most of its core banking customers, whom the ring-fencing policy primarily seeks to protect, are outside of Europe.

Strategically, SCB does not operate branch banking in the UK but keeps the hub of its investment banking operations in London. Traditionally, for upward of 150 years, their commercial banking operations remained mainly in Asia, China, Taiwan, the Middle East, South Korea, and some African countries, including South Africa, Ghana, and Nigeria.

Nevertheless, though SCB was not directly affected by the ring-fencing policy, its accounts presented a unique opportunity to compare and contrast its results with those of other UK banks within the case studies group required to comply with it.

These were the circumstances under which SCB retained its status as one of the case studies that deserved inclusion in this study.

4.16 Standard Chartered Bank Plc: Historical Background and Basic Statistics

Standard Chartered Bank is a Public Limited Liability Company registered in England under registration number 966425, having its Group Headquarters at 1 Basinghall Avenue London, EC2V 5DD, United Kingdom. SCB is listed on the London and Hong Kong Exchanges.[766] The bank is also listed on the Bombay and National Exchange in India.[767] In the period leading to the global financial crisis, Standard Chartered Bank ranked among the top 25 companies in the FTSE100 index by market capitalisation.[768]

The origin of Standard Chartered Bank dates way back to 1853 when a Royal Charter was granted to one of its founders, James Wilson, a Scotsman. He opened pioneering bank branches in Shanghai, Mumbai and Kolkata in 1858 and opened others in Hong Kong and Singapore over the next decade.[769] About that same period, a different bank, Standard Bank of British South Africa, was founded in 1862 by another Scotsman, John Paterson, who was also granted a Royal Charter in 1853, which led to his establishing the first branch of the bank in Cape province, South Africa in 1862.[770] Eventually, the two separate banks merged in 1969, with the adopted name Standard Chartered Bank.

Right from their inception, both banks focused their banking operations outside the UK. They have found a strong foothold in Asia Pacific countries such as Hong Kong, Singapore, Malaysia, and Korea. In addition, they established branches in other places around the world, including China, India, the Middle East, and Africa. Even today that reflects the current geographical spread of their business operations, with less than 20% of their operating income coming from Europe and the Americas.[771, 772]

The Statutory Auditors for the bank are KPMG Audit Plc, London, Chartered Accountants, 15 Canada Square, London E14 5GL.[773] The financial accounting

---

[766] Standard Chartered Bank, 'Annual Report and Financial Accounts' 2007, p. 164
[767] Standard Chartered Bank 'Annual Report and Financial Accounts' 2012, p. 1
[768] Standard Chartered Bank 'Annual Report and Financial Accounts' 2008, p. 4
[769] https://www.theguardian.com/business/2012/aug/07/standard-chartered-short-history
[770] Ibid. (The Guardian)
[771] Standard Chartered Bank 'Annual Report and Financial Accounts' 2018
[772] Standard Chartered Bank 'Annual Report and Financial Accounts' 2008, p. 4.
[773] Standard Chartered Bank 'Annual Report and Financial Accounts' 2018, p. 235

year starts from 1st January to 31st December annually. The accounts are denominated in US dollars. Apart from regulators in the countries around the world where they operate, the Group's lead regulators are the Prudential Regulatory Authority (PRA) and the Financial Conduct Authority (FCA) in the UK.[774]

Following enhanced regulatory requirements in the banking sector in the aftermath of the global financial crisis of 2007–2009, a more onerous burden was imposed on the independent external auditors to, among other requirements, provide a more comprehensive report in their audit. The report concerns wide-ranging issues, including a specific report on the financial statement, the accounting report standards used, liquidity and insolvency risks, loans impairment provision, valuation of complex or illiquid financial instruments, an estimate of future profitability and the scope of the audit. There was no adverse report from the auditors in the accounts for the period evaluated.

4.17 The Size, Markets and Business Model of Standard Chartered Bank Over Time

With about 160 years of experience in some of the world's most dynamic markets in the Middle East, Asia and Africa, Standard Chartered Bank, an international banking group, operates a universal banking model across about 1,700 branches in sixty-eight markets, relying on both organic growth by ploughing back part of its profit into the business and also exploiting the benefits of mergers and acquisitions.[775]

For example, in 1999, SCB acquired a 75% majority interest in Narkornthon Bank in Thailand. In the year 2000, it purchased Grindlays in India. In 2004, in conjunction with a consortium partner, PT Astra, the bank took a controlling interest in Bank Permata, Indonesia. SCB also purchased Korea First Bank in 2005. [776] In 2006, it merged with Union Bank in Pakistan. In 2007, it took a controlling interest in the Taiwanese bank, Hsinchu International Bank, and in that same year, SCB acquired Pembroke and Harrison Lovegrove and American Express Bank.[777]

---

[774] Standard Chartered Bank 'Annual Report and Financial Accounts' 2017, p. 68
[775] Standard Chartered Bank 'Annual Report and Financial Accounts' 2012, p. 1
[776] Standard Chartered Bank 'Annual Report and Financial Accounts' 2005, p. 5
[777] Standard Chartered Bank 'Annual Report and Financial Accounts' 2007, p. 6

In addition to their increased appetite for mergers and acquisitions of commercial banks, SCB also formed strategic alliances with non-core banking institutions like Fleming Family & Partners Ltd (FF&P), a leading wealth management services provider, and acquired an interest in Travelex, a non-bank foreign exchange specialist.[778]

As demonstrated by all these, the period leading to the global financial crisis was a time of exponential growth for SCB. The bank enjoyed ever-increasing growth in its primary markets in China, Thailand, Indonesia, South Korea, Pakistan, India, Taiwan, Malaysia, Nigeria, Ghana, South Africa and the United Arab Emirates. They have maintained a presence for about 160 years in some of the countries listed.

Although SCB was not in the same category in terms of size as HSBC, RBS, and Barclays, it had an impressive success story for the period under review. The four banks, SCB, RBS, HSBC, and Barclays, operated similarly in terms of growth and operational strategies. In addition, they operated a universal banking model, and they all had extensive international outreach. However, unlike RBS and Barclays, HSBC and SCB focused more on markets outside Europe and America.

At the peak of its success in 2014, SCB held assets of about US$726 billion and employed about 90,000 people worldwide, compared to just US$147 billion in assets in 2005. This phenomenal growth in the space of ten years was partly due to its universal banking model and acquisitions and mergers strategies. SCB only kept a minimal share in the turbulent American markets, so when there was a financial crisis, the bank was one of the least affected banks.[779]

---

[778] Standard Chartered Bank 'Annual Report and Financial Accounts' 2005, p. 15
[779] Standard Chartered Bank 'Annual Report and Financial Accounts' 2014.

Table 8: Tabulated Data Extracted from the Annual Reports and Consolidated Financial Accounts of the Standard Chartered Group From 2004 to 2018 (Financial Year Ending on 31st December Annually)

Year	Operating Income US$ (b)	Operating Profit Before Tax US$ (b)	Total Asset US$ (b)	Impairment Charges US$ (b)	Branches	Employees 000
1	2	3	4	5	6	7
2004	5.4	2.3	147.1	0.3		
2005	6.9	2.7	215.0	0.4	1,200	44
2006	8.6	3.2	266.0	0.6	1,400	59
2007	11.0	4.0	329.2	0.8	1,600	70
2008	14.0	4.8	435.0	1.8	1,600	74
2009	15.1	5.1	436.7	2.1	1,600	77
2010	16.0	6.1	516.5	1.0	1,700	85
2011	17.6	6.8	599.0	1.0	1,500	87
2012	19.0	6.9	636.5	1.4	1,700	89
2013	18.8	6.0	674.4	2.7	1,600	87
2014	18.3	4.2	725.9	2.9	1,200	90
2015	15.3	(1.5)	640.5	5.5	-	84
2016	14.0	0.4	646.7	3.0	-	87
2017	14.4	2.4	663.5	1.7	-	86
2018	14.8	2.5	688.8	0.8	-	85

Earnings Per Share (Cent)	Dividend Per Share (Cent)	Total Deposit US$ (b)	Total Loan US$ (b)	Income from Wholesale Banking £ (b)	Contribution Insurance US$ (000)	Income from Wealth Management US$ (000)
8	9	10	11	12	13	14
129.6c	57.50c	100.2	88.7	1.2	-	0.9
148.5c	64.00c	138.8	133.5	1.4	-	1.4
169.0c	71.04c	173.6	159.0	1.8	-	1.9
201.1c	79.35c	205.6	189.6	5.2	-	2.6
202.4c	61.62c	265.9	220.8	7.5	-	2.8
167.9c	66.03c	289.7	249.2	9.3	-	2.2
196.3c	69.15c	335.5	292.4	10.0	-	1.1
200.8c	76.00c	378.0	329.7	10.8	-	1.3
199.7c	84.00c	414.1	352.3	11.8	-	1.3
164.4c	86.00c	424.6	374.4	11.5	-	1.3
102.2c	86.00c	459.7	368.6	6.0	-	1.7
(91.9c)	13.70c	388.2	321.9	5.3	-	1.7
(14.5c)	Nil	408.7	325.3	6.5	-	0.5
23.5c	11.00c	401.5	306.2	6.5	-	0.5
18.7c	21.00c	420.7	318.0	6.9	-	0.5

4.18 Constituents of Table 8

Table 8 above contains the tabulated data regarding the financial summaries extracted from the Annual Reports and Financial Accounts of SCB for fifteen years from 2004 to 2018.

The first three years' accounts from 2004 to 2006 represent the years immediately preceding the global financial crisis. Remarkably, SCB continued to perform creditably well through the crisis period until 2015, when, for the first time, they had a negative OPBT. By 2017–2018, they started gaining momentum again, returning to making a modest OPBT.

Appendix 3, at the back of this book, contains page reference numbers indicating the pages in the Annual Reports and Financial Accounts where the financial summaries were extracted.

The Table comprises fourteen vertical columns with self-explanatory headings indicating the variables contained in each column. The horizontal rows are the values of Key Performance Indicators (KPI) recorded annually.

Figures 18–25 below are graphical presentations of the variables in Table 8 in chart forms to illustrate visually the relationships between the variables indicated on the headings of each chart. In addition, beneath each chart is a summary of the results generated from the chart.

Appendices 18 to 25, at the back of this report, present the variables of each chart's 'X' and 'Y' axes.

Figure 18: SCB Group: The Relationship Between Income and Operating Profit Before Tax 2004–2018 US $ (B)

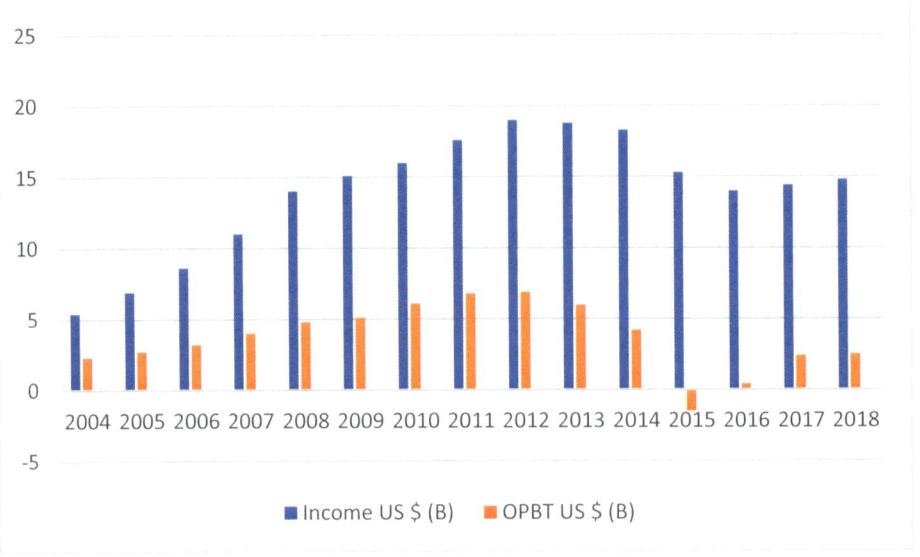

The chart indicates nine unbroken years of income growth peaked at US$19 billion in 2012. In 2013 and 2014, there were dips in the operating income of about US$200 million in 2013 and a slide of US$500 million in 2014. After that, there was a huge fall in income by US$3 billion in 2015. The impairment charges increased from $2.9 billion in 2014 to $5.5 billion. Income only started to pick up gradually in 2017 and 2018. Correspondingly, OPBT maintained unbroken growth for nine years from 2004–2012. The bank suffered a negative OPBT in 2015, following a decline of US$3 billion in operating income and a sharp increase in the impairment charges, as mentioned earlier. The bank went back to making modest positive OPBT from 2016 to 2018.

Figure 19: SCB Group: The Relationship Between Assets, Deposits and Loans 2004–2018 US$ (B)

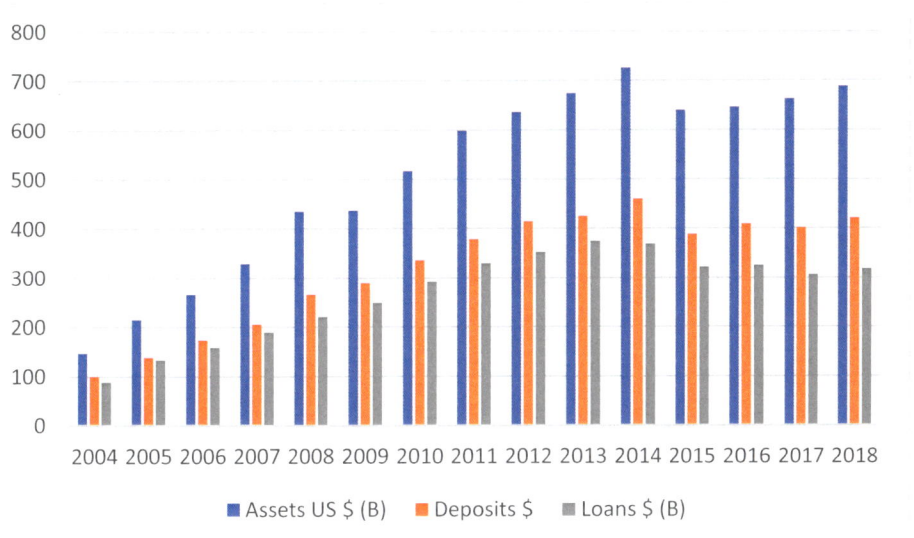

Except in 2015, when the total assets fell from $726 billion to $641 billion, the bank maintained fairly consistent growth in the total assets employed, having quadrupled from about $147 billion in 2004 to $689 billion in 2018. In the same vein, from 2008 to 2018, the deposits had a good margin above the aggregate loans, indicating that the bank maintained a healthy liquidity ratio.

Figure 20: SCB Trend of Growth/Decline in the Total Assets For 2004–2018 US$ (B)

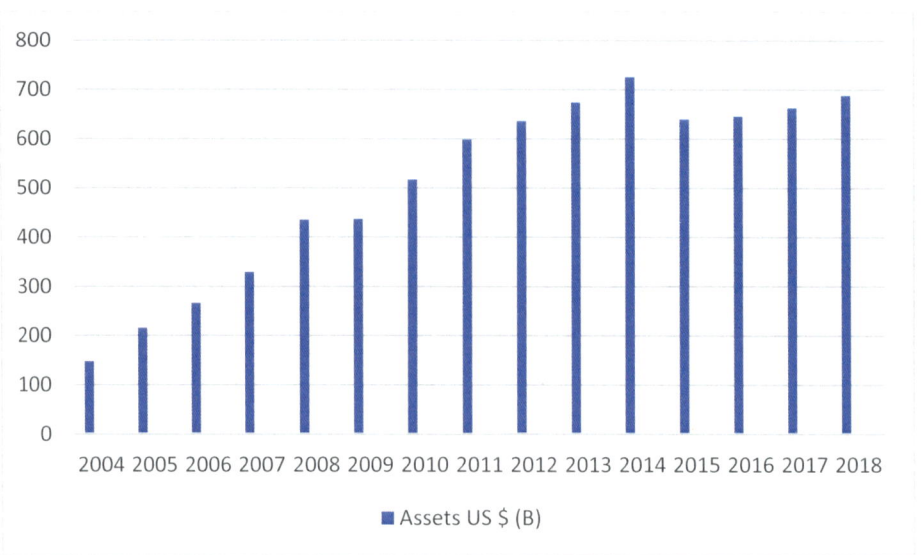

This chart relates to the total assets held by SCB from 2004 to 2018. The asset value stands alone. It shows consistent growth from 2004 to 2014 and then a dip, which started to pick up in 2017.

Figure 21: SCB Trend of Growth/Decline in Impairment Charges 2004–2018 US$ (b)

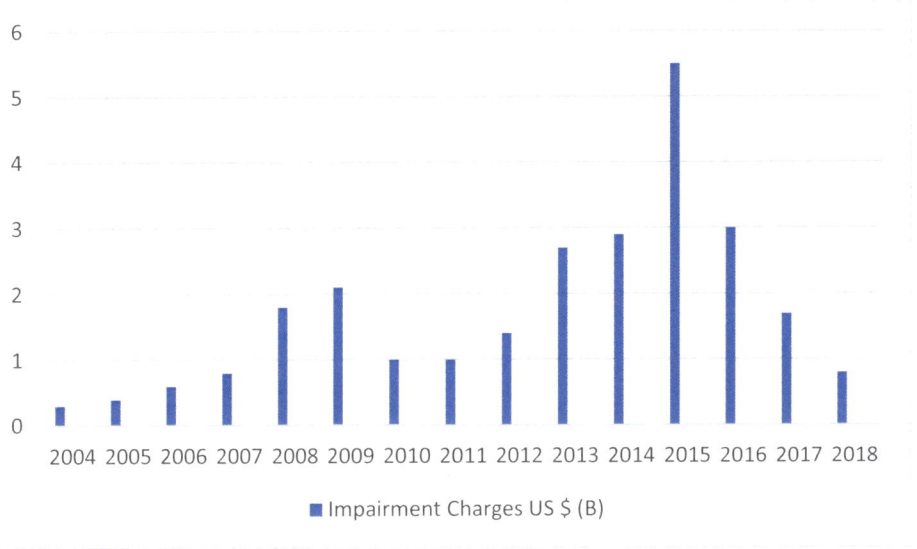

This chart indicates a sharp increase in the impairment charges, which in 2015 amounted to $5.5 billion. This helps us to understand why SCB went into negative OPBT, particularly in 2015. Impairment charges are a provision against credit risks such as weakened recoverable loans and advances. It is also a proportion of the profit set aside against losses arising from the diminished value of the bank's financial assets (this is different to provisions made for the depreciation of buildings and machinery).

On this occasion, the impairment charges related to depreciation in the local currencies against the dollar and viewed against a reduction of US$ 3 billion in the operating income in that same year helps us understand why SCB OPBT ended up in a negative OPBT of US$ 1.5 billion in 2015.

Figure 22: SCB Group: The Proportion of Contribution of Investment Banking Division to the Operating Profit Before Tax 2004–2018

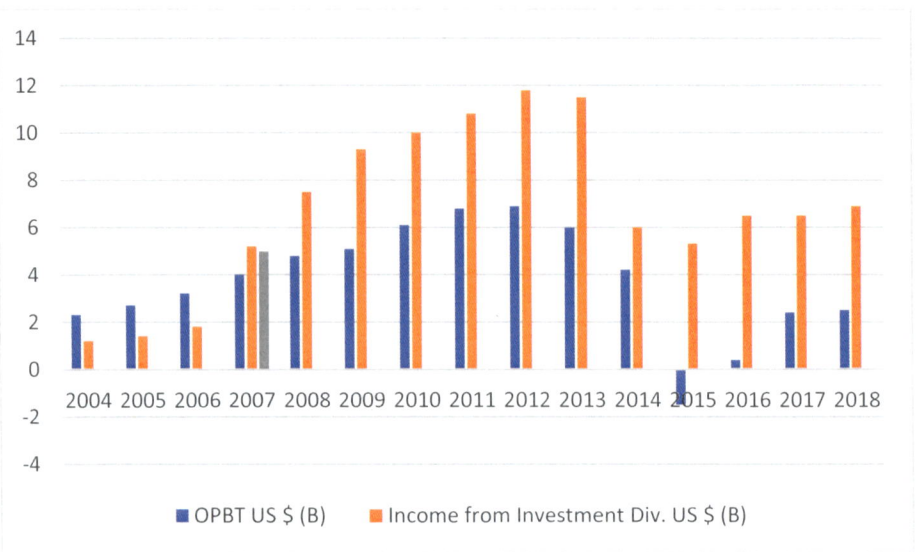

This chart implies that from 2007 to 2018, income from the investment division accounted for most of SCB's income. SCB was heavily dependent on income from that division. Income from that division peaked in 2009 to 2013, when it was $9.3 billion, $10 billion, $10.8 billion, $11.8 billion, and $11.5 billion.

Figure 23: SCB Group: Employee Profile 2005–2018

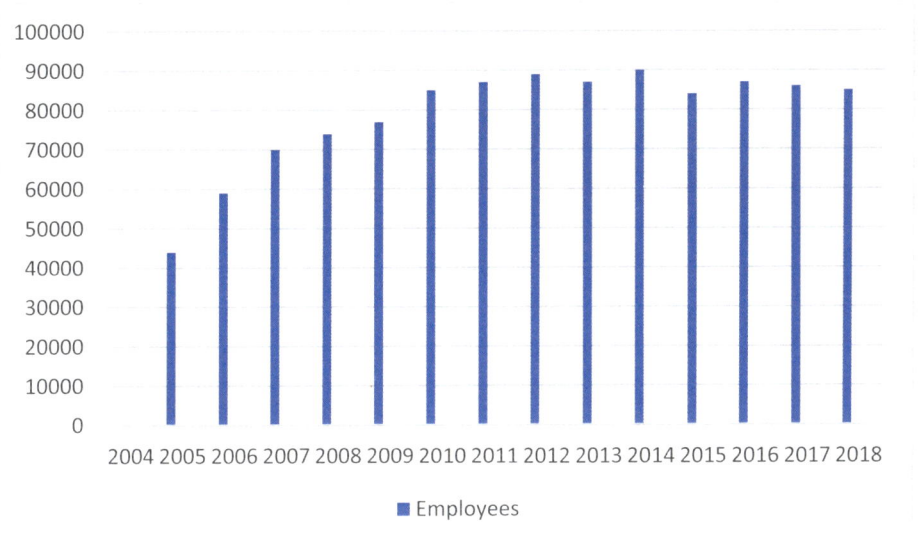

The chart reflects growth/decline in SCB's staff profile based on the data available from 2005 to 2018. SCB had 44,000 staff members in 2005. The number of staff peaked at 90,000 in 2014. As reflected in the downward slide in income and OPBT from 2015, the number of staff also went down marginally to 85,000 employees. In general terms, the staff's numerical strength was stable over the 15 years under review.

Figure 24: SCB Group: Trend of Growth/Decline in Earnings Per Share and Divided Per Share 2004–2018

Considering the global financial crisis that affected most financial institutions from 2007 to 2009, the bank's consistent growth in EPS and commensurate level of dividends from 2004 to 2014 are remarkable. The bank experienced a downturn in 2015 and 2016, but it started to pick up again in 2017.

Figure 25: SCB Group: Trend of Growth/Decline in Income from Wealth Management 2004–2018 US$ (b)

The undulating movement in the income earned from wealth management is a response to increased/decreased growth in revenue for the period under review. SCB earned US$ 2.8 billion from this arm of its operations in 2008, its highest within the period under review. After that, there was a sharp decline of $600 million in income in 2009, having earned US$2.2 billion. There was a further downward trend, coming to US$1.1 billion in 2010. The second wave of income movement witnessed a very slight increase in income, increasing to US$ 1.3 billion in 2011. After that, there was a slight upsurge to US$1.7 billion in 2014. Finally, in 2015–2018, wealth management income crashed to an all-time low of US$0.5 billion yearly.

4.19 Analysis and Interpretation of the Extracted Information Collated from the Annual Financial Accounts of Standard Chartered Bank Plc in Light of the Aim and Objectives of the Study

The trend in income level generated by a business is an important performance indicator that enables assessors to see whether the business is gaining or losing its hold on the market share. More importantly, this performance marker enables managers to assess whether assets are effectively deployed to generate sufficient income that meets the bank's budgeted income level and whether the income generated by the business justifies the costs.[780]

Column 2 is the record of the annual operating income. Remarkably, from 2005 to 2012, SCB maintained an eight-unbroken record of income increases, starting with $5.4 billion in 2004 and increasing to $19 billion by 2012. The increase in income is considered commensurate with the increase in operating assets.

As mentioned previously under paragraph 4.17, page 262 in 2005, SCB acquired interests in other financial institutions, including Korea First Bank, Union Bank in Pakistan and Taiwan (2006).[781] In addition, SCB also acquired interests in Hsinchu International Bank and formed alliances with non-banking financial institutions such as Fleming Family & Partners Ltd and Travelex. These acquisitions and alliances helped to boost SCB's revenue, as their operating income more than doubled by 2007 when it reached $11 billion.

Moreover, Asia, including China, had widely diversified economies during that period. As a result, there was a high degree of insulation and resilience due to more robust domestic demand and strong policy response to market challenges at the time.[782]

The bank witnessed accelerated growth in this period, with staff strength more than doubled, reaching almost sixty thousand by 2006. From 2001 to 2006, SCB reported that customers grew from about 7 million to over 14 million in five years. In addition, the number of branches increased to over 1,400 from just 550 in 2001.[783] What all this meant for SCB was an impressive growth in operating income, which climaxed at $19 in 2012.

Although from 2012 to 2014, revenue dipped to $18.3 billion, it is remarkable that SCB had such sustained growth throughout the global recession period. It appears as if the recession hardly touched SCB. According to SCB, their resilience during the global financial crisis was due to their disciplined risk-taking approach and limited exposure to direct and indirect Asset-Backed

---

[780] Op. Cit. E. McLaney and P. Atrill 2016, p. 70, (n. 701).
[781] Standard Chartered Bank 'Annual Report and Financial Accounts' 2006, p. 6
[782] Standard Chartered Bank 'Annual Report and Financial Accounts' 2007, p. 9
[783] Standard Chartered Bank, 'Annual Report and Financial Accounts' 2006, p. 9

Securities (ABS), including Collateralised Debt Obligations (CDO) at the time, which amounted to only $6 billion.[784]

Part of the strategy that enabled SCB to thrive during the inclement global financial crisis was monitoring the basics of banking—costs, capital, operational risks, and liquidity.[785]

However, from 2015 to 2018, their revenue suffered a significant reversal of fortune, dwindling to $14 billion in 2015. However, by 2018, they had slightly recovered, and operating income started a turnaround, making $14.8 billion.

Operating Profit Before Tax followed the same pattern as Operating Income. OPBT maintained an unbroken record of consistent growth for eight straight years from 2004 to 2012. The OPBT almost doubled from $2.3 billion earned in 2004 to $4 billion in 2007. This continued to increase modestly between 2008 to 2012 when the bank made the highest OPBT of $6.9 billion. After that, OPBT was reduced to $6 billion in 2013. Worst of all, SCB had a negative OPBT of $1.5 billion in 2015, having had the worst fall in their revenue by $3 billion in the same year, 2015. Thus, the reasons behind the OPBT loss of $1.5 billion are understandable. Foremost, there was a drop of $3 billion in revenue occasioned by weakened local currencies against the dollar at that time.

Secondly, the bank and the US authorities reached a settlement agreement over sanctions for breaches relating to compliance on regulatory issues. This amounts to $667 million, a significant dent in SCB's profit.[786] In addition, SCB faced other civil monetary penalties of $5.2 billion.[787, 788]

Worst of all, the impairment losses on loans, advances and other credit provisions increased phenomenally from $2.9 billion in 2014 to $5.5 billion in 2015. The very high impairment losses were due to some irrecoverable loans and a drastic fall in the value of local currencies against the dollar in Asia and Africa, their dominant markets.[789]

The situation worsened because of stricter regulations, low interest rates, subdued world trade, and trade tension between America and China, which

---

[784] Standard Chartered Bank, 'Annual Report and Financial Accounts' 2007, p. 11
[785] Standard Chartered Bank, 'Annual Report and Financial Accounts' 2008, p. 9
[786] Standard Chartered Bank, 'Annual Report and Financial Accounts' 2012, p. 8.
[787] Standard Chartered Bank, 'Annual Report and Financial Accounts' 2014, p. 3.
[788] Standard Chartered Bank, 'Annual Report and Financial Accounts' 2018, p. 9 & 305
[789] Standard Chartered Bank, 'Annual Report and Financial Accounts' 2012, p. 9

impacted market confidence.[790] Notwithstanding, SCB returned to making profits in 2016 and began to pick up modestly as the OPBT increased from $0.4 billion in 2016 to $2.4 billion in 2017 and $2.5 billion in 2018.

Column 4 shows that total assets in 2004 stood at $147 billion. However, over the next ten years, the assets grew to $729.9 billion due to organic and extensive mergers, acquisitions and strategic alliances, mainly in Asian markets and in America, as previously mentioned. From 2015, the value of the assets witnessed some decline, reduced to $640.5 billion. However, in 2016, it started to pick up, reaching $646.7 billion and ultimately attained $688.8 billion in 2018. As explained previously, the worsened economic environment in Asia, SCB's primary market, coupled with unfavourable exchange rate movement, significantly affected the bank's performance from 2013 to 2018.

Column 5 relates to impairment charges. This is a contingent provision set aside annually from OPBT to defray potential losses due to non-performing accounts, irrecoverable loans, advances, and losses arising from diminution in the value of financial assets (not physical assets such as land, buildings, and equipment).

The impairment provision is contingent because a loan classified as irrecoverable may eventually be recovered. The impairment provision for that account would be added back to the bank's profit when previously bad and doubtful debt is recovered. As a matter of prudence and good practice, banks are encouraged to make generous provisions for losses that may arise from their business, which entails giving loans and advances to customers. The proportion of the amount provided would usually be based on the degree of riskiness of their exposure concerning loans and advances to customers.[791]

In the case of SCB, the sum provided as impairment charges from 2004 to 2007 were $0.3 billion, $0.4 billion, $0.6 billion, and $0.8 billion each year. This researcher cannot ascertain the adequacy of this level of provision at that time, given that the impairment charges were not growing at the same pace as the total assets. SCB did not explain these seemingly inadequate provisions in the financial accounts. Similarly, from 2008 to 2014, the impairment provisions for non-performing accounts ranging between $1 billion and $2.9 billion are also considered very modest, bearing in mind that the bank's assets had grown exponentially over the years. Be that as it may, if the impairment provisions were

---

[790] Standard Chartered Bank, 'Annual Report and Financial Accounts' 2018, p. 4.
[791] Op. Cit., Bank of International Settlement, 2017, (n. 361).

inadequate over time, SCB had only deferred the 'doomsday' until 2015, when the bank had to cough up $5.5 billion as impairment charges.

The significantly high impairment provision may be due to bank supervisors' intervention in line with the requirements under Basel III. As explained in Chapter 2, under Basel I and II, banks were given the discretion to use an internal model to determine how they wanted to determine the Risk Weighted Averages of their loan profile.[792] However, after the global financial crisis of 2007–2009, it was discovered that some banks were not entirely honest in grading their assets' quality. Thereupon, under Basel III reforms, banks' supervisors were given powers to look closely at the methodology engaged and powers to require banks to provide 'buffers' to cover risks, as they may determine.[793] This could have happened to SCB in 2015, but we cannot be entirely sure about that without SCB's comments on that aspect of their account.

What is known, however, is that as a direct consequence of the relatively huge impairment provision of $5.5 billion in 2015, the bank sustained operating losses before tax of $1.5 billion for the first time in the years under review.

Column 6 is related to the number of branches and outlets SCB operated. In 2003, SCB made the point that it had only 450 branches. However, in 2005, following strategic mergers and acquisitions, their network of branches increased to 1,200.[794] From then, the network of branches continued to increase until it peaked at 1,700 in 2010 and 2012. By 2014, the branches had reduced to 1,200. Following that, no further statistics were provided as to whether the branches increased or decreased. Understandably, due to the increase in the impact of technology, the importance of an increasing or diminishing number of branches is reduced.

Column 7 concerns the number of staff engaged by the Group. SCB's employment profile hit 90,000 in 2014 from about 44,000 in 2005. These people were employed in over 50 countries around their highly diversified markets.[795] Given the SCB strategy of keeping its investment banking arm mainly in the UK while branch banking was kept elsewhere, the staff complement in the UK was only about 2,000 people.

---

[792] Please see pages 116 – 117.

[793] Please see pages 75 – 76, 116 – 117.

[794] Standard Chartered Bank, 'Annual Report and Financial Accounts' 2005, p. 5.

[795] Standard Chartered Bank, 'Annual Report and Financial Accounts' 2007, p. 1.

Columns 8 and 9 are related to EPS and DPS. Over eleven years, from 2004–2014, SCB maintained an unbroken profit-making record. Except for 2016, the bank paid generous dividends to equity shareholders, ranging from 0.11 cents in 2017 to 0.86 cents in 2013 and 2014. As a result, the average DPS for the years under review was about 60 cents yearly.

Columns 10 and 11 relate to total deposits and loans. The key issue with these two variables is the consideration of whether or not aggregate loans exceeded total deposits. This is about the liquidity risk and whether there are concerns about SCB's ability to meet cash withdrawal demands of its customers. It should be borne in mind that the representative figures for each year are the total of loans and deposits for just one day in the year, the 31st of December annually. That means there may have been instances in the year when the ratio of aggregate deposits to loans may not necessarily be as impressive. However, that would be difficult to determine based on the figures presented in the annual reports and accounts for the years under review. That said, SCB was generally in a comfortable position.

Based on the statistics in columns 10 and 11 in Table 8, for the fifteen years under review, the aggregate deposit figures in each year exceeded the loan figures by very comfortable margins. For example, from 2008 to 2011, the deposits exceeded loans by an average of $50 billion. From 2012 to 2016, the deposits exceeded loans by an average of $70 billion. In 2017 and 2018, the average figure with which the deposits exceeded loans was almost $100 billion. These figures give the impression of a well-resourced bank with good liquidity.

Column 12 is the extract of income from the investment banking division of SCB from 2004 to 2018. This division contributed $1.2 billion in 2004 and $1.4 billion in the subsequent year. In 2009, however, the contribution from this arm of SCB significantly rose to $9.3 billion. This was after the strategic mergers, takeovers, acquisitions, and alliances with other financial institutions which SCB engaged in to grow itself, especially in the period 2005 leading to 2009, as pointed out earlier in the review.

From 2010 to 2013, the contributions from the bank's investment banking arm were even better, with over $10 billion in annual contributions from the division, until 2014, when, as it were, the bubble ruptured. The downturn led to a 50% reduction in the division's contributions. The reason for the slump in the general performance of SCB from 2013 onward was linked with the general inclement market conditions in Asia at that time and the depreciation in the value of the local currencies within SCB's main markets against the USA dollar.

Column 13 indicates a nil return as SCB appears not to have engaged in the insurance business in its portfolio or that they were not reported separately.

Column 14 relates to income derived from wealth management services provided to wealthy private customers. Again, SCB made significant inroads into this niche market, having grown from a revenue earning capacity of a little less than a billion dollars in 2004 to an earning capacity of $2.8 billion in 2008. In 2013, SCB had $58 billion in Assets Under Management (AUM) from high-net-worth individuals, which generated an income of $1.3 billion.[796] The plan was to increase the AUM to $300 billion by 2020. However, as with other segments of SCB, the private banking sector income-generating capacity went down from $1.7 billion in 2015 to a mere $0.5 billion from 2016 to 2018.

4.20 Findings and Conclusions Regarding Standard Chartered Bank Group in the Light of the Aim of the Study

(i) SCB is a UK-registered bank regulated by the PRA and FSA and regulatory authorities in other countries where they were hosted. The bank has a long history, having its roots linked to two Scottish pioneers who were licensed to operate financial institutions as far back as the 1850s and 1860s.[797]

(ii) SCB is a universal bank listed on the London Stock Exchange, Hong Kong Stock Exchange, and Bombay National Stock Exchange in India. Notwithstanding that the bank's core deposits are more than £25 billion, SCB is not directly affected by the ring-fencing policy.[798] This is because the bank was outside the policy's scope. In addition, the core deposit bank's customers that the ring-fencing policy seeks to protect are based outside Europe.

---

[796] Standard Chartered Bank 'Annual Report and Financial Accounts', 2013, p. 9

[797] Please see page 261.

[798] Please see page 261.

Thus, other than a requirement to comply with other laws and banking regulations in the UK, SCB was not directly affected by the need to prepare and comply with the ring-fencing policy.[799]

(iii) Although the bank is a registered UK bank, it derives between 80–90% of its income from overseas in Asia, China, Africa, and the Middle East, where most of its consumer banking services have been provided over the last 150 years.[800, 801]

(iv) Strategically, SCB coordinates its investment banking services from the UK.[802]

(v) Generally, in all the areas of the available statistics concerning the Key Performance Indicators (except for impairment charges of $5.5 billion recorded in 2015), SCB performed creditably well. For example, the operating income grew consistently from only $5.4 billion in 2004 to $19 billion in 2012 but dropped sharply by $3 billion in 2015.[803]

(vi) SCB maintained an unbroken stretch of growth in its OPBT between 2004 and 2012, which climaxed at $6.9 billion. Similarly, earnings per share peaked at about $2.02 per ordinary share. The company's strong earning capacity allowed SCB to pay a generous average DPS of about $0.69 to its ordinary shareholders between 2007 and 2009 amidst the prevalent difficulties during the global financial crisis. From 2010 to 2014, DPS reached $0.86.[804]

(vii) Similarly, SCB had a very comfortable liquidity ratio such that deposits/loan ratios in 2004 were 1.14:1 and in 2018 it was 1.32:1. As pointed out previously, the difference between aggregate deposits was about $100 billion above total loans in 2017 and 2018.[805]

In conclusion, this researcher wants to point out the remarkable presence of regulatory arbitrage in the circumstances of SCB, as discussed below.

---

[799] Please see page 260.
[800] Standard Chartered Bank 'Annual Report and Financial Accounts' 2006, pages 4 & 5
[801] Standard Chartered Bank 'Annual Report and Financial Accounts' 2008, page 4
[802] Please see page 260
[803] Please see Table 8, pages 264 – 265.
[804] Please see Table 8, pages 264 – 265.
[805] Please see Table 8, pages 264 – 265.

For example, economic arbitrage occurs when a trader exploits price differences on the same instruments so that while selling an overpriced security, he simultaneously buys the underpriced security.[806] As a result, that trader later reaps a huge profit by selling the under-priced security at a much higher price. Arbitrage is not illegal, nor does it amount to breaking any rules.

SCB coordinates its investment banking activities from the UK, while its core banking customers are spread in other jurisdictions. The bank is listed on the London Stock Exchange and in other places such as Hong Kong and India.[807] Thus, the bank has the advantage of carrying out its investment banking businesses in the UK with enhanced capacity to raise much-needed finance in the UK (with the exclusion of deposits from consumer banking customers).

The opportunity gives SCB to use London as a corridor to funnel pounds sterling to fund its operations in Asia, China, the Middle East and Africa. It could also go the other way round so that access to funding in those other markets could be channelled through to London to fund wholesale banking in the UK, without the strenuous burden of the need to be ring-fencing compliant at home as other competitors in the UK.

The question may be, "Why couldn't other universal banks like Barclays and RBS use foreign deposits to subsidise their investment banking activities?"

The circumstances of SCB were very different to Barclays and RBS in some ways in the years under evaluation.

SCB was well-resourced with attractive balance sheets. Unlike Barclays and RBS, which could hardly break even during the global financial crisis. SCB scaled through the crisis almost effortlessly. With such credentials, SCB would naturally be the 'darling' of financiers and underwriters, whether in Europe, America or Asia, having few difficulties assuming they wanted to raise more funds.

Secondly, SCB was a well-managed and stable bank, unlike Barclays and RBS, which floundered for over ten years. The same reasons Barclays and RBS struggled to raise funds in the UK would also be the obstacles they would encounter elsewhere, whether in Europe, America, or Asia. This is because they would present the same financial records analysed in this study to potential lenders wherever they go. The potential financiers and underwriters would also

---

[806] Op. Cit., G. Arnold, 2005, p. 720, n. 31)

[807] Please, see page 261.

see the holes and difficulties in their accounts and may not want to throw good money after a struggling business.

Thirdly, it is not the case that RBS and Barclays cannot use funding from elsewhere to support their operations here in the UK. After all, that was what Barclays did by accessing £6.1 billion from Qatar through the private arrangement as discussed under Section B.

The argument is that apart from the fact that Barclays and RBS had load of difficulties already discussed, compliance with the ring-fencing policy would even make things worse for Barclays and RBS seeking external funding abroad compared with SCB and other European Banks that are not obliged to be ring-fencing compliant.

The evidence of the inherent advantages to SCB is that, in the face of the global financial crisis in 2007–2009, SCB was growing while other banks in the same market in the UK were shrinking and struggling to remain afloat. Meanwhile, SCB was thriving. SCB declared an unbroken eight-year record of increasing profits and comfortably paying increasing dividends from 2004–2014. On the contrary, RBS could hardly break even in 10 years. Similarly, Barclays could only pay little to nothing as dividends.

In the case of SCB, for ten years during and after the global financial crisis, making profits and paying increasing levels of dividends year in and year out was not a problem. It only raises questions about whether there was a level playing field. While RBS and Barclays were subjected to the UK's stringent rules, including the ring-fencing policy, SCB was not subjected to the ring-fencing policy. Furthermore, whilst RBS and Barclays had to dispose of their assets for some reasons, as previously discussed, SCB did not need to because of its impressive all-round performance.

Assuming that SCB faced criticisms in line with the issues highlighted, SCB might argue that, even if it were true, the bank did nothing wrong regarding regulation arbitrage. In any event, SCB has always had its businesses spread worldwide for more than 150 years from its inception.[808] Furthermore, even if SCB were found to have benefited from regulatory arbitrage, the bank did nothing illegal in that respect.

SCB could also defend their unbroken impressive profitability record from 2004–2014 on the basis that, unlike their competitors that were exposed to toxic

---

[808] Please see pages 261 – 263.

collateralised assets of more than £100 billion in some instances, SCB's extent of exposure to such assets was only limited to $6 billion.[809] As SCB did not share in the excruciating burden of toxic collateralised assets when compared with other banks that did, it should not be seen as out of the ordinary that SCB was making record profits while their competitors were struggling.

Also, regarding the $5.5 billion impairment charges that stood out of the lot in 2015, SCB could defend them as a one-off issue that arose due to depreciation in the currencies of their local markets against the US dollar, which is nothing unusual.

Section D: HSBC Holdings Plc (Group Accounts)

4. 21 HSBC Plc: Historical Background, Size and the Corporate Services Provided by the Bank

HSBC Holdings Plc is currently the largest UK bank. As of 2018, HSBC was the 7th rank among the largest banks in the world.[810]

The abbreviation HSBC stands for "Hong Kong and Shanghai Banking Corporation." Although the bank has a long history dating to 1865, when it was established in Hong Kong and where it then had its headquarters, HSBC was only incorporated in England on 1st January 1959 under the UK Companies Act.[811] At registration, the Company House issued the bank with company registration number 617987. The Group Headquarters, formerly located at 1 Queen's Road in the City of Victoria in the Central district of Hong Kong, was relocated to the UK in 1993 following the merger and acquisition of Midland Bank Plc.[812] The headquarters is currently at number 8, Canada Square London, E14 5HQ.[813]

The idea behind the establishment of HSBC started in 1864 when a Scottish Merchant Seaman called Thomas Sutherland was sailing along the coast of South China. He sensed a growing need for a bank that could cater to the needs of the rapidly growing international trade between Europe and Asian countries,

---

[809] Standard Chartered Bank, 'Annual Report and Financial Accounts' 2007, p. 11
[810] Please see Table 3, page 151.
[811] HSBC, Annual Accounts, 2017, p. 270
[812] HSBC, Annual Accounts, 2008, p. 458
[813] HSBC, Annual Accounts, 2018, p. 318

especially at the ports of Hong Kong, Shanghai and Japan. Thus inspired, with the support of well-established business communities across his social network in Hong Kong, Sutherland soon floated a corporation with an initial capital of 20,000 ordinary shares at HKD250 each, which sold out promptly.[814]

The bank's first branch was established in Hong Kong on March 3, 1865, while another soon followed in Shanghai in April of the same year. The bank also opened another branch in London in July 1865. At that time, the London branch was more of an outstation branch planted primarily to assist with the recruitment and training of staff in London and to facilitate the procurement of foreign exchange needed for trading between Europe and Asia.[815]

The point is that, at inception, HSBC was primarily founded to provide international banking services in Asia, providing financial services to support the export of a variety of goods to Europe, including silk and tea from China, sugar from the Philippines and jute and cotton from India.[816] In a short time, the bank became very successful in its business. At the start of the 20th century, it expanded to sixteen countries and had substantial resources to support infrastructural development in its primary place of birth, Asia. This included providing developmental loans to national governments to finance capital projects such as railways in some Asian countries.[817]

Although HSBC's far-reaching tentacles now extend globally, in keeping with the vision of the pioneer of the bank, a larger proportion of the bank's businesses are still located in Asia. HSBC operates a universal banking model with global businesses that provide wide-ranging financial services segmented along four main divisions, including (i) Retail banking and wealth management, (ii) Commercial banking, (iii) Global banking and market, and (iv) Global private banking.[818]

The following statistics can help readers understand HSBC's enormous size in recent history and appreciate the magnitude of the bank's global operations. At the peak of its success, HSBC had about US$2.7 trillion in assets,[819] over

---

[814] https://www.hsbc.com/who-we-are/our-history
[815] Ibid.
[816] Ibid.
[817] Ibid.
[818] HSBC Annual Accounts, 2016, p. 3
[819] HSBC Annual Accounts, 2012, p. 374.

310,000 employees,[820] and about 221,000 shareholders spread across 127 countries and territories worldwide.[821]

HSBC was listed on the Bermuda, London, New York, Hong Kong and Paris stock exchanges. Before the global financial crisis, HSBC operated from a network of branches in about 10,000 locations spanning almost 100 countries in five regions, including Hong Kong, the rest of Asia Pacific, North America, Latin America and Europe.[822] Also, before the global financial crisis, the bank served over 128 million customers worldwide,[823] which has now drastically reduced to about 39 million customers following the demerger, de-risking and selling off several non-core banking businesses, primarily in the North and Latin American countries.[824]

Importantly too, the above-stated statistics vis-a-vis the far-reaching potential consequences of the failure of such a mammoth size bank to the local and international banking system could understandably be a matter of deep concern to the public, the banking sector regulators and policymakers leading to supporting the argument for the ring-fencing policy adopted in the UK.

Just as RBS ran into difficulties by acquiring ABN, Ambro and Barclays had their share of trouble buying parts of Lehman Brothers' businesses. HSBC suffered losses during the global financial crisis because of its involvement in the subprime housing market. This happened through its merger with Household Finance Corporation, which HSBC acquired in 2003.

On a positive note, the restructuring processes that took place in HSBC in the period leading to 2019, inspired by policy measures taken to mitigate the effect of a possible failure in the banking sector, have arguably provided some relief on the risk factor of a failure occurring in the HSBC banking group. These policy measures also cut across other banking groups.

However, an important difference in the sales of HSBC non-core businesses is that (except where there were losses, such as in the case of Household Finance Corporation), the sales proceeds mostly remained in the business, which made the total assets remain almost unchanged. This was unlike the cases in RBS and Barclays, where a substantial part of the realised gains from selling their assets

---

[820] HSBC Annual Account, 2006, p. 265.
[821] HSBC Annual Accounts, 2010, the introductory page.
[822] HSBC Annual Accounts, 2006, the introductory page
[823] HSBC Annual Accounts, 2007, the introductory page
[824] HSBC Annual Accounts, 2018, p. 2.

went into cutting losses. Thus, while Barclays and RBS sold their non-core businesses, the assets' total value declined rather than increased because the sale proceeds were used to plug holes created by huge losses.

Part of the subjects discussed in Section D is the summary of how HSBC fared in the 15 years from 2004 to 2018 and the regulatory environment the bank operated under in the aftermath of the global financial crisis.

This section also discusses the threat that the bank may still pose to the world economy and issues identified in the HSBC financial records during the 15 years spanning the global financial crisis and about 10 years after that.

HSBC is primarily regulated and supervised by FCA and PRA (Departments in the Bank of England). This is in addition to the Federal Reserve Board in the USA and the Hong Kong Monetary Authorities. In 2008, HSBC reported having regulatory relationships that covered about 540 supervisory agencies, including central banks in jurisdictions worldwide where they have offices, branches or subsidiaries.[825] These regulatory activities covered lending practices, financial stability, capital adequacy, transparency in financial market dealings and depositors' protection, among many other areas. According to HSBC, the estimated costs of these regulatory and supervisory relationships to the bank were about US$635 million in 2005 alone.[826]

The bank's financial year starts on the 1st of January and ends on the 31st of December annually. For the period under review, the reporting currency was USA dollars.

As reported in the literature review in Chapter 2, Paragraph 2.16.1, pages 61 – 62. under 'Accounting Standards', the contributions of failed accounting reporting scandals in the USA-based energy company, Enron and the events that led to the collapse of BCCI have led to more scrutiny on the quality of the auditing standards adopted by banks' auditors.

Regarding HSBC, for the period under review, the accounts in 2004–2014 were audited by KPMG Audit Plc. From 2015–2018, PricewaterhouseCoopers LL P, Chartered Accountants and Statutory Auditors based in London, took over as the principal reporting auditors. Among many other areas of importance, the report of their audits includes a risk assessment of the bank at a global level, which separately covers individual legal entities within the group and the parent company.

---

[825] HSBC Annual Accounts, 2008, p. 188.
[826] HSBC Annual Accounts, 2005, p. 13.

In addition, Auditor's fieldwork was reported to have stretched over widespread locations. The auditors stated that they assessed operational processes critical to the financial reporting of HSBC. The auditors also claimed to have assessed the methodology to determine the fair value of financial assets and measurements of capital adequacy and liquidity ratios adopted by HSBC.[827] The point being emphasised is that it is increasingly recognised that effective auditing that is deep and far-reaching is a *sine qua non* to the ongoing efforts and processes needed to keep the banking sector safe. In 2017, HSBC reported auditor fees of US$129.7 million, demonstrating the extent and value of the works carried out by the auditors.[828]

Overall, the auditors gave no adverse reports for the years under review.

In the following paragraphs, the data extracted from HSBC accounts for 2004–2018 are in tables and graphs. It concluded with an analysis of the data.

---

[827] HSBC Annual Accounts, 2018, p. 213
[828] HSBC Annual Accounts, 2017, p. 129

Table 9: Tabulated Data Extracted from the Annual Reports and Consolidated Financial Accounts of HSBC Group From 2004 to 2018 (Financial Year Ending on 31st December Annually)

Year 1	Total Income US$ (b) 2	Operating Profit Before Tax US$ (b) 3	Total Assets US$ (b) 4	Impairment Charges US$ (b) 5	Branches 6	Employees 000 7
2004	51	19	1,280	6		253
2005	58	21	1,502	8		284
2006	65	22	1,861	11	10,000	312
2007	79	24	2,354	17	10,000	322
2008	82	9	2,527	25	9,500	325
2009	66	7	2,364	26	9,500	310
2010	68	19	2,455	14		307
2011	72	22	2,556	12	7,200	288
2012	68	21	2,693	8	6,600	270
2013	65	23	2,671	6	6,300	235
2014	61	19	2,634	4	6,100	258
2015	60	19	2,410	4	4,700	255
2016	48	7	2,375	3	-	235
2017	51	17	2,522	2	3,900	229
2018	54	20	2,558	2	-	235

Earnings Per Share (Cent) 8	Dividend Per Share (Cent) 9	Total Deposit US$ (b) 10	Total Loan US$ (b) 11	Investment Banking US$ (b) 12	Contribution Insurance US$ (b) 13	Global Private Banking US$ (000) 14
1.18c	0.63c	777	816	5	1	1
1.36c	0.69c	809	866	5	1	1
1.40c	0.76c	997	1,053	7	1	1
1.65c	0.87c	1,228	1,219	6	0.5	2
0.47c	0.93c	1,245	1,087	3	4	1
0.34c	0.34c	1,284	1,076	10	(2)	1
0.73c	0.36c	1,338	1,167	10	(0.6)	1
0.92c	0.39c	1,367	1,121	7	2	1
0.74c	0.45c	1,447	1,150	9	(1)	1
0.84c	0.49c	1,612	1,292	9	(2)	0.1
0.69c	0.50c	1,428	1,087	6	(1)	1
0.65c	0.51c	1,344	1,015	8	(1)	0.3
0.07c	0.51c	1,332	950	6	(2)	0.3
0.48c	0.51c	1,434	1,053	6	(3)	0.3
0.63c	0.51c	1,419	1,054	6	1	0.3

4.22 Constituents of Table 9

Table 9 comprises tabulated financial data extracted from HSBC's annual reports and financial accounts for 15 years starting from 2004 to 2018. The table contains fourteen vertical columns with self-explanatory headings regarding some key economic performance indicators obtained annually for the fifteen years under review.

The first three years, 2004–2006, is the period that preceded the global financial crisis. According to the HSBC accounting records, the bank generally performed credibly well in those three years, including 2007, when the crisis began. Although HSBC struggled considerably in 2008, 2009 and 2016, the bank came out of the general economic doldrums unaided by the government's bailout packages and successfully paid dividends throughout the 15 years under review. A more detailed analysis of the bank's performance is given in the next paragraph, 4.27.

Appendix 4, at the back of this book, provides the page numbers of the annual reports and financial accounts from which the financial data were extracted.

Figures 26–30 present the data in chart forms to illustrate the relationships between the data at a glance. The visual presentation assisted in understanding the basis of the bank's performance, how well it performed in some areas of its business activities and the extent to which the bank did not perform so well in other areas and why that may have been the case.

The variables in each chart's X and Y axes are presented in separate Appendices 26–30 at the back of this book.

Figure 26: HSBC Group: The Relationship Between Operating Income and PBT 2004–2018 US$ billion

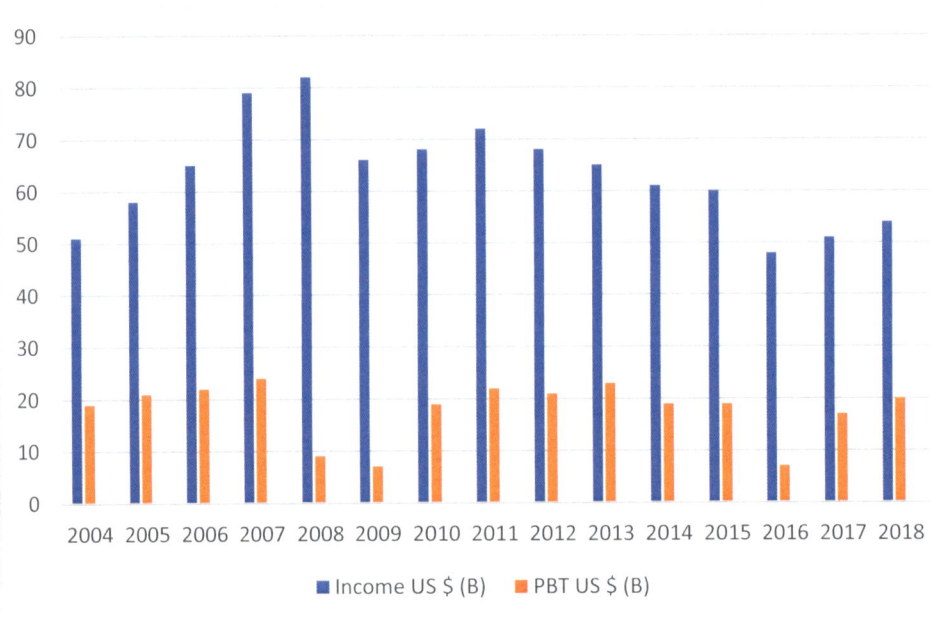

The chart indicates growth in HSBC's operating income from 2004 to 2008 when their income constantly increased annually from US$51 billion in 2004 to $82 in 2008. After that, from 2009 to 2015, the annual operating income ranged between $60 billion and $72 billion. Then, however, the operating income nose-dived sharply in 2016, when the bank had $48 billion in income as opposed to the $60 billion made in the previous year, 2015. This dismal performance was due to the losses incurred in the North American market, where HSBC lost $7 billion and in Brazil, where the bank sustained a loss of about $1 billion.

Also, operating profit before tax ranged between $24 billion in 2007 and $7 in 2009 and 20016. The poor performance in 2008 and 2009 had its roots in the defunct sub-prime lenders Household Finance Corporation, acquired by HSBC in 2003. Losses from this outfit cost HSBC about $50 billion. Part of the underlying difficulties at the height of the global financial crisis resulted in impairment charges of $25 and $26 billion in 2008 and 2009. Written-down goodwill exacerbated this in 2009. In addition, there were (i) scaled-down operations by disposing of non-core banking assets, which considerably reduced its global number of clients from 128 million to 39 million in 2018. (ii) reduced interest rate and (iii) depreciation in Asia countries' currencies against US dollars.

Figure 27: HSBC Group: The Relationship Between Assets, Deposits and Loans 2004–2018 US$ billion '000

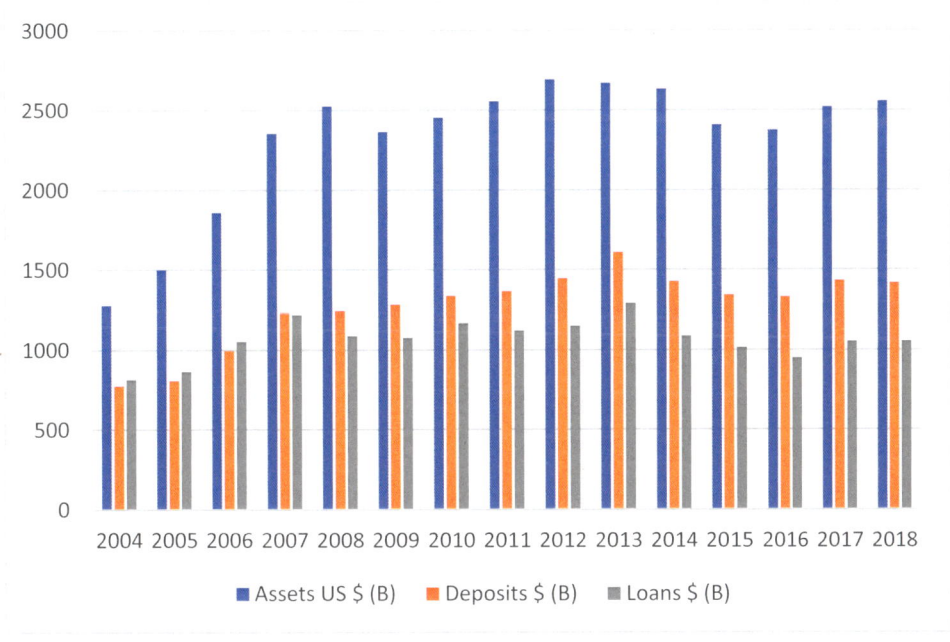

Remarkably, HSBC doubled its total assets in the 15 years under review, so its assets grew from $1.3 trillion in 2004 to $2.6 trillion by 2018. Moreover, except from 2004 to 2006, when the aggregate loans slightly exceeded deposits,

HSBC was firmly in control of its liquidity position from 2009–2018. This is because HSBC had excess deposits of between $200–$400 billion above the total loans annually throughout that period.

The enormous deposits, far more than loans and advances, indicate that HSBC was in a sound liquidity position. Depending on where this excess liquidity is stationed within the group, whether in the ring-fenced or non-ring-fenced bank, HSBC has an excellent capacity to support large customers. Either way, HSBC is generally better positioned to support its large customers. In addition, the constraints imposed by the ring-fencing policy would be minimal on HSBC, unlike RBS and Barclays.

Figure 28: HSBC Group: Trend of Growth/Decline in Impairment Charges 2004–2018 US$ billion

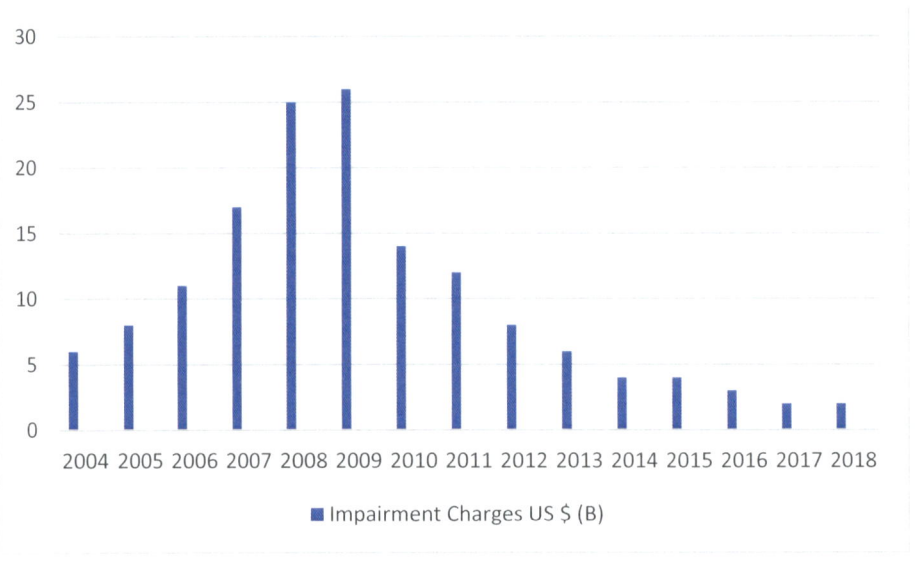

Impairment charges rose sharply in 2008 and 2009. This was due to the revaluation of derivatives in 2008 and the writing down of goodwill in 2009.

Figure 29: HSBC Group: The Proportion of Contributions to PBT from Investment Banking Division, Insurance Business and Private Banking 2004–2018 US$ billion

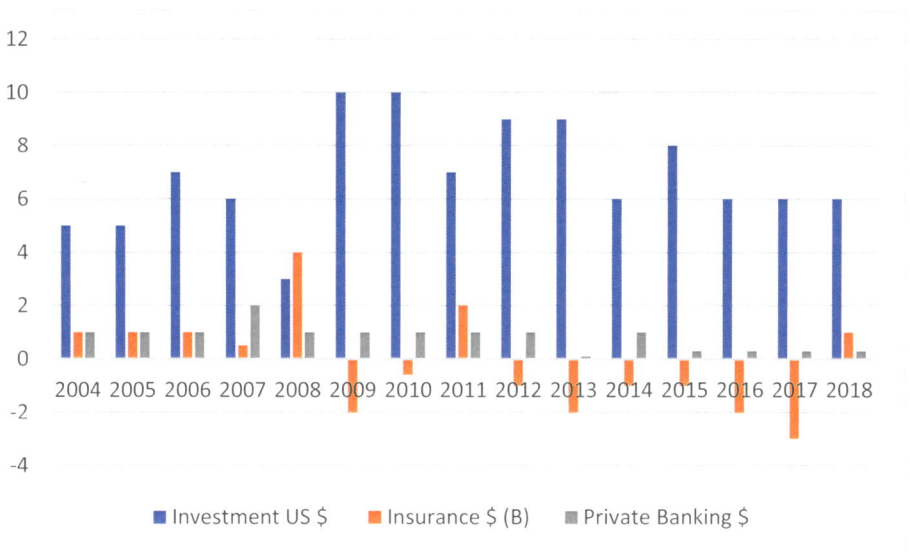

The HSBC investment banking division made some considerable contributions of $10 billion each in 2009 and 2010 and remained relatively stable in its contributions to the PBT. The strength of HSBC lies in its retail banking business. Generally, the insurance business was the weakest as it consistently made losses for eight of the 15 years evaluated. The private banking division also only made very modest contributions to the PBT. Moreover, that division stagnated for four years, running from 2013 to 2018.

Figure 30: HSBC Group: Employee Profile 2004–2018

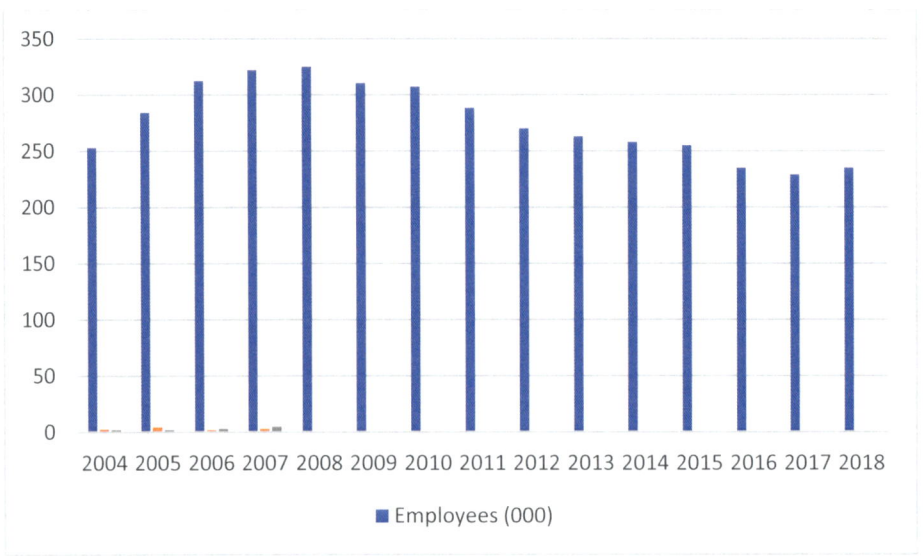

At its highest level in 2008, HSBC had approximately 325,000 employees, which reduced to about 229,000 in 2017. Notwithstanding that the physical network of branches and office locations climbed down from 10,000 to about 3,900 and customer numbers reduced from 128 million to about 39 million, commendably, the least number of staff HSBC had in the fifteen years under evaluation was 229,000 employees in 2017. This started picking up again, reaching 235,000 in 2018.

Figure 31: HSBC Group: Investment Banking Contributions to the Profit Before Tax 2004–2018 US$'000 billion

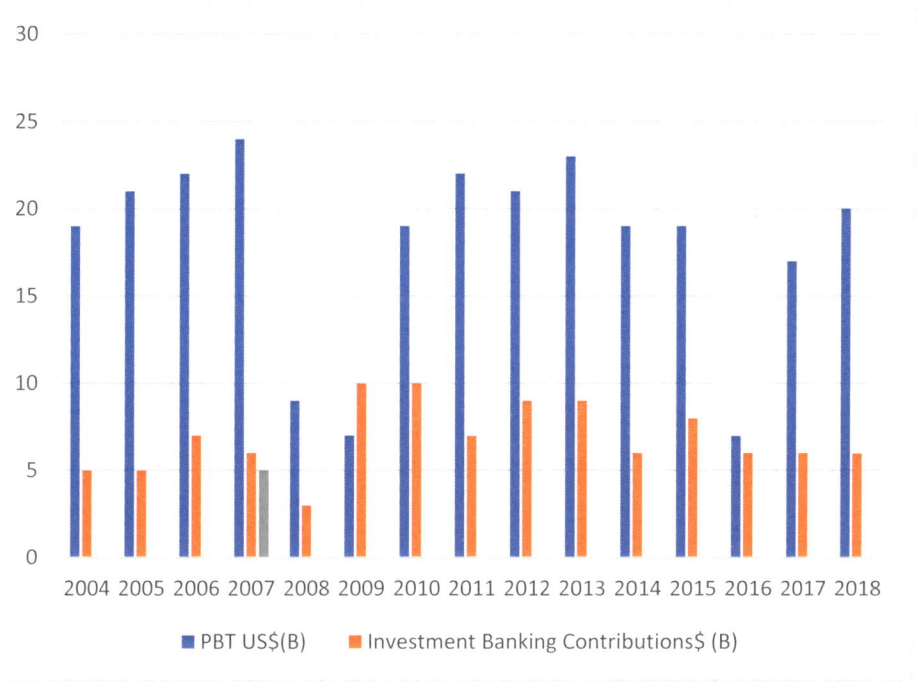

Although investment banking made significant contributions towards the profit before tax, generally, the contributions were not predominant.

4.23 Analysis and Interpretation of the Extracted Financial Data Collated from the Annual Accounts of HSBC Group

4.23.1 Analysis for 2004–2006

This was before the dawn of the global financial crisis. The bank reported a setback brought about by losses incurred from their earlier purchase of Household Finance Corporation, a sub-prime mortgage business acquired in the USA, which slowed down their growth in 2006.[829] As well, the liquidity position of the bank in the period 2004–2006 was below acceptable standards as

---

[829] HSBC, Annual Accounts, 2006, p. 8

aggregate loans exceeded total deposits throughout that period. The impairment charges increased from $6 billion in 2004 to $11 billion in 2006.

That is almost double the amount charged in 2004. As mentioned earlier, the increase can be associated with provisions for envisaged losses from their investment in sub-prime mortgages and the fact that the assets grew substantially from $1.3 trillion in 2004 to $1.9 trillion in 2006. While the bank appeared to have a growing income and growing assets, there is a noticeable degree of underlying difficulty as the profit before tax was not increasing at the same pace as the assets. Part of the causes of the slowing down in the earning powers of the assets was due to weakened asset quality, low interest rates and regulatory pressure to boost capital and liquidity requirements.

Apart from these occurrences, generally, the bank maintained a steady growth rate in their income. As a result, they had consistent growth in their operating profit before tax, even if it was only marginal. On the positive side, the bank was still making profits. As a result, it was able to declare dividends to shareholders. From 2004 to 2006, they declared dividends of 0.63 cents, 0.69 cents and 0.76 cents, respectively. Above all, HSBC aimed to retain up to 60% of its profits in the business, which was very helpful to the company in subsequent years to support the Common Equity Tier 1.

4.23.2 Analysis for 2007–2009

This was a period of unprecedented upheaval in the banking sector, which created a credit crunch and a general slowdown in the global economy. It brought many financial institutions down to their knees, and some, including RBS, had to be bailed out at a high cost to the public.

The economic climate of that period amplified the weaknesses in HSBC's financial position. In addition, HSBC carried the burden of their misadventure of buying HFC into the heat of the global financial crisis in 2007–2009. It was a venture that HSBC regretted very much because of the string of losses over time, which was estimated to be about $50 billion. In 2009, reflecting on the losses, S. K Green, the then Group Chairman, said,

"With the benefits of hindsight, this is an acquisition we wish we had not undertaken." [830]

---

[830] HSBC, Annual Report and Financial Accounts, 2008, p. 9.

Income reached its peak in the period 2007 and 2009 when the bank had an income of $79 billion, $82 billion and $66 billion, respectively, with total assets for the same period climbing to $2.4 trillion, $2.5 trillion and $2.4 trillion, which generated declared profits before tax of $24 billion, $9 billion and $7 billion.

Foremost, HSBC had a sudden expansion in the balances on its derivative accounts during this period which contributed to the increase in asset growth. For example, in 2006, the balance on the derivative account was only $104 billion, but by 2008, it had risen to $495 billion and later revalued downward to $251 billion in 2009.[831, 832] HSBC reported that these financial instruments increased in value because of an upward review of the price of the financial instruments, not necessarily because there were any changes in the notional value of the underlying contracts.[833] As a result, the value had to be written down in the following accounting period to reflect the reality of the then-prevailing market conditions.[834]

Although a peak of $82 billion in the operating income was significantly high in the period, they were vastly eroded by impairment charges which also peaked at $26 billion. HSBC reported that some of the reasons for the increase in impairment charges were due to heightened credit card balances and a rise in bankruptcies in Hong Kong.[835] Similarly, housing price depreciation restricted refinancing options for customers coupled with job losses in the labour market.[836] In addition, HSBC reported that they had business challenges in their North American market, where they sustained a loss of $7 billion and in Brazil, where they had a loss of over $1 billion.[837] At the same time, the economic climate in Europe at home affected HSBC's performance just as it affected other banks in the UK.

HSBC kept afloat through refocused operations in emerging markets such as South Korea, Vietnam, Malaysia, Brazil and India. In addition, the bank benefited from the economic boom in China and gains due to the increase in oil

---

[831] HSBC Accounts 2007, p. 334
[832] HSBC Accounts 2009, p. 355
[833] HSBC Accounts 2008, p. 40
[834] HSBC Accounts 2008, p. 10.
[835] HSBC Accounts 2007, p. 61
[836] HSBC Accounts, 2008, p. 34
[837] HSBC Accounts 2007, p. 6

prices for five consecutive years in the Middle East.[838] In addition, HSBC sold some of its matured investments during this period, including selling 20% of its assets in Yantai City Commercial Bank in China.[839]

On a good note, HSBC gained control over the liquidity status of the bank in the period 2007–2009 without any need for recourse to the government for a bailout. In addition, in the heat of the global financial crisis, HSBC paid its highest dividends of 0.93 cents in 2008. Meanwhile, Tier 1 Capital under Basel II was consistently gaining strength as it increased from $91 billion in 2007 [840] to $95 billion and $122 billion in 2008 and 2009, respectively.[841]

Notably, customer deposits increased substantially from $997 billion in 2006 to $1.3 trillion. The over $300 billion increase was due to an inflow from abroad, customers who withdrew from volatile investments and brought such proceeds to HSBC, attracted by the strength and stability of the bank.[842]

4.23.3 Analysis for 2010–2013

The period 2010–2013 was the time of regulatory reforms. First, it was a period of uncertainty. Then, there were international collaborations, consultations with stakeholders, deliberations, and the determination of the appropriate regulatory response to the global financial crisis. Finally, it was the period that the Financial Services (Banking Reform) Act 2013 was conceived. This was also when the UK government imposed levies on the UK banks to stabilise the banking sector further. In addition to all these, there was the impact of fines and redress to customers for past misdeeds. Thus, issues around the tightening of Common Equity Tier 1 also significantly boosted confidence in the banking sector, but this had cost implications for the banks.

Regarding HSBC, 2010/2011 marked a time of bank management changes. It was the time of the incoming new administration of D J Flint, the new Group Chairman, Stuart Gulliver, the new Chief Executive Officer and the exit of the bank's former Chairman Stephen Green and Michael Geoghegan, the former Chief Executive Officer of the bank. Both retired key officers navigated the

---

[838] HSBC Accounts, 2007, p. 8
[839] HSBC Accounts, 2007, p. 7
[840] HSBC Accounts 2007, p. 288
[841] HSBC Accounts 2009, p. 290
[842] HSBC Accounts 2008, p. 41.

bank's affairs throughout the global financial crisis. They had spent 28 and 37 years in the bank's service at their retirement, including the period they led the bank.[843]

2010 to 2013 witnessed a relatively stable financial performance for HSBC after the bank's difficulties between 2007 and 2009. Operating income, profit before tax, and total assets remained reasonably stable. HSBC had its highest asset level of $2.7 trillion in 2012. However, with much higher assets, the bank started to make as much profit as it did in the pre-global financial crisis era. Notwithstanding the increased asset level, the impairment charges decreased drastically to $6 billion in 2013 instead of $26 billion in 2009.

A contributory factor to the improvement witnessed in HSBC's account was the benefit of higher trade volumes in Asia markets. As a result, as reported by the bank, Asia contributed the largest proportion to the operating profit before tax.[844] In addition, the asset level grew to its highest level through the controlled disposal of sixteen non-strategic investments. It also yielded further profits, enabling the bank to pay more dividends and boost the Core Tier 1 capital in the period.[845]

Although the bank paid a levy of $571 million in 2012, the negative impact on the bank's profit was almost negligible because of the bank's huge size and large-scale operations. In addition, the bank reported that the levy of $571 million was equivalent to $0.03 per ordinary share, which would have been available for distribution as dividends or used to increase the capital for the year if it had not been set aside for the levy.[846]

The deposit base increased substantially from $1.3 trillion in 2009 to $1.6 trillion in 2013, a difference of $300 billion. While RBS and Barclays were shrinking, HSBC was growing and attracting deposits on a large scale. HSBC attributed their success to focusing on the Asian market, which did not face as much upheaval as Europe and America. Also, the disposal of their non-core banking businesses was not under any compulsion, as was the case

---

[843] HSBC Accounts, 2010, p. 4
[844] HSBC, Accounts 2010, p. 7
[845] HSBC, Accounts, 2012, p. 7
[846] HSBC Account, 2012, p. 5

with RBS and Barclays. For example, when HSBC could not get a good offer for the divestment in Turkey, they stopped the sale and invested more to increase the marketability of the planned asset disposal.

4.23.4 Analysis for 2014–2018

Operational performance between 2014–2018 was not particularly attractive for HSBC. Exception for the impairment charges, which went down to $2 billion apiece in 2017 and 2018 (the lowest ever for the period under review), most of the key statistics went down. Operating income went to an all-time low of $48 billion in 2016. Correspondingly, operating profit also came down to $7 billion in 2016 but started growing again in 2017 and 2018, when operating profit increased to $17 billion and $20 billion, respectively. Assets climbed down from $2.7 trillion in 2013 to $2.4 trillion. There was a reduction in the deposit accounts, but not as dramatic as in the other key areas. Loans and overdrafts reduced considerably from $1.3 trillion in 2013 to $950 billion in 2016. This peaked marginally at $1 trillion in 2017 and 2018. The reduction of about $300 billion between 2013 and 2016 could only have resulted in lower revenue generation.

So, in addition to the poor interest rate generally and the decline in the mortgage market, HSBC also faced a decline in its main Asian markets during a trade war between China and America throughout the tenure in office of President Donald Trump. In addition, there was a deterioration in the Asian currencies against the US dollar. In 2014, HSBC faced fines, settlements, and customers' redress in the total sum of $3.7 billion for uncovered past misdeeds, which could not have come at a worse period for HSBC.[847]

To compound matters for HSBC, they suffered losses in their operations in Europe and Latin America during that period. Part of the European losses related to a writing-off of a substantial historical goodwill.[848] The new auditors, PWC, picked up issues with HSBC over a historical goodwill account that stood at $15.5 billion, some of which related to the acquisition of Safra Republic Holdings in 1999. The auditors were of the view that a review of this account

---

[847] HSBC Accounts, 2014, p. 7.
[848] HSBC Accounts 2016, p. 7.

balance was long overdue. That led to writing off $800 million on the account related to Europe.[849]

4.24 Conclusions

HSBC faced almost the same trajectory as SCB in the period under review. This is unsurprising, given that both banks had similar main markets in Asia.

RBS and Barclays faced the worst period of operations during the global financial crisis and immediately after that but gradually recovered in 2017 and 2018. On the other hand, SCB and HSBC scaled through the heat of the period of the global financial crisis relatively well. Still, they faced a general decline in their performance from 2014, mainly due to weakened Asian currencies' depreciation against the dollar. In addition, the slowdown in Asia's economy and the tension between the US and China contributed to the decline.

HSBC was also embroiled in the same reputation-damaging ethical issues as were found to be the case in RBS and Barclays. This included matters such as interest rate manipulation scandals, facilitation of tax evasion schemes, money laundry allegations, surreptitious inflation of the value of their derivative accounts and regulation compliance failure. In addition, was the proliferation of merger and acquisition deals (not necessarily a bad business to do in themselves, but too often, they end up having crippling bad deals). Finally, HSBC was found complicit in matters related to mis-sold products that warranted customers' redress and huge fines.[850] Alongside RBS and Barclays, HSBC was also considered vulnerable to failure. As such, classified as a high-risk Global Systemically Important Bank, more so that the bank operates from multiple jurisdictions.

Despite some similarities with RBS and Barclays, HSBC stood out in some respects. In keeping with the founder's vision, HSBC's businesses were mainly focused on China, its place of birth, and emerging markets in Asia. This policy largely insulated the bank from some of the effects of the global financial crisis that mainly affected America and Europe.

In the case of HSBC, there was stability in the tenure of office of its leadership. This is because the top executives in the bank were mainly

---

[849] HSBC Accounts 2016, p. 179

[850] HSBC Accounts 2014, p. 5

'homegrown' hands who were familiar with their markets and the organisation's culture.

The spread of the HSBC businesses was well diversified, but at the same time, it strategically focused on developing a large volume of personal banking. This was unlike RBS and Barclays, which were over-reliant on investment banking.

For example, as of 2005, the income generation profile of the four strategic divisions in HSBC was as follows:

Personal Financial Services $9.9 billion
Commercial Banking $4.9 billion
Corporate Investment Banking $5.0 billion
Private Banking/Wealth Management $0.9 billion
Total $20.7 billion

Over the period under review, the all-around performance of HSBC demonstrated that big banks could be managed safely with or without applying the ring-fencing policy. HSBC scaled through the global financial crisis without requesting a government bail-out.

Chapter 5
Comparative Evaluation of the Performance of the Four Case Studies

5.1 Introduction

Following the turbulent global financial crisis from 2007–2009 and as the dust settled, the study, with the benefit of hindsight, evaluated the varied long-term impacts of the crisis on the performance of four of the largest UK banks to highlight what went wrong during and after the Global Financial Crisis.

Evaluating the Group financial accounts of the Royal Bank of Scotland Plc, HSBC Plc, Barclays Group, and Standard Chartered Bank Plc from 2004–2018, the outcomes demonstrate what could go wrong in a megabank. It indicates the crippling price of failure, the downward journey of the banks in the period under review and the long, challenging route to recovery.

The study evaluated the desirability or otherwise of the ring-fencing policy as a suitable regulatory measure in response to the global financial crisis (GFC), especially in the circumstances of the Global Systemically Important Banks (GSI-Bs) in the UK.[851]

Through evaluation of the financial accounts of the case studies from 2004 to 2018, the study aimed to determine the varied long-term impacts of the GFC on the performance of four of the largest UK banks chosen as case studies. Lest we forget too quickly, the study lays out some of the direct consequences and costs of the downward journey of these banks as a lesson on record for the future.

Following the evaluation of the accounts of the case studies and in light of the aim of the study stated, this chapter evaluates the shared characteristics among the case studies, the Royal Bank of Scotland, Barclays Bank, Standard Chartered Bank and HSBC Holdings Plc. This section stresses how skilful

---

[851] Please see page 9.

integration of different facets of the business operations management in one bank and the robustness of the implementation strategies adopted in the bank can enable that bank to excel above others. It also states how a deficiency in those management capabilities can make an appreciable difference between success and failure among the banks under study.[852]

The chapter underscores the contingency management theorists' approach, which emphasises how the availability of management talents in a bank can aid the bank in managing change effectively during an unpredictable season and acutely turbulent market environment. Possession of such management capability can ultimately lead to better performance than other less-endowed organisations facing similar circumstances, as was the case during the financial crisis.[853, 854]

This chapter also contrasts the circumstances of each bank, identifying distinctive characteristics that differentiate each bank in the case studies. Such differences include the dominant markets each of the banks was exposed to and the different levels of credit risk exposure to subprime financial instruments in the period leading to the crisis. Another example includes the impact the restrictions imposed on RBS had on its performance due to the bank obtaining bailout support from the UK government.

The chapter also evaluates how these differences helped or became a burden in responding to the regulatory changes and other non-regulatory market environmental factors that the banks faced during and in the aftermath of the financial crisis in 2007–2009. This served as the background that assisted in understanding why HSBC thrived during and after the global financial crisis. It also facilitates understanding of how the performance of SCB, a bank excluded from needing to be ring-fencing compliant, was remarkably better compared with the performance of the other banks, RBS and Barclays, that struggled for almost ten years after the financial crisis.

---

[852] N. Slack, et al., 'Operations Management 3rd Ed.' Pearson Education, 2001, p. 151

[853] B. Burnes, 'Managing Change 4th Ed' (Pearson Education, 2004)

[854] P. Drucker, 'Managing in Turbulent Times' (Routledge, 2011)

5.2 Similarities in the Circumstances of the Case Studies: People, Objectives, Structure and Business Models

Mullins noted that there may be manifest cultural differences between different types of organisations. However, at least three fundamental factors are common in most organisations: people, objectives, and structure.[855] Typically, organisations employ people and organise or structure their operations to efficiently implement the strategic business plan and to achieve their organisation's goals.

This principle applies to the four banks that formed the case studies. One critical difference between the banks is how each of the organisations configured processes, systems, styles of management, methods of operation and the behaviour of the members of the organisation in order to achieve their objectives.[856] The interactions of these factors within each bank can either make or break the organisation.

In addition, referring to the behaviour of complex organisations in a turbulent period and management practice, Ansoff states the importance of engaging with the basic SWOT analysis model in strategic business planning, decision making and problem-solving processes in business organisations.[857, 858]

- S represents Strengths, identification of inherent competitive advantages that exist within the organisation, including skills, abilities, and activities that the organisation does very well,
- W stands for Weaknesses–these are disadvantages, success factors that are lacking or not in a sufficient quantity within the organisation,
- O is concerned with external Opportunities–favourable chances or business openings that the organisation can take advantage of and
- T represents external threats, such as changes in regulation and undiversifiable market conditions that negatively impact the

---

[855] Op. Cit., L. Mullins, Prentice-Hall, 2016, (n. 52).
[856] ibid
[857] H. Ansoff, 'Business Strategy' (Penguin, 1969)
[858] M. Abdi, et al., 'SWOT Methodology: A State-of-the-art Review for the Past, a Framework for the Future'(2011) 1 (24–48) Journal of Business Economics and Management.

organisation's success, as was the case when the banks were exposed to harsh market conditions brought about by the global financial crisis.[859]

Working with the two-grid matrix in the SWOT model can help organisations identify ways to maximise their advantages while realistically seeking ways to reduce external threats to the barest minimum that may expose the banks to potential failure. While simultaneously finding a way to improve on critical success factors that are lacking or insufficient in the organisation.

It is arguable that the impact of the financial crisis and the regulatory changes that came with it on each of the banks and their responses to them largely depended on the different circumstances of each bank and the capabilities of the leadership steering the affairs of each of the banks. An example is the case of Standard Chartered Bank, which hardly changed its leadership team over the period under review. John Peace was the bank's Chairman for eight years, from 2008 to 2015. Through the turbulent period, Peter Sands remained the CEO for nine years, from 2006 to 2014. The same situation applied to HSBC as the bank had its key leadership team unchanged for a long time. More often, HSBC appointed 'homegrown' Chief Executives from within the organisation. These were long-standing employees who understood their markets and the organisation's culture.

On the other hand, RBS and Barclays witnessed frequent leadership changes. Barclays' case was the worst regarding the frequency of changes in the leadership team. From 2005 to 2018, they had five chairmen and four CEOs. The most recent change was in 2019.[860]

In the SWOT analytic model, the interaction of processes and the availability of managerial capabilities in an organisation do not assume simplification of the challenges involved in managing a complex multinational universal banking group. It does, however, emphasise the important differences that having capable hands at the helm of affairs can make in managing giant conglomerate banks during uncertain and turbulent periods such as the banking sector faced between 2007 to 2018.[861]

---

[859] P. Drucker, 'Managing for Results' (Butterwort-Heinemann, 1994)
[860] Barclays Plc 'Barclays Announces Leadership Changes' (2019)
[861] T. Chermack, and B. Kasshanna, 'The Use and Misuse of SWOT Analysis and Implications for HRD Professionals' (2007) Vol. 10 (4) 383–399 Human Resources Development International.

Secondly, they point out how failed business strategies can bring an organisation to its knees, as was the case with RBS when the bank in consortium with other banks made the strategic decision to purchase ABS Ambro in 2007 and ended up with losses of about £40 billion in 2008.[862] Another example, in 2013, under the leadership of David Walker, the Chairman, and the Group Chief Executive, Anthony Jenkins, Barclays floated 564 wholly owned subsidiaries and 288 joint venture companies to run the non-core businesses of the bank.[863] That business model failed. Ultimately, the bank incurred total losses of £12 billion in the disposal of Barclays's classified non-core business arm.[864] As a result, both the Chairman and the Group CEO who promoted the model were relieved of their posts.

Thirdly, and very importantly, it is also meant to reiterate that other than regulatory changes that created additional burdens on the banks evaluated, there were endemic managerial issues in both RBS and Barclays, as highlighted in the previous paragraph.

The four banks that formed the case studies are reputable UK-registered banks and long-established financial institutions that have been operating in the banking business for centuries. RBS has been around for almost three hundred years, and Barclays is well over three hundred years old. SCB started about one hundred sixty years ago, while HSBC started in 1865, slightly over 150 years ago.

Apart from the influence of the regulatory and supervisory guidance emanating from the collaborative efforts of international governments spearheaded by the Basel Committee on Banking Supervision, the four banks in the case studies are supervised in the UK by the Financial Conduct Authority and the Prudential Regulation Authority. They are also subject to the various regulatory and supervisory authorities of host countries where they operate their businesses worldwide.

Common characteristics among these leading UK banks include the fact that they are all internationally active. In addition, they are massive financial institutions with an extensive geographical spread in their fields of business operations. This was demonstrated in the sections allocated to each of the banks

---

[862] RBS 'Annual Report and financial Accounts' (2008)

[863] Barclays Plc 'Annual Report and Financial Accounts' (2015, p. 341–347)

[864] Barclays 'Annual Report and Financial Accounts' (2018, p. 2)

in Chapter 4, Sections A, B, C and D.[865] Their business tentacles are in almost identical markets across the globe, especially in Asia, the Middle East, Africa, America and in Europe except that HSBC and SCB concentrated their businesses in Asia more than other parts of the world where they operated.

The four banks also shared the same universal banking model. They grew their businesses organically and through acquisitions, mergers and affiliations with other financial institutions. The universal banking model enabled them to undertake diverse financial services across wholesale and consumer banking products and services.[866]

They all operated an extensive branch banking model, with their headquarters in the UK. They provide wide-ranging services, including personalised banking services to individual customers, commercial banking to small and medium-sized customers, and tailored specialist services to large corporate organisations and institutional customers. SCB is slightly different in that the bank maintains its investment banking hub in the UK whilst most of its retail banking customers are outside Europe. RBS's major markets are in Europe and America, whilst HSBC has its market spread worldwide but is primarily domiciled in Asia.

As of November 2019, Barclays, SCB, and HSBC were rated global systemically important banks. This is in the sense that each had significantly huge assets and operated in multiple jurisdictions, such that should any of these banks fail, their collapse could potentially trigger a global financial crisis.[867]

To put the size of these banks into context, at its peak in 2007, just before the global financial crisis, RBS's number of branches reached 2,278,[868] and the numerical strength of its customer base clocked at about 44 million in 53 countries across the globe.[869] In 2008, total assets amounted to £2.4 billion; at its height, RBS had over 226,000 employees. Earnings Per Share were at their highest of £1.94, and the highest dividend paid was 0.77 p per ordinary share.

---

[865] Please see pages A, RBS– 199, B, Barclays–225, C, SCB–260 and D, HSBC–283.
[866] Type of services rendered RBS, see pages 201 – 203, Barclays see pages 226 – 227, SCB see pages 262 – 263, and HSBC pages 284 – 285.
[867] Op. Cit., Financial Stability Board, 2019, (n. 34)
[868] The Royal Bank of Scotland, 'Annual Report and Accounts' (2007, p. 15)
[869] Ibid (2007, p.11)

Similarly, at its zenith in 2008, Barclay's asset was £2.1 trillion.[870] At that time, it had about 160,000[871] employees globally, with 1,733 branches across the UK as of 2009,[872] while it served about 48 million customers globally.[873]

In the case of Standard Chartered Bank, at its peak, it had total assets of about US$726 billion with 90,000 employees spread across diverse world regions, including Asia, the Middle East, Africa, America, and Europe.

At its peak in 2012, HSBC's assets clocked $2.7 trillion. Deposits peaked at $1.6 trillion, and the bank had 325,000 employees in 2006 and about 10,000 service outlets.

As the core deposits of each of the four banks were above the minimum threshold of £25 billion from 2013 to 2018, all these banks should ordinarily have been subjected to preparation to be ring-fencing compliant by 1st January 2019. However, in view of the fact that SCB had negligible core banking customers in Europe, the ring-fencing policy did not apply to SCB.

5.3 The Differences in the Circumstances of the Four Case Study Banks: RBS, Barclays, SCB and HSBC

Notwithstanding the significant similarities between the four banks, there were differences in the level of their performances. The impact of the global financial crisis on banks and their ability to respond to it was influenced by their circumstances and investment choices in the immediate period leading up to the global financial crisis. For example, the level of involvement and exposure to the derivative markets and subprime securitised Collateral Debt Obligation (CDO) in the period leading to the global financial crisis varied substantially. The worst affected in this regard were RBS through the bank's purchase of ABN Ambro and Barclays through its purchase of failed Lehman Brothers.[874]

5.4 The Royal Bank of Scotland

Before the global financial crisis began, RBS had cumulative underlying problems regarding managerial issues, poor asset quality, inadequate capital and

---

[870] Barclays Plc, 'Annual Report and Financial Accounts', (2008, p.205)

[871] Ibid (2008, p.23)

[872] Barclays Plc, 'Annual Report and Financial Accounts' (2009, p.4)

[873] Barclays Plc, 'Annual Report and Financial Accounts', (2008, p.4)

[874] Please see pages 214 and 227.

liquidity issues and problems with its compulsive aggression towards mergers and acquisitions. However, the full impact of these ailments on the bank started to surface at the beginning of the global financial crisis when RBS could no longer access an immediate supply of funds from the wholesale financial market to meet its cash requirements.

The burden of the liquidity crunch went into overdrive in 2008.[875] As pointed out in Section B of Chapter 4 under the analysis of RBS, this was when the impact of the toxic assets acquired from the Netherland Bank, ABS Amro, started to crystallise, and the need to urgently seek a bailout dawned on the bank, the regulatory authorities and the government.[876] In 2008, the book of accounts also started witnessing significant stress. As may be observed in Table 5, page 204 - 205, a liquidity problem emerged as the total deposits were £898 billion compared to loans of £1.013 trillion.[877]

Impairment charges skyrocketed from about £2 billion in 2006 and 2007 to £8 billion in 2008. That year, RBS made a previously unmatched operating loss of £40.7 billion.[878]

Given the perilous liquidity position of RBS at that time, the bank, as it were, had its back against the wall as there was no opportunity to seek assistance from other banks. The availability of interbank assistance had frozen because of the dislocation in the market then. The catastrophic tactical mistake RBS management made was that, in conjunction with other partners, they purchased ABS Amro for about $100 billion in cash.[879]

If the successful bid for ABS Amro had been paid for in cash and shares, the story about RBS might have been very different, especially if the cash spent to buy ABS Amro had been in hand to deal with immediate needs and RBS had not had to take a government-funded bailout. It may also be argued that there were more than enough long-term underlying issues in RBS before the crisis began, which were enough to throw RBS into its difficulties.

These include the poor quality of its assets, a general loss of confidence in the bank due to past misdeeds, the free fall in the share price of the bank, which went down from £18 to 0.67 p over the years, inadequate equity capital, poor

---

[875] Please see page 217.
[876] Please see page 214.
[877] Please see pages 204 – 205.
[878] Please see Table 5, pages 204 – 205.
[879] Please see pages 215 – 216.

liquidity, huge nonperforming assets, growing accumulated losses and the burden of the fines, penalties and huge litigation costs that the bank faced due to its past misdeeds.[880] Part of the consequences for RBS was that for almost ten years, they were unable to break even, unable to earn income to meet the cost of capital, and unable to pay dividends. Some of the consequences are that it would be extremely difficult for RBS to raise fresh funds in the capital market. In the circumstances of RBS, the bank is likely to be under more pressure with additional costs of implementation of the ring-fencing policy when compared with other competitors, as explained in the body of the book.

5.5 Barclays Group

At face value of the book of accounts, in 2006, just before the financial crisis began, Barclays had an outstanding performance with a 37% increase in the Operating Profit Before Tax.[881]

Just like RBS, Barclays also made offers in the proposed acquisition of ABN Ambro, but they had to walk away from the deal because, while Barclays made a share-based offer, RBS, in a consortium with others, made a cash-based offer, which was accepted.[882]

Although not as much as RBS, Barclays was severely hit by securitisation and subprime debt issues. Dealing with this burden threw open other difficulties the bank had to contend with. Foremost, although income generation increased from £23 billion in 2008 to £29 billion in 2009, costs were escalating. First, impairment charges grew at a galloping rate, increasing from £5 billion to £8 billion in 2009. Secondly, liquidity was under tremendous strain as deposits stood at £399 billion against loans, far ahead at £461 billion. It was not until 2011 before Barclays started to have a grip on the poor liquidity problem.[883]

Thirdly, because of the deteriorated liquidity position, the cash-strapped bank desperately bid to seek help from the Qatar government. That move helped with a cash booster of £6.1 billion.[884] Although Barclays was taken to court by the UK Serious Fraud Office in 2017 and by the UK Antifraud Office in 2018

---

[880] Please see pages 215 – 216.
[881] Table 6 Column 3 page 231.
[882] Barclays Plc (2007, p.7) Annual Report and Financial Account
[883] Table 6, pages 231 – 232.
[884] Please see pages 228 – 230.

for seeking assistance from a foreign government and for assisting in purchasing its shares,[885] the bank got away lightly. This was unlike RBS, which took the UK government bailout at very unfavourable terms, leading to the forced sale of many of its branches, including some non-core banking arms of the bank both locally and overseas.[886]

Unlike RBS, Barclays kept making some profits and continued to pay dividends to its shareholders, even if it was only a modest one.[887]

In addition to these difficulties was the need to comply with regulatory changes, including Basel III, reviewed capital requirements and the ring-fencing policy.

5.6 Standard Chartered Bank

The period leading to the global financial crisis was a time of exponential growth for SCB, with ever-increasing expansion in their primary markets in China, Thailand, Indonesia, South Korea, Pakistan, India, Taiwan, Malaysia, Nigeria, Ghana, South Africa and the United Arab Emirates.[888] They have maintained a presence in some of these countries for about 160 years.[889]

Although SCB was also affected by the burden associated with Asset-Backed Securities, in relative terms, their case was very mild compared to RBS and Barclays described earlier.

SCB had total ABS exposure of $5.9 billion in 2007, $3.3 billion in 2008 and $2.7 billion in 2009, as opposed to hundreds of billions that others had.[890] Throughout the global financial crisis in 2007–2009 and the ensuing recession period, remarkably, SCB continued to flourish all around. As indicated in Table 8, page 196, from 2004–2012, total income and Operating Profit Before Tax continued to grow steadily for nine years.[891] Income rose from $5.4 billion in 2004 to $19 billion in 2012. Similarly, OPBT increased from $2.3 billion in 2004 to $6.9 billion in 2012. Thus, SCB maintained a fairly consistent growth in the

---

[885] Ibid.
[886] See page 242.
[887] See Table 6, Pages 231 – 232.
[888] See pages 262 – 263.
[889] ibid.
[890] SCB Accounts 2007, p. 54, 2008, p. 57, 2009, p. 61
[891] See Table 8, page 264 – 265.

dividend payout ratio.[892] Like HSBC, SCB was not under pressure to sell off any of its businesses; neither did they have a massive staff level reduction, nor did the other two banks.[893] Throughout the fifteen years under review, SCB had no liquidity problem. Except in 2015 and 2016, when their performance dipped due to difficulties that arose in the Asian markets and a one-off comparatively high impairment charges of $5.5 billion in 2015, SCB was a success story.[894]

The most likely factors contributing to the SCB success story include their very low exposure to subprime assets, stability in the bank's leadership and the strategic advantages that accrued from keeping the hub of their very lucrative investment banking division in the UK.[895] Thus, SCB was insulated from the strict regulatory regime in the UK and the need to be ring-fencing compliant because their retail banking customers were mostly outside Europe; generally, SCB was well-resourced.[896]

5.7 HSBC

HSBC was also involved in similar reputation-damaging ethical issues found in the cases of RBS and Barclays. For example, HSBC was accused of facilitating tax evasion schemes in their Switzerland private banking business. In addition, they were involved in the interest rate manipulation scandal. They were indicted over matters relating to money laundering, fell short on regulation compliance, and were found complicit in matters relating to mis-sold financial products. As such, HSBC also faced the consequences of breaches in conduct matters, which led to huge fines and penalties.

Like SCB, HSBC's dominant markets were in Asia, especially China. China, where HSBC maintained a dominant presence, was not as severely affected as Europe during the global financial crisis in 2007–2009. However, the account evaluation revealed that HSBC was, to some extent, adversely affected by the global financial crisis through its businesses in Europe, America and Latin America, especially in Brazil.

---

[892] Ibid (Table 8) Pages 264 – 265.

[893] Ibid (Table 8) pages 264 – 265.

[894] Ibid.

[895] Please see page 263. In relative terms, SCB had the least exposure to subprime securities

[896] Please see page 263.

HSBC suffered losses during the global financial crisis because of its involvement in the sub-prime housing market through its merger with Household Finance Corporation, which HSBC acquired in 2003.[897]

Except for 2004–2006, when total loans slightly exceeded deposits, as indicated below, for the remaining twelve years, deposits always exceeded loans as of the balance sheet dates. For example, in 2004, deposit accounts amounted to $777 billion, while aggregate loan accounts amounted to $816. In 2005, deposit accounts were $809 billion, whereas loans amounted to $866 billion; in 2006, the deposit was $997 billion, and the loan was $1 trillion.[898]

Contributions from the bank's insurance division are not impressive as it made overall losses in 8 years out of the 15 years under review. As well, the contribution from the private banking division was only marginal. Although the investment banking division contributed a relatively sizeable portion to the PBT at $5 billion to $10 billion annually, HSBC's main strength was providing core and corporate banking services. Another key strength of HSBC was their leadership team. They safely navigated the bank's affairs through the crisis period hitch-free and throughout the 15 years under review. As a result, the bank made profits and was thus able to declare generous dividends and ploughed back retained earnings, which improved their Core Tier 1 Capital annually.

Notwithstanding the issues enumerated, HSBC generally fared very well compared to RBS and Barclays. Moreover, throughout the period under review, the bank was self-sufficient, as it did not require a bailout from the UK government or any other external support.

The all-around performance of HSBC over the period under review demonstrated that big banks could be managed safely with or without the application of the ring-fencing policy. Moreover, given that HSBC is well-resourced, the impact of the ring-fencing policy on the bank may be minimal.

Annually, the equity capital progressively increased through retained profit and funds from selling non-core financial assets.

---

[897] Please see page 285.
[898] Please see Table 9, pages 288 – 289.

5.8 Conclusions

(i) This chapter points out that at a turbulent period, as was the case during and in the immediate period after the 2007–2009 global financial crisis, managing change in conglomerate universal banks in response to regulatory and non-regulatory market environments required talented leadership. There is also a need for an abundance of competent middle-level managers across the board to navigate such a challenging period.[899] The availability or lack of such skilful hands and the role they played deserves mentioning, even if ascertaining the extent of these critical success factors in the banks evaluated is outside the scope of this study.

(ii) Analysis of SCB financial accounts in Chapter 4 Section D and evaluation of the unique circumstances of the bank in this chapter led to a conclusion that, comparatively, SCB stood in a better position to weather the storm during the global financial crisis than RBS and Barclays. This is primarily because SCB's exposure to subprime assets was relatively low.[900] Also, as their retail banking customers were outside Europe, SCB was not faced with the burden of being ring-fencing compliant.[901] In the same vein, HSBC also thrived during and after the crisis as the bank was well-resourced. Moreover, its operations were primarily domiciled in Asia, where the effects of the global financial crisis were less pronounced. The bank also had the benefit of excellent and successful leaders.

(iii) The cumulative effects of inadequate equity capital and liquidity ratio, low interest rate, ineffective management, exposure to a high level of subprime assets, the upward review of the composition of capital requirements under Basel III, large-scale divestment during a tumultuous recession period and the need to be compliant with conditionalities attached to taking government bailout placed considerable pressure on RBS. These led to low profitability, low return on investment, inability to cover the cost of capital, large-scale

---

[899] Please see page 306.
[900] Please See page 263.
[901] See page 261.

reduction in employee number and diminished global influence.[902] Similarly, Barclays suffered from poor leadership, low interest rates, weak assets, enormous consequences for breaches of rules and over-bloated asset levels, which, in the end, were written down.

---

[902] See pages 204 – 205, Table 5 RSB; Pages 231 – 232, Table 6 Barclays and SCB page 264 – 265, Table 8.

Chapter 6
Findings and Conclusions

6.1 Introduction

Through evaluation of the financial accounts of the case studies from 2004 to 2018, the study aimed to determine the varied long-term impacts of the GFC on the performance of four of the largest UK banks chosen as case studies. So as not to forget too quickly, the study lays out some of the direct consequences and costs of the downward journey of these banks from 2004 to 2018 and the difficult road back to recovery as a lesson on record for the future.[903]

The study evaluated the desirability of retaining the ring-fencing policy as a suitable regulatory measure in response to the global financial crisis (GFC), particularly in the circumstances of the Global Systemically Important Banks (GSI-Bs) in the UK.[904]

In light of these aims and objectives of the study stated above and also found in Chapter 1, pages 8 - 9, this chapter is concerned with presenting a summary of the findings and conclusions drawn on each of the following,

(i) the varied long-term impacts of the GFC on the performance of four of the largest banks in the UK chosen as case studies, the downward journey of each of these banks from 2004 to 2018 and their challenging route to recovery,

(ii) the desirability or otherwise of the ring-fencing policy as a suitable regulatory measure in response to the global financial crisis (GFC), particularly in the circumstances of the Global Systemically Important Banks (GSI-Bs) in the UK,

---

[903] Please see pages 8 – 9.
[904] Please see pages 13 – 15, Ring-fencing in Brief, and Pages 152 – 154, Evaluation on whether the ring-fencing policy can prevent the reoccurrence of financial crises.

(iii) the appropriateness of the ring-fencing policy as a measure that is capable of deterring financial crises in the future,
(iv) some of the commonly accepted general causes of the GFC found in the literature reiterate the picture of the burden that the negligence of bankers brought upon themselves, an estimate of the extent of the losses brought upon the global financial system, the hardship created for businesses, individuals, equity owners in the banks that were hit hardest, and employees that lost out during the GFC,
(v) although mergers and acquisitions, deficiencies in leadership performance and inadequate internal control mechanisms were not a specific part of the issues under consideration at the beginning of the study, these factors emerged in the course of the study as very significant factors among the problems that some of the case studies had which could have permanently ruined at least two of the banks in the case studies, and finally,
(vi) the chapter makes recommendations on the ways forward into the future.

6.2 The Varied Long-term Impacts of the GFC on RBS, Barclays, SCB, HSBC and the Undulating Trips of these Case Studies to Recovery from 2004 to 2018

This section graphically presents how the global financial crisis affected each bank in the case studies differently, their downward journeys and the route to their turnaround from 2004–2018.

Figure 32: The Impacts of GCF on the Case Studies and Their Difficult Trips Through 2004–2018

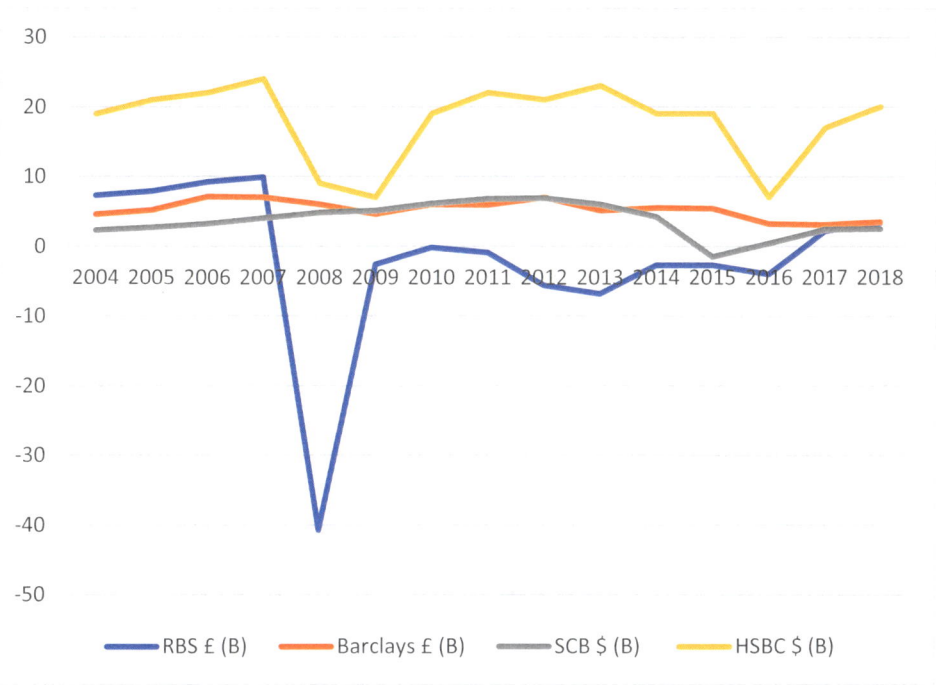

The variables on the 'Y' axis of the graph are the annual Operating Profit Before Tax measured in billions for each of the banks in the case studies, while the horizontal axis is the time frame from 2004–2018. In the case of RBS and Barclays, the unit of measurement of their performance is £ sterling, while for SCB and HSBC, it is in US$.

The graph above indicates the undulating movements of the individual bank during their varied journeys from 2004–2018. This should not be confused with comparing the banks' profitability against each other. That is not the aim of the graph because each of the banks operated with different asset levels. Also, their level of operations was measured differently in terms of the currency units.

The graph demonstrates how RBS went down to minus £40 billion OPBT in 2008 and, for several years between 2008–2016, operated below the water level, having had negative OPBT until 2017, when the bank had a turnaround with positive OPBT of £2.2 billion and £3.4 billion in 2018.[905] In the case of Barclays,

---

[905] Please see page 204 Table 5, Column 3, OPBT.

though the bank operated at a positive OPBT throughout the entire journey from 2004–2018, it only barely broke even due to huge impairment charges, losses from the sale of non-core assets, and pressure from the need to meet enhanced capital and liquidity requirements. Moreover, huge regulatory fines due to regulatory infringements resulted in Barclays only being able to pay lacklustre DPS ranging from 2.5p to 6.5p from 2009–2018 as opposed to 34p paid in 2007.[906] HSBC also felt the negative impact of the crisis in the sense that their OPBT was $24 billion in 2007, but it drastically fell to $9 billion and $7 billion in 2008 and 2009, respectively. Notwithstanding, throughout the period under review, the bank did not for once have any negative OPBT.[907] On the contrary, SCB dipped into negative OPBT once in 2015.[908]

One of the most remarkable points about the graph is that, for all the banks, 2017 was the turning point. This was when they all started to return to increasing their annual OPBT. At that point, impairment charges also returned to the pre-crisis era and were even lower. The question now is whether the darkest part of the night is over for the banks and whether they have started to match forward into the dawn of a new era. Only time will tell.

6.3 The Desirability of the Ring-fencing Policy as a Suitable Regulatory Measure in Response to the Global Financial Crisis in the UK

For example, Goodhart accepted that the ring-fencing policy would most likely support stability in the banking sector. This is because any dislocation arising in the non-ring-fenced banks is unlikely to cause disruptions to the continuation of payment and retail banking services in the ring-fenced banks.[909] The ring-fencing policy would also make it less likely for any need to provide expensive government-funded bailouts to rescue non-ring-fenced banks should they run into difficulties out of their own making.[910]

However, it is suggested that the ring-fencing policy in the banking sector needs amending so that only the risky investment banking arms in the non-ring-

---

[906] Please see pages 231 – 232, Table 6.
[907] Please see pages 288 – 289, Table 9, Column 3.
[908] Please see pages 264 – 265, Table 8, Column 3.
[909] Op. Cit., C. Goodhart, 2012, (n. 50)
[910] Ibid.

fenced banks are removed. The policy has a likely long-term damaging impact on the banking sector and the UK economy. The likely adverse impacts highlighted in the study include the following:

(1) The UK banks would be at a disadvantage competing with other banks at the international level. This is especially so with huge universal banks in other countries where their laws are less restrictive and in places where they do not favour the implementation of the ring-fencing policy as it is in the UK.[911]

Part of the challenges the UK banks would then face is that they must abide by the internationally agreed banking regulations just like other global systemically important banks elsewhere. However, in addition, the UK banks would, at a higher cost, need to comply with the ring–fencing policy, whereas those other banks are not required to do so.

(2) The transfer of cheap depositors' funds from the non-ring-fenced banks to the ring-fenced banks would naturally lead to the breakdown of synergy in the huge and well-resourced universal banks in the UK. It is therefore contended that though both classes of banks can lend, the ability of the restructured banks to support the needs of the biggest multinational corporate customers as a unit would be considerably diminished.[912]

(3) Part of the consequences would be the additional cost to huge conglomerate customers needing huge capital outlay. In addition, such large customers would then face additional difficulties in searching for multiple sources of finance instead of dealing with just one or relatively fewer banks where complications arising from perfecting security against loans and advances can be minimised.[913]

(4) The ring-fencing policy is likely to reduce the performance of the non-ring-fenced banks. This is because cheap core deposits are no longer available to subsidise loans and advances, including huge, accumulated mortgage portfolios that only generate low-interest income due to the prevailing low interest rate orchestrated by the global financial crisis.

---

[911] Please see pages 139 – 141.

[912] The point about synergy was extensively discussed on pages 145 – 146 and 254, for example.

[913] Please see pages 223 – 224.

However, it is appreciated that the bankers have the discretion to choose the side of the fence where they want the loan assets to be, whether within the ring-fenced or non-ring-fenced banks.[914]

(5) This researcher also contends that the financial sector encompasses, for example, banking, the stock market, pension funds, insurance, and credit card service providers. These subsectors have a symbiotic relationship, depending on one another. The point is that although the ring-fenced banks can provide both corporate and retail banking services and can provide allowed services to the banks within the group, by separating banks along the ring-fenced and non-ring-fenced bank, the ring-fencing policy limits the support that comes from the ring-fenced banks to the entire financial system. This is because restrictions are placed on the ring-fenced banks regarding providing facilities to other financial institutions, branches, and subsidiaries outside the EEA.[915] The effect is that should the non-ring-fenced bank run into financial difficulties, it cannot depend on the ring-fenced bank to provide the non-ring-fenced bank with financial assistance.

The above-mentioned issues suggest that the policymakers consider reviewing the ring-fencing policy in the economy's best interest, especially following the considerable restructuring in the banks that have de-risked and improved stability in the banking sector so far. In the past ten years after the GFC, many policy measures have been taken to de-risk banks, which were already evaluated in Chapter 2, literature review. These policies and regulations were designed to mitigate the risks of possible failure in the banking sector. For example, some of the policies relate to improved capital and liquidity adequacy, better supervisory regimes, and considerable restructuring through demergers and substantial divestment from non-core assets.[916]

---

[914] Op. Cit., Ring-fencing Guidance (n. 40)
[915] Ibid. Ring-fencing Guidance para. 1.6 (n. 40), Please see pages 13 – 14, and 22 – 23.
[916] Please see pages 75 – 77, 113 – 114, 115 – 119.

6.4 Suitability or otherwise of the Ring-fencing Policy as a Measure that is Capable of Deterring Financial Crises in the Future

The suitability of the ring-fencing policy in response to the global financial crisis is a significant part of the thrust of the study. This was discussed in the body of the book in Chapters 1 and 2. The conclusion is that the general idea that gave birth to the ring-fencing policy has some potential benefits. However, the study highlighted the policy's significant drawbacks, including its potential to make the UK's GSI-Bs less competitive than their peers elsewhere, as enumerated in paragraph 6.3.

Goodhart agreed that the ring-fencing policy would limit the probable contingent liability that the UK taxpayers may face in another global financial crisis.[917]

Indeed, the ring-fencing policy has appeals and benefits, but the question is, "At what cost?"

In July 2013, the UK government came up with the estimated costs of the ring-fencing policy stated as follows:

- Direct private costs to UK banks-about £1.7 billion-£4.4 billion annually.
- Indirect cost on GDP about £0.4 billion-£1.9 billion annually.
- Reduction in tax receipt about £150 million-£690 million annually.
- The assumed benefits of adopting the ring-fencing policy stated in the document are (i) greater financial stability, (ii) a reduction in the likelihood of government providing bailout as crises become less frequent and severe, (iii) a reduction in implicit subsidies to the huge banks and reducing the probability of future crises by 15% which would generate an annual benefit of £7.1 billion.[918]

One side of the argument is that if the ring-fencing policy can keep in abeyance financial crisis, then the cost is probably worth it because it would be

---

[917] Op. Cit., C. Goodhart, 2012, (n. 50).
[918] Ibid.

far lower than the costs of a rescue package where there is a situation that requires a bailout after a possible financial crisis.[919]

On the other hand, Campbell and Moffatt's contention is that given the improvement in prudential regulation since 2009 after the crisis and the ongoing efforts directed towards recovery and resolution efforts in the banks, which arguably have led to significant improvement in their stability, they do not see how the enormous cost of ring-fencing can be justified.[920]

Arguably, the regulatory and supervisory environment has improved considerably since the GFC. So also, there has been considerable recovery from losses incurred from the nonperforming assets over the past ten years. In addition, there has been a huge divestment from risky investments in Barclays and RBS. So, hopefully, the issues around mis-sold products and regulatory fines have been put behind these banks. With all these developments, hopefully, in no distant future, the regulators may wish to consider easing the regulatory burden imposed on the UK banks regarding the ring-fencing policy.

6.5 The Commonly Accepted Causes of the Global Financial Crisis in 2007–2009

As discussed on pages 34 to 35, among several factors attributed as the causes of the financial crisis are failings arising from the inadequate cross-border and unified international financial regulation, products and services that escaped the boundary of regulation and supervision, poor banking supervision,[921] securitisation of sub-prime mortgage assets, poor lending practices, failings in the administration/governance of financial institutions, general laxity in internal control mechanisms,[922] behavioural issues relating to a corporate culture where there are tensions in power dynamics and internal politics, external socio-economic pressure leading to financial institutions intentionally circumventing rules[923] and less than acceptable standards of the activities of credit rating agencies.[924]

---

[919] Op. Cit., C. Hofmann, 2017, (n. 32).
[920] Op. Cit., Campbell and Moffatt 2019, (n. 59).
[921] Op. cit., Arora, A. 2010, (n. 24)
[922] Op. cit., R. Grosse, 2012, (n. 152)
[923] Op. Cit., S. Ashby, 2009, (n. 153)
[924] Op. cit., G. Baber, 2013 (n. 22).

Other than the spillover of the causes of the crisis that emanated in America, in the particular circumstances of the UK, the trigger of the crisis was a loss of confidence in the banks and a reaction to the chain of events that started with the short-term money market freeze which prevented banks in dire need of liquidity from accessing funds from the wholesale money market.[925] These banks' problems were compounded by poor liquidity, inadequate capital and underlying weaknesses in assets/nonperforming loans.

The underlying issue was the precarious liquidity position of these distressed banks, their inadequate operating capital, poor management decisions, weak assets, disproportionate nonperforming loan accounts and on top of that, from December 2007 to February 2008, major investment banks owned up that their structural credit assets were overstated and needed to be written downs.[926] Understandably, this led to credibility issues and doubts about what to believe about bankers who, prior to the GFC, were paying themselves obscene bonuses at a time when Hudson thought that bankers could not be relied on to file honest reports that may likely damage their business interest.[927]

6.6 Some of the Dire Consequences of the Global Financial Crisis in 2007–2009 to Different Classes of People and Organisations

Some of the dire consequences of the fallouts precipitated by the GFC to the bankers themselves include loss of credibility and personal disgrace faced by some principal bank officials who lost their jobs in the process, including Fred Goodwin, who did not only lose his job as the CEO of RBS but also had an additional embarrassment of having his knighthood annulled.[928] In addition, Bob Diamond and Marcus Agius, the former CEO and Chairman of Barclays, also were relieved of their posts.[929]

Globally, huge, incalculable losses were sustained, including examples of twenty-four of some of the most industrialised nations in the world whose financial system's stock market capitalisation fell, as depicted on Table 1, pages

---

[925] Op. Cit., Financial Services Authority, 2011, pp 314–315, (n. 155)

[926] Ibid.

[927] Op. Cit., A. Hudson, 2013, (n. 20), Please see page 107.

[928] Please see page 156.

[929] Please see page 250.

36–37. For example, the USA was assessed to have lost $1.2 trillion in their banking system market capitalisation, the UK lost $551 billion, Japan lost $402, and France lost $275 billion.[930]

Also, an unquantifiable level of hardship was caused to businesses in the UK, out of which some went into liquidation. The equity owners in RBS and Barclays had their investments reduced in value, as painted in the analysis of the accounts of the banks in Chapter 4. In the case of RBS, from 2008 to 2017, they were not paid dividends for 10 years.[931] RBS' share, which was £4 in 2000, rose to £18 just before the crisis but crashed to only 67p.[932] In the case of Barclays, though the shareholders received some dividends, they were pittances. In Barclays, from 2009–2018, DPS ranged from 2.5p to 6.5p as opposed to 34p paid out to shareholders in 2007.[933]

Worst is the burden shared by ordinary bank workers who lost their jobs at RBS and Barclays. By the time the dust settled, RBS, whose employees had peaked at 226,000, came down to 65,000, while in Barclays, the total employees' level that reached 156,000 globally came down to 84,000.[934]

This shows the financial system's importance to the public generally and why it is in everyone's interest to safeguard the banking sector as much as possible.

6.7 The Gold Rush: Mergers, Acquisition and Leadership Failure in the Banking Sector Before The Global Financial Crisis

This section deals with issues that emerged from the study, which can potentially contribute to instability in the banking sector and need the specific attention of bankers, regulators and banks' supervisors.

Although mergers and acquisitions, deficiencies in leadership performance and inadequate internal control mechanisms were not a specific part of the issues under consideration at the beginning of the study, these factors emerged in the course of the study as very significant factors among the problems that some of

---

[930] Please see Table 1 on page 52.
[931] Please see Table 5, pages 204 – 205, column 9.
[932] Please see the discussion on page 220.
[933] Please see Table 6, pages 231 – 232, column 9.
[934] Please see Table 5, pages 204 – 205, and Table 6, pages 231 – 232.

the case studies had which could have permanently ruined at least two of the banks in the case studies, especially RBS and Barclays. Apart from these, the issues that led to the collapse of Barings Capital discussed in the literature review were inefficient internal control mechanisms. The Union Bank of Switzerland also lost over $2 billion due to the same problem in their internal control systems.[935]

6.7.1 The Benefits of Mergers and Acquisitions and Potential Harms

Apart from growth cultivated through ploughing back part of the profits generated into the businesses, the evidence found in the study is that in more than a century, all the banks in the case studies adopted policies that promoted the growth of their banks through mergers and acquisitions.[936] However, while the policy was beneficial to the banks in some cases, it also proved to be the undoing of RBS and Barclays. In the case of RBS, their purchase of NatWest in 2000 was highly successful, and the deal brought Fred Godwin, a former CEO, into the limelight. In contrast, their purchase of ABN Amro, among other factors, nearly brought RBS into ruin.[937]

The critics of deregulation policy often point out that the abrogation of the Glass Stealgall Act 1933 may have been the primary cause of the catastrophe of the global financial crisis in 2007–2009.[938] The argument was that repealing the Act opened the lid that had previously restrained commercial banks from directly engaging in risky investment banking.

A historical review of each case study in Chapter 4, Sections A, B, C and D revealed that dating back to over a hundred years ago, each of the banks under study had a long history of acquiring and taking over other financial institutions. Over that period, the strategy of mergers aided the expansion of these banks.[939]

However, in later years, say, in about 30 years since the adoption of deregulation policy and the repeal of the Glass Stealgall Act 1933, the

---

[935] Please see pages 98 - 99

[936] Please see, for example, RBS, page 200 and Barclays, pages 227 – 228.

[937] Ibid.

[938] Please see page 137, M. Steger and R. Roy, 2010, line 454.

[939] Please see pages 200 for RBS, pages 227 – 228, for Barclays, 261 - 262 for SCB and pages 284 - 286 for HSBC.

commercial banks under study ventured into buying chains of financial institutions that are not core banking institutions, including banks that were deeply enmeshed in investment banking, which came with it, ruinous sub-prime assets that almost crashed RBS that bought ABN Ambro, Barclays that bought part of Lehman Brothers businesses and HSBC that bought Household Finance Corporation as expounded in Chapter 4.[940]

On the one hand, some of the other mergers and acquisitions were generally beneficial to the banks. However, mergers and acquisitions can have severe implications and constitute potential risks capable of bringing a bank down, as demonstrated by the case studies. Given the enormous potential risks associated with mergers and acquisitions to the banking sector and its contributory role in the near collapse of some of the global systemically important banks in the UK during and in the aftermath of the global financial crisis in 2007–2009, the question is concerned with what the attitude of the policymakers should now be when designing the legal framework for the banking sector in order to keep these huge financial conglomerate banks in the UK safe from future catastrophe.

6.7.2 The Response of the Banking Regulators to M&A and Why.

As demonstrated in the cases of RBS, Barclays, SCB, and HSBC, notwithstanding the enormous potential hazards identified in M&A that can immensely contribute to the vulnerability of GSI-Bs when such deals go wrong, the equally substantial accruable benefits of M&A cannot be ignored.

In the real world of business, there are various reasons why people and businesses generally want to dispose of their assets. The disposal of assets could be voluntary or forced disposal. Sometimes, sellers may be under intense pressure to dispose of their personal properties ranging from moveable chattels such as television sets, cookers, refrigerators, and vehicles or real estate such as land and buildings. Depending on the reasons for selling, these valuable assets can often come to the market at giveaway prices because the seller needs immediate cash. Investors can be on the lookout to take advantage of such opportunities. However, there could be hidden adverse features in the property that is on sale, which may only come to light long after the purchase of a

---

[940] Ibid.

seemingly cheap article had gone through and, worse of all, without a right of recourse to the seller after the deal, has been finalised.

It is not in any way different in the financial sector. There are wide-ranging reasons why a bank may want to take over another financial institution. A financial institution may want to take over another organisation for reasons, including an opportunity to cheaply buy a company that is under a winding-up order or in receivership. The desire to buy another company may be motivated by a wish to buy a cash-rich organisation or extend market outreach across international boundaries.

A takeover may be induced by tax advantages that may accrue from the takeover, an opportunity may arise to buy a company with choice landed property that is of interest to the buyer, there may be a need to diversify into some desired business areas and so many other reasons that could be advantageous to the predator company.[941] Growing a bank through mergers and acquisitions is nothing new. It is a popular means of stimulating growth, as in all the case studies.[942] In the past, it served the interest of the banks very well.[943]

The huge risks that may come with M&A include the purchaser's inability to achieve the desired level of integration and failure to realise full synergy among the constituents in a merger.[944] Also, when M&A becomes too frequent, as was in the case studies, the combined risk increases, and so are the uncertainties.[945] Part of the difficulties in M & A is that not all the underlying facts about the targeted financial institution may be known to the purchaser when considering whether to buy. Therefore, the responsibility lies with the purchaser to exercise due diligence. This happened in the case of ABN Ambro, purchased by RBS. RBS did not appreciate the extent of the poor quality of the assets when they bought ABN Ambro. Barclays and HSBC had precisely the same problem

---

[941] Op. Cit., E. McLaney, 2016, p. 207, (n. 701).

[942] Y. Ahmed and T. Elshandidy, 'The Effect of Bidder Conservatism on M & A Decisions: Text-based Evidence from US 10–K Fillings'. 46, 176–190, (2016) International Review of Financial Analysis.

[943] Please see pages 200 for RBS, pages 227 – 228, for Barclays, 261 – 262, for SCB and pages 284 – 286, for HSBC.

[944] C. Ott, 'The Risks of Mergers and Acquisitions: Analysing the Incentives for Risk, Reporting in Items 1A of 10-K Fillings'. (2020) 106, 158–181, Journal of Business Research.

[945] Ibid.

in their purchase of Lehman Brothers and HSBC in the case of their purchase of Household Finance Corporation in 2003.[946]

Abraham and Shrives contended that during the early stages, when the acquiring organisation is expected to exercise due diligence, it is doubtful whether the acquiring managers are always entirely honest in declaring all potential risks identified, which may hinder commitment to buying an organisation.[947]

This point may be very relevant in the case studies regarding the purchase of ABN Ambro by RBS, Lehman Brothers by Barclays and HFC by HSBC. The question is, in the process of exercising caution and due diligence prior to committing themselves to the mergers and acquisitions of the troubled banks, whether the managers were entirely honest in giving due weight to all the risks identified or they did not see those risks and then ended up paying too much for the Dutch bank and in the same way with the other banks.

Similarly, Robert et al. contended that the motivation behind the agitation to purchase another bank might relate to the high compensation usually paid to the CEO when such ventures are successful.[948] These authors also suggested that CEOs may be motivated by the desire to become personally famous and to acquire the 'Too big to fail' status for their bank to reap the benefits of associated subsidies. [949]

The former CEO of RBS, Fred Goodwin, was accused of being too ambitious in search of fame. It was suggested that such a drive may have led to his aggressive pursuit of mergers and acquisitions, which eventually brought the bank he led (RBS) into disrepute and ruin.[950]

In the Financial Services Authority's report relating to their enquiry into the causes of the failure at RBS, which concluded in December 2011, the banking sector regulator identified M & A of ABN as a significant contributory factor to the causes of the near collapse of the bank. However, FSA did not propose to

---

[946] See pages 201, 214, 217 RBS, Page 296 for HSBC, pages 243/244 for Barclays.

[947] S. Abraham and P. Shrives, 'Improving the Relevance of Risk Factor Disclosure in Corporate Annual Reports'. (2014) 46 (1) 91–107.

[948] D. Robert, E. Douglas and M. Philips, 'Mergers and Acquisitions of Financial Institutions: A Review of the Post 2000 Literature' (2009) Vol 36 (23) 87–110. Journal of Financial Services Research.

[949] Ibid.

[950] Please see pages 214 and 217.

stop banks altogether from engaging in M & A. FSA made the point that RBS did not exercise necessary caution before taking on the immense risks associated with the cross-border acquisition, neither did the management of RSB sufficiently engage the regulators to enable them to probe further into that purchase.[951] Even if RBS did, the FSA at that time did not see itself as responsible for providing a detailed assessment or approving ABN Amro's purchase.[952]

Following that event, banks may still engage in M&A. However, significant deals would now be subjected to a more intrusive assessment by a special supervisory focus group that would rigorously assess associated risks during the exercise of the due diligence stage, and the supervisors would now need to approve important M&A before a supervised bank can progress the deal.[953]

Although the bank's management would still need to take responsibility for the decision to commit themselves to an M&A, the introduction of the backup, which involves an independent assessment of risks associated with M&A in the ways suggested, would, in this researcher's view (i) eliminate subjective evaluation by CEOs who may be over-optimistic about the value of the assets and risks attached to financial institutions that are prime targets of the predator company (ii) the involvement of independent assessors would provide safety measures by having another layer of assessors who have no emotional attachment and no specific benefits to gain or anything to lose whether the acquisition of targeted financial institutions goes through or fails to go through (iii) as a consequence of the additional layer of independent assessors, banks can still enjoy the benefits that are available in M&A while safety measures are also improved.

The alternative could have been a compulsory cessation of M&A in giant banks because of the enormous risks of failure that may be induced by M&A, as happened in RBS, Barclays and HSBC. However, given the advantages available in M&A, this researcher believes that it would not be economically prudent to dispense with M&A altogether.

Thus, the new supervisory approach, which involves getting the permission of the bank supervisor for M&A to scale through, would be a welcomed development as part of the strategies to keep considerable banks in the UK that are globally systemically important safe.

---

[951] Op. Cit., Financial Services Authority, December 2011, p. 25 & p. 264, (n. 155)
[952] Ibid.
[953] Ibid.

6.7.3 The Impact of Poor Management Decisions, Which Often Led to Incessant Changes in the Leadership of Banks

The importance of the quality of the leadership in a bank, the stability in the office of the foremost leaders, and a culture of planned succession cannot be over-emphasised in relation to the success or failure of a bank.[954] One wrong appointment is all it takes to face the risk of collapse. Examples are found in the cases of Nick Leeson and Kawu Adoboli relating to Barings Capital and UBS.[955] In both cases, they were not part of the leadership team of their organisations; they were just given the powers to commit their banks on a vast scale, but they were not adequately supervised.

In recognition of this crucial issue, FSMA 2000 Part V and the Banking Reform Act 2013 took this matter into account under Part 4 of the Banking Reform Act, which deals with the issues of regulating and vetting those to take up senior management roles in the banking sector.[956] By involving supervisory agencies in scrutinising those to hold key roles in the bank, this researcher accepts that this necessary step will ensure that the most capable people are given the roles of gatekeepers on financial issues of grave consequences which are of concern to the public.

In the circumstances of the four case studies, HSBC and Standard Chartered Bank were more successful at leadership retention, with an average of about 8–9 years of service as Chairmen/Chief Executive Officers. In most cases, these officers would have served for upward of about 20–25 years in their organisation, so they are deeply familiar with the bank's market, the ethos of the bank, their aspirations and organisation culture.[957]

In the case of RBS, although before the near collapse of RBS, the bank's leadership was stable, in the period leading to the global financial crisis, those who had served in the capacity of the Chairmen and Chief Executive Officers did not appear to have had prior background training in banking and finance or other subjects that are directly related to banking and finance and neither did they have prior experience in leading a bank. For example, Sir George Matthewson,

---

[954] These issues were discussed in Chapter 5, page 306.

[955] Please see pages 98 - 99 regarding Nick Leeson and pages 98 – 99 regarding Adoboli.

[956] These Parts of the Banking Reform Act 2013 were discussed on page 31.

[957] Please see page 306.

who was the CEO from 1992 and became the Chairman from 2001–2006, was a Mathematician and Applied Physicist.[958] Similarly, Tom McKillop, the Chairman from 2006–2008, held a PhD in Chemistry.

After the global financial crisis, matters started to improve when Philip Hampton, who holds an MBA and was previously an investment banker, took over the leadership following the crisis. At the same time, Stephen Hester, an Economist; Ross McEwan, a holder of an MBA from Harvard; and Prof Howard Davies, a seasoned professor of economics and central banking, all had a stint in joining hands to revamp RBS.

Worst of all, in Barclays, there were instances where Chairmen/CEOs served for just one year, and others could only serve for two years. It is not difficult to figure out that each time a new leader is brought in, foremost, such leaders would be faced with the difficult task of gaining the trust and cooperation of those they met on the ground and would be under additional challenge to meet the expectation of the shareholders who would naturally expect new leaders to bring into the bank new ideas and purposeful leadership in order to create a turn-around in an ailing bank under a turbulent economic environment.

For example, in 2014, under the leadership of David Walker, the Chairman, and Anthony Jenkins, the Group Chief Executive of Barclays, the company went through what John McFarlane, the subsequent Chairman, described as one of the largest restructurings in history when the company floated almost 600 non-core banking subsidiaries to manage its non-core banking assets.[959] Ultimately, the project turned out to be a disaster for Barclays.[960]

The argument is that headhunting for the right people to manage the affairs of a vast multinational banking corporation and a succession programme cannot be left to a game of chance or a matter of trial-and-error, as this area is an important critical success factor that has the potential to make or undo a bank. As such, this researcher opines that there should be a well-planned policy that is subjected to periodic reviews if that does not exist already. For example, in 2010/2011, when there was a change in leadership at HSBC, a senior staff member, Vincent Cheng, was about to retire after 33 years in service. However, the bank management persuaded him to take up an advisory role to the incoming

---

[958] Royal Bank of Scotland, 'Annual Accounts', 2005, p.7
[959] Barclays Plc, 'Annual Report and Financial Accounts (2016, p. 2).
[960] Please see pages 249 – 250.

Group Chief Executive on regional matters, where Vincent was considered to have considerable expertise.[961]

As pointed out previously, it is consoling to have the provisions under Part 4 of the Banking Reform Act 2013 wherein banks' supervisors are required by law to be involved in vetting responsible position holders before they can function in critical positions in the bank. It is one thing to have such a policy in place. It is also essential to support such policy with the backing of legislation. However, on the other hand, the most crucial part that should be of concern to all stakeholders is the process of how such a policy would be implemented in practice.

6.7.4 Suggestions About Internal Control Mechanisms

Internal control mechanisms are part of the micro areas of management in huge banks that may easily escape proper scrutiny. The problem is not about a bank not having some internal control system. It would be highly unusual for a bank not to have internal control systems.

The real issue concerns the working, adequacy, and effectiveness of the processes of the systems engaged in a bank, whether they are fit for purpose, whether they can timeously discover anomalies, and how issues identified are promptly resolved. Therefore, it is suggested that this area of banking practice should be subjected to periodic evaluation and auditing. If necessary, external management consultants could be engaged in addition to the auditor's annual review in this area of operation management.

For example, in the case of Adoboli of UBS cited earlier, he was given the sole responsibility to commit his bank up to a limit of $100 million. His case exemplifies all that could go wrong in an internal control system. In his case, there was almost no supervision by his managers, and other team members were unaware of his dubious activities that went on for three years before he exposed himself. As a result, although his trading limit was $100 million, he exposed his employers to a potential loss of $12 billion at one point.[962]

---

[961] HSBC, Annual Accounts, 2010, p. 4.

[962] Please see the discussion of this on pages 98 – 99.

In any internal control environment in a bank of any size, it should never be possible for any individual to have such enormous powers as to commit his bank to such an extent. This is because the personal circumstances of individuals can change over time. Also, personal character can, for some reason, deteriorate.

For example, not many people are immune to exhaustion, depression, or their consequences. This is more so because different people handle these vicissitudes of life differently. In addition, individuals can run into personal financial difficulties, family problems, divorce and so on, which in some cases can lead to gambling, developing bad drinking habits and so on as coping strategies. Hosts of other operational risks can lead to someone hiding important documents or even shredding documents. That is why the barest minimum of security measures in an internal control system should embrace a Dual Control Mechanism (DCM) at all levels of operation involving exposure of a bank's assets to a significant level of risk.

Thus, before the release of a substantial amount, including the granting of loans and overdrafts running up to $100 million or exposure of a bank to an amount in the region of $12 billion, the barest minimum would be dual control of senior managers. Where it reaches up to $12 billion, such an amount should gain the board's attention. In any transaction involving a huge amount, such as $100 million, a system is suggested so that at least two to three senior managers must authorise a significant amount before it can scale through. The disadvantage of this suggestion is that it may slow down processing time. However, it has the potential advantage of avoiding huge losses and reducing bank failure incidences, as in Adoboli and Nick Lesson.[963] It is indeed astonishing and a matter of deep concern if an individual can continue to act alone, authorising significant payments for up to three years without any of the colleagues knowing what he was doing, and the person was not supervised.

Even if a bank has a very robust capital base and the liquidity is impeachable, all those could disappear very quickly, as happened in the case of Nick Leeson at Barings Capital. It is unlikely that during the period that Nick ran down his employer's assets, he ever woke up in the morning at any time and thought of checking the capital or liquidity level before he engaged in the activities that filtered away the bank's resources. That was possible because he could work alone and do as he pleased without anyone overseeing him. By the time his

---

[963] Please see pages 97 – 98.

wrongdoing came to light, it was too late. The point here is that an effective regulatory architecture must be holistic, not just capital and liquidity adequacy alone. It must also embrace efficient supervision, perfectly working internal control mechanisms and quality leadership.

In any internal control environment in a bank of any size, it should never be possible for any individual to have such enormous powers as to act solely and bring a bank into liquidation.

6.8 Justification of the Hypothesis Proposed at the Beginning of the Study

The hypothesis at the beginning of the study was, "Notwithstanding some benefits that may accrue from the ring-fencing policy, the banking sector and, by extension, the economy in the UK may likely face long-term detriments arising from the implementation of the ring-fencing policy."[964]

The study found that, indeed, as Goodhart suggested, applying the ring-fencing policy would most likely support stability in the banking sector. This is because any case of dislocation arising in the non-ring-fenced banks is unlikely to cause disruptions to the continuation of payment and retail banking services in the ring-fenced banks.[965] Moreover, the ring-fencing policy would also make it less likely for any need to provide expensive government-funded bailouts to rescue non-ring-fenced banks should they run into difficulties out of their own making.[966]

However, it is suggested that unless the ring-fencing policy in the banking sector is amended so that only the risky investment banking arms in the non-ring-fenced banks are removed, some of the likely long-term damaging impacts on the banking sector and the UK economy highlighted in the study include the following:

---

[964] Please see page 17.
[965] Op. Cit., C. Goodhart, 2012, (n. 44)
[966] Ibid.

(1) The UK banks would be at a disadvantage competing with other banks at the international level, especially huge universal banks in other countries where their laws are less restrictive and do not favour the implementation of the ring-fencing policy as it is in the UK.[967]

Part of the challenges that UK banks would then face is that they are obligated to abide by the internationally agreed banking regulations just like other globally systemically important banks elsewhere. In addition, the UK banks would need to comply with the ring–fencing policy at additional costs, whereas those other banks are not required to do so.

(2) Due to the breaking up of synergy in the huge and well-resourced universal banks in the UK as a result of the remover of cheap depositors' funds from the non-ring-fenced banks to the ring-fenced bank, it is contended that though both classes of banks have the capacity to lend, the ability of the restructured banks to support the needs of the biggest multinational corporate customers as an individual unit would be considerably diminished.[968]

(3) Part of the consequences would be the additional cost to huge conglomerate customers in dire need of huge capital outlay, but which would face the additional difficulties involved in searching for multiple sources of finance instead of dealing with just one or relatively fewer banks where complications arising from perfecting security against loans and advances can be minimised.[969]

(4) The ring-fencing policy is likely to reduce the performance of the non-ring-fenced banks in situations where cheap core deposits are no longer available to subsidise loans and advances, including huge, accumulated mortgage portfolios that are only generating low-interest income due to the prevailing low interest rate orchestrated by the global financial crisis. It is appreciated that the bankers have the discretion to choose the side of the fence where they want the loan assets to be, whether within the ring-fenced bank or the non-ring-fenced bank.[970]

---

[967] Please see pages 139 – 141.
[968] The point about synergy was extensively discussed on pages 145, 153, 254 and 259.
[969] Please see pages 21, 224 and 322.
[970] Ring-fencing Guidance Statutory Guidance Instrument 2014/2080 Part II Article 7(2) and Article 9.

(5) This researcher contends that the financial sector encompasses banking, the stock market, pension funds, insurance, credit card service providers, and so on. These subsectors have a symbiotic relationship, depending on one another. The point is that although the ring-fenced banks have the capacity to provide both corporate and retail banking services and can provide allowed services to the banks within the group, by separating banks along the ring-fenced and non-ring-fenced bank, the ring-fencing policy limits the support that comes from the ring-fenced banks to the entire financial system. This is because restrictions are placed on the ring-fenced banks regarding providing facilities to other financial institutions, branches, and subsidiaries outside the EEA.[971] The effect is that should the non-ring-fenced bank run into financial difficulties; it cannot depend on the ring-fenced bank to provide the non-ring-fenced bank with financial assistance.

The above-enumerated issues led to the suggestion that the policymakers should consider a review of the ring-fencing policy in the best interest of the economy, especially following the huge restructuring in the banks that have de-risked and improved stability in the banking sector so far. Also, in the past ten years after the GFC, there has been a considerable number of policy measures already evaluated in Chapter 2, the literature review, that are designed to mitigate the risks of possible failure in the banking sector, especially regulations relating to improving capital and liquidity adequacy, a better supervisory regime in addition to the considerable restructuring through demergers and substantial divestment from non-core assets.[972]

6.9 Recommendations on the Way Forward and Further Research

It is understood that it may still take some time to appreciate the full impact of the regulatory changes, including the full effects of the ring-fencing policy on the UK banks and the economy.

This study suggests that a better approach could have been to use legislative powers to stop the banks from engaging in risky speculative investment trading

---

[971] Op. Cit., Ring-fencing Guidance para. 1.6 (n. 40), Please see pages 9 & 16.
[972] Please see pages 75 – 76, 112 - 113 and 116 – 118.

while on application, licences could be given to qualified banks that are interested in incorporating a separate entity that could engage in speculative proprietary trading and derivative accounts should they wish to do so. In effect, the risky investment elements should be taken off the mainstream banks, not the core deposit accounts.

That way, core depositors' accounts would be protected in the same way that the ring-fencing policy would. The added advantages are that the cheap core deposits would then be available for traditional corporate lending, where huge multinational corporate customers' financial needs could be catered for. Also, the UK universal banks would have been able to retain their competitiveness in relationships with the other European counterparts that did not adopt the ring-fencing policy.

Also, following recovery from the recession and a possible reduction in the scale of penalties imposed on banks, the banking sector's performance may take a new positive turn. It is therefore suggested that considering the sector's economic performance in the next five to ten years may aid policymakers in deciding whether to retain or repeal the ring-fencing policy.

In addition to the foregoing, this researcher would, in summary, suggest that the most diligent attention should be paid to the following as discussed in the body of the book:

(1) Keen attention to be paid to mergers and acquisitions in banks by supervisors to forestall issues that arose with the purchase of ABN Ambro by RBS and Lehman Brothers purchased by Barclays at costs considered too high for the value of those financial institutions and the high risks that came with them to RBS and Barclays.[973]
(2) Bank supervisors should continue to demand improvement in the quality of corporate governance to ensure that only competent hands are able to add value to the security of a bank's assets and are allowed to be appointed to the boards of banks and other positions of responsibility.[974]

---

[973] Please refer to pages 242 and 329 for the purchase of ABN Ambro and page 244 for Lehman Brothers
[974] Please refer to page 31.

(3) Banks' supervisors should continue to demand improvement in the quality of training and development of compliance officers in the banking sector.[975]

(4) Emphasis should be placed on the importance of empowering internal auditors so that the outcomes of their audits that raise serious concerns receive the direct attention of the board concerned and the bank's supervisors.[976]

(5) Supervisory agencies should see that banks follow the policy of enhanced incentives and protection of whistle-blowers in the banking sector, as discussed in the book.[977]

(6) As also discussed by Admati, diligent attention should be paid by banks' supervisors to ensure that banks under their supervision are compliant with capital and liquidity ratios requirements considered appropriate in the circumstances of each bank, based on their risk levels.[978]

(7) The principle of the dual control mechanism expounded earlier should form part of the basic foundations for managing the internal control system.[979]

If other researchers pick up interest in this area of study and keep under watch performance in the banking sector for the next 5–10 years, the outcome of a collective research endeavour may hopefully spearhead policy change on ring-fencing in the future, assuming that it is considered desirable to do so.

6.10 Contributions to Knowledge

For emphasis on the important contributions to knowledge derived from this study, this paragraph is a signpost to the section of this report that contains 'Contributions to knowledge' in Chapter 1, Paragraph 1.11 on pages 32–34. To avoid a tedious re-copying of that section, kindly refer to the pages cited.

---

[975] Please see page 31.
[976] Please refer to pages 109 - 110.
[977] Please see pages 110 - 112.
[978] Op. Cit., A. R. Admati 2014, (n. 17). Please see pages 7, 63 and 115 - 117.
[979] Please refer to pages 334 – 335

Bibliography

Abdi, M., Azadegan-Mehr, M. and Ghazinoory, S. (2011) **SWOT Methodology: A State-of-the-art Review for the Past, a Framework for the Future**, Journal of Business Economics and Management 1(24–48).

Abraham, S. and Shrives, P. (2014) **Improving the Relevance of Risk Factor Disclosure in Corporate Annual Reports**. The British Accounting Journal Review, (2014) 46 (1) 91–107.

Ackrell, M. and Hannah, L. (2001) **Barclays the Business of Banking: 1690–1996**, Cambridge: Cambridge University Press.

Admati, A. R. (2014) **The Compelling Case for Stronger and More Effective Leverage Regulation in Banking**. The Journal of Legal Studies, Vol. 43 (2).

Ahmed, Y. and Elshandidy, T. (2016) **The Effect of Bidder Conservatism on M & A Decisions: Text-based Evidence from US 10–K Fillings**. 46, 176–190, International Review of Financial Analysis.

Alexander, D., Britton, A., and Mourik, C. (2014) **International Financial Reporting and Analysis** (6th Ed). Andover, Hampshire: Cengage Learning.

Alexander, P. (2015) **Splitting Banks Divides Opinion in the E.U.** The Banker https://www.thebankcr.com/World/Splitting-banks-divides-opinion-in-the-EU/(language)/eng-GB?ct=true

Andreades, A. (1909) **History of the Bank of England**, London: P. S. King & Sons

Ansoff, H. I. (1969) **Business Strategy**. London: Penguin

Arnold, G (2005) **Corporate Financial Management** (3rd Ed), Harlow: Prentice-Hall, Pearson Education Ltd.

Arnold, G (2013) **Corporate Financial Management** (5th Ed), Harlow: Prentice-Hall, Pearson Education Ltd

Arora, A. (1997) **Practical Banking and Building Society Law**, Oxford: Oxford University Press.

Arora, A. (2010) **The Global Financial Crisis: A New Global Regulatory Order?** Journal of Business and Law, 8, 670–699.

Arora, A. (2014) **Banking Law**, Harlow: Pearson Education

Arthur, T and Booth, P (2010) **Does Britain Need a Financial Regulator?** London: The Institute of Economic Affairs.

Arthur Andersen (1996) **Findings and Recommendations of the Review of Supervision and Surveillance** https://www.bankofengland.co.uk/-/media/boe/files/archive/banking-act-report/1996-1997.pdf

Artis, M. J. (1965) **Foundations of British Monetary Policy**, Oxford: Basil Blackwell

Ashby, S. (2009) **The Turner Review on the Global Banking Crisis: A Response from the Financial Services Research Forum.** Financial Services Research Forum https://www.nottingham.ac.uk/business/businesscentres/gcbfi/documents/researchreports/paper61.pdf

Atiyah, P., Adams, J., and Macqueen, H. (2005) **The Sale of Goods** (11th ed) Harlow: Pearson Education

Atkinson, T. N. (2008) **Using Creative Writing Technique to Enhance the Case Study Method in Research Integrity and Ethics Courses**, J Acad (2008) 6:33–50

Baber, G. (2013) **A Critical Examination of the Legislative Response in Banking and Financial Regulation to Issues Related to Misconduct in the Context of the Crisis of 2007–2009,** Journal of Financial Crime Vol. 20 (2), 237–252

Baber, G. (2013) **Interbank Offered Rates: H.M. Treasury's Decisive Act**. Company Lawyer 34 (1), 25–26.

Bagheri, M. and Nakajima, C. (2002) **Optimal Level of Financial Regulation under the GATS: A Regulatory Competition and Cooperation Framework for Capital Adequacy and Disclosure Information,** Journal of International Economic Law Volume 5 Issue 2 (507)

Baily, M., Litan, R. and Johnson M. (2008) **The Origins of the Financial Crisis**, Washington DC: The Brookings Institution

Ball, R. (2006) **International Financial Reporting Standards (IFRS): Pros and Cons for Investors,** Accounting and Business Research, 36: Sup, 5–27.

Bank of England (2021) **Executing Bail-in: An Operational Guide From the Bank of England. BoE Resolution**. https://www.bankofengland.co.uk/-/media/boe/files/paper/2021/executing-bail-in-an-operational-guide-from-thebank-of-england.pd

Bank of England (2018) **The Prudential Regulation Authority's Approach to Banking Supervision** London: Bank of England.

Bank for International Settlement (2013) **Basel III: The Liquidity Coverage Ratio and Liquidity Risk Monitoring Tools** (BIS).

Bank for International Settlement (2017) **Basel III: Finalising Post-Crisis Reforms**.
https://www.bis.org/bcbs/publ/d424.pdf

Barclays Bank Plc (2005–2018) **Annual Report and Financial Accounts**, London: Barclays.
https://home.barclays/content/dam/home-barclays/documents/investor-relations/IRNewsPresentations/2019News/Barclays%20leadership%20changes.pdf Accessed 22/6/2020

Barclays Bank Plc (2019) Barclays Announces Leadership Changes.
https://home.barclays/content/dam/home-barclays/documents/investor-relations/IRNewsPresentations/2019News/Barclays%20leadership%20changes.pdf

Barclays Bank UK Plc (2020) **Annual Report and Financial Accounts**, London: Barclays.

Barth, J., Capiro, G. and Levine, R. (2004) **Bank Regulation and Supervision: What Works Best?** Journal of Financial Intermediation, Vol 13 Issue 2 205–248.

Barth, J., Capiro, G. and Levine, R. (2006) **Rethinking Banking Regulation**. Cambridge: University Press, Cambridge.

Basel Committee on Banking Supervision (1988) **International Convergence of Capital Measurement and Capital Standards (Basel I)** http://www.bis.org/publ/bcbs04a.pdf. Accessed 01/06/2020.

Basel Committee on Banking Supervision (2004) **International Convergence of Capital Measurement and Capital Standards: A Revised Framework Basel II**

Basel Committee on Banking Supervision (2010) **Basel III: A Global Regulatory Framework for more Resilient Banks and Banking System.** Bank for International Settlement.

Berg, B. (2001) **Qualitative Research Methods for the Social Sciences**, Needham Heights: Pearson Educational.

Berk, J. and DeMarzo, P. (2014) **Corporate Finance** (3rd Ed) Harlow Essex: Pearson Educational

Bessis, J. (2007) **Risk Management in Banking** (2nd Ed). Chichester: John Wiley & Sons Ltd

Bingham, Lord Justice (1992) **Inquiry into the Supervision of the Bank of Credit and Commerce International.** London: HMSO

Blaikie, N. (1993) **Approaches to Social Enquiry.** Cambridge: Polity Press

Blaikie, N. (2007) **Approaches to Social Enquiry** (2nd Ed), Cambridge: Polity Press

Blaikie, N. (2007) **Approaches to Social Enquiry** (2nd Ed), Cambridge: Polity Press.

Blaikie, N. (2010) **Designing Social Research** (2nd ed) Cambridge: Polity Press

Blair, M., Cranston, R., Ryan, C. and Taylor, M. (1998) **Blackstone's Guide to the Bank of England Act 1998.** London: Blackstone Press Ltd

Blair, W., Allison, A., Palmer, K. and Richards-Carpenter, P. (1993) **Banking and the Financial Services Act.** London: Butterworths

Blake, D. (2000) **Financial Market Analysis** (2nd ed) Chichester: John Wiley & Sons.

Booth, P. (2006) **Were 364 Economists All Wrong?** London: The Institute of Economic Affairs.

Brinded, L. (2015) **The Sorry History of the Near Destruction of Investment Banking at RBS.** Business Insider.com.au. https://www.businessinsider.com.au/why-rbs-failed-as-an-investment-bank-2015- 3.

Brink, B. (2000) **The Tragedy of Liberalism: An Alternative Defence of a Political Tradition,** New York: State University of New York, Albany.

Brusden, J. (2017) **European Commission Withdraws Bank Separation Proposal**. London: Financial Times https://www.ft.com/content/ddbedcd9-2dea-3b68-b8e2-2e1bc1eda13f Accessed 04/06/2020

Bryman, A. (1998) **Quantity and Quality in Social Research**, London: Routledge

Bryman, A. (2016) **Social Research Methods** (5th Ed) Oxford: Oxford University Press

Burnes, B. (2004) **Managing Change** (4th Ed) Harlow: Pearson Educational Ltd

Campbell, A. and Moffatt, P. (2019) **Bank Insolvency: The Introduction of Ring-fencing in the UK: An Example to be Followed?** Journal of Business Law, 4, 241–261.

Capie, F (2002) **Capital Controls: A Cure Worse than the Problem?** London: The Institute of Economic Affairs

Carabellese, P. and Zhang, D. (2019) **The Legal Nature of the Recovery and Resolution Plans.** International Company and Commercial Law Review 30 (7) 380–398

Carroll, A. (2003) **Constitutional and Administrative Law** (3rd Ed) Harlow: Pearson Education Ltd.

Casu, B., Girardone, C., and Molyneux, P. (2015) **Introduction to Banking** (2nd ed). Harlow: Pearson Education

Chalmers, A. (2013) **What is this Thing Called Science?** (4th Ed) Maidenhead Berkshire: Open University Press McGraw-Hill Education.

Chermack, T. and Kasshanna, B. (2007) **The Use and Misuse of SWOT Analysis and Implications for H.R.D. Professionals** Human Resources Development International, Vol. 10(4) 383–399.

Chiu, I. and Wilson, J. (2019) **Banking Law and Regulation.** Oxford: Oxford University Press.

ColClough, C. and Manor J. (1993) **States or Markets? Neo-Liberalism and the Development Policy Debate**, Oxford: Oxford University Press.

Cooper, C. (2008) **Extraordinary Circumstances: The Journey of a Corporate Whistle-blower,** (2008). New Jersey: John Wiley & Sons.

Collins, M. (1988) **Money and Banking in the U.K.: A History** (Volume 6). London: Routledge.

Committee on Banking Regulations and Supervisory Practices (1975) **Report to the Governors on the Supervision of Banks' Foreign Establishment** https://www.bis.org/publ/bcbs00a.pdf. Accessed 01/06/2020

Coskun, D. (2010) **Credit-Rating Agencies in the Basel II Framework: Why the Standardised Approach is inadequate for Regulatory Capital Purposes**. Journal of International Banking Law and Regulation, 25(4), 157–169.

Cosserat, G. (2006) **Modern Auditing**, (2nd Ed) Chichester: John Wiley & Sons Ltd.

Cotter, D. (2012) **Advanced Financial Reporting: A Complete Guide to IFRS,** Harlow: Prentice Hall

Coyle, D. (2014) **G.D.P.: A Brief but Affectionate History**, Princeton, New Jersey: Princeton University Press

Craig, P. and De Burca, G. (2008) **E.U. Law**. Oxford: Oxford University Press.

Cranston, R. (2002) **Principles of Banking Law** (2nd Ed) Oxford: Oxford University Press.

Creswell, J. W. (2007) **Qualitative Inquiry & Research Design: Choosing Among Five Approaches** (2nd Ed) Thousand Oaks, California: Sage Publications

Crotty, M. (1998) **The Foundations of Social Research**. London: Sage Publications

Cullen, J. (2014) **Executive Compensation in Imperfect Financial Markets**. Cheltenham: Edward Elgar Publishing Ltd.

Cullen, J. (2018) **Securitisation, Ring-fencing, and Housing Bubbles: Financial Stability Implications of UK and EU Bank Reforms**, Journal of Financial Regulation, Vol. 4 73–118.

Dabbs, J. (1982) **Making Things Visible**, in J. Van Maanen (Ed), Varieties of Qualitative Methodology, Beverley Hills, CA: Sage Publications

Davies, R. (2018) **Barclays Avoids Trial Over £6 Billion Qatar Rescue Package**. (The Guardian 26/10/2018) https://www.theguardian.com/business/2018/oct/26/barclays-avoids-trial-over-6bn-qatar-rescue-package

Deakin, S. and Morris, G. (2005) **Labour Law** (4th ed) Oxford and Portland, Oregon: Hart Publishing.

Deardorff, A. V. (1980) **The General Validity of the Law of Comparative Advantage**. The Journal of Political Economy, Vol. 88, No 5 pp 941–957

Delanty, G. and Strydom, P. (2003) **Philosophies of Social Science: The Classic and Contemporary Readings**, Maidenhead, Berkshire: Open University Press.

Denscombe, M. (2007) **The Good Research Guide For Small-Scale Social Research Projects.** Berkshire: Open University Press McGraw-Hill Education

Denscombe, M (2011) **The Good Research Guide: For Small Scale Social Research Projects** (3rd Ed) Maidenhead, Berkshire: Open University Press McGraw-Hill Education.

Dewey, J. (1917) **Creative Intelligence: Essays on the Pragmatic Attitude**, New York: Henry Holt.

Docherty, D. and Viort, F. (2014) **Better Banking: Understanding and Addressing the Failures in the Risk Management, Governance and Regulation**. Chichester: John Wiley.

Drucker, P. (1994) **Managing for Results.** Oxford: Butterworth-Heinemann.

Drucker, P. (2011) **Managing in Turbulent Times**. London: Routledge.

Drury, C. (2004) **Management and Cost Accounting** (6th Ed). London: Thomson

Easterby-Smith, M., Thorpe, R., and Jackson, P. (2008) **Management Research** (3rd Ed) London: Sage Publications.

Ellinger, E., Lomnicka, E., and Hare, C. (2011) **Ellinger's Modern Banking Law** (5th Ed) Oxford: Oxford University Press.

Elliott, B. and Elliott, J. (2017) **Financial Accounting and Reporting** (18th Ed) Harlow: Pearson Education.

Elliott, C., Quinn, F., Allbon, E. and Dua, S. (2018) **English Legal System** (19th Ed). Harlow: Pearson Longman

Fidler, P. (1982) **Practice and Law of Banking**, (11th Ed) Plymouth: Macdonald & Evans

Financial Conduct Authority (2015) **Ring-fencing: Guidance on the F.C.A.'s Approach to the Implementation of Ring-fencing Transfer Schemes**

Financial Conduct Authority (2015) **Ring-fencing: Disclosure to Consumers by Non-Ring-Fenced Bodies, Consultation Paper** https://www.fca.org.uk/publication/consultation/cp15-23.pdf

Financial Services Authority (2011) The Failure of the Royal Bank of Scotland: Financial Services Authority Board Report
https://www.fca.org.uk/publication/corporate/fsa-rbs.pdf

Financial Stability Board (2011) **List of Global Systemically Important Banks** https://www.fsb.org/work-of-the-fsb/policy-development/addressing-sifis/global-systemically-important-financial-institutions-g-sifis/

Financial Stability Board (2019) **List of Global Systemically Important Banks** https://www.fsb.org/wp-content/uploads/P221119-1.pdf

Flick, U. (2009) **An Introduction to Qualitative Research** (4th Ed) Los Angeles: Sage Publications

Friedman, M. (1962) **Capitalism and Freedom**. Chicago: University of Chicago Press

Friedman, M. (2007) **Price Theory**, New Brunswick (U.S.A.) and London: Aldine Transaction

Friedman, T. (2006) **The World is Flat: The Globalised World in the Twenty-First Century**. London: Penguin.

Galbraith, J. (1954) **The Great Crash 1929**, London: Penguin Books Ltd.

Gall, M., Gall, J., and Borg, W. (2002) **Educational Research: An Introduction** (8th Ed). New York: Longman.

Garson, R. and Fladgate, C. (2018) **Whistleblowing: The Dodd-Frank Model—A Brief Primer and Is it Replicable Elsewhere?** Butterworth Journal of International Banking & Financial Law. 2018, 33 (11), 705–707.

George, E A J and Hardcastle, A, (1999) **Report of the Board of Banking Supervision Inquiry into the Circumstances of the Collapse of Barings**, London: HMSO

Gill, J. and Johnson, P. (2010) **Research Methods for Managers** (4th ed), London: Sage Publications

Glaser, B. and Strauss, A. (1967) **The Discovery of Grounded Theory**, Chicago: Aldine.

Glesne, C. and Peshkin, A. (1992) **Becoming Qualitative Researchers: An Introduction.** White Plains: New York: Longman

Goddard, J., Molyneux, P., and Wilson, J. (2009) **The Financial Crisis in Europe: Evolution, Policy Responses and Lessons for the Future**. Journal of Financial Regulation and Compliance 17(4), 362–380.

Goddard, J. and Wilson, J. (2016) **Banking: A Very Short Introduction**. Oxford: Oxford University Press.

Goodhart, C., Kay, J. and Duguid, A. (1988) **Financial Regulation or Over-Regulation?** London: Institute of Economic Affairs.

Goodhart, C. (2012) The Vickers' Report: An Assessment. Law and Financial Market Review Vol. 6 (1).

Gray, D. (2009) **Doing Research in the Real World** (2nd Ed) London: Sage Publications

Gray, J. and Hamilton, J. (2006) **Implementing Financial Regulation: Theory and Practice**. Chichester: John Wiley & Sons, Ltd

Grosse, R. (2012) **Bank Regulation, Governance, and the Crisis: A Behavioural Finance Review**, Journal of Financial Regulation & Compliance JFRC 20(1), 4–25

Guba, E. and Lincoln, Y. (1994) **Competing Paradigms in Qualitative Research.** In N. K Denzin & Y. S Lincoln (eds) **Handbook of Qualitative Research**, Thousand Oaks: Sage Publications

Guba, E. and Lincoln, Y. (2004) **Competing Paradigms in Qualitative Research.** In Hesse-Biber, S. and Leavy, P. (ed) **Approaches to Qualitative Research: A Reader on Theory and Practice** New York: Oxford University Press

Guiso, L., Sapienza, P., and Zingales, L. (2006) **The Costs of Banking Regulation**, National Bureau of Economic Research Massachusetts Cambridge, MA Working paper 12501

Gurrea-Martinez, A. and Remolina, N. (2019) **The Dark Side of Implementing Basel Capital Requirements: Theory, Evidence, and Policy**. Journal of International Economic Law, Oxford University Press, Vol 22, Issue 1, 2019.

Hadjiemmanuil, C. (1996) **Banking Regulation and the Bank of England**, London: L.L.P. Ltd Legal & Business Publishing Division

Hall, M. J. B. (1996) **U.K. Banking Supervision After the Arthur Andersen Report**. Journal of International Banking and Financial Law 11 JIBFL 525

Hannagan, T. (2008) **Management: Concepts and Practices** (5th Ed) Harlow England: Pearson Education, Prentice Hall.

Harvey, D. (2005) **A Brief History of Neoliberalism**. Oxford: Oxford University Press.

Haynes, A. (2015) **Banking Reforms Struggles On**, Statute Law Review, (2015) 36 (2): 123.

Haynes, A. (2016) **Banking and Financial Services Regulation**, Company Lawyer 37 (9) 265–266. Company Lawyer.

Heffernan, S. (1996) **Modern Banking in Theory and Practice**, Chichester: John Wiley & Sons.

Hillier, D., Grinblatt, M., and Titman, S. (2012) **Financial Markets and Corporate Strategy**, (2nd European Ed) Maidenhead Berkshire: McGraw-Hill

H.M. Treasury (2011) **A New Approach to Financial Regulation: The Blueprint for Reform**. White Paper Cnmd 8083

HM Treasury (2011) **The Comptroller and Auditor General's Report on Accounts to the House of Commons: The Financial Stability Interventions** https://www.nao.org.uk/wp-content/uploads/2011/07/HMT_account_2010_2011.pdf Accessed 13/11/2017.

HM Treasury, (2013**) Banking Reform: Draft Secondary Legislation'** https://assets.publishing.service.gov.uk/government/uploads/system/uploads/atta chment_data/file/223566/PU1488_Banking_reform_consultation_-_online-1.pdf

H.M. Treasury (2013) **The First Sale of Shares in Lloyds Banking Group,** Report by the Comptroller and Auditor General, National Audit Office https://www.nao.org.uk/wp-content/uploads/2013/12/10315-001-Lloyds-Book-ES.pdf

H.M. Treasury (2017) **The First Sale of Shares in Royal Bank of Scotland**, Report by the Comptroller and Auditor General, National Audit Office https://www.nao.org.uk/wp-content/uploads/2017/07/The-first-sale-of-shares-in-Royal-Bank-of-Scotland.pdf

Hofmann, C. (2017) **Global Systemically Important Banks (GSIBs): Operating Globally, Regulated Nationally?** Journal of Business Law 2017, 2, 155–179

Hopt, K. J. (2013) **Corporate Governance of Banks and Other Financial Institutions After the Financial Crisis**, Journal of Corporate Law Studies, 13 (2) 219–253

Hornby, A. S. (1998) **Oxford Advanced Learner's Dictionary**: Oxford: Oxford University Press.

House of Common (1985) Hansard: vol. 83 cc 1442–50. https://api.parliament.uk/historic-hansard/commons/1985/jul/26/johnson-matthey-bankers accessed 15/3/2019

House of Commons, "The FSA's Report into the Failure of RBS–Treasury", (2012, para. 117) https://publications.parliament.uk/pa/cm201213/cmselect/cmtreasy/640/64007.htm

Howard, M., Masefield, R., and Chuah, J. (2006) **Butterworths Banking Law**. London: Lexis Nexis Butterworth.

Howe, K. (1988) **Against the Quantitative–Qualitative Incompatibility thesis or Dogmas Die Hard,** Educational Researcher, 17, 10- 16

Howells, P. and Keith, B. (2007) **Financial Markets and Institutions**, Essex: Pearson Education Ltd

HSBC Holding Plc (2005–2018) **Annual Report and Financial Accounts**, London: HSBC.

Hubbard, G R (2002) **Money, the Financial System and the Economy** (4th Ed) New York: Addison Wesley.

Hudson, A. (2013) **Banking Regulation and Ring-Fence**, Compliance Officer Bulletin 107, 1–23.

Hudson, A. (2013) **The Law of Finance**, (2nd Ed) London: Thomson Reuters

Hupkes, E. (2009) **Complicity in Complexity: What to do about the 'Too Big to Fail' Problem.** Journal of International Banking and Financial Law 9 JIBFL 515.

International Accounting Standards Board, (2010) **Conceptual Framework For Financial Reporting,** London: https://people.unica.it/gianluigiroberto/files/2015/09/Conceptual-FrameworkIASB-2010-1.pd.

Islam, M., Gilisinan, J., Shahin, W. and Fisher, J. (2019) **After Regulatory Wrangling in the Financial Sector Following the Great Recession**. Company Lawyer 40(3), 81–87.

Jankowicz, A. (2005) **Business Research Project** (4th Ed). London: Thomson Learning.

Jefferson, M. (2015) **Criminal Law**. (12th Ed) Harlow: Pearson Education Ltd.

Johnson, I. and Roberts, W. (1982) **Money and Banking: A Market-oriented Approach**, New York: C.B.S. College Publishing

Joint Committee on Financial Services and Market Report April 1999 https://publications.parliament.uk/pa/jt199899/jtselect/jtfinser/328/32802.htm

Jones, A. and Suffrin, B. (2008) **E.C. Competition Law**, (3rd Ed) Oxford: Oxford University Press

Joyce, J. O (2013) **The I.M.F. and Global Financial Crises: The rise of the Phoenix?** New York: Cambridge University Press.

Karr, J. (2005). **Performance Measurement in Banking: Beyond R.O.E**. Journal of Performance Measurement, 18(2), 56-70.

Kaufman, H. (1977) **Financial Crises: Market Impact, Consequences, and Adaptability** in **Financial Crises: Institutions & Markets in a Fragile Environment.** Edited by Altman, E. I and Sametz, A. W. New York: John Wiley & Sons.

Keller, A. (2019) **De-biasing Macroprudential Policy Part 1: An Evidence-based Approach and the Precautionary Principle.** Journal of International Banking Law and Regulation 34(1), 5–16.

Kerlinger, F (1986) **Foundations of Behavioural Research** (3rd ed) New York: Rinehart and Winston

Keynes, J. M. (1936) **The General Theory of Employment, Interest and Money**. London: Macmillan

Kidder, L. and Judd, C. (1986) **Research Methods in Social Relations** (5th Ed) New York: C.B.S. Publishing

Kirk, J. and Ross, J. (2013) **Modern Financial Regulation**, Bristol: Jordan Publishing

Kohn, M (1994) **Financial Institution and Market**, New York: McGraw-Hills Inc.

Kvale, S. and Brinkmann, S. (2009) **Interviews: Learning the craft of Qualitative Research Interviewing** (2nd Ed) Los Angeles: Sage Publications

Larosiere, J. (2015) **Structural Bank Reforms: An Illusory Solution**, Journal of International Banking and Financial Law, (2015) vol. 30 Issue 10, 636.

Lemus, E. (2014) **The Financial Collapse of the Enron Corporation and Its Impact in the United States Capital Market.** Global Journal of Management and Business Research: Accounting and Auditing, Vol 14, Issue 4.

Ligere, E. (2014) **Legislative Comment, The Future of Banking in the E.U.?** Journal of International Banking Law and Regulation JIBLR 29 (5), 308–311.

Lincoln, Y, and Guba, E. (1985) **Naturalistic Inquiry**, Beverly Hills: Sage Publications

Lomnicka, E. (2000) **Making the Financial Services Authority Accountable**. Journal of Business Law Jan. 65–81.

Loveland, I. (2015) **Constitutional Law, Administrative Law, and Human Rights** (7th ed) Oxford: Oxford University Press.

MacNeil, I. (2011) **The Trajectory of Regulatory Reform in the U.K. in the Wake of the Financial Crisis,** European Business Organization Law Review, 11, pp 483–526

Mamica, L. and Tridico, P. (2016) **Economic Policy and the Financial Crisis**. London: Routledge

Manicas, P (2007) **The Social Sciences Since World War II: The Rise and Fall of Scientism** In **The Sage Handbook of Social Science Methodology** (ed) Outhwaite, W and Yurner, S (2007) London: Sage Publications

Marshall, C. and Rossman, G. (2016) **Designing Qualitative Research** (6th Ed) Los Angeles: Sage Publication

Mason, J (1997) **Qualitative Researching**, London: Sage Publications

Mathias, P. (2001) **The First Industrial Nation: The Economic History of Britain 1700–1914**, (2nd Ed.) London: Routledge Taylor & Francis Group

Matthews, K. and Thompson, J. (2008) **The Economics of Banking** (2nd Ed) Chichester: John Wiley & Sons Ltd

Maxwell, A. and Eichhorn, M. (2010) **Measuring Operational Risk in the Context of Basel II: Do Banks Move along the Spectrum of Available Approaches.** Journal of International Banking Law and Regulation 25(2), 83–88.

McCartan, K and Robson, C. (2017) **Real World Research** (4ᵗʰ Ed) London: John Wiley & Sons

McDonald, O. (2019) **Should LIBOR Come to an End?** Company Lawyer 40 (8), 237–238.

McKee, M. (2020) **The Implications of Moving to SONIA**. Journal of International Banking Law and Regulation 35 (6), 223–230.

McLaney, E. and Atrill, P. (2016) **Accounting and Finance: An Introduction** (8ᵗʰ Ed). Harlow: Pearson

McLoughlin, J. (1975) **Introduction to Negotiable Instruments**. London: Butterworths

Mead, G. (1917) **Scientific Method and the Individual Thinker**. In J. Dewey (Ed), Creative Intelligence: Essays in the Pragmatic, New York: Henry Holt

Melville, A. (2015) **International Financial Reporting: A Practical Guide** (5ᵗʰ Ed) Harlow: Pearson Educational

Mertens, D. (2003) **Mixed Methods and the Politics of Human Research: The Transformative-Emancipatory Perspective**. In Tashakkori, A. and Teddlie, C. (Eds), Handbook of Mixed Methods in Social and Behavioural Research, Thousands Oak, CA: Sage Publications

Miles, M. and Huberman, A. (1994) **Qualitative Data Analysis: An Expanded Sourcebook**, London: Sage Publications

Miller, J. (2011) **Vickers' Report Slammed**. New Law Journal, 161 NLJ 1228 (2)

Mills, J. (1976) **Wurtzburg and Mills Building Society Law** (14ᵗʰ Ed) London: Stevens & Sons

Mills, J. S. (1974) **On Liberty.** Harmondsworth: Penguin

Mishkin, F. S and Eakins, S. G (2012) **Financial Markets and Institutions** (7th Ed) Harlow Essex: Pearson Education Ltd.

Mishkin, F. S., Matthews, K., and Guiuliodori, M. (2013) **The Economics of Money, Banking and Financial Markets,** Harlow: Pearson Educational.

Mishkin, F. S and Eakins, S. G (2018) **Financial Markets and Institutions** (9ᵗʰ Ed) Harlow Essex: Pearson Education Ltd.

Moore, N. (1987) **How to Do Research** (2ⁿᵈ Ed) London: Library Association Publishing.

Moosa, I. (2010) **The Myth of Too Big to Fail**. Journal of Banking Regulation, 11 (4), 319–333.

Morris, G. (2005) **U.K. Accounting Practice**. London: Lexis Nexis Butterworths

Morris, C. R. (2008) **The Trillion Dollar Meltdown**. New York: Perseus Books Group.

Morris, S. (2016) **Financial Services Regulation in Practice**, Oxford: Oxford University Press

Morrison, J. (2009) **International Business: Challenges in a Changing World**, Basingstoke: Palgrave Macmillan

Mullins, L. J. (2016) **Management and Organisational Behaviour** (11th Ed.) Harlow: Prentice-Hall, Pearson Education Ltd

Mumford, A. (1997) **When to Use the Case Study Method**. ECCHO: The Newsletter of the European Case Clearing House, Autumn/Fall pp. 16–17.

Murphy, D (2009) **Unravelling the Credit Crunch**, London: C.R.C. Press, Taylor & Francis Group.

Mwenda, K. (2006) **Legal aspects of Financial Services Regulation and the Concept of a Unified Regulator.** Washington: The World Bank.

National Audit Office (2011) **HM Treasury, the Comptroller and Auditor General's Report on Accounts to the House of Commons**, NAO Report: The Treasury's 2010-11 Accounts: the financial stability interventions

Nattrass, R. (2010) **The Too Big to Fail Problem: Fault Lines Open Up**. Journal of International Banking and Financial Law (6) JIBFL 353.

Neuendorf, K. (2002) **The Content Analysis Guidebook.** Thousand Oaks, California: Sage Publications

Ogus, A. I. (1994) **Regulation: Legal Form and Economic Theory**, Oxford: Clarendon Press

O'Leary, Z. (2009) **The Essential Guide to Doing Research**. Los Angeles: Sage Publications.

Ormerod, D. and Laird, K. (2018) **Smith, Hogan & Ormerod Criminal Law** (15th Ed). Oxford: Oxford University Press.

Ott, C. (2020) **The Risks of Mergers and Acquisitions: Analysing the Incentives for Risk, Reporting in Items 1A of 10 -K Fillings**. (2020) 106, 158–181, Journal of Business Research.

Pakravan, K (2014) **Bank Capital: The Case Against Basel**, Journal of Financial Regulation & Compliance JFRC 22(3), 208–218

Palfreman, D and Ford, P (1992) **Elements of Banking** (2nd) London: Pitman Publishing.

Penn, G. (1989) **Banking Supervision: Regulation of the U.K. Banking Sector under the Banking Act 1987**, London: Butterworts

Penn, G., Shea, A., and Arora, A. (1987) **The Law Relating to Domestic Banking (Banking Law Volume I)** London: Sweet & Maxwell.

Perry, F. (1972) **Law and Practice Relating to Banking** (2nd Ed) Middlesex: Penguin Books

Persaud, A. (2010) **A Critique of Current Proposal to Reform Bank Regulation**, Journal of International Banking and Financial Law, (2010) 3 JIBFL 147.

Persaud, A. (2015) **Reinventing Financial Regulation: A Blueprint for Overcoming Systemic Risk.** California: Apress Publishers.

Petitjean, M. (2013) **Bank Failures and Regulation: A Critical Review**. Journal of Financial Regulation & Compiance JFRC 21 (1), 16–38.

Picciotto, S (1998) **Globalisation, Liberalisation and Regulation**: Conference paper delivered at the Conference on Globalisation, The Nation-State, and Violence Organised by the Review of International Political Economy, Sussex University, 16th April 1998

Pilbeam, K. (2013) **International Finance** (4th Ed) Basingstoke, Hampshire: Palgrave Macmillan

Plato-Shimar, R. (2018) **Principles of Financial Regulation**. Journal of International Banking Law and Regulation, 2018 (33(3)) 108–110.

Popper, K. (1994) **The Open Society and its Enemies**. Princeton, New Jersey: Princeton University Press.

Prager, J. (1982) **Fundamentals of Money, Banking and Financial Institutions**. New York: Harper & Row Publishers

Ramasastry, A. and Slavova, S. (1999) **European Bank for Reconstruction and Development's (EBRD) Survey Result: Market Perceptions of Financial Law in the Region,** Journal of International Banking and Financial Law (7) JFBL (297).

Ree, J. and Urmson, J. (2005) **The Concise Encyclopedia of Western Philosophy**, (3rd Ed) London & New York: Routledge.

Reichardt, C, and Rallis, S. (1994) **Qualitative and Quantitative Inquiries are not Incompatible: A call for New Partnership.** In C. S. Reichardt & S. F Rallis (eds), **The Qualitative-Quantitative Debate: New Perspective**, San Francisco: Jossey-Bass

Revell, J. (1973) **The British Financial System**, London: The Macmillan Press Ltd

Richardson, D. (1976) **Guide to Negotiable Instruments and the Bill of Exchange Acts** (5th Ed). London: Butterworths

Ritchie, J and Lewis, J (2003) **Qualitative Research Practice: A Guide for Social Science Students and Researchers,** London: Sage Publications

Ritchie, J., Lewis, J., Nicholls, C., and Ormston, R. (2014) Qualitative Research Practice: **A Guide for Social Science Students and Researchers.** (2nd Ed) London: Sage Publications

Robert, D. Douglas, E and Philips, M. (2009) **Mergers and Acquisitions of Financial Institutions: A Review of the Post 2000 Literature**. Journal of Financial Services Research Vol 36 (23) 87–110.

Robson, C. (2002) **Real World Research**. (2nd Ed) Malden U.S.A.: Blackwell Publishing

Rochon, L., and Olawoye, S. (2012) **Monetary Policy and Central Banking: New Directions in Post Keynesian Theory**, Cheltenham Glos: Edward Elgar Publishing

Rogers, J. (1995) **The Early History of the Law of Bills and Notes: A Study of the Origins of Anglo-American Commercial Law**. Cambridge: Cambridge University Press

Roseveare, H. (1991) **The Financial Revolution 1660–1760,** London: Longman.

Royal Bank of Scotland Plc (2005–2018) **Annual Reports and Financial Accounts.**

Royal Bank of Scotland Plc (2005–2018) **Annual Reports and Financial Accounts.**

Salz, A. and Collins, R. (2013) **An Independent Review of Barclays' Business Practices**

Saunders, A. and Cornett, M. (2011) **Financial Institution Management: A Risk Management Approach**, (7th Ed) New York: McGraw-Hill

Saunders, A. and Walter, I. (1993) **Universal Banking in America: What Can we Gain? What Can We Lose?** New York: Oxford University Press

Saunders, M., Lewis, P. and Thornhill, A. (2009) **Research Methods For Business Students** (5th Ed) Harlow Essex: Pearson Education Ltd.

Saunders, M., Lewis, P. and Thornhill, A. (2023) **Research Methods For Business Students** (9th Ed) Harlow Essex: Pearson Education Ltd.

Schwerter, S. (2011) **Basel III's Ability to Mitigate Systemic Risk**, Journal of Financial Regulation and Compliance, 19 (4), 337–354

Scott, J. (1990) **A Matter of Record: Documentary Sources in Social Research**. Cambridge: Polity Press.

Sharp, J., Peters, J., and Howard, K. (2002) **The Management of a Student Research Project** (3rd Ed). Aldershot: Gower.

Sikka, P. (2013) **Written evidence submitted to Parliamentary Commission on Banking Standards;**
http://www.publications.parliament.uk/pa/jt201314/jtselect/jtpcbs/27/27ix_we_h13.htm accessed on 8th November 2019.

Silverman, D. (2013) **Doing Qualitative Research** (4th Ed) London: Sage Publications

Silverman, D. (2014) **Interpreting Qualitative** data (5th Ed) London: Sage Publications

Singh, D. (2007) **Banking Regulation of the U.K. and U.S. Financial Markets**, Hampshire: Ashgate

Sinkey, J. (1998) **Commercial Bank Financial Management** (5th Ed) New Jersey: Prentice Hall.

Slack, N., Chambers, S., and Johnston, R. (2001) **Operations Management** (3rd Ed) Harlow: Pearson Education Ltd.

Smart, P. E. (1983) **Chorley & Smart Leading Cases in the Law of Banking,** (5th Ed) London: Sweet & Maxwell.

Smith, A. (1776) **An Enquiry into the Nature and Causes of the Wealth of Nations**, London: Dent ed (1933) cited in Davies, G (1996) *A History of Money*, Cardiff: the University of Wales Press

Smith, I. T. and Thomas, G. H (2003) **Industrial law**, (8th Ed), Colchester: Lexis Nexis

Snieder, R. and Larner, K. (2009) **The Art of Being Scientist: A Guide for Graduate Students and their Mentors.** Cambridge: Cambridge University Press

Sommer, R. and Sommer, B. (2002) **A Practical Guide to Behavioural Research: Tools and Techniques** (5th Ed) Oxford: Oxford University Press.

Standard Chartered Bank Plc (2005–2018) **Annual Reports and Financial Accounts.**

Steger, M. and Roy, R. (2010) **Neoliberalism: A Very Short Introduction**. Oxford: Oxford University Press.

Stiglitz, J. (2009) The Stiglitz Report: **Report of the Commission of Experts to the President of the U.N. on Reforms of the International Monetary Fund and Financial System**. New York: United Nations

Tanega, J. (2005) **Securitisation Disclosures and Compliance under Basel II: A Risk Based Approach to Economic Substance Over Legal Form: Part I**. Journal of International Banking Law and Regulation 20(12), 617–627.

Tashakkori, A. and Teddlie, C. (1998) **Mixed Methodology: Combining Qualitative and Quantitative Approaches,** London: Sage Publications

Tattersall, J., Smith, R., Ilako, C., Stollov, V., Devine, M., Barfield, R., Matten, C.,

Triffitt, G., and Quinn, R. (2004) **Basel II: A Briefing for Practitioners**. Compliance Officer Bulletin C.O.B 21 (Nov), 1–41.

Teather, D. Clark, A. and Treanor, J. (2008) **Barclays to Buy Lehman Brothers' Assets.** London: The Guardian 17/09/2008.

Tesch, R. (1990) **Qualitative Research: Analysis Types and Software Tools**, Bristol: Falmer Press

Thieffry, G. (2019) **The Impact of the Latest Basel Accords on Commodity Trade Finance: An Update**. Journal of International Banking law and Regulation 34(7), 237–242

The Guardian (2011) R.B.S. Collapse: Timeline https://www.theguardian.com/business/2011/dec/12/rbs-collapse-timeline

Tomasic, R. (2008) **Corporate Rescue, Governance and Risk-taking in Northern Rock: Part 2.** Company Lawyer 2008, 29 (11), 330–337.

Transfield, D., Denyer, D. and Smart, P. (2003) **Towards Methodology for Developing Evidence-informed Management Knowledge by Means of Systemic Review**. British Journal of Management, Vol. 14, No. 3, pp. 207–222.

Turner, A. (2009) **The Turner Review, Regulatory Response to the Global Banking Crisis**. Financial Services Authority.

Turner, A. (2012) **Oral Evidence Before Parliamentary Commission on Banking Standards** http://www.publications.parliament.uk/pa/jt201314/jtselect/jtpcbs/27/121119.htm

Valdez, S. and Molyneux, P. (2016) **An Introduction to Global Financial Market** (8th Ed) London: Palgrave.

Verrill, L. (2008) **Regulation Hits the Rocks?** Insolvency Intelligence 2008, 21(1), 16

Vickers, J (2011) **The Independent Commission on Banking**: **The Vickers' Report**

Wacks, R. (2017) **Understanding Jurisprudence: An Introduction to Legal Theory** (5th ed) Oxford: Oxford University Press

Wadsley, J. and Penn, G.A. (2000) **The Law Relating to Domestic Banking** (2nd Ed), London: Sweet & Maxwell

Wilcox, J. (1984). **The P/B-ROE Valuation Model**. Financial Analysis Journal, Jan-Feb, 58-66.

Wilson Committee Report (1980) **The Functioning of the Financial Institutions** CMND 7937. London: HMSO

Wilson, J. (2010) **Essentials of Business Research: A Guide to Doing Your Research Project:** London: Sage Publications.

Wolcott, H. (1994) **Transforming Qualitative Data: Description, Analysis and Interpretation**, Thousand Oaks, California: Sage Publications

Wood, F. and Sangster, A. (2007) **Business Accounting 2** (11th Ed) Harlow: Prentice-Hall Publications

Yeoh, P. (2018) **Global Banking Reforms: Mission Accomplished?** Journal of International Banking Law and Regulation, 33(9), 305–313.

Young, S. and Cafferty, D. (2005) **Money Laundering: Reporting Officer's Handbook,** London: LexisNexis Butterworth

Zufferey, J. (2011) **Regulating Financial Markets in Times of Stress is a Fundamentally Human Undertaking**. European Company and Financial Law Review Vol.8 Issue 2.

Z/Yen (2017) **The Global Financial Centre Index 22** www.longfinance.net/images/gfci/_22.pdf Accessed 17/12/2017

Case law

A v B (Bank of England Intervening) [1992] 1 All ER 778

Bank of England v Riley [1992] 1 All ER 769, CA

BCCI (Overseas) Ltd v Price Waterhouse (No 2) [1998] PNLR 564

Foley v Hill (1848) 2 H.L.C. 28

Lee v Lee's Air Farming (1916) A.C. 12

Price Waterhouse v BCCI Holdings (Luxembourg) S.A. [1992] BCLC 583

R v. Kwaku Mawuli Adoboli [2014] EWCA Crim 1204

Salomon v Salomon (1897) AC 22

Three Rivers DC v Bank of England (No.3) (C.A. and H.L. (E.J.)) 2003 2 AC

Tournier v National Provincial & Union Bank of England: CA [1924]1KB 461
United Dominion Trust v. Kirkwood [1966] 1 Q.B. 431; 1 ALL ER 968

Legislation

Banking Act 2009 Part 1 s.1, s.2 (a) (b) & (c), Part 1, s.2 (1)
Bank of England Act 1998 Part 1A s.9a–9n, Part II s.10; Part III s.21
Bill of Exchange Act 1882 s.2
Building Societies Act 1986
Company Act 1947
Company Act 1948
Company Act 1985
Company Act 2006
Criminal Justice Act 1993
Directive 2014/49/E.U. of the European Parliament and of the Council on Deposit Guarantee Scheme
Dodd-Frank Wall Street Reform and Consumer Protection Act 2010 (U.S.A.)
Drug Trafficking Act 1994
Employment Protection Act 1975
Employment Rights Acts 1996
European Economic Community, "Own Funds of Credit Institutions", (1989) Directive 89/299/EEC
Financial Service Act 1986
Financial Services Modernisation Act 1999 (American legislation)
Financial Services Markets Act 2000 s.2 (a) (b) (c) (d), Part II s.19
Financial Services (Banking Reform) Act 2013, Part 1 (2), (i) & (ii)
Insolvency Act 1986
Limited Liability Company Act 1855
Proceeds of Crime Act 2002 ss. 327–332, 333A–E, 335–340
Public Interest Disclosure Act 1998, s. 43B–s.43H
Statutory Instrument 2014/2080 FSMA 2000 (Excluded Activities and Prohibitions) Part II Article 4
Terrorism Act 2000 s.18
The Banking Act 1979
The Banking Act 1987 Part 1 s.41, 42 & 43; s.45, s.46 & s.47
The Banking (Special Provision) Act 2008

The Bank of England Act 1946 s.4 (3)
The Bank Charter Act 1844
The Financial Choice Act 2018 (U.S.A.)
The Financial Services (Banking Reform) Act 2013 s.71, s. 73
The Glass-Stealgall Act 1933 (U.S.A.)
The Wall Street Amendment and Transparency Act 2010 (U.S.A.)
Unfair Contract Terms Act 1977, s.3 (1); s.11 (1); s.12(1);

Web pages

https://www.bis.org/bcbs/history.htm. Accessed 01/06/2020.
https://www.bankofengland.co.uk/about Accessed 15/4/2019.
BCBS, 'History of Basel Committee' https://www.bis.org/bcbs/history.htm. Accessed 01/06/2020
https://www.bankofengland.co.uk/banking-services#:~:text=We%20provide%20banking%20services%20to,role%20as%20a%20reserve%20currency. Accessed 03/07/2020
https://fxssi.com/top-20-largest-world-banks-in-current-year 21/4/2020
https://www.prarulebook.co.uk/rulebook/Content/Chapter/213753/14-05-2019 History

Appendix 1: The Royal Bank of Scotland Group: References to Page Numbers on the Annual Reports and the Financial Accounts

	2004	2005	2006	2007	2008	2009	2010
Income	p.145	p.145	p.139	p.120	p.174	p.241	p.127
Operating Profit Before Tax	p.145	p.145	p.139	p.120	p.174	p.241	p.127
Total Assets	p.146	p.146	p.140	p.121	p.175	p.243	p.127
Impairment Charges	p.58	p.58	p.50	p.35	p.174	p.73	p.126
Number of Branches		p.11	p.19	p.15			
Number of Employees	p.81	p.81	p.40	p.3	p.149	p.262	p.120
Earnings Per Share	p.145	p.1	p.139	p.1	p.174	p.241	
Dividend Per Share	p.145	p.1	p.139	p.1			
Total Deposit	p.146	p.146	p.140	p.121	p.175	p.243	p.127
Total Loan	p.146	p.146	p.140	p.121	p.175	p.243	p.127
Contribution from Investment Banking	p.70	p.70	p.12	p.2	p.50	p.86	p.7
Contribution from Insurance Division	p.38	p.38	p.31	p.12	p.17	p.36	

| Contribution from Wealth Management | p.76 | p.76 | p.2 | p.2 | p.12 | p.26 | p.7 |

2011	2012	2013	2014	2015	2016	2017*	2018
p.169	p.353	p.202	p.342	p.260	p.290	p.176	p.176
p.169	p.353	p.202	p.342	p.260	p.290	p.176	p.176
p.171	p.355	p.204	p.344	p.262	p.292	p.178	p.178
p.169	p.353	p.202	p.342	p.260	p.290	p.176	p.176
p.163	p.346	p.196	p.4	p.87	p.117	p.188	p.188
						p.176	p.176
							p.176
p.171	p.355	p.204	p.344	p.262	p.292	p.178	p.178
p.171	p.355	p.204	p.344	p.262	p.292	p.178	p.178
p.8	p.28	p.10					
p.12	p.24	p.10					

From 2004–2018

Note

(i) The figures for the year ended December 2004 were extracted from the Annual Report and Financial Accounts for 2005, hence pages referred to are actually on the Group Financial Report and Annual Financial Accounts for the Year 2005

(ii) Statistics for 2017 was derived from 2018 Annual Report and Financial Accounts. This is because the Annual Report and Financial Accounts for 2017 was comprehensively redrafted such that operating loss before tax of £1,396 billion (p.81, 2017 Financial Accounts) became £2,239 billion (p.176, 2018 Financial Accounts) after the adjustments. Since this is considered to be a material adjustment in the accounts of the Group, hence this researcher opted to work with the adjusted figures.

(iii) From 2008 to 2017, the Group was in difficulty and mostly recorded losses and as such, there was no dividend paid from 2008 to 2017.

(iv) Due to divestment, the insurance arm of the Group was sold out as such, from 2009 contributions from that arm of the Group stopped. That situation similarly affected the investment arm of the Group. Due to restructuring, Wealth Management ceased to be reported separately having been merged with another department in the Group

Appendix 2: Barclays Group: References to Page Numbers on the Annual Reports and the Financial Accounts from 2004–2018

	2004	2005	2006	2007	2008	2009	2010
Total Income	p.96	p.96	p.162	p.176	p.204	p.204	p.74
Operating Profit Before Tax	p.96	p.96	p.162	p.176	p.204	p.204	p.74
Total Assets	p.98	p.98	p.163	p.177	p.205	p.206	p.76
Impairment Charges	p.96	p.96	p.162	p.176	p.204	p.204	p.74
Number of Branches	p.4*	p.4*	p.4	p.24		p.4	
Number of Employees	p.109	p.109	p.49	p.2	p.23	p.5	p.29*
Earnings Per Share	p.96	p.96	p.10	p.176	p.204	p.204	p.164*
Dividend Per Share	p.96	p.96	p.10	p.2	p.2	p.204	p.164*
Total Deposit	p.98	p.98	p.12	p.177	p.205	p.206	p.76
Total Loan	p.98	p.98	p.12	p.177	p.205	p.206	p.76
Contribution from Investment Banking	p.114	p.114	p.4	p.3	p.5	p.3	p.9
Contribution from Insurance Division		p.183	p.183	p.183			

Contribution from Wealth Management		p.115	p.115	p.4	p.3	p.5	p.10*	p.10

2011	2012	2013	2014	2015	2016	2017	2018
p.164	p.2	p.245	p.224	p.220	p.240	p.137	p.226
p.164	p.2	p.246	p.224	p.220	p.240	p.137	p.226
p.170	p.204	p.247	p.227	p.223	p.242	p.139	p.228
p.164	p.202	p.245	p.224	p.220	p.240	p.137	p.226
p.29	p.34	p.2	p.71	p.76	p.90*	p.90*	p.90
p.164	p.203	p.246	p.224	p.220	p.240	-	p.226
p.164	p.2	p.245	p.222	p.350	p.376	-	p.359
p.170	p.204	p.247	p.227	p.223	p.242	p.139	p.228
p.170	p.204	p.247	p.227	p.223	p.242	p.139	p.228
p.173	p.207	p.249	p.229	p.225	p.234*	p.234*	p.234
p.173	p.207	p.249					

Note

(i) The figures for the year ended December 2004 were extracted from the Annual Report and Financial Accounts for 2005, hence pages referred to are actually on the Group Financial Report and Annual Financial Accounts for the Year 2005

(ii) The figures relating to contribution of insurance division for the 2005, 2006 and 2007 were extracted from the Annual Report and Financial Accounts for the 2007 p.183

(iii) EPS and D.P.S. for 2010 found on page 164, 2011 Accounts

(iv) In 2012 audited adjusted figures were used relating to total income, Profit Before Tax and Earning Per Share since the difference in the amounts are substantial and can significantly impact on the analysis

(v) Number of employees stated as 119,300 as at 2016, 79,900 as at 2017 and 83,500 for 2018 were found on p. 90, 2018 Accounts

(vi) Contributions of investment banking for years 2016, 2017 and 2018 are found on p.234 of 2018 Accounts

(vii) The number of employees for 2010 was found in the Financial Accounts for 2011

(viii) Consequent to the bottom-line loss declared in 2017, there was no dividend paid hence there is no statistics for EPS and D.P.S. in 2017

(ix) Number of branches for 2004, 2005 and 2006 were extracted from 2006 Annual report and financial accounts

(x) Profit Before Tax in 2009 was £4.6 billion for continuing operations while in addition to that was income £6.78 billion earned from discontinued operations

Appendix 3: Standard Chartered Bank Group:
References to Page Numbers on the Annual Reports and the Financial Accounts from 2004–2018

	2004	2005	2006	2007	2008	2009	2010
Income	p.64*	p.64	p.76	p.88	p.96	p.112	p.139
Operating Profit Before Tax	p.64*	p.64	p.76	p.88	p.96	p.112	p.139
Total Assets	p.65*	p.65	p.77	p.89	p.97	p.114	p.141
Impairment Charges	p.64*	p.64	p.76	p.88	p.96	p.112	p.139
Number of Branches		p.42	p.9	p.66	p.4	p.76	p.126
Employees		p.42	p.1	p.3	p.2	p.1	p.39
Earnings Per Share	p.64*	p.64	p.76	p.88	p.96	p.112	p.139
Dividend Per Share	p.1*	p.1	p.1	p.3	p.2	p.1	p.4
Deposit	p.65*	p.65	p.77	p.89	p.97	p.114	p.141
Loan	p.65*	p.65	P.77	p.89	p.97	p.114	p.141
Contribution from Investment Banking	p.24*	p.24	p.31	p.5	p.5	p.1	p.1
Contribution from Insurance Business							

Contribution from Wealth Management	p.24	p.24	p.37*	P.37	p.25*	p.25	p.29	

2011	2012	2013	2014	2015	2016	2017	2018
p.163	p.197	p.229	p.225	p.235	p.199	p.200	p.236
p.163	p.197	p.229	p.225	p.235	p.199	p.200	p.236
p.165	p.199	p.231	p.227	p.237	p.201	p.202	p.238
p.163	p.197	p.229	p.225	p.235	p.199	p.200	p.236
p.152	p.4	p.213	p.210				
p.2	p.3	p.3	p.23	p.1	p.315	p.217	p.7
p.163	p.197	p.229	p.225	p.235	p.199	p.200	p.236
p.2	p.2	p.2	p.2	p.5	p.5	p.5	p.30
p.165	p.199	p.231	p.227	p.237	p.201	p.202	p.238
p.165	p.199	p.231	p.227	p.237	p.201	p.202	p.238
p.2	p.2	p.2	p.2	p.3	p.2	p.2	p.2
p.29	p.50*	p.50	p.37	p.3	p.2	p.2	p.2

Note:

(i) Information regarding 2004 Annual Accounts were extracted from 2005 Annual Financial Accounts
(ii) Operating Income from wealth management for 2012 was obtained from 2013 Annual Financial Accounts
(iii) Operating Income from wealth management for 2008 was obtained from p.25 of 2009 Annual Financial Accounts
(iv) Operating Income from wealth management for 2006 was obtained from p.37 of 2007 Annual Financial Accounts
(v) Operating Income from wealth management for 2004 was obtained from p.24 of 2005 Annual Financial Accounts

Appendix 4: HSBC Group: References to Page Numbers in the Annual Financial Reports 2004–2018

	2004	2005	2006	2007	2008	2009	2010
Total Income	p. 1	p. 1	p.294	p.337	p.333	p.66	p.238
Operating Profit Before Tax	p.236	p.236	p.294	p.337	p.333	p.353	p.238
Total Assets	p.237	p.237	p.295	p.338	p.334	p.355	p.240
Impairment Charges	p.236	p.236	p.294	p.337	p.333	p.24	p.238
Number of Branches							
Number of Employees	p.10	p.10	p.265	P365	p.303	p.388	p.206
Earnings Per Share	p.236	p.236	p.294	p.337	p.2	p.2	p.238
Dividend Per Share	p.236	p.236	p.294	p.337	p.2	p.2	p.1
Total Deposit	p.237	p.237	p.295	p.338	p.334	p.355	p.240
Total Loan	p.237	p.237	p.295	p.338	p.334	p.355	p.240
Contribution from Investment Banking	p.45	p.44	p.45	p.33	p.84	p.82	p.48
Contribution from Insurance Division	p.236	p.236	p.294	p.337	p.333	p.82	p.48
Private Banking	p.45	p.44	p.45	p.33	p.84	p.82	p.48

2011	2012	2013	2014	2015	2016	2017	2018
p.279	p.372	p.417	p.335	p.337	p.184	p.176	p.214
p.279	p.372	p.417	p.335	p.337	p.2184	p.176	p.214
p.281	p.374	p.419	p.337	p.339	p.186	p.178	p.216
p.279	p.372	p.417	p.335	p.337	p.184	p.176	p.214
p.1	p.1	p.1	p.1	p.5		p.2	
p.29	p.335	p.27	p.1	p.60	p.40	p.2	p.2
p.279	p.2	p.417	p.335	p.337	p.184	p.176	p.214
p.2	p.1	p.2	p.1	p.3	p.3	p.3-	p.3
p.281	p.374	p.419	p.337	p.339	p.186	p.178	p.216
p.281	p.374	p.419	p.337	p.339	p.186	p.178	p.216
p.57	p.76	p.94	p.76	p.74	p.20*	p.20	p.20
p.57	p.76	p.94	p.76	p.74	p.21*	p.21	p.214
p.72*	p.72	p.72*	p.72	p.72	p.18*	p.18	p.21

Notes

(a) Data for the year 2004 were extracted from Annual accounts for year 2005
   (i) Contribution from investment banking for 2016 was extracted from 2017 accounts at page 20
   (ii) Contribution from insurance business for 2016 was extracted from 2017 accounts at page 21
   (iii) Contribution from private banking for 2011 was extracted from 2012 accounts at page 72
   (iv) Contribution for private banking for 2013 was extracted from 2014 accounts at page 72

Appendix 5: Data for Figure 5: The Royal Bank of Scotland Group: The Relationship Between Income and Operating Profit Before Tax 2004–2018 £ (b)

Year	Income	Profit Before Tax
2004	23.4	7.3
2005	25.9	7.9
2006	28	9.2
2007	31.1	9.9
2008	25.9	-40.7
2009	38.7	-2.6
2010	23.7	-0.2
2011	21.8	-0.9
2012	17.9	-5.6
2013	19.8	-6.8
2014	15.1	-2.7
2015	12.9	-2.7
2016	12.6	-4
2017	13.1	2.2
2018	13.4	3.4

Appendix 6: Data for Figure 6: The Royal Bank of Scotland Group The Relationship Between Assets, Deposits and Loans 2004–2018 £ (b)

Year	Assets	Deposits	Loans
2004	588	382	408
2005	777	453	488
2006	871	516	549
2007	1901	995	1049
2008	2402	898	1013
2009	1696	756	820
2010	1307	558	606
2011	1433	581	587
2012	1312	623	564
2013	1020	537	506
2014	1051	452	421
2015	815	408	364
2016	799	420	382
2017	738	392	322
2018	694	384	318

Appendix 7: Data for Figure 7: The Royal Bank of Scotland Group Trend of Growth and Decline in the Total Assets 2004–2018 £ (b)

Year	Total Assets
2004	588
2005	777
2006	871
2007	1901
2008	2402
2009	1696
2010	1307
2011	1433
2012	1312
2013	1020
2014	1051
2015	815
2016	799
2017	738
2018	694

Appendix 8: Data for Figure 8: The Royal Bank of Scotland Group: The Contributions of Earnings from the Investment Banking to the Profit Before Tax 2004–2013 £ (b)

Year	Profit Before Tax	Earning from Investment Banking
2004	7.3	4.2
2005	7.9	5.2
2006	9.2	6.1
2007	9.9	5.6
2008	-40.7	-8.7
2009	-2.6	5.7
2010	-0.2	3.2
2011	-0.9	1.5
2012	-5.6	1.5
2013	-6.8	0.7
2014	-2.7	
2015	-2.7	
2016	-4	
2017	2.2	
2018	3.4	

Appendix 9: Data for Fig. 9: The Royal Bank of Scotland Group Impairment Charges 2004–2018 £ (b)

Year	Impairment Charges
2004	1.5
2005	1.7
2006	1.9
2007	2.1
2008	8
2009	14
2010	9.4
2011	7.2
2012	5.3
2013	8.4
2014	
2015	
2016	0.5
2017	0.5
2018	0.4

Appendix 10: Data for Figure 10: The Royal Bank of Scotland Group Trend of Growth and the Decline in the Employees' Profile 2005–2018

Year	Number of Employees
2004	-
2005	137000
2006	135000
2007	226400
2008	199800
2009	184500
2010	113600
2011	113700
2012	137200
2013	106100
2014	110027
2015	93659
2016	77900
2017	69700
2018	65400

Appendix 11: Data on Fig. 11. Barclays Group:
The Relationship Between Income and Operating Profit Before Tax From 2004–2018 £ (b)

Year	Income	Profit Before Tax
2004	14,108	4,580
2005	17,333	5,280
2006	21,595	7,136
2007	23,000	7,076
2008	23,115	6,077
2009	29,123	11,642
2010	31,450	6,079
2011	32,292	5,879
2012	29,043	7,048
2013	27,935	5,167
2014	25,288	5,502
2015	25,454	5,403
2016	21,451	3,230
2017	20,937	3,166
2018	21,136	3,494

Appendix 12: Data for Fig. 12 Barclays Group:
The Relationship Between Assets, Deposits and Loans From 2004–2018 £ (b)

Year	Assets	Deposits	Loans
2004	538,181	329,721	343,041
2005	924,357	316,152	300,001
2006	996,787	338,537	313,226
2007	1,227,361	385,535	385,518
2008	2,052,980	450,415	509,522
2009	1,378,929	398,875	461,359
2010	1,490,038	423,777	465,741
2011	1,563,527	458,117	479,380
2012	1,490,321	464,290	466,218
2013	1,312,267	482,736	468,264
2014	1,357,906	486,094	469,878
2015	1,120,012	465,322	440,566
2016	1,213,126	471,392	436,035
2017	1,129,343	467,332	401,762
2018	1,133,283	394,838	326,406

Appendix 13: Data for Fig. 13–Barclays Group: Trend of Growth/Decline in the Total Assets for 2004–2018 £ (b)

Year	Total Assets
2004	538,181
2005	924,357
2006	996,787
2007	1,227,361
2008	2,052,980
2009	1,378,929
2010	1,490,038
2011	1,563,527
2012	1,490,321
2013	1,312,267
2014	1,357,906
2015	1,120,012
2016	1,213,126
2017	1,129,343
2018	1,133,283

Appendix 14: Data for Figure 14–Barclays Group:
Trend of Growth/Decline in Impairment Charges from 2004–2018 £ (b)

	Impairment Charges
2004	1.1
2005	1.6
2006	2.2
2007	2.8
2008	5.4
2009	8.1
2010	5.7
2011	5.6
2012	3.6
2013	3.1
2014	2.2
2015	2.1
2016	2.4
2017	2.3
2018	1.5

Appendix 15: Data for Fig. 15–Barclays Group:
The Proportion of the Contributions of the Investment Banking to the Operating Profit Before Tax 2004–2018 £ (billion)

Year	PBT	Investment Banking
2004	4.6	1
2005	5.2	1.3
2006	7.1	2.2
2007	7	2.3
2008	6	1.3
2009	4.6	2.5
2010	6	4.8
2011	5.9	3
2012	7	4
2013	5.2	2.5
2014	5.5	1.4
2015	5.4	1.6
2016	3.2	2.7
2017	3.2	2
2018	3.5	2.6

Appendix 16: Data on Fig. 16–Barclays Group: Trend of Growth/Decline in the Employees' Profile 2004–2018

Year	Employees
2004	82,700
2005	120,300
2006	131,700
2007	135,000
2008	156,300
2009	144,200
2010	147,500
2011	141,100
2012	139,200
2013	139,600
2014	132,200
2015	129,400
2016	119,300
2017	79,900
2018	83,500

Appendix 17: Data on Fig. 17 Barclays Group: Trend of Growth/Decline in Earnings Per Share and Dividend Per Share in Pence 2004–2018

Year	Earnings Per Share Pence	Dividend Per Share Pence
2004	0.51	0.24
2005	0.544	0.266
2006	0.719	0.31
2007	0.689	0.34
2008	0.593	0.115
2009	0.862	0.025
2010	0.304	0.055
2011	0.251	0.06
2012	0.345	0.065
2013	0.167	0.065
2014	0.173	0.065
2015	0.166	0.065
2016	0.104	0.03
2017		
2018	0.094	0.065

Appendix 18: Data for Figure 18 S.C.B. Group: The Relationship Between Income and Operating Profit Before Tax 2004–2018

Year	Income US$ (b)	OPBT US$ (b)
2004	5.4	2.3
2005	6.9	2.7
2006	8.6	3.2
2007	11	4
2008	14	4.8
2009	15.1	5.1
2010	16	6.1
2011	17.6	6.8
2012	19	6.9
2013	18.8	6
2014	18.3	4.2
2015	15.3	-1.5
2016	14	0.4
2017	14.4	2.4
2018	14.8	2.5

Appendix 19: Data for Figure 19 S.C.B. Group: The Relationship Between Assets, Deposits and Loans 2004–2018

Year	Assets US$ (b)	Deposits US$ (b)	Loans US$ (b)
2004	147.1	100.2	88.7
2005	215	138.8	133.5
2006	266	173.6	159
2007	329.2	205.6	189.6
2008	435	265.9	220.8
2009	436.7	289.7	249.2
2010	516.5	335.5	292.4
2011	599	378	329.7
2012	636.5	414.1	352.3
2013	674.4	424.6	374.4
2014	725.9	459.7	368.6
2015	640.5	388.2	321.9
2016	646.7	408.7	325.3
2017	663.5	401.5	306.2
2018	688.8	420.7	318

Appendix 20: Fig. 20 S.C.B. Group: Trend of Growth/Decline in the Total Assets Employed 2004–2018 US$ (b)

Year	Assets US$ (b)
2004	147
2005	215
2006	266
2007	329
2008	435
2009	436.7
2010	516.5
2011	599
2012	636.5
2013	674.4
2014	725.9
2015	640.5
2016	646.7
2017	663.5
2018	688.8

Appendix 21: Fig 21 S.C.B. Group: Trend in Growth/Decline in Impairment Charges 2004–2018 US$ (b)

Year	Impairment Charges US$
2004	0.3
2005	0.4
2006	0.6
2007	0.8
2008	1.8
2009	2.1
2010	1
2011	1
2012	1.4
2013	2.7
2014	2.9
2015	5.5
2016	3
2017	1.7
2018	0.8

Appendix 22: Fig 22 S.C.B. Group: The Proportion of Contributions of the Investment Division to the OPBT US$ 2004–2018

Year	OPBT US$	Income from Investment Division US$
2004	2.3	1.2
2005	2.7	1.4
2006	3.2	1.8
2007	4	5.2
2008	4.8	7.5
2009	5.1	9.3
2010	6.1	10
2011	6.8	10.8
2012	6.9	11.8
2013	6	11.5
2014	4.2	6
2015	-1.5	5.3
2016	0.4	6.5
2017	2.4	6.5
2018	2.5	6.9

Appendix 23: Fig 23 S.C.B. Group: Employees' Profile

Year	Employees
2004	
2005	44,000
2006	59,000
2007	70,000
2008	74,000
2009	77,000
2010	85,000
2011	87,000
2012	89,000
2013	87,000
2014	90,000
2015	84,000
2016	87,000
2017	86,000
2018	85,000

Appendix 24: Fig. 24 S.C.B. Group: Trend of Growth/Decline in Earnings Per Share and Divided Per Share 2004-2018

Year	EPS in Cent	D.P.S. in Cent
2004	129.6	57.5
2005	148.5	64
2006	169	71.04
2007	201.1	79.35
2008	202.4	61.62
2009	167.9	66.03
2010	196.3	69.15
2011	200.8	76
2012	199.7	84
2013	164.4	86
2014	102.2	86
2015	-91.9	13.7
2016	-14.5	
2017	23.5	11
2018	18.7	21

Appendix 25: Fig. 25 S.C.B. Group: Trend of Growth/Decline in Income from Wealth Management 2004–2018 US$ (b)

Year	Income from Wealth Management US$ (b)
2004	0.9
2005	1.4
2006	1.9
2007	2.6
2008	2.8
2009	2.2
2010	1.1
2011	1.3
2012	1.3
2013	1.3
2014	1.7
2015	1.7
2016	0.5
2017	0.5
2018	0.5

Appendix 26: HSBC Group: The Relationship Between Operating Income and PBT 2004–2018 US$ billion

	Income	PBT
2004	51	19
2005	58	21
2006	65	22
2007	79	24
2008	82	9
2009	66	7
2010	68	19
2011	72	22
2012	68	21
2013	65	23
2014	61	19
2015	60	19
2016	48	7
2017	51	17
2018	54	20

Appendix 27: HSBC Group: The Relationship Between Assets, Deposits and Loans 2004–2018 US$ billion '000

	Assets	Deposits	Loans
2004	1280	777	816
2005	1502	809	866
2006	1861	997	1053
2007	2354	1228	1219
2008	2527	1245	1087
2009	2364	1284	1076
2010	2455	1338	1167
2011	2556	1367	1121
2012	2693	1447	1150
2013	2671	1612	1292
2014	2634	1428	1087
2015	2410	1344	1015
2016	2375	1332	950
2017	2522	1434	1053
2018	2558	1419	1054

Appendix 28: HSBC Group: Trend of Growth/Decline in Impairment Charges 2004–2018 US$ billion

	Impairment Charges
2004	6
2005	8
2006	11
2007	17
2008	25
2009	26
2010	14
2011	12
2012	8
2013	6
2014	4
2015	4
2016	3
2017	2
2018	2

Appendix 29: HSBC Group: Contributions to the PBT by Investment Banking, Insurance Business and Private Banking 2004–2018 US$ billion

	Investment	Insurance	Private Banking
2004	5	1	1
2005	5	1	1
2006	7	1	1
2007	6	0.5	2
2008	3	4	1
2009	10	-2	1
2010	10	-0.6	1
2011	7	2	1
2012	9	-1	1
2013	9	-2	0.1
2014	6	-1	1
2015	8	-1	0.3
2016	6	-2	0.3
2017	6	-3	0.3
2018	6	1	0.3

Appendix 30: Figure 30, HSBC Group: Employee Profile 2004–2018

	Employee
2004	253
2005	284
2006	312
2007	322
2008	325
2009	310
2010	307
2011	288
2012	270
2013	263
2014	258
2015	255
2016	235
2017	229
2018	235

Appendix 31: HSBC Group: Investment Banking Contributions to PBT 2004–2018

	PBT	Investment Banking Contribution
2004	19	5
2005	21	5
2006	22	7
2007	24	6
2008	9	3
2009	7	10
2010	19	10
2011	22	7
2012	21	9
2013	23	9
2014	19	6
2015	19	8
2016	7	6
2017	17	6
2018	20	6

Appendix 32: Fig 32 The Impacts of GFC on the Case Studies and their Difficult Recovery Trips Through 2004–2018

Time	RBS £ billions	Barclays £ billions	SCB $ billions	HSBC $ billions
2004	7.3	4.6	2.3	19
2005	7.9	5.2	2.7	21
2006	9.2	7.1	3.2	22
2007	9.9	7	4	24
2008	-40.7	6	4.8	9
2009	-2.6	4.6	5.1	7
2010	-0.2	6	6.1	19
2011	-0.9	5.9	6.8	22
2012	-5.6	7	6.9	21
2013	-6.8	5.1	6	23
2014	-2.7	5.5	4.2	19
2015	-2.7	5.4	-1.5	19
2016	-4	3.2	0.4	7
2017	2.2	3.1	2.4	17
2018	3.4	3.5	2.5	20